Contents

Acknowledgements

The publisher wishes to thank the following for their help with the reading and production of the book: Jean Cox, Michael Gilbert, Claire McCarthy and Liz Smith. Thanks are also due to Richard Holt for his designs for this new series, and to Sandy Hood who has helped produce spreadsheet and word-processing material for Unit 7.

The publisher is indebted to the Association of Accounting Technicians for its generous help and advice to our authors and editors during the preparation of this text, and for permission to reproduce extracts from the Standards of Competence for Accounting. The publisher is grateful to a number of organisations which have been helpful in providing information and in granting permission to reproduce material: Barclays Bank PLC, the Department of Trade and Industry, Hereford and Worcester Chamber of Commerce, and the Independent Publishers Guild. The VAT forms, Sales Lists and Intrastat Declarations reproduced in this book are Crown Copyright and are reproduced here with the kind permission of the Controller of Her Majesty's Stationery Office.

The development of the content of this book would not have been possible without the help and advice of a number of practising AAT lecturers. In particular the editorial team would like to thank Claire Eccleston of Hereford College of Technology and Kevin Fisher of Gloucester College of Arts and Technology for their useful suggestions and practical contributions.

Lastly, the publisher would pass special thanks to Roger Petheram, who as main consultant for this text and an experienced accounting lecturer at Worcester College of Technology, has provided invaluable help in reading, checking and providing practical advice in the writing and production process.

Authors

David Cox has more than twenty years' experience teaching accountancy students over a wide range of levels. Formerly with the Management and Professional Studies Department at Worcester College of Technology, he now lectures on a freelance basis and carries out educational consultancy work in accountancy studies. He is author and joint author of a number of textbooks in the areas of accounting, finance and banking.

Michael Fardon has extensive teaching experience of a wide range of banking, business and accountancy courses at Worcester College of Technology. He now specialises in writing business and financial texts and is General Editor at Osborne Books. He is also an educational consultant and has worked extensively in the areas of vocational business curriculum development.

Costing & Reports

Tutorial

NVQ Accounting Units 6 & 7

David Cox

Michael Fardon

osborne
BOOKS

Published by Osborne Books Limited
Unit 1B Everoak Estate
Bromyard Road
Worcester WR2 5HP
Tel 01905 748071
Email books@osbornebooks.co.uk
Website www.osbornebooks.co.uk

Design by Richard Holt
Cover image from Getty Images

Printed and bound in Malta by Gutenberg Press Limited

British Library Cataloguing in Publication Data
A catalogue record for this book is available from the British Library

ISBN 978 1872962 863

Introduction

Osborne tutorials

Costing & Reports Tutorial has been written to provide a study resource for students taking courses based on the NVQ Level 3 Accounting Unit 6 'Recording and evaluating costs and revenues' and Unit 7 'Preparing reports and returns'. The companion Osborne text *Financial Records & Accounts* covers Unit 5 'Maintaining financial records and preparing accounts'.

Costing & Reports Tutorial deals with the recording and analysis of direct and indirect costs, including the allocation, apportionment and absorption of overhead costs. An important aspect is the use of costing information to help with decision-making – in the short-term and long-term.

The completion by individuals and organisations of reports and returns is covered in the second part of this book. The text explains how data is recorded and presented for internal reporting and how various returns are completed for external bodies. The concluding part of the book explains the principles of Value Added Tax and the completion of the VAT Return.

The chapters of *Costing & Reports Tutorial* contain:

• a clear text with worked examples and case studies

• a chapter summary and key terms to help with revision

• student activities – with answers at the end of the book

The tutorial text – with questions and answers – is therefore useful for classroom use and also for distance learning students.

Osborne Workbooks

Costing & Reports Workbook, which accompanies this tutorial text, contains extended student activities, practice Skills Tests, and practice Examinations. If you would like the *Costing & Reports Workbook*, please telephone the Osborne Books Sales Office on 01905 748071 for details of mail ordering, or visit the 24-hour online shop at www.osbornebooks.co.uk

Osborne Tutor Packs

The answers to the Activities, Skills Tests and Examination tasks in the *Workbook* are available in a separate *Tutor Pack*. Contact the Osborne Books Sales Office on 01905 748071 or visit the website for details of how to obtain the Tutor Pack.

surfing with www.osbornebooks.co.uk

The Osborne Books website is constantly developing its range of facilities for tutors and students. Popular features include free downloadable resources and the on-line shop. Log on and try us!

NVQ units covered

UNIT 6
RECORDING AND EVALUATING COSTS AND REVENUES

element 6.1

record and analyse information relating to direct costs and revenues

PC	Chapter
A	1,2,3,4,7
B	2,3,4,7
C	2,3,4,6,7
D	2
E	2,3,4

element 6.2

record and analyse information relating to the allocation, apportionment and absorption of overhead costs

A	5
B	5,6
C	5
D	5,7
E	5,7
F	5
G	5

element 6.3

prepare and evaluate estimates of costs and revenues

A	6,8,9
B	8,9
C	8,9
D	8,9
E	8,9
F	8,9
G	8,9

UNIT 7
PREPARING REPORTS AND RETURNS

element 7.1

prepare and present periodic performance reports

PC	Chapter
A	10,11,14
B	10,11,14
C	12
D	11,14
E	11,14
F	12,13

element 7.2

prepare reports and returns for outside agencies

A	15
B	15
C	15
D	15

element 7.3

prepare VAT returns

A	16,17
B	16,17
C	16,17
D	16,17

Unit 6

Recording and evaluating costs and revenues

this chapter covers . . .

- *the purpose of cost accounting and its role in providing information to the managers of a business*
- *cost units and cost centres*
- *identification and coding of costs and revenues*
- *the categories into which costs can be classified*
  - *by element*
  - *by function*
  - *by nature*
- *how the cost of goods and services is calculated*
- *the layout of a total cost statement*

Set out below are the NVQ competences covered by this chapter.

NVQ PERFORMANCE CRITERIA COVERED

unit 6: RECORDING AND EVALUATING COSTS AND REVENUES

element 6.1

record and analyse information relating to direct costs and revenues

A   identify direct costs in accordance with the organisation's costing procedures

KNOWLEDGE AND UNDERSTANDING – THE BUSINESS ENVIRONMENT

1   the nature and purpose of internal reporting

2   management information requirements

PURPOSE OF COST ACCOUNTING

Cost accounting, as its name implies, enables the managers of a business to know the cost of the firm's output – whether a product or a service – and the revenues from sales. Once costing information is available, managers can use it to assist with

- decision-making
- planning for the future
- control of expenditure

Cost accounting is widely used by all types of businesses – the cost of a hospital operation, the cost of building a new hospital ward, the cost of tuition to a student, the cost of a swim at a sports centre, the cost of a passenger's bus journey, the cost of a new road are all just as important as the cost of making a product. A business – whether it provides a service or makes a product – needs to keep its costs under review; in order to do this it needs accurate cost information. Thus a cost accounting system will provide answers to questions such as:

What does it cost us to provide a student with a day's accountancy course?

What does it cost us to carry out a hip replacement operation?

What does it cost us to make a pair of trainers?

What does it cost us to serve a cheeseburger and fries?

What does it cost us to provide a week's holiday in the Canaries?

The cost accounting system helps managers with production planning and decision-making, such as:

- short-term decisions, eg "how many do we need to make and sell in order to break-even?"; "shall we increase production of Aye or Bee, bearing in mind that shortages of skilled labour mean that we can't do both?"
- long-term decisions, eg "we need to buy a new machine for the factory – shall we buy Machine Exe or Machine Wye?"

The Case Study that follows shows how cost accounting enables the managers of a business to have better information about its activities.

Case Study

S & T MANUFACTURING COMPANY

situation

The following information is given for S & T Manufacturing Company, a two-product (S and T) company, for last year:

				£	£
Sales revenue:	S				100,000
	T				200,000
					300,000
Less:	Cost of materials	S		50,000	
		T		95,000	
	Labour costs	S		40,000	
		T		50,000	
	*Cost of overheads	S		20,000	
		T		30,000	
					285,000
Profit					15,000

* Overheads include factory rent, depreciation of machinery, and other production costs.

How would you present this information in a way which will be of more use to the management of the business? What conclusions do you draw for this business?

solution

The information is best presented in a way which analyses the cost and profit of each product:

	S	T	Total
	£	£	£
Cost of materials	50,000	95,000	145,000
Labour costs	40,000	50,000	90,000
Cost of overheads	20,000	30,000	50,000
Total cost	110,000	175,000	285,000
Sales	100,000	200,000	300,000
Less Total cost	110,000	175,000	285,000
Profit/(loss)	(10,000)	25,000	15,000

On the basis of this information, product S should be discontinued because it is making a loss. However, there may be other factors which will have to be considered, eg sales of product T may be linked to sales of S; the overheads of T are likely to increase if S is discontinued because of the way in which the cost of overheads has been split between the two products.

This Case Study emphasises two important functions of cost accounting:

• to find out the costs (in this case for each product)

• to give responsibility to someone for those costs (here for the manager of product S to investigate the reasons for the loss of £10,000)

COST ACCOUNTING AND FINANCIAL ACCOUNTING

The Case Study of S & T Manufacturing Company, above, illustrates some of the differences between cost accounting and financial accounting. These two types of accounting, although they produce different reports and statements, obtain their data from the same set of transactions carried out by the business organisation over a given period. This is illustrated in the diagram below.

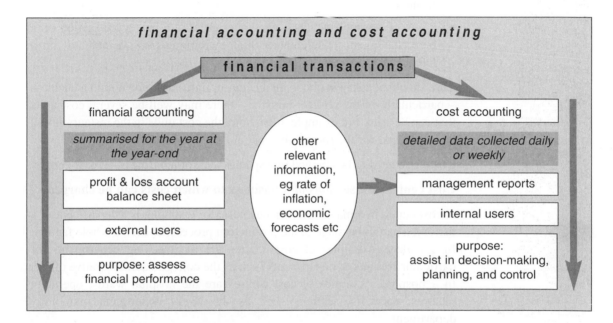

financial accounting and cost accounting

financial transactions

financial accounting		cost accounting
summarised for the year at the year-end	other relevant information, eg rate of inflation, economic forecasts etc	*detailed data collected daily or weekly*
profit & loss account balance sheet		management reports
external users		internal users
purpose: assess financial performance		purpose: assist in decision-making, planning, and control

Financial accounting uses the financial data relating to transactions carried out over a period of time. The information is processed through the accounting records and extracted in the form of financial statements – profit and loss account and balance sheet. The statements are often required to be produced by law, eg the Companies Act, and are available to external users such as shareholders, creditors, bank, Inland Revenue, Companies House.

Cost accounting uses the same data to produce reports containing financial information on the recent past and projections for the future. The reports are available to internal users only, such as managers, directors, and owners (but not to shareholders generally). There is no legal requirement to produce this information and the content of the report and the principles used can be suited to the activities of the business or organisation and the requirements of its managers. The information is prepared as frequently as it is required, and speed is often vital as the information may go out-of-date very quickly.

COST UNITS AND COST CENTRES

Before we begin our study of costing we need to understand the terms: cost units and cost centres.

Cost units are units of output to which costs can be charged.

A cost unit can be:

- a unit of production from a factory such as a car, a television, an item of furniture

- a unit of service, such as a passenger-mile on a bus, a transaction on a bank statement, an attendance at a swimming pool, a call unit on a telephone

Care should be taken in choosing the appropriate cost unit. Within a business – particularly in the service industry – there may well be several cost units that can be used. For example, in an hotel the cost units in the restaurant will be meals, and for the rooms, the cost units will be guest nights.

Costs also need to be charged to a specific part of a business – a **cost centre.**

Cost centres are sections of a business to which costs can be charged.

A cost centre in a manufacturing business, for example, is a department of a factory, a particular stage in the production process, or even a whole factory. In a college, examples of cost centres are the teaching departments, or particular sections of departments such as the college's administrative office. In a hospital, examples of cost centres are the hospital wards, operating theatres, specialist sections such as the X-ray department, pathology department.

Collecting costs together in cost centres assists with control of the business or organisation. The manager of a cost centre can be held responsible for its costs.

IDENTIFICATION AND CODING OF COSTS AND REVENUES

coding of costs

Both cost units and cost centres have costs charged to them. This process is carried out in two steps:

- *identification* of the cost unit or cost centre to which the cost is to be charged

- *coding* the cost so that it is charged to the correct cost unit or cost centre

Code numbers are used in cost accounting because:

- they are easier to process than a description of a cost
- once coded there is no doubt as to which cost unit or cost centre the item relates
- they are easily input into a computer accounting system

Various systems are used to code costs. It is for a business to use the system that meets its needs – a smaller business will use a less sophisticated system than does a larger business. Most codes incorporate two sets of numbers that indicate:

- which cost centre or cost unit incurred the cost
- what cost has been used, eg wages, materials

For example, a business uses the following codes:

- code for administration office, 500
- code for sales department, 550
- code for salaries, 200

Thus the cost code for administration salaries is:

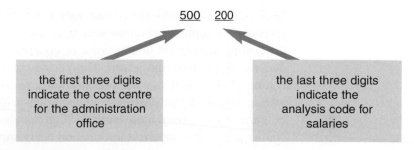

500   200

the first three digits indicate the cost centre for the administration office

the last three digits indicate the analysis code for salaries

Using the same principles, the cost code for sales department salaries is 550200. By using coding in this way, the correct cost centre is charged with the cost.

coding of revenues

In a similar way to coding of costs, revenue from sales needs to be coded so that information is available to management on:

- which product has been sold
- which department, or salesperson, made the sale

For example, a restaurant uses the following codes:

- code for revenue from meals, 700
- code for revenue from the bar, 800
- code for Jason, a waiter, 082

Thus the revenue code for meals sold by Jason is:

082 700

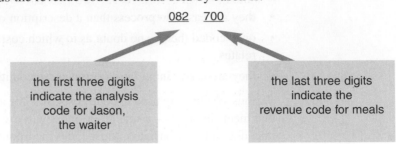

the first three digits indicate the analysis code for Jason, the waiter

the last three digits indicate the revenue code for meals

Using the same principles, the revenue code for bar sales made by Jason is 082800.

You can often see the use of revenue codes in use in a shop, or a bar, or a restaurant – the salesperson first keys in his or her personal code number on the till and then records the items sold by either scanning them through a bar code reader, or by pressing the appropriate keys. The information on sales revenues is then available to the managers of the business.

features of a good coding system

The source documents for coding vary depending on the type of cost or revenue – examples of common sources of data are given on page 29. Within the costing department of a business or organisation, it is necessary to code documents received and issued. The person carrying out the coding – the coding clerk – will use the organisation's *coding manual*, or the *policy manual* (the book that states how all operations within the organisation are to be carried out). They must work to high standards of accuracy – wrong coding will lead to incorrect information being supplied to managers, which could in turn lead to wrong decision-making.

The way in which documents are coded varies from one organisation to another. For some, the code number is written on the document and marked clearly; others use a rubber stamp to provide a layout on which can be indicated the code number and the initials of the person entering the code.

For a coding system to work well:

- coding should follow a logical sequence – similar items, such as cost centres, should be grouped together within the coding system
- codes should be unique, ie a particular code number should relate only to one item going to one particular cost/revenue centre
- codes should provide the correct level of detail, ie the cost/revenue centre code and the analysis code
- coding of documents must be accurate
- code numbers must be complete, ie the full code to be indicated and not just the cost/revenue centre code or the analysis code

- coding of documents must be carried out regularly within the timescales required by the organisation

The objective of coding is to provide correct analysis so as to give information from the costing system to managers. By analysing costs and income to cost/revenue centres we can answer questions such as "how much was basic pay in the sales department last month?"; "how much was factory overtime last week?"; "what sales did the Birmingham office make of product Exe last month?"

CLASSIFICATION OF COSTS

Within any business, whether it manufactures a product or provides a service, there are certain costs involved at various stages to produce the units of output. The diagram below shows the costs of a manufacturing business which are incurred by the three main sections or 'areas' of a manufacturing business.

These three separate sections are:

- **factory** – where production takes place and the product is 'finished' and made ready for selling
- **warehouse** – where finished goods are stored and from where they are despatched when they are sold
- **office** – where the support functions take place – marketing, sales, administration, finance and so on

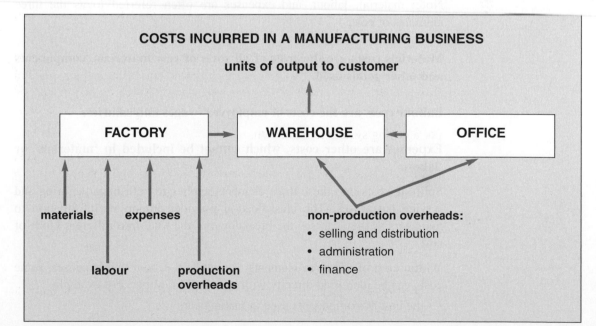

COSTS INCURRED IN A MANUFACTURING BUSINESS

units of output to customer

FACTORY → WAREHOUSE ← OFFICE

materials · expenses · labour · production overheads

non-production overheads:
- selling and distribution
- administration
- finance

Note that while the diagram on the previous page shows the costs of a manufacturing business, it can be adapted easily to fit non-manufacturing organisations, such as a shop, a hospital, a school or college, a church, a club. While the units of output of these organisations differ from those of a manufacturer, nevertheless they still incur costs at various stages of the 'production' process.

In order to prepare information for the managers of a business, costs must be *classified*, ie organised into sets in a way which the managers will find useful.

This can be done in three ways:

- by element
- by function
- by nature

classification of costs by element

Businesses and organisations incur many different kinds of cost in the production of goods or 'output', including costs of the warehouse and the office. The most basic way of splitting up costs is according to the type of expenditure under the headings:

- materials, eg the components to make a car
- labour, eg wages of an employee
- expenses, eg rent and rates, telephone charges, insurance

Note: material, labour, and expenses are often referred to as the three elements of cost.

Materials costs are the costs of all sorts of raw materials, components and other goods used.

Labour costs are the costs of employees' wages and salaries.

Expenses are other costs, which cannot be included in 'materials' or 'labour'.

Splitting costs into these three elements applies to both manufacturing and service businesses. The classification provides important information to managers as they can see the breakdown of the total into different kinds of cost.

Within each of the three elements of materials, labour and expenses, some costs can be identified directly with each unit of output. For example:

- the cost of components used in making cars

- the wages of workers on a production line in a factory

These are termed **direct costs**. In manufacturing, the total of all the direct costs is called the **prime cost** of the output.

A direct cost is a cost that can be identified directly with each unit of output.

Prime cost is the total of all direct costs.

Costs which cannot be identified directly with each unit of output are **indirect costs** or overheads.

Indirect costs (overheads) are all costs other than those identified as 'direct costs'. They cannot be identified directly with specific units of output.

There are many examples of overheads, including:

- telephone charges
- insurance premiums
- cost of wages of non-production staff, such as managers, secretaries, cost accountants and so on
- running costs of delivery vehicles
- depreciation charge for fixed assets

Note particularly the last two examples. In cost accounting, as in financial accounting, we distinguish between capital and revenue expenditure. In our analysis of costs we are referring to revenue expenditure, and therefore include the running costs and depreciation of fixed assets, rather than the capital cost of their purchase.

We now have six possible classifications for costs, each of the three elements of materials, labour and expenses being split into direct and indirect costs. These are illustrated for a manufacturing business in the table on the next page, while the Case Study on page 22 is for a service business.

classification of costs by function

Another method of classifying costs is to look at the costs incurred in different sections of the organisation, according to their 'function', or the kind of work being done.

In manufacturing, the main function is *production* of the goods. The business could not be run, however, without secretaries, administrators, accountants, sales and delivery staff and so on – these are examples of *non-production* costs.

	DIRECT COSTS	INDIRECT COSTS
MATERIALS	The cost of raw materials from which the finished product is made.	The cost of all other materials, eg grease for machines, cleaning materials.
LABOUR	Wages paid to those who work the machinery on the production line or who are involved in assembly or finishing of the product.	Wages and salaries paid to all other employees, eg managers and supervisors, maintenance staff, administration staff.
EXPENSES	Any expenses which can be attributed to particular units of output, eg royalties payable to the designer of a product, fees linked directly to specific output and paid to people who are not employees.	All other expenses, eg rent, rates, telephone, lighting and heating costs, depreciation of fixed assets, insurance, advertising, etc. These are costs which cannot be linked directly with units of output.
TOTAL	**TOTAL DIRECT COST = PRIME COST**	**TOTAL INDIRECT COST = TOTAL OVERHEADS**

When costs are classified by function, the main headings generally used are:

> production
> administration
> selling and distribution   ⎤—— non-production costs
> finance   ⎦

Other functions can be added to suit the needs of a particular business. For example, a 'Research and Development' heading could be used if a company spent large sums of money in researching and developing new products.

Non-manufacturing organisations – such as a hospital or a college – may use other 'function' headings, according to the kind of work each section of the organisation carries out.

Please note that, in classifying costs by their function, we are looking at the same set of costs for the organisation as before. We are simply presenting them in different groupings.

It is an important function of accounting that information should be presented in the form most suitable for the purpose for which it is required. For some management purposes, classification of costs by function provides better information.

classification of costs by nature

In cost accounting, it is important to appreciate the nature of costs – in particular to understand that not all costs increase or decrease directly in line with increases or decreases in output. By nature, costs are:

- fixed, or
- semi-variable, or
- variable

The diagram below shows the differences between these.

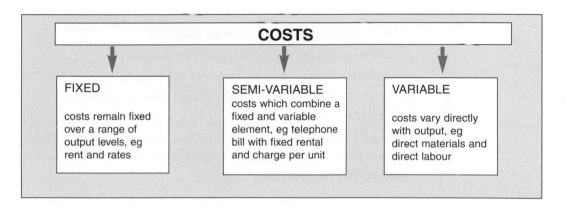

It is important to know the nature of costs and how they are affected by changes in the level of output. For example, a business decides to increase its output by 25% – will all costs increase by 25%? Fixed costs, such as rent and rates, are likely to remain unchanged, provided that there is capacity for the increased output within the existing building. Variable costs, such as direct materials and direct labour, are likely to increase by 25% as they generally vary directly with output (unless any economies of scale can be achieved). Semi-variable costs, such as the telephone bill, will increase as the extra business generates more 'phone calls; however, the increase should certainly be much less than 25%.

REASONS FOR CLASSIFYING COSTS

The question might be asked, "Why classify costs in three ways?" The answer is that we can see the same business from three different viewpoints – this will help management to run the business better:

- **by element**

  looking for the high cost elements in order to make savings, eg labour might be identified as being too high

- **by function**

  looking at the different departments to see which are the high-spending departments – perhaps savings can be made

- **by nature**

  identifying the costs as being fixed, semi-variable, or variable – the business might be able to make savings by altering the balance between fixed and variable costs

Thus classifying costs helps management with:

- decision-making, when implementing changes
- planning, when preparing forecasts and budgets
- control, when checking results against what was planned

The two Case Studies which follow illustrate the classification of costs by element (Albion Restaurant) and by function (Thyme plc). The nature of costs – fixed, semi-variable, and variable will be considered in more detail later in the book (Chapters 4 and 8).

Case Study

ALBION RESTAURANT:
COST CLASSIFICATION BY ELEMENT

situation

Albion Restaurant is a large restaurant. Some of the costs incurred by Albion Restaurant are listed below:

(a)   wages of the cleaner

(b)   cost of heating the restaurant

(c)   wages of the chefs

(d)   telephone charges

(e)   paper table covers and napkins

(f)   cost of ingredients for meals

(g)   cleaning materials

(h)   advertising costs

(i)   maintenance contract for ovens

(j)   wages of waiters and waitresses

As an accounts assistant at Albion Restaurant, you are to:

- suggest a suitable cost unit for a restaurant.
- classify the costs into the six categories shown in the table below; give your answer by entering the costs into the table:

	DIRECT COSTS	INDIRECT COSTS
MATERIALS		
LABOUR		
EXPENSES		

solution

An appropriate cost unit for a restaurant would be one meal.

	DIRECT COSTS	INDIRECT COSTS
MATERIALS	(f) cost of ingredients for meals	(e) paper table covers and napkins (g) cleaning materials
LABOUR	(c) wages of the chefs (j) wages of waiters and waitresses*	(a) wages of the cleaner
EXPENSES		(b) cost of heating the restaurant (d) telephone charges (h) advertising costs (i) maintenance contract for ovens

* see next page

* You may have classified (j) 'wages of waiters and waitresses' as 'indirect wages'. This is an equally valid answer. A cost accounting system is designed to suit a particular organisation. There are some costs that may be treated as either direct or indirect costs, depending on the particular situation and the information required from the system. Costs which could be linked directly to cost units may be treated as overheads if this is easier and saves time without losing any useful information. Whichever treatment is used, it is important to be consistent so that, next time the cost is incurred, it is dealt with in the same way.

Case Study

THYME PLC:
COST CLASSIFICATION BY FUNCTION

situation

Thyme plc is a manufacturer of TV sets.

Some of the indirect costs incurred by Thyme plc are listed below:

(a)   depreciation charge for delivery vehicles

(b)   salary of the personnel manager

(c)   materials used for maintaining factory machinery

(d)   cost of computer disks for office computers

(e)   interest payable on a bank overdraft

(f)   salary of the sales manager

(g)   cost of power used for running factory machinery

(h)   maintenance contract for office photocopier

As an accounts assistant at Thyme, you are to classify the costs by function and give your answer by entering the costs into a table.

solution

PRODUCTION COSTS	(c) materials used for maintaining factory machinery (g) cost of power used for running factory machinery
SELLING AND DISTRIBUTION COSTS	(a) depreciation charge for delivery vehicles (f) salary of the sales manager
ADMINISTRATION COSTS	(b) salary of the personnel manager (d) cost of computer disks for office computers (h) maintenance contract for office photocopier
FINANCE COSTS	(e) interest payable on a bank overdraft

CALCULATING THE COST OF GOODS AND SERVICES

Using the principles of costing will help to calculate the cost of a product – whether goods or services. Only when the cost of producing each unit of output is known, can a business make decisions about the selling price.

The steps towards calculating the cost of goods and services are:

identify the unit of output

The cost units for a particular business or organisation must be identified. As we have seen earlier, these are the units of output to which costs can be charged. Only by recovering costs through the sales of output can a business make a profit.

calculate the number of units of output for a particular time period

Once the unit of output is identified, the business is then able to calculate how many units can be produced or provided in a given time period, such as a day, week, month, quarter or year. For example, a garage will work out how many hours of mechanics' time are available, or a car manufacturer will calculate how many cars it can produce in a year.

calculate the direct costs for a particular time period

Having established the number of units of output for a particular time period, the next task is to calculate the direct costs, or prime cost, for that time period. As we have seen earlier in this chapter, the direct costs comprise:

direct materials	identifiable with the product
direct labour	the wages paid to those who make the product
direct expenses	attributable to the product

The amounts of the direct costs are added together to give the total direct costs (prime cost) of the output for the time period.

calculate the indirect costs for a particular time period

The indirect costs, or overheads, of the production or service must be calculated for the particular time period. Indirect costs comprise:

indirect materials   materials used that are not attributed directly to production

indirect labour   wages and salaries paid to those who are not directly involved in production

indirect expenses   expenses of the business not attributed directly to production

Once the indirect costs have been calculated, we must then ensure that their total cost is charged to the cost units for a particular time period. Only by including indirect costs in the total cost of the output can a business recover their cost from the sales made.

The amounts of the indirect costs are added together to give the total indirect costs (overheads) for the time period.

calculate the total cost of a unit of output

Once the direct and indirect costs for a time period are known, the total cost of a unit of output can be calculated, as follows:

$$\frac{direct\ costs\ +\ indirect\ costs}{number\ of\ units\ of\ output} = total\ cost\ of\ a\ unit\ of\ output$$

The total cost is also known as the absorption cost – because it absorbs (includes) both the direct costs and the indirect costs. Once total cost is known, the business can use the information to help it make pricing and other decisions. Note that, for stock valuation purposes, only those indirect costs which relate to production are to be included in total cost (see page 58).

calculating the cost – a summary

The process of calculating the cost of output is illustrated in the diagram shown on the next page.

costs for a service business

While the units of 'output' of businesses or organisations that produce a service are not manufactured products, they still incur the costs of:

• materials

• labour

• expenses

Some of the costs of a service business can be linked directly to the 'output' or the cost units of the organisation, but others are classified as overheads.

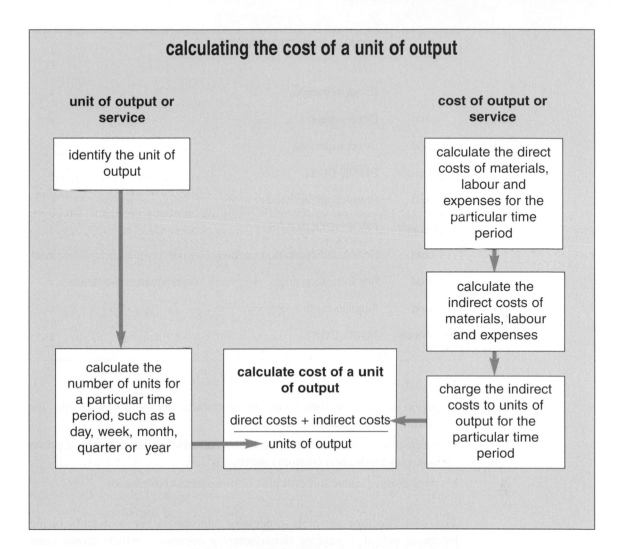

calculating the cost of a unit of output

unit of output or service

identify the unit of output

calculate the number of units for a particular time period, such as a day, week, month, quarter or year

calculate cost of a unit of output

$$\frac{\text{direct costs} + \text{indirect costs}}{\text{units of output}}$$

cost of output or service

calculate the direct costs of materials, labour and expenses for the particular time period

calculate the indirect costs of materials, labour and expenses

charge the indirect costs to units of output for the particular time period

TOTAL COST STATEMENT

The total cost statement brings together all the costs involved in producing the output of a business. It can be prepared on the basis of:

- a single cost unit, eg the cost of making one car in a car factory

- a batch, eg the cost of making 1,000 'special edition' cars

- the whole factory, eg the cost of all the car factory's output for a given time period

The total cost statement is prepared using the following layout:

TOTAL COST STATEMENT		£
	Direct materials	x
add	Direct labour	x
add	Direct expenses	x
equals	PRIME COST	x
add	Production overheads	x
equals	PRODUCTION COST	x
add	Selling and distribution costs ⌐	x
add	Administration costs ——————┤ non-production overheads	x
add	Finance costs ———————————	x
equals	TOTAL COST	x

Note that:

- *prime cost* is the direct cost of manufacturing products, before the addition of production overheads
- *production cost* is the factory cost of manufacturing the products, ie prime cost plus production (factory) overheads
- *total cost* is production cost plus non-production overheads

The cost structure above is especially appropriate for a manufacturing business; indeed a separate *manufacturing account* – which shows costs through to production cost – is prepared prior to the profit and loss account. Manufacturing accounts are covered in more detail in Chapter 7.

By taking total cost away from sales revenue we can create a profit statement. This shows the profitability of the business after all costs have been taken into account. The profit statement is:

PROFIT STATEMENT		£
	Sales revenue	x
less	Total cost	x
equals	PROFIT	x

SOURCES OF DATA FOR COSTING

In order to code, analyse and classify costs and revenues we need to obtain the information from a data source. There will be many of these within a business or organisation – potential sources include:

- materials
  - purchase orders
  - goods received notes
  - returns notes
  - invoices received
  - materials requisitions
  - stock records
  - job sheets
  - ledgers

- labour
  - clock and time cards
  - payroll analysis sheets
  - income tax and National Insurance Contributions
  - job sheets
  - ledgers

- expenses
  - invoices received
  - receipts
  - cash book
  - petty cash book
  - cheque counterfoils
  - bank transfers made
  - bank statements
  - ledgers

- income
  - invoices issued
  - cash receipts issued
  - bank paying-in book
  - bank transfers received
  - bank statements
  - ledgers

Note: at this stage in your studies you may not be familiar with all these sources of data – specialist terms will be explained in subsequent chapters.

Chapter Summary

- Cost accounting is essential to provide information for managers of organisations in order to assist with decision-making, planning and control.
- Costs may be charged directly to cost units or to sections of the business defined as cost centres.
- Costs may be classified by element, or by function, or by nature, depending on the purpose for which the information is required.
- The three categories of cost: materials, labour and expenses can each be split into direct costs and indirect costs. Indirect costs are also called 'overheads'. This gives a six-way split of costs:

DIRECT MATERIALS	INDIRECT MATERIALS
DIRECT LABOUR	INDIRECT LABOUR
DIRECT EXPENSES	INDIRECT EXPENSES
TOTAL DIRECT COSTS or PRIME COST	TOTAL OVERHEADS

- Overheads may be classified by dividing them amongst the functions or sections of the business:
  - factory (or production)
  - selling and distribution
  - administration
  - finance
  - other section headings as appropriate to the organisation
- By nature, costs are fixed, or semi-variable, or variable.
- Total cost of producing a unit of output $= \dfrac{\text{direct costs + indirect costs}}{\text{number of units of output}}$
- A total cost statement lists the total of the direct costs and the overheads. Sales revenue minus total cost equals profit.

Key Terms

cost unit	unit of output to which costs can be charged
cost centre	section of a business to which costs can be charged
materials costs	the costs of all sorts of raw materials, components and other goods used
labour costs	the costs of employees' wages and salaries
expenses	other costs, which cannot be included in 'materials' or 'labour'
direct cost	a cost that can be identified directly with each unit of output

indirect cost (overhead)	a cost that cannot be identified directly with each unit of output
prime cost	the total of all direct costs
fixed costs	costs which remain fixed over a range of output levels
semi-variable costs	costs which combine a fixed and variable element
variable costs	costs which vary directly with output
total cost statement	list of the total of the direct costs and the overhead

Student Activities

1.1   Select an organisation – either where you work, or one with which you are familiar.

(a)   Prepare a diagram, similar to that shown on page 17, identifying the main functions of the organisation and the costs incurred by each section.

(b)   Describe the cost units and cost centres used by the organisation.

1.2   Suggest one cost unit and two cost centres for:

- a college of further education
- a mixed farm, growing crops and raising cattle

1.3   (a)   Why is it important to analyse costs in different ways, eg by element, by function and by nature?

(b)   Classify each of the following costs by nature (ie fixed, or semi-variable, or variable):

- raw materials
- factory rent
- telephone
- direct labour, eg production workers paid on the basis of work done
- indirect labour, eg supervisors' salaries
- commission paid to sales staff

Taking the costs in turn, explain to a friend, who is about to set up a furniture manufacturing business, why you have classified each as fixed, or semi-variable, or variable. Answer the comment, "What difference does it make anyway, they are all costs that have to be paid."

1.4 Severn Manufacturing Limited makes chairs for school and college use. The chairs have plastic seats, and tubular steel legs. You are to classify the manufacturing costs into:

- direct materials
- indirect materials
- direct labour
- indirect labour
- direct expenses
- indirect expenses

The cost items to be classified are:

COST ITEM	CLASSIFICATION (write your answer)
Tubular steel	
Factory supervisor's salary	
Wages of employee operating the moulding machine which produces the chair seats	
Works canteen assistant's wages	
Rates of factory	
Power to operate machines	
Factory heating and lighting	
Plastic for making chair seats	
Hire of special machinery for one particular order	
Cost of grease for the moulding machine	
Depreciation of factory machinery	
Depreciation of office equipment	

If you believe alternative classifications exist, argue the case and state if you need further information from the company.

1.5 Betterwell NHS Trust is a large hospital with many departments. Costs of the general operating theatre have been identified and you are to classify them into:

- direct materials
- indirect materials
- direct labour
- indirect labour
- direct expenses
- indirect expenses

The cost items to be classified are:

COST ITEM	CLASSIFICATION (write your answer)
Dressings	
Disposable scalpels	
Surgeon's salary	
Floor cleaning materials	
Laundry	
Depreciation of staff drinks machine	
Theatre heat and light	
Porter's wages	
Anaesthetic gas	
Depreciation of theatre equipment	
Maintenance of theatre equipment	
Cost of CDs for music in theatre	
Anaesthetist's salary	

If you believe alternative classifications exist, argue the case and state if you need further information.

1.6 Wyvern Water Limited bottles natural spring water at its plant at Walcoll at the base of the Wyvern Hills. The natural spring is on land owned by a local farmer to whom a royalty is paid for each bottle of water produced.

You are working in the costing section of Wyvern Water and are asked to analyse the following cost items into the appropriate columns and to agree the totals:

Cost item	Total cost	Prime cost	Production overheads	Admin costs	Selling and distribution costs
	£	£	£	£	£
Wages of employees working on the bottling line	6,025				
Wages of employees in the stores department	2,750				
Cost of bottles	4,050				
Safety goggles for bottling line employees	240				
Advertisement for new employees	125				
Depreciation of bottling machinery	500				
Depreciation of sales staff's cars	1,000				
Royalty paid to local farmer	750				
Cost of trade exhibition	1,500				
Computer stationery	210				
Sales staff salaries	4,095				
TOTALS	21,245				

1.7   The following figures relate to the accounts of Hughes Limited, a manufacturing business, for the year ended 31 December 2004:

	£
Raw materials used in the factory	118,830
Rent and rates of factory	16,460
Factory wages	117,315
Factory power	3,825
Factory heat and light	1,185
Factory expenses and maintenance	4,095
Salaries and wages of office staff	69,350
Advertising	11,085
Office expenses	3,930
Depreciation of factory plant and machinery	3,725
Sales revenue	426,350

You are to:

(a)   Prepare a total cost statement for the year which shows:

- prime cost

- production cost

- total cost

Discuss any assumptions that you make and state if you need further information from the company.

(b)   Prepare a profit statement for the year (on the assumption that all the goods manufactured have been sold).

2 Materials costs

Businesses and other organisations hold stocks of materials in the form of raw materials and components, products bought for resale, and service items. Often the value of such materials is high, representing a considerable investment of money. In this chapter we look at:

- the purchasing and control of stocks of materials
- re-ordering procedures
- the records that are kept for stocks of materials
- the purposes of stock taking and stock reconciliation
- the valuation of stock
- the use of stores ledger records
- the book-keeping entries for materials costs

NVQ PERFORMANCE CRITERIA COVERED

unit 6: RECORDING AND EVALUATING COSTS AND REVENUES

element 6.1

record and analyse information relating to direct costs and revenues

A   identify direct costs in accordance with the organisation's costing procedures

B   record and analyse information relating to direct costs

C   calculate direct costs in accordance with the organisation's policies and procedures

D   check cost information for stocks against usage and stock control practices

E   resolve or refer queries to the appropriate person

MATERIALS STOCKS

Materials is the cost of:

- raw materials and components bought for use by a manufacturing business
- products bought for resale by a shop or a wholesaler
- service items, such as stationery, bought for use within a business or organisation

In costing we need to distinguish between direct materials and indirect materials. Thus a manufacturer classifies the cost of materials from which the finished product is made as direct materials; other materials used – grease for machines, cleaning materials, etc – are classified as indirect materials, and form part of the overheads of the business.

The buying of materials is normally undertaken by a firm's Purchasing Department, although in smaller businesses the responsibility will be carried out by an individual or the owner. The job of the buyer(s) is to ensure that the purchases made by the business are bought at the lowest possible cost, consistent with quality and quantity.

At any time, most businesses will hold materials in stock ready for use or resale. The diagram shown on the next page examines the holding of stocks by three types of business: a manufacturing business which makes stock, a trading business such as a shop, which buys and sells stock, and a service business or organisation.

PLANNING OF PURCHASES AND CONTROL OF STOCKS

Planning for the purchase of materials and the control of stocks of materials is critical to the efficiency of a business. However, holding stocks is expensive:

- they have to be financed, possibly by using borrowed money (on which interest is payable)
- there are storage costs, including rent and rates, security, insurance

Within an organisation there are conflicting demands on its policy for stocks of materials. On the one hand, the finance department will want to minimise stock levels to keep costs as low as possible; on the other hand, production and marketing departments will be anxious to keep stocks high so that output can be maintained and new orders satisfied speedily before customers decide to buy elsewhere.

STOCKS HELD BY BUSINESSES

Manufacturing Business	Trading Business	Service Business
raw materials and components These stocks are held by a manufacturer to reduce the risk of production delays if a supplier fails to deliver on time. A vehicle manufacturer may hold a stock of plastic bumpers, for example.	**goods for sale** These are items the retailer or wholesaler has bought in (eg from the manufacturer) and has available for sale to the customer. For example:	**consumable materials** These are materials that are either for use in the organisation or for sale to the customer as part of the service provided. For example:
work-in-progress These are stocks of part-finished goods on the production line. In a car factory these would be cars partly assembled, for example.	■ *retailers* a supermarket will have a stock of cans of orange drink for sale ■ *wholesalers* a timber merchant will have quantities of wood for sale to customers	■ *for use in the organisation* in a college there will be a stock of paper for the photocopiers ■ *items for sale* an optician will sell reading glasses as part of the service provided
finished goods These are goods that have been completed and are ready for sale to customers. A vehicle manufacturer would have completed cars ready for sale, for example.		

There are a number of methods of planning purchases and of stock control. Which is adopted will depend on the size and sophistication of the organisation. It is important that an organisation knows how much stock it has at any time – either by making a physical stock count, or by keeping computer records (which need physical verification at regular intervals) – and it must know when it will have to re-order more stocks. The organisation then needs to know the quantity that needs to be re-ordered. The methods used include:

estimation   Some small businesses do not keep much stock, and the owner may estimate the quantity and timing of materials purchases. This is not a recommended method for a well-managed business or organisation.

'two bin' system	The principle here is to keep two 'bins' of a stock unit. When the first bin has run out, new stocks of materials are ordered and will be supplied before the second 'bin' runs out. The term 'bin' is used loosely, and can apply to any measure of stock. This is a very basic principle, but it works well in many situations.
perpetual inventory	'Inventory' is another word for stock. This system records receipt and issue of stock as the items pass in and out of the organisation, and re-orders are made accordingly. Records of stock are kept manually, or more commonly now on computer file activated by reading of bar codes. Many supermarkets and manufacturing businesses work on this basis, and order stock on a 'Just-In-Time' basis (see page 43).
formulas	Organisations need to calculate when to order materials, and how much to order; formulas can be used to help with this. These are explained in the sections which follow.

MATERIALS PURCHASES: LEVEL METHOD OF RE-ORDERING

This method orders materials in fixed quantities, eg 750 reams of photocopying paper (a ream is 500 sheets). For such a system to operate, the organisation should know:

- the *lead time*, ie how long it takes for new stock to be delivered after being ordered
- the appropriate *re-order quantity*
- the *minimum stock level,* ie the lowest level that stock should fall to before the new order from the supplier is delivered (the minimum stock level is also known as a *buffer stock* to meet unexpected emergencies)
- the *maximum stock level* that can be held – this can be calculated (see below) but may well be determined by the amount of storage space available in the warehouse, shop or office stationery 'cupboard'
- the *re-order level*, ie the point at which a new order is to be placed – this is often the most critical factor to determine

Many organisations use manual or computer stock control systems to keep a running record of the amount of each material held in stock, the lead time for re-ordering, and the minimum stock level. The level method of re-ordering is illustrated as follows:

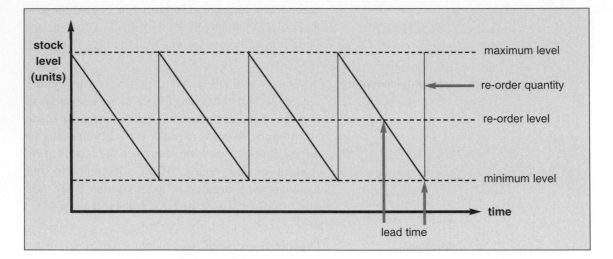

re-order level

The re-order level is calculated so that replacement materials will be delivered just as the stock level reaches the minimum level. The calculation of re-order level is:

(maximum usage x maximum lead time) + minimum stock level

re-order quantity

At the re-order level, a purchase order for new stock is forwarded to the supplier. The quantity to be purchased is the re-order quantity; which is calculated as:

maximum stock level − minimum stock level

maximum and minimum stock levels

By the time new stock is delivered, the remaining stock should have fallen to the minimum level, so that the new stock restores the level to the maximum.

The maximum and minimum stock levels can be set as follows:

- *maximum stock level = minimum stock level + re-order quantity*
- *minimum stock level = re-order level − (average usage x average lead time)*

However, maximum stock may be determined by other factors, eg the amount of storage space available, a policy decision not to hold more than a certain number of days' (or weeks' or months') usage.

example

A4, white photocopying paper

daily usage	30 reams (a ream is 500 sheets)
lead time	5 days
re-order quantity	750 reams*
minimum stock level	150 reams**
maximum stock level	900 reams***

Re-order level = (30 daily usage x 5 days' lead time) + 150 minimum stock

= (30 x 5) + 150

= 150 + 150

= 300 reams (re-order level)

When the balance of stock falls to 300 reams, a purchase order for 750 reams is forwarded to the supplier of the paper.

*   re-order quantity   = maximum stock level – minimum stock level

                                             = 900 – 150

                                             = 750 reams

**   minimum stock level   = re-order level – (average usage x average lead time)

                                             = 300 – (30 x 5 days)

                                             = 150 reams

*** maximum stock level   = minimum stock level + re-order quantity

                                             = 150 + 750 = 900 reams

It is important not to treat stock calculations in isolation – there does need to be consideration of wider issues which may affect the business or organisation. Such issues include:

- needs of the business – for example, if a stock item is being used less frequently than before, the stock calculations will need to be revised to suit current and future needs

- obsolescence of stock – for example, if spare parts are kept for a particular make and model of vehicle, stock levels will need to be run down if the vehicles are being replaced by those of a different make and model

- seasonal variations affecting usage and stock levels – for example, a business using oil for heating may be offered a cheaper price when usage is low in the summer which may make it worthwhile to stock up; by contrast, when usage is high in the winter, the supplier's price and lead times may increase

MATERIALS PURCHASES: ECONOMIC ORDER QUANTITY (EOQ)

It is clear that the re-order quantity is critical to the efficiency of stock-holding:

- if re-order amounts are *too large*, too much stock will be held, which will be an expense to the business
- if re-order amounts are *too small*, the expense of constantly re-ordering will outweigh any cost savings of lower stock levels, and there will be the danger that the item might 'run out'

The most economic re-order quantity – *the economic order quantity (EOQ)* – can be calculated by a mathematical formula which involves a number of different costs and other figures:

- *ordering cost* – the administration cost of placing each order, eg stationery, postage, wages, telephone
- *stock holding cost* – the cost of keeping the stock on the shelves expressed as the cost of holding one item of stock per year; examples of stock holding costs include rent and rates, insurance, wages, deterioration, obsolescence, security
- *annual usage* – the number of stock units used per year

The formula is:

$$\text{Economic Order Quantity (EOQ)} = \sqrt{\frac{2 \times \text{annual usage} \times \text{ordering cost}}{\text{stock holding cost}}}$$

On a calculator with a square root function, this formula can be worked out easily. Calculate the figures in the formula first, and then press the square root button ($\sqrt{}$).

For example, for a particular stock item, the ordering cost of each order is £30, the stock holding cost is £2 per stock item per year, and annual usage is 2,000 units. The EOQ formula is applied as follows:

$$\text{Economic Order Quantity (EOQ)} = \sqrt{\frac{2 \times 2,000 \times £30}{£2}}$$

$$= \sqrt{\frac{120,000}{2}}$$

continued on next page

$$= \sqrt{60,000}$$

$$= \quad 245 \text{ units}$$

As a result of using EOQ, a balance is struck between the cost of placing an order and the cost of holding stock; EOQ represents the most efficient level of order to place – in the example here it is 245 units.

As well as the formula method, EOQ can be found using other methods – by tabulation and by graph.

MATERIALS PURCHASES: JUST-IN-TIME (JIT)

Just-In-Time is a system of materials purchasing favoured by manufacturing businesses and large supermarket chains. Using JIT, materials needed by a manufacturer are delivered to the production line, or – for retailers – delivered to the store, just as they are needed. The essentials of the successful operation of JIT are:

*   the right quantities
*   in the right place
*   just-in-time

For JIT to operate effectively, the manufacturer or supermarket needs quality suppliers who can be contracted to deliver materials in accordance with demand schedules. In this way stock levels are kept to a minimum, with consequent savings in stock holding costs. The disadvantage is that the JIT system is susceptible to supply chain problems – eg bad weather or a labour dispute – there are no buffer stocks to absorb such difficulties.

Manufacturers who use JIT often try to attract component suppliers to the same area. The car manufacturer Fiat has gone a step further than this by building a car factory in southern Italy with the component firms on the same site.

Retailers who use JIT – such as major supermarket chains – have arrangements with their suppliers to supply goods more or less on demand. Information technology systems used by these businesses help them to anticipate the quantities they have to order: electronic tills provide up-to-the-minute stock usage for each product 'line' and so stock levels are constantly monitored. Orders are sent to suppliers, often through EDI (Electronic Data Interchange) systems, and delivered within a short space of time. If there is a run on a particular item – eg soft drinks in a heat wave – the system will ensure that new stock is delivered very rapidly.

Factors to consider in relation to JIT include:

- reliability of the supplier
- quality of goods supplied
- effect on the business of disruption of supplies caused by factors such as bad weather or strikes
- flexibility of suppliers to react positively to changes in orders caused by increases or decreases in demand
- minimal stock taking requirements
- alternative uses for resources released, eg storage areas no longer needed
- overall efficiency of the JIT system in the context of maintaining the firm's output

STOCK RECORDS

Most organisations will have records of their stocks of materials. Such records may be kept either by using a computer stock control system, or manually on individual stock records. Under both methods – computer and manual – a separate record is maintained for each of the different materials kept in stock. The system is used whether the materials are held for resale by a retailer, or for use in production by a manufacturer. When supplies of the material are received they are entered in the stock record, and when items are sold (or issued to production) they are deducted from the stock record.

A typical stock record is shown on the next page. The stock item is A4 white photocopying paper which is used within the organisation.

Note the following on the stock record:

stock description	refers to the description of the stock, for example photocopying paper
stock units	refers to how the stock is stored or packed, eg photocopying paper is packed in reams (packets of 500 sheets)
stock reference no	refers to the identification number allocated to the stock by the business – often marked on the stock, and sometimes by means of a barcode
location	refers to where the stock can be found in the stores, eg row A, bin 6 refers to the location in the storeroom or warehouse

STOCK RECORD

Stock description .. A4 white photocopying paper ..

Stock units .... reams ....

Stock ref. No. .... P1026 ....

Location .... row A, bin 6 ....

Minimum	150 reams
Maximum	900 reams
Re-order level	300 reams
Re-order quantity	750 reams

| DATE | GOODS RECEIVED | | GOODS ISSUED | | BALANCE |
	Reference	Quantity	Reference	Quantity	
2004					
1 Apr					300
2 Apr			MR 101	40	260
5 Apr			MR 104	30	230
6 Apr			MR 116	50	180
7 Apr			MR 121	40	140
8 Apr	GRN 17901	750			890
9 Apr	MRN 58	5			895

goods received   the two columns record the Goods Received Note (GRN) reference and the quantity of items received – or where goods are returned into stock, the reference of the Materials Returns Note (MRN)

goods issued   the two columns record the Materials Requisition (MR) reference and the number of items issued; an example of a Materials Requisition is shown below

balance   is the number of items which remain in stock

MATERIALS REQUISITION

Department: Printing

Document no: MR 101

Date: 2 April 2004

Code no	Description	Quantity	For cost office use only Value of issue (£)
P 1026	A4 white photocopying paper	40 reams	

Authorised by: *R Omar*   Received by: *Pete Bashir*

STOCK TAKING AND STOCK RECONCILIATION

stock taking

A business or organisation will check regularly that the quantity of stock held is the same as the number recorded on the stock records. This is done by means of a stock take – counting the physical stock on hand to check against the balance shown by the records, and to identify any theft or deterioration.

Stock taking is carried out on either a periodic basis or continuously.

A *periodic basis* involves carrying out a stock take of all items held at regular intervals (often twice a year).

Continuous stock taking is a constant process where selected items are counted on a rotating basis, with all items being checked at least once a year (expensive, desirable or high-turnover items will need to be checked more frequently).

The number of items actually held is recorded on a stock list by the person doing the stock take. An extract from a stock list is shown on the next page; it shows the A4 paper seen in the stock record. The stock list will, of course, contain many items when the stock take has been completed.

stock list as at *9 April 2004*					**checker** *H Ramsay*		
product code	item description	location	unit size	units counted	stock record balance	discrepancy	checker's initials
P1026	*A4 white photocopying paper*	*row A, bin 6*	*ream*	*895*	*895*	*nil*	*HR*

checker's signature *H Ramsay*   **Authorised for write-off**

stock reconciliation

The object of the stock take is to see if the stock records represent accurately the level of stock held. The two columns on the stock list – 'units counted' and 'stock record balance' enable this comparison to be carried out; the process is known as a *stock reconciliation*. It is an important process because

- an accurate stock figure can then be used to value the stock
- it will highlight any discrepancies which can then be investigated

Discrepancies and queries should be noted on the stock list and referred to the supervisor and any other people who may need to know, eg the storekeeper, or the firm's auditors who are organising the stock take. If the discrepancy is small it will be authorised for write-off. Larger discrepancies will need to be investigated, as they could have been caused by:

- an error on the stock record, such as a failure to record a stock movement or an error in calculating the balance of stock
- theft of stock
- damaged stock being disposed of without any record having been made

stock holding queries

Inevitably, even in the best-run system, queries will arise about stock. These queries may come from within the organisation, eg the production department, or externally, eg suppliers.

It is important that such queries are resolved swiftly and efficiently by referring directly to the correct department, as indicated in the following diagram:

QUERY	DEPARTMENT/SECTION
stock levels	stores
materials usage	production, purchase ordering, goods inwards, auditors
materials prices	purchasing, accounts
quality and rejects	goods returns, stores (scrap)
stock returns	returns outwards, accounts

VALUATION OF STOCK

The stock of materials held by a business or organisation invariably has considerable value and ties up a lot of money. At the end of the financial year, it is essential to value the stock for use in the calculation of profit in the final accounts. As we have just seen, a process of stock taking is used to make a physical check of the stock held, which is then compared with the stock records. The stock held is then valued as follows:

number of items held x cost per item = stock value at cost

The auditors may make random checks to ensure that the stock value is correct.

The general rule is that stock can be valued at *either*:

- what it cost the business to buy the stock (including additional costs to bring the product or service to its present location or condition, such as delivery charges), *or*
- the net realisable value – which is the actual or estimated selling price (less any extra costs, such as selling and distribution) – ie what you would get for it

Stock valuation is normally made at the *lower of cost and net realisable value*. This valuation is taken from Statement of Standard Accounting Practice (SSAP) No 9, entitled 'Stocks and long-term contracts'. This method of valuation applies the 'prudence' concept of accounting. It is illustrated as follows:

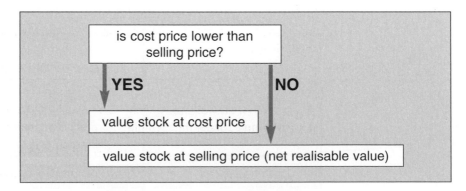

The difficulty in stock valuation is in finding out the cost price of stock – this is not easy when quantities of a particular stock item are continually being bought in – often at different prices – and then sold. Some organisations have stock in a number of different forms, eg manufacturing businesses have stocks of raw materials, work-in-progress and finished goods.

METHODS OF STOCK VALUATION

issuing of materials and goods

The costing process requires that a value is given to raw materials (for a manufacturer) and goods (for a shop) when they are 'issued'. This means the point at which they are handed over to the production line or placed on the shop shelves. Traditionally the materials and goods were issued from 'stores' – a storage area or stockroom – where they had been kept by the business since delivery from the supplier. The phrase 'issued from stores' is still used, although nowadays materials and stocks are often delivered at the very last minute (Just-In-Time) to save storage and finance costs.

The cost of the materials or goods at the time of issue is normally the purchase cost – ie the price the business paid the supplier. But costs do vary – so which cost do you take and what valuation do you give the materials or goods?

The three most commonly used methods for deciding which 'cost' to use for raw materials used in the production process or sold from shop shelves are:

FIFO (First In, First Out)

In this method, the first (oldest) cost prices are used first when goods are issued from stores. This means that the remaining stock is valued at the most recent cost prices.

LIFO (Last In, First Out)

In this method, the most recent (last) cost prices are used first when goods are issued from stores. This means that the remaining stock is valued at older cost prices.

AVCO (Weighted Average Cost)

In this method, a weighted average cost is calculated for the goods in stock at a given time, using the formula:

$$\text{weighted average cost} = \frac{\text{total cost of goods in stock}}{\text{number of items in stock}}$$

The weighted average cost is then used to attach a value to issues from stores. A new weighted average must be calculated each time that further purchases are made.

The use of a particular method of stock valuation does not necessarily correspond with the method of physical distribution adopted in a firm's stores. For example, in a car factory one car battery of type X is the same as another, and no-one will be concerned if the storekeeper issues one from the last batch received, even if the FIFO system has been adopted. However, perishable goods are always physically handled on the basis of first in, first out, even if the accounting stock records use another method.

Having chosen a suitable stock valuation method, a business will continue to use that method unless there are good reasons for making the change. This is in line with the 'consistency' concept of accounting.

recording stock values – stores ledger record

In order to be able to calculate accurately the price at which stocks of materials are issued and to ascertain a valuation of stock, a stores ledger record – or stock card – is used, as shown below. This method of recording stock data is also used in the Case Study which follows.

	STORES LEDGER RECORD								
Date	**Receipts**			**Issues**			**Balance**		
	Quantity	Cost*	Total Cost	Quantity	Cost*	Total Cost	Quantity	Cost*	Total Cost
		£	£		£	£		£	£

*cost = cost price

Note that the layout of the stores ledger record – or stock card – may vary slightly from one business to another. Also, many businesses use a computer system for their stock records.

Case Study

H RASHID COMPUTER SUPPLIES: STORES LEDGER RECORDS

situation

H Rashid runs a computer supplies company. One of the items he sells is the 'Zap' data disk.

To show how the stores ledger records would appear under FIFO, LIFO and AVCO, and the closing stock valuation at 31 May 2004, the following data is used for each method:

January	Opening stock of 40 units at a cost of £3.00 each
February	Bought 20 units at a cost of £3.60 each
March	Sold 36 units for £6 each
April	Bought 20 units at a cost of £3.75 each
May	Sold 25 units for £6 each

What will be the profit for the period using each stock valuation method?

solution

Note: In the first two methods – FIFO and LIFO – units issued at the same time may be valued at different costs. This is because the quantities received, with their costs, are listed separately and used in a specific order. There may be insufficient units at one cost, eg see the May issue using both FIFO and LIFO methods.

FIFO

STORES LEDGER RECORD

Date	Receipts			Issues			Balance		
2004	Quantity	Cost	Total Cost	Quantity	Cost	Total Cost	Quantity	Cost	Total Cost
		£	£		£	£		£	£
Jan	Balance						40	3.00	120.00
Feb	20	3.60	72.00				40	3.00	120.00
							20	3.60	72.00
							60		192.00
March				36	3.00	108.00	4	3.00	12.00
							20	3.60	72.00
							24		84.00
April	20	3.75	75.00				4	3.00	12.00
							20	3.60	72.00
							20	3.75	75.00
							44		159.00
May				4	3.00	12.00			
				20	3.60	72.00			
				1	3.75	3.75	19	3.75	71.25

Note: In the 'Balance' columns, a new list of stock quantities and costs is started after each receipt or issue. When stock is issued, costs are used from the **top** of the list downwards.

LIFO

STORES LEDGER RECORD

Date	Receipts			Issues			Balance		
2004	Quantity	Cost	Total Cost	Quantity	Cost	Total Cost	Quantity	Cost	Total Cost
		£	£		£	£		£	£
Jan	Balance						40	3.00	120.00
Feb	20	3.60	72.00				40	3.00	120.00
							20	3.60	72.00
							60		192.00
March				20	3.60	72.00			
				16	3.00	48.00	24	3.00	72.00
April	20	3.75	75.00				24	3.00	72.00
							20	3.75	75.00
							44		147.00
May				20	3.75	75.00			
				5	3.00	15.00	19	3.00	57.00

Note: In the 'Balance' columns, a new list of stock quantities and costs is started after each receipt or issue. When stock is issued, costs are used from the **bottom** of the list upwards. However, the new balance list each time must be kept in date order.

AVCO

In this method, each quantity issued is valued at the weighted average cost per unit, and so is the balance in stock. The complete list of different costs does not have to be re-written each time.

STORES LEDGER RECORD

Date	Receipts			Issues			Balance		
2004	Quantity	Cost	Total Cost	Quantity	Cost	Total Cost	Quantity	Cost	Total Cost
		£	£		£	£		£	£
Jan	Balance						40	3.00	120.00
Feb	20	3.60	72.00				40	3.00	120.00
							20	3.60	72.00
							60	3.20	192.00
March				36	3.20	115.20	24	3.20	76.80
April	20	3.75	75.00				24	3.20	76.80
							20	3.75	75.00
							44	3.45	151.80
May				25	3.45	86.25	19	3.45	65.55

Note: Weighted average cost is calculated by dividing the quantity held in stock into the value of the stock. For example, at the end of February, the weighted average cost is £192 ÷ 60 units = £3.20, and at the end of April it is £151.80 ÷ 44 = £3.45.

The closing stock valuations at the end of May 2004 under each method show total cost prices of:

FIFO	£71.25
LIFO	£57.00
AVCO	£65.55

There is quite a difference, and this has come about because different stock methods have been used.

effect on profit

In the example above, the selling price was £6 per unit. The effect on gross profit of using different stock valuations is shown below.

		FIFO	LIFO	AVCO
		£	£	£
Sales: 61 units at £6		366.00	366.00	366.00
Opening stock:	40 units at £3	120.00	120.00	120.00
Purchases:	20 units at £3.60 and 20 units at £3.75	147.00	147.00	147.00
		267.00	267.00	267.00
Less Closing stock: 19 units		71.25	57.00	65.55
Cost of sales		195.75	210.00	201.45
Gross profit = Sales – Cost of sales		170.25	156.00	164.55

Notice that the cost of sales figure in each case is also obtainable by adding up the values in the 'Issues' column. You can also check in each case that, both in Units and in Values:

opening stock + receipts – issues = closing stock

The Case Study shows that in times of rising prices, FIFO produces the highest reported profit, LIFO the lowest, and AVCO between the other two. However, over the life of a business, total profit is the same in total, whichever method is chosen: the profit is allocated to different years depending on which method is used.

The choice of method depends on which method is considered to give the most useful information for management purposes.

ADVANTAGES AND DISADVANTAGES OF FIFO, LIFO AND AVCO

FIFO (first in, first out)

advantages

- it is realistic, ie it assumes that goods are issued in order of receipt
- it is easy to calculate
- stock valuation comprises actual costs at which items have been bought
- the closing stock valuation is close to the most recent costs

disadvantages

- costs at which goods are issued are not necessarily the latest prices
- in times of rising prices, profits will be higher than with other methods (resulting in more tax to pay)
- the method is cumbersome as the list of different costs must be maintained

LIFO (last in, first out)

advantages

- goods are issued at the latest costs
- it is easy to calculate
- in manufacturing, materials are issued at more up-to-date costs, giving a more realistic production cost

disadvantages

- illogical, ie it assumes goods are issued in reverse order from that in which they are received
- the closing stock valuation is not usually at most recent costs
- when stocks are being run down, issues will 'dip into' old stock at out-of-date costs
- may not be acceptable to the Inland Revenue for taxation purposes as the method overstates cost of sales and understates profit
- the method is cumbersome as the list of different costs must be maintained

AVCO (weighted average cost)

advantages

- over a number of accounting periods reported profits are smoothed, ie both high and low profits are avoided
- fluctuations in purchase costs are evened out so that issues do not vary greatly
- logical, ie it assumes that identical units, even when purchased at different times, have the same value
- closing stock valuation is close to current market values (in times of rising prices, it will be below current market values)
- the calculations can be computerised more easily than the other methods

disadvantages

- a new weighted average has to be calculated after each receipt, and calculations may be to several decimal places
- issues and stock valuation are usually at costs which never existed
- issues may not be at current costs and, in times of rising prices, will be below current costs

The important point to remember is that a business must adopt a consistent stock valuation policy, ie it should choose one method of finding the cost price, and not change it without good reason. FIFO and AVCO are more commonly used than LIFO; in particular, LIFO usually results in a stock valuation for the final accounts which bears little relationship to recent costs – for this reason it is not favoured by SSAP 9. However, LIFO has the advantage that it gives a more realistic production cost – this is because materials are issued at more up-to-date prices. It is also appropriate to apply LIFO principles when costing materials in a quotation to be given to a potential customer: in times of rising prices you wouldn't want to quote old prices – for example, under FIFO – and then, when the quotation is accepted, find that there is no more of the older-priced materials left.

Now study the table on the next page to consolidate what you have learnt so far.

a comparison of the methods of stock valuation

	FIFO	LIFO	AVCO
method	The costs used for goods sold or issued follow the order in which the goods were received.	The costs used for goods sold or issued are opposite to the order in which the goods were received.	Does not relate issues to any particular batch of goods received, but uses a weighted average cost.
calculation	It is easy to calculate costs because they relate to specific receipts of materials or goods.	It is easy to calculate costs because they relate to specific receipts of materials or goods.	More complex because of the need to calculate weighted average costs.
stock valuation	Stock valuations are based on the most recent costs of materials or goods received.	Stock valuations are based on older costs of materials or goods received.	Weighted average costs are used to value closing stock.
profits and taxation	In times of rising prices this method will result in higher reported profits than the other methods, resulting in more tax being payable. This method is acceptable for tax purposes.	In times of rising prices this method will result in lower reported profits than the other methods. This may not be acceptable for tax purposes.	The weighted average method will smooth out some of the peaks and troughs of profit and loss. This method is acceptable for tax purposes.
administration	Use of this method will mean keeping track of each receipt until the goods are issued or sold.	Use of this method will mean keeping track of each receipt until the goods are issued or sold.	There is no need to track each receipt as a weighted average cost is used. This also means it is easier to computerise the stock records.
cost of sales	In a time of rising prices this method will use older, out of date prices for cost of sales or goods issued.	In a time of rising prices this method will use more up-to-date prices for cost of sales or goods issued.	This method will give an average price for the cost of sales.

CATEGORIES OF STOCK

Statement of Standard Accounting Practice No 9 requires that, in calculating the lower of cost and net realisable value, note should be taken of:

– separate items of stock, or

– groups of similar items

This means that the stock valuation 'rule' must be applied to each separate item of stock, or each group or category of similar stocks. The total cost cannot be compared with the total net realisable value, as is shown by the Case Study which follows.

Case Study

PAINT AND WALLPAPER SUPPLIES: VALUING YEAR-END STOCKS

situation

The year-end stocks for the two main groups of stock held by the business Paint and Wallpaper Supplies are found to be:

	Cost £	Net realisable value £
Paints	2,500	2,300
Wallpapers	5,000	7,500
	7,500	9,800

How will the stock be valued for the year-end accounts?

solution

The correct stock valuation is £7,300, which takes the 'lower of cost and net realisable value' for each group of stock, ie

	£
Paints (at net realisable value)	2,300
Wallpapers (at cost)	5,000
	7,300

You will also note that this valuation is the lowest possible choice, indicating that stock valuation follows the *prudence concept* of accounting.

STOCK VALUATION FOR MANUFACTURING BUSINESSES

We saw earlier that, under SSAP 9, stock is normally valued at the lower of cost and net realisable value. This principle applies to a manufacturer for the three types of stock that may be held at the year-end:

- raw materials
- part-finished goods or work-in-progress
- finished goods

For raw materials, the comparison is made between cost (which can be found using techniques such as FIFO, LIFO, or AVCO) and net realisable value.

For stocks of both part-finished and finished goods, SSAP 9 requires that the cost valuation includes expenditure not only on direct materials but also on direct labour, direct expenses and production overheads. Thus for part-finished and finished goods, 'cost' means 'production cost', ie the total of:

- direct materials
- direct labour
- direct expenses
- production overheads (to bring the product to its present location or condition)

Such 'cost' is then compared with net realisable value – less any further costs necessary to complete the item or get it in a condition to be sold – and the lower figure is taken as the stock valuation. (Remember that different items or groups of stock are compared separately).

Case Study

ABC MANUFACTURING: STOCK VALUATION FOR A MANUFACTURER

situation

ABC Manufacturing started in business on 1 July 2003 producing security devices for doors and windows. During the first year 2,000 units were sold and, at the end of the year, on 30 June 2004, there were 200 units in stock which were finished and 20 units which were exactly half-finished as regards direct materials, direct labour and production overheads.

Costs for the first year were:

	£
Direct materials used	18,785
Direct labour	13,260
Production overheads	8,840
Non-production overheads	4,420
Total cost for year	**45,305**

At 30 June 2004 it was estimated that the net realisable value of each completed security device was £35. There were no stocks of direct materials.

Calculate the stock valuation at 30 June 2004 for:

- part-finished goods
- finished goods

solution

PART-FINISHED GOODS/WORK-IN-PROGRESS

To calculate the value of both part-finished and finished goods we need to know the production cost, ie direct materials, direct labour and production overheads. This is:

	£
Direct materials used	18,785
Direct labour	13,260
Production overheads	8,840
Production cost for year	**40,885**

All these costs are included because they have been incurred in bringing the product to its present location or condition. Non-production overheads are not included because they are not directly related to production.

Thus, a production cost of £40,885 has produced:

Units sold	2,000
Closing stock of completed units	200
Closing stock of part-finished goods –	
20 units exactly half-finished equals 10 completed units	10
Production for year	**2,210**

The **cost per unit** is:

$$\frac{£40,885}{2,210} = \textbf{£18.50 per unit}$$

The 20 half-finished units have a cost of (20 ÷ 2) x £18.50 = **£185**.
They have a net realisable value of (20 ÷ 2) x £35 = £350.
The value of part-finished goods will, therefore, be shown in the accounts as £185, which is the lower of cost and net realisable value.

FINISHED GOODS
The completed units in stock at the end of the year have a production cost of 200 x £18.50 = £3,700, compared with a net realisable value of 200 x £35 = £7,000. Applying the rule of lower of cost and net realisable value, finished goods stock will be valued at the cost price, **£3,700**.

OTHER STOCK VALUATION METHODS

As well as the FIFO, LIFO and AVCO methods used to determine the valuation of closing stock, other methods which could be used include:

standard cost

This uses a pre-determined cost based on estimates of expected cost levels – referred to as standard cost. This level of cost is determined in advance so as to aid planning, cost control and pricing.

An example would be in a factory making cars. The costs of materials are assessed – based on past production and future predictions to establish a standard cost. The same process is carried out on anticipated wage levels. Finally a standard cost for materials and labour can be prepared which then would form the basis for any decision on car prices, and also be used to assess control of cost levels during actual production.

SSAP 9 stresses that standard costs should be reviewed frequently, to ensure that they bear a reasonable relationship to actual costs during the period.

Note: standard costs are studied in detail at NVQ Level 4 Accounting.

replacement cost

This method considers the price at which the items of stock can be replaced, either by purchase or by manufacture. SSAP 9 considers this method unacceptable because replacement cost is not necessarily the same as actual cost. For example, in times of rising prices, replacement cost will be higher than actual cost, which means that a profit is taken before the stock is sold.

This method, similarly to LIFO, gives a more up-to-date production cost for the work done.

BOOK-KEEPING FOR MATERIALS COSTS

In this section we look at the cost book-keeping entries to record stock transactions – the purchase of materials on credit from suppliers, and the issue of materials to work-in-progress. These entries form part of the book-keeping system for costing. Chapter 7 looks in detail at an integrated book-keeping system.

When making cost book-keeping entries, remember to use the principles of double-entry book-keeping:

• a debit entry records a gain in value, an asset or an expense

• a credit entry records the giving of value, a liability or an income item

With stocks of materials, there are two main entries to record:

• **purchase of materials on credit from a supplier**
    – debit materials account (ie an asset is gained)
    – credit creditor's account (ie a liability is incurred)

• **issue of materials to work-in-progress**
    – debit work-in-progress account (ie an asset of materials is gained)
    – credit materials account (ie value of materials is given to work-in-progress account)

Three accounts are involved in these transactions
    – materials account
    – work-in-progress (or part-finished goods) account
    – creditor's account/purchases ledger control account

The cost book-keeping entries are shown diagrammatically as follows:

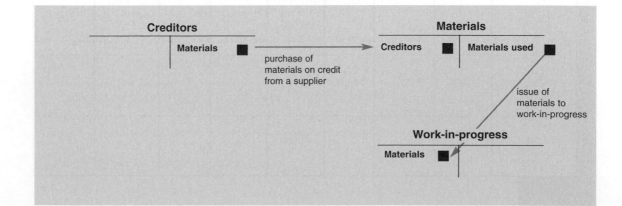

BLUE JEANS LIMITED:
BOOK-KEEPING FOR MATERIALS COSTS

situation

Blue Jeans Limited manufactures and sells denim jeans and jackets. The company uses the first in, first out (FIFO) method for valuing issues of materials to production and stocks of materials.

The company has been very busy in recent weeks and, as a consequence, some of the accounting records are not up-to-date. The following stores ledger record has not been completed:

STORES LEDGER RECORD

Product: **Blue denim**

	Receipts			Issues			Balance	
Date 2004	Quantity metres	Cost per metre £	Total Cost £	Quantity metres	Cost per metre £	Total Cost £	Quantity metres	Total Cost £
Balance at 1 Oct							20,000	10,000
11 Oct	10,000	0.60	6,000				30,000	16,000
14 Oct				25,000				
19 Oct	20,000	0.70	14,000					
25 Oct				20,000				

All issues of blue denim are for the manufacture of blue jeans. The following cost accounting codes are used to record material costs:

code number	description
2000	stock of blue denim
2200	work-in-progress – blue jeans
4000	creditors/purchases ledger control

As an accounts assistant at Blue Jeans Limited, you are asked to complete the stores ledger record and to fill in the table (below) to record separately the two purchases and two issues of blue denim in the cost accounting records.

2004	Code	Debit	Credit
11 October	2000		
11 October	4000		
14 October	2000		
14 October	2200		
19 October	2000		
19 October	4000		
25 October	2000		
25 October	2200		

solution

The stores ledger record is completed as shown on the next page.

Note that there may be a need to calculate the balance from more than one receipt cost. For example, on 11 October, the balance is made up of:

				£
20,000	metres at £0.50 per metre	=		10,000
10,000	metres at £0.60 per metre	=		6,000
30,000	metres	=		16,000

Similarly, on 19 October, the balance is made up of:

				£
5,000	metres at £0.60 per metre	=		3,000
20,000	metres at £0.70 per metre	=		14,000
25,000		=		17,000

STORES LEDGER RECORD

Product: **Blue denim**

Date	Receipts Quantity metres	Receipts Cost per metre £	Receipts Total Cost £	Issues Quantity metres	Issues Cost per metre £	Issues Total Cost £	Balance Quantity metres	Balance Total Cost £
2004								
Balance at 1 Oct							20,000	10,000
11 Oct	10,000	0.60	6,000				30,000	16,000*
14 Oct				25,000	20,000 x 0.50 / 5,000 x 0.60	10,000 / 3,000 / 13,000	5,000	3,000
19 Oct	20,000	0.70	14,000				25,000	17,000**
25 Oct				20,000	5,000 x 0.60 / 15,000 x 0.70	3,000 / 10,500 / 13,500	5,000	3,500

* £10,000 + £6,000   ** £3,000 + £14,000

The cost book-keeping entries are:

Creditors (4000)

£	£
	6,000
	14,000

Stock of blue denim (2000)

£	£
6,000	*13,000
14,000	**13,500

Work-in-progress – blue jeans (2200)

£	£
13,000	
13,500	

* £10,000 + £3,000   ** £3,000 + £10,500

The cost book-keeping entries are recorded on the table as follows:

2004	Code	Debit	Credit
11 October	2000	£6,000	
11 October	4000		£6,000
14 October	2000		£13,000
14 October	2200	£13,000	
19 October	2000	£14,000	
19 October	4000		£14,000
25 October	2000		£13,500
25 October	2200	£13,500	

Chapter Summary

- Businesses and other organisations hold stocks of raw materials and components bought for production, products bought for resale, and service items bought for use within the business.

- Two important stock costs are the ordering cost and the stock holding cost.

- Materials purchases can be made using techniques such as:
  - the level method of re-ordering
  - Economic Order Quantity (EOQ)
  - Just-In-Time (JIT)

- The level of stock is recorded on a stock record, which also indicates
  - the level at which new stock should be ordered
  - the quantity of stock that should be re-ordered

- Stock levels of materials are monitored regularly by means of stock taking; stock reconciliation notes any discrepancies and reports them for further investigation.

- Stock valuation is normally made *at the lower of cost and net realisable value* (SSAP 9).

- Stock valuation methods include:
  - FIFO (first in, first out)
  - LIFO (last in, first out)
  - AVCO (weighted average cost)
  - standard cost
  - replacement cost

- For a manufacturer, cost comprises the direct manufacturing costs of materials, labour and expenses, together with the production overheads which bring the product to its present location or condition.

- Cost book-keeping entries are made to record stock transactions such as:
  - the purchase of materials on credit from suppliers
  - the issue of materials to work-in-progress/part-finished goods

Key Terms	
materials	the cost of: – raw materials and components used in production – products bought for resale – service items bought for use within the business
level method of re-ordering	the re-ordering of materials in fixed quantities
Economic Order Quantity (EOQ)	a balance between ordering costs and stock holding costs; calculated by the formula: $$\sqrt{\dfrac{2 \times \text{annual usage} \times \text{ordering cost}}{\text{stock holding cost}}}$$
Just-In-Time (JIT)	the process of delivering goods in the right quantities, in the right place, just-in-time
stock record	record held for each stock item which shows receipts of supplies and sales (or issues to production)
stock taking	the process of counting physical stock on hand
stock reconciliation	comparison of the physical stock on hand with the stock record balance and identification of the reason(s) for discrepancies
stock value	number of items held x stock valuation per item

cost	the amount it cost to buy the stock (including additional costs to bring the product to its present location or condition)
net realisable value	selling price (less any extra costs, such as selling and distribution)
FIFO	'First in, first out' method of attaching a value to each issue of materials or goods from stores, using the oldest cost prices first
LIFO	'Last in, first out' method of attaching a value to each issue of materials or goods from stores, using most recent cost prices first
AVCO	'Average cost' method of attaching a value to each issue of materials or goods from stores, using a weighted average of the cost prices of all items in stock at the date of issue
stores ledger record (stock card)	method of recording stock data in order to ascertain the cost at which stocks of materials are issued, and to ascertain a valuation of stock
cost book-keeping	double-entry system to record costing transactions; uses the principles of double-entry book-keeping

Student Activities

2.1 Calculate, for stock items D and E, the re-order stock level and the re-order quantity to replenish stock levels to the maximum level, from the following information:

- daily usage of D = 3 units, of E = 4 units

- total stock should never exceed 95 days' usage

- 10 days' stock should always be held

- there is space available in the store for 350 units of each item of stock

- lead time is 7 days

2.2   (a)   Prepare a stock record from the following information:

- *product:* A4 Yellow Card, code A4/Y3, location row 7, bin 5

- *units:* reams

- *maximum stock level:* 35 days' usage

- *daily usage:* 3 units

- *lead time:* 10 days

- *minimum stock level:* 12 days' stock

- *opening balance on 1 May 2004:* 84 reams

Note: a blank stock record, which may be photocopied, is provided in the Appendix.

(b)   Calculate maximum, minimum and re-order levels of stock, together with re-order quantity (to replenish stock to the maximum level)

(c)   Enter the following materials requisitions for May 2004 on the stock record remembering to re-order when necessary and to show the order arriving ten days later (Goods Received Note 4507):

4 May	Materials Requisition 184	18 reams
6 May	Materials Requisition 187	20 reams
10 May	Materials Requisition 188	10 reams
17 May	Materials Requisition 394	20 reams
20 May	Materials Requisition 401	11 reams
26 May	Materials Requisition 422	6 reams

2.3   Complete the following sentences:

(a)   Stock levels and movements are recorded on a ....

(b)   A person carrying out a stock check will record the stock on a ....

(c)   The process of comparing stock on the shelves with stock in the records is known as

....

(d)   The usual basis for stock valuation is at the lower of .... and ....

....

2.4 From the following information prepare stores ledger records for product X using:

(a) FIFO

(b) LIFO

(c) AVCO

- 20 units of the product are bought in January 2004 at a cost of £3 each

- 10 units are bought in February at a cost of £3.50 each

- 8 units are sold in March

- 10 units are bought in April at a cost of £4.00 each

- 16 units are sold in May

Notes:

- a blank stores ledger record, which may be photocopied, is provided in the Appendix

- where appropriate, work to two decimal places

2.5 XY Limited is formed on 1 January 2004 and, at the end of its first half-year of trading, the stores ledger records show the following:

2004	TYPE X		TYPE Y	
	Receipts (units)	**Issues (units)**	**Receipts (units)**	**Issues (units)**
January	100 at £4.00		200 at £10.00	
February		80	100 at £9.50	
March	140 at £4.20			240
April	100 at £3.80		100 at £10.50	
May		140	140 at £10.00	
June	80 at £4.50			100

At 30 June 2004, the net realisable value of each type of stock is:

type X	£1,750
type Y	£1,950
	£3,700

You are to:

- Complete stores ledger records for products X and Y using (a) FIFO, (b) LIFO, (c) AVCO.

- The business has decided to use the FIFO method. Show the amount at which its stocks should be valued on 30 June 2004 in order to comply with standard accounting practice.

Notes:

- a blank stores ledger record, which may be photocopied, is provided in the Appendix

- where appropriate, work to two decimal places

2.6   Breeden Bakery Limited makes 'homestyle' cakes which are sold to supermarket chains.

The company uses the first in, first out (FIFO) method for valuing issues of materials to production and stocks of materials.

As an accounts assistant at Breeden Bakery you have been given the following tasks.

Task 1

Complete the following stores ledger record for wholewheat flour for May 2004:

STORES LEDGER RECORD

Product: Wholewheat flour

Date	Receipts			Issues			Balance	
	Quantity kgs	Cost per kg £	Total Cost £	Quantity kgs	Cost per kg £	Total Cost £	Quantity kgs	Total Cost £
2004								
Balance at 1 May							10,000	2,500
6 May	20,000	0.30	6,000				30,000	8,500
10 May				20,000				
17 May	10,000	0.35	3,500					
20 May				15,000				

Task 2

All issues of wholewheat flour are for the manufacture of fruit cakes. The following cost accounting codes are used to record materials costs:

code number	description
3000	stock of wholewheat flour
3300	work-in-progress – fruit cakes
5000	creditors/purchases ledger control

Complete the table below to record separately the two purchases and two issues of wholewheat flour in the cost accounting records.

2004	Code	Debit	Credit
6 May	3000		
6 May	5000		
10 May	3000		
10 May	3300		
17 May	3000		
17 May	5000		
20 May	3000		
20 May	3300		

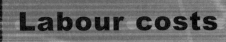

3 Labour costs

this chapter covers . . .

In this chapter we explain:

- *the factors that affect labour costs*
- *the ways in which the direct labour employees of a business or organisation can be remunerated*
- *how payroll information is gathered*
- *the advantages and disadvantages of different labour remuneration methods*
- *overtime and idle time*
- *the book-keeping entries for labour costs*

NVQ PERFORMANCE CRITERIA COVERED

unit 6: RECORDING AND EVALUATING COSTS AND REVENUES

element 6.1

record and analyse information relating to direct costs and revenues

A   *identify direct costs in accordance with the organisation's costing procedures*

B   *record and analyse information relating to direct costs*

C   *calculate direct costs in accordance with the organisation's policies and procedures*

E   *resolve or refer queries to the appropriate person*

ACCOUNTING FOR LABOUR COSTS

We saw in Chapter 1 how costs may be classified as materials costs, labour costs and expenses. All businesses incur labour costs: the costs of wages and salaries of all their employees.

factors that affect labour costs

There are many factors that need to be considered by a business when deciding how much to pay employees. The starting point will always be the amount that is paid by other businesses in the area for similar grades of employees but, at the same time, the wider economic implications of supply and demand will affect wage rates.

The factors to consider include:

- wage rates paid by other local businesses

- comparisons with national average wage rates

- the national minimum wage rate imposed by government

- any government incentives to take on additional employees, such as young people or the long-term unemployed

- local employment conditions – high unemployment in the area will drive down wage rates; conversely low unemployment, and especially a shortage of skilled labour, will increase wage rates

- housing and transport costs in the locality

- the impact of interest rate changes, and exchange rates (eg against the euro) on business confidence

- for a new business, it might be prudent to choose to locate in an area of high unemployment – in addition to lower wage rates, there may be government incentives in the form of reduced rents and rates, training and other grants

Before taking on labour, a business must decide how to calculate gross pay for its employees. The methods of labour remuneration are looked at in detail on the next page.

Earnings are usually calculated according to time worked or work done, or a combination of both.

From time-to-time, employees will expect their pay rates to be reviewed and then, most probably, increased. Usually such a process takes place each year when wage rates are negotiated. In the negotiations, both the employer and the representatives of the employees will take into account such things as:

- the rise in the cost of living, for example, as measured by the Retail Price Index (RPI)

- the overall employment situation

- the profitability of the business – can it afford to pay increased wage rates?

While the employer will be seeking a package of measures that gives the business a more efficient workforce, employees will be looking for higher wages together with enhanced benefits.

LABOUR REMUNERATION

Direct labour cost is the wages paid to those who work on a production line, are involved in assembly, or are involved in the output of a service business.

The three main methods of direct labour remuneration are:

time rate

Time rate (sometimes known as a day rate) is where the employee is paid on the basis of time spent at work. Overtime may be paid for hours worked beyond a standard number of hours, or for work carried out on days which are not part of the working week, eg Saturdays or Sundays. Overtime is often paid at rates such as 'time-and-a-quarter', 'time-and-a-half', or even 'double-time'.

'Time-and-a-half', for example, means that 1.5 times the basic hourly rate is paid.

piecework rate

The employee is paid an agreed sum for each task carried out or for each unit of output completed.

In some cases, employees may have a guaranteed minimum wage.

bonus system

The employee is paid a time rate and then receives a bonus if output is better than expected. Such systems are often linked into standard costing – covered at NVQ Level 4 Accounting – where the quantity of work that can be achieved at a standard performance in an hour (a standard hour) is estimated; the bonus is then expressed as an agreed percentage of the standard hours saved.

Bonus systems base employees' earnings on a combination of time taken and work done.

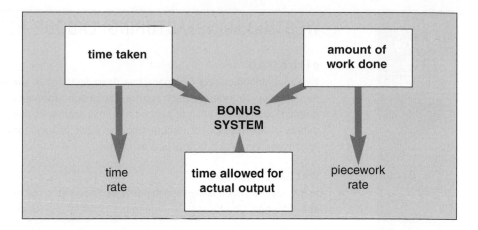

Most other employees, eg factory supervisors, sales staff, office staff, are usually paid on a weekly or monthly basis. Such wages and salaries – classed as indirect labour costs – may be increased by bonus payments; for example, a production bonus for factory supervisors, commissions for sales staff, a profit-sharing scheme for all employees.

There are many variations on the three methods outlined above and, indeed, changing patterns of employment create different remuneration methods from those that would have been the norm just a few years ago. For example, the contracting out of many business support services – such as cleaning, security, computers – means that the costing of such services by the provider may incorporate time rates and bonus systems whereas previously the employees would have been paid on a weekly or monthly basis.

In order to calculate gross wages, information about hours worked and/or work done must be recorded. The documents used include:

- *time sheets,* where employees record the hours they have worked
- *clock cards,* where employees 'clock in' at the start of work, and 'clock out' at the end – these are often computerised
- *piecework tickets,* completed by employees who work on a batch of output
- *job cards,* where each employee records the amount of time spent on each job
- *route cards* – which are used to follow a product through the production process – on which employees record the amount of time they spend working on the product
- *computer cards* – 'swipe' cards which link direct into the computerised payroll are increasingly being used by employers to record attendance

WESTMID MANUFACTURING: LABOUR REMUNERATION

situation

Westmid Manufacturing Company has three factories in the West Midlands making parts for the car industry. Each factory was bought from the previous owners and, as a result, each has a different method for remunerating its direct labour workforce. The details of the method of remuneration in each factory, together with data on two employees from each factory, are as follows:

WALSALL FACTORY

In this factory, which is involved in heavy engineering, employees are paid on the basis of a time rate. Employees are required to 'clock in' and 'clock out' each day.

John Brown is a machine operator and his clock card for last week shows that he worked 39 hours; his hourly rate of pay is £8 per hour.

Stefan Wozniak is a skilled lathe operator and his clock card shows that he worked 42 hours; his hourly rate of pay is £10 per hour, with overtime for hours worked beyond 40 hours at 'time-and-a-half'.

DUDLEY FACTORY

This factory operates a number of light engineering production lines making car components such as windscreen wiper blades, headlamp surrounds, interior mirrors etc. The production line employees are all paid on a piecework basis; however, each employee receives a guaranteed time rate which is paid if the piecework earnings are less than the time rate. This may happen if, for example, there are machine breakdowns and the production line has to be halted.

Tracey Johnson works on the line making headlamp surrounds. For each one that passes through her part of the process, she is paid 30p; her guaranteed time rate is 37 hours each week at £6 per hour. Last week's production records show that she processed 870 units.

Pete Bronyah is on the line which makes interior mirrors. For his part of the process he receives £1.00 for each one, with a guaranteed time rate of 37 hours at £6 per hour. Last week there was a machine failure and he was only able to process 150 units.

WOLVERHAMPTON FACTORY

In this factory a number of engineering production lines are operated. The direct labour force is paid on a time rate basis, but a bonus is paid if work can be completed faster than the standard performance. Thus a standard time allowance is given for each task and, if it can be completed in less time, a bonus is paid: the bonus in this factory is for the savings achieved to be shared equally between employer and employee. Wages are, therefore, paid on the following basis: time rate + 50% of (time saved x time rate). If no bonus is due, then the time rate applies.

Martin Lee worked a 38 hour work last week; his time rate is £10 per hour. He is allowed a standard time of 30 minutes to carry out his work on each unit of production; last week he completed 71 units.

Sara King has a time rate of £11 per hour; last week she worked 40 hours. She is allowed a standard time of 15 minutes to carry out her work on each unit of production; last week she completed 184 units.

What were the gross earnings of each employee?

solution

WALSALL FACTORY

John Brown	39 hours x £8.00 per hour	=	£312.00
Stefan Wozniak	40 hours x £10.00 per hour = £400		
	2 hours x £15.00 per hour = £30	=	£430.00

DUDLEY FACTORY

Tracey Johnson	Piecework rate, 870 units x 30p per unit	=	£261.00
	Guaranteed time rate, 37 hours x £6.00 per hour	=	£222.00
	Therefore piecework rate of £261.00 is paid.		

Pete Bronyah	Piecework rate, 150 units x £1.00 per unit	=	£150.00
	Guaranteed time rate, 37 hours x £6.00 per hour	=	£222.00
	Therefore guaranteed time rate of £222.00 is paid.		

WOLVERHAMPTON FACTORY

Martin Lee	Time rate, 38 hours x £10.00 per hour	=	£380.00
	Bonus, time allowed 71 units x 30 minutes each = 35 hours 30 minutes		
	Therefore no time saved, so no bonus payable.		
	Time rate of £380 paid.		

Sara King	Time rate, 40 hours x £11.00 per hour	=	£440.00
	Bonus, time allowed 184 x 15 minutes each = 46 hours		
	Therefore time saved is 6 hours		
	Bonus is 50% of (6 hours x £11.00)	=	£33.00
	Therefore wages are £440.00 + £33.00	=	£473.00

The Case Study illustrates some of the direct labour remuneration methods in use, however it should be appreciated that there are many variations on these to be found.

DIRECT LABOUR REMUNERATION METHODS: ADVANTAGES AND DISADVANTAGES

time rate

Time rate is often used where it is difficult to measure output, and where quality is more important than quantity. Variations include a high time rate, used to motivate employees where a higher standard of work is required.

advantages:
- easy to understand and to calculate
- no requirement to establish time allowances and piecework rates
- the employee receives a regular wage, unaffected by fluctuations in output
- the employer pays a regular amount, making planning for cash flows easier
- can be used for all direct labour employees
- quality of the finished product does not suffer as a result of hurried work

disadvantages:
- both efficient and inefficient employees receive the same wage
- no incentive is given to employees to work harder
- slower working will not affect basic wage, but may lead to overtime
- more supervisors are needed to ensure that output is maintained

piecework rate

Piecework rate is used where the quantity of output is important, and there is less emphasis on quality. Variations include:

- piecework with guaranteed time rate, which ensures that employees are paid if production is stopped through no fault of their own, eg machine breakdown, or shortage of materials

- differential piecework system, where a higher rate is paid for all output beyond a certain level, eg 50p per unit for the first 100 units each day, then 60p per unit thereafter; used to motivate employees to produce more than a basic level of output

- attendance allowances, paid to encourage employees on piecework to attend each day, thus ensuring that the production-line can be staffed and operated every working day

advantages:

- payment of wages is linked directly to output
- more efficient workers earn more than those who are less efficient
- work is done quicker and less time is wasted

disadvantages:

- not suitable for all direct labour employees
- pay is reduced if there are production problems, eg machine breakdown or shortage of materials
- quality of the finished product may be low
- morc inspectors may be needed
- control systems needed to check the amount produced by each worker
- more complex pay calculations
- may be difficulty in agreeing piecework rates with employees
- the employer cannot plan ahead for wages so easily, as they may be irregular amounts

bonus systems

Bonus systems are used to encourage employees to be more efficient in an environment where the work is not so repetitive. Variations include an accelerating premium bonus – which is an increased bonus paid for higher levels of output, and group bonuses paid to groups of employees who achieve increased output – the group could be as large as the entire workforce of a large company, or as small as a work team of two or three people.

advantages:

- wages linked to output, but minimum wage is guaranteed each week
- work is done quicker and less time is wasted
- more efficient workers earn more
- a bonus system can often be applied to the entire workforce

disadvantages:

- bonus is not paid if circumstances beyond employee's control prevent work, eg machine breakdown or shortage of materials
- quality of finished product may be low
- more inspectors may be needed and additional control procedures
- pay calculations may be more complex
- there may be difficulty in agreeing bonus rates with employees

- group bonus schemes may cause conflict within the group, if some workers consider that others are working too slowly

qualities of a good labour remuneration scheme

These include:

- reward should be related to effort and fair to all staff
- the scheme should be easy to manage and administer, and cheap and efficient to run
- it should be easy for employees to understand how pay is calculated
- payment should be made at regular intervals and soon after the event, eg employees on piecework should be paid in the week after the production has been achieved
- the principles of the scheme should remain constant, but there should be flexibility to deal with changes in production techniques

summary

The three main methods of remuneration, together with some alternative systems, are summarised in the table on the next page.

As an accounts assistant, always remember that payroll information is confidential and any queries should be referred to the appropriate person – for example, the payroll manager, or the accounts supervisor.

OVERTIME AND IDLE TIME

In Chapter 1 we divided labour costs between:

- **direct costs,** labour costs of production-line employees
- **indirect costs,** labour costs of other employees, such as supervisors, office staff, etc

Whilst this distinction appears clear enough, there are times when a proportion of the labour costs of production-line employees is classed as an indirect cost (rather than a direct cost) and is included amongst the overheads of the business. This is done if part of the cost of wages of the direct workers cannot be linked to specific work.

overtime payments

When production-line employees work overtime they are usually paid at a rate above the time rate. For example, overtime might be paid at 'time-and-a-half'; thus an employee with a time rate of £8 an hour will be paid overtime at £12 an hour. The additional £4 per hour is called **overtime premium**. For

continued on page 82

methods of remuneration – a summary

	TIME RATE	PIECEWORK RATE	BONUS SYSTEM
situation	This system is used where it is difficult to measure the quantity of output and where quality is more important than volume of output.	This system is used where the work is repetitive and quantity of output is more important than quality.	This system is used to motivate employees, where the work is not so repetitive as in piecework but is measurable.
gross pay calculation	Hours worked x rate per hour This is easy to calculate and understand.	Number of items produced x rate per item This is easy to calculate and understand.	Basic pay + proportion of the time saved Time saved is the difference between time allowed and time taken to do a task. More complex to calculate and understand.
motivation	Pay is not linked to output and therefore there is no incentive to work hard. Slower workers may get paid overtime at higher rates.	Pay is related directly to output. There is a direct incentive to work as the amount of output determines the amount paid.	There is some incentive to work in order to earn a bonus as well as basic pay.
quality of output	There is no pressure on time and so quality should be maintained.	The fact that pay is related to output means it is important that quality standards of output are met.	The link between pay and output means that the quality of output needs to be checked.
control	It is important that the volume and quality of output is maintained.	It is important that the volume and quality of output is maintained.	It is important that the volume and quality of output is maintained.
administration	There is no need to set time allowances for output.	There is a need to set time allowances for work done and to keep these up to date.	There is a need to set time allowances for work done and to keep these up to date.
payment to employees	A regular amount is earned by the employee.	The amount earned by the employee varies with the output the employee produces.	There is some regular income but pay can be increased by additional effort.
ALTERNATIVE SYSTEMS	**High day rate** – employees are paid a higher than average rate per hour but agree to produce a given amount of output at a given quality.	**Attendance allowance** – to ensure employees turn up. **Guaranteed day rate** – to give employees a minimum payment. **Differential piecework** – to pay efficient workers more for output beyond a given level of output, ie an extra amount per unit.	**Group bonus schemes** – used where employees work as a group. This can include all workers, eg cleaners. This may create problems as the most efficient workers may be held back by the less efficient workers.

normal cost accounting purposes, any overtime worked is charged at £8 an hour to direct labour, and £4 an hour to indirect labour.

Example:

A group of employees on a production line have a working week consisting of 40 hours each. Anything over that time is paid at time-and-a-half. One employee has worked 43 hours during the week at a normal rate of £8.

- Direct wages cost is 43 hours at £8 = £344
- Overtime premium is 3 hours at £4 (half of £8) = £12, which is charged to indirect labour

In this way, the cost of overtime is spread across all output and is not charged solely to the output being worked on during the overtime period. As another issue, management will wish to know why there was the need to work overtime, and will seek to control such an increase in labour costs.

However, where a customer requests overtime to be worked to get a rush job completed, then the full overtime rate (£12 an hour in the above example) is charged as direct labour, and passed on as a cost to the customer.

Other additional payments made to employees – such as a bonus – will be treated in a similar way to overtime and will normally be treated as an indirect labour cost.

idle time

Idle time occurs when production is stopped through no fault of the production-line employees – for example, a machine breakdown, or a shortage of materials. Employees paid under a piecework or a bonus system will receive time rate for the period of the stoppage. Such wages costs are normally charged to overheads as indirect labour.

Similarly, time spent by direct workers on non-productive work would also usually be treated as an overhead.

BOOK-KEEPING FOR LABOUR COSTS

In this section we look at the cost book-keeping entries to record labour costs – the transfer of labour costs to work-in-progress and to overheads. These entries form part of the book-keeping system for costing; Chapter 7 looks in detail at an integrated book-keeping system.

A **wages control account** – which may also include salaries – is used to charge labour costs to the various cost centres of a business or organisation.

In this way:

- direct labour costs are charged to work-in-progress
- indirect labour costs are charged to production overheads
- administration labour costs are charged to non-production overheads

The cost book-keeping entries are:

- **transfer of direct labour costs to work-in-progress**
    - debit work-in-progress account
    - credit wages control account

- **transfer of indirect labour costs to production overheads**
    - debit production overheads account
    - credit wages control account

- **transfer of administration labour costs to non-production overheads**
    - debit non-production overheads account, eg administration
    - credit wages control account

The cost book-keeping entries are shown diagrammatically as follows:

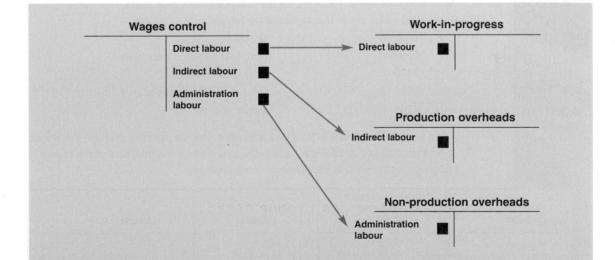

Note: Here all of the labour costs have been transferred to work-in-progress and overheads. From time-to-time, however, some part of labour costs may relate to capital expenditure (see page 94) – for example, own workforce used to build an extension to the premises; here the book-keeping entries for the relevant labour costs are:
- debit premises account (or relevant capital expenditure account)
- credit wages control account

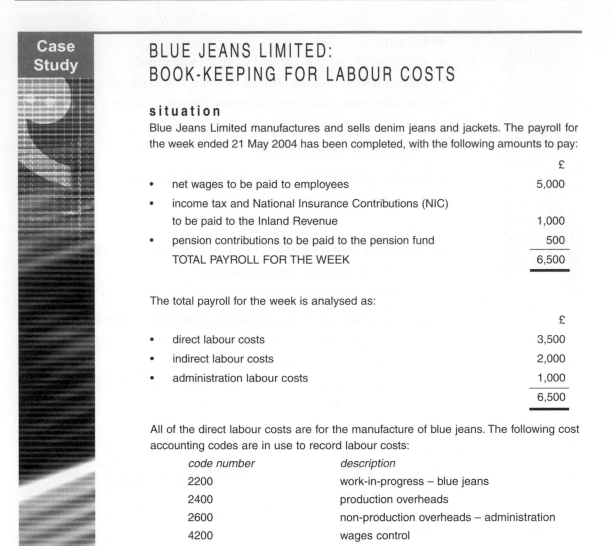

Case Study

BLUE JEANS LIMITED:
BOOK-KEEPING FOR LABOUR COSTS

situation

Blue Jeans Limited manufactures and sells denim jeans and jackets. The payroll for the week ended 21 May 2004 has been completed, with the following amounts to pay:

		£
•	net wages to be paid to employees	5,000
•	income tax and National Insurance Contributions (NIC) to be paid to the Inland Revenue	1,000
•	pension contributions to be paid to the pension fund	500
	TOTAL PAYROLL FOR THE WEEK	6,500

The total payroll for the week is analysed as:

		£
•	direct labour costs	3,500
•	indirect labour costs	2,000
•	administration labour costs	1,000
		6,500

All of the direct labour costs are for the manufacture of blue jeans. The following cost accounting codes are in use to record labour costs:

code number	description
2200	work-in-progress – blue jeans
2400	production overheads
2600	non-production overheads – administration
4200	wages control

As an accounts assistant at Blue Jeans Limited, you are asked to prepare the wages control account and to fill in the table below to show how the total cost of the payroll is split between the various cost centres of the business.

2004	Code	Debit	Credit
21 May	2200		
21 May	4200		
21 May	2400		
21 May	4200		
21 May	2600		
21 May	4200		

solution

Wages control account is prepared as follows:

Dr   **Wages Control Account**   Cr

	£		£
Cash/bank (net wages)	5,000	Work-in-progress (direct labour)	3,500
Inland Revenue		Production overheads	
(income tax and NIC)	1,000	(indirect labour)	2,000
Pension contributions	500	Non-production overheads	
		(administration)	1,000
	6,500		6,500

The cost book-keeping entries are:

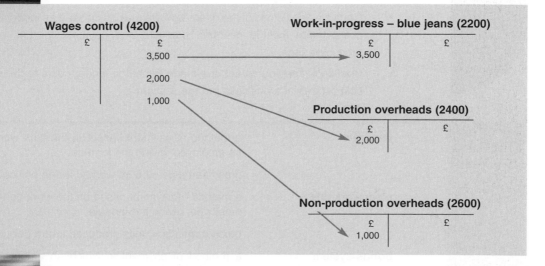

These are recorded on the table as follows:

2004	Code	Debit	Credit
21 May	2200	£3,500	
21 May	4200		£3,500
21 May	2400	£2,000	
21 May	4200		£2,000
21 May	2600	£1,000	
21 May	4200		£1,000

In this way, the total cost of the payroll is split between the various cost centres of the business.

Chapter Summary

- Labour costs are incurred in every kind of business and are influenced by levels of wages and by the method of remuneration.
- Levels of wage rates paid to employees are influenced by a number of factors including the rates paid by similar local businesses, compulsory minimum rates and national averages.
- The main methods of remuneration are based either on time or amounts of work done or on a combination of both.
- Different methods of remuneration have advantages and disadvantages for the employer and the employee. The employer needs to control the cost of wages, but also to motivate employees to produce work of suitable quality within a reasonable time.
- A good remuneration scheme should be fair, easy to understand and efficiently managed.
- Certain wages costs of the direct workers may be classed as indirect labour costs: these include overtime premium and payment for idle or non-productive time.
- Cost book-keeping entries are made to charge labour costs to the various cost centres of a business or organisation.

Key Terms

time rate	a method of payment based on the time worked by an employee, giving the formula:
	gross earnings = hours worked x rate per hour
piecework rate	a method of payment based on the work done by an employee, giving the formula:
	gross earnings = units produced x rate per unit
bonus system	a method of payment in which an employee may earn a bonus by completing work in less time than the time allowed – usually the bonus is calculated as a share of the hours saved, multiplied by the rate per hour
standard hour	the quantity of work that can be achieved by one worker in one hour, at a standard level of performance
time sheet	method by which employees record the hours they have worked
clock card	where employees 'clock in' at the start of work, and 'clock out' at the end
piecework ticket	documentation completed by employees who work on a batch of output
job card	documentation completed by employees which records the amount of time spent on each job

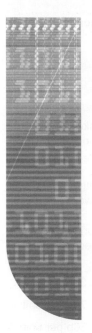

route card	documentation which follows a product through the production process – employees record the amount of time they spend working on the product
overtime premium	the additional pay above normal rates which is paid to employees working overtime, for example, the premium part of 'time-and-a-half' is the extra 'half' of the hourly rate
idle time	time during which work is stopped, due to reasons such as machine breakdown or shortage of materials; employees usually receive time rate for idle time, and the cost is normally classified as an indirect cost
wages control account	used to charge labour costs to the various cost centres:

– direct labour to work-in-progress

– indirect labour to production overheads

– administration labour to non-production overhead

Student Activities

3.1 A manufacturing business pays its production workers on a time rate basis. A bonus is paid where production is completed faster than the standard hour output; the bonus is paid at half of the time rate for production time saved. How much will each of the following employees earn for the week?

Employee	Time rate	Hours worked	Standard hour output	Actual production
N Ball	£8.00 per hour	35	30 units	1,010 units
T Smith	£9.00 per hour	37	40 units	1,560 units
L Lewis	£10.00 per hour	40	20 units	855 units
M Wilson	£7.00 per hour	38	24 units	940 units

3.2 Harrison & Company is a manufacturing business. Currently it pays its production-line workers on a time rate basis. Recently the employee representatives have approached the management of the company with a view to seeking alternative methods of remuneration. Suggestions have been made that either a piecework system, or a time rate with a production bonus system would be more appropriate.

The office manager has asked you, as an accounts assistant, to draft a memorandum to the management giving advantages and disadvantages of:

• time rate

• piecework

• time rate, plus production bonus

as methods of remunerating production-line employees. In particular, you are asked to describe two circumstances under which the piecework basis would not be in the interests of employees.

3.3 (a) A company pays its production-line employees on a piecework basis, but with a guaranteed time rate. How much will each of the following employees earn during the week?

Employee	Time rate	Hours worked	Production	Piecework rate
L Fry	£10.00 per hour	40	1,200 units	30p per unit
R Williams	£8.00 per hour	37	450 units	70p per unit
P Grant	£9.50 per hour	36	725 units	50p per unit

(b) What are the problems a company might face in operating a piecework system of remuneration?

3.4 Print 'n Go is a print shop that specialises in printing headed notepaper for businesses. It employs two printers, Steve Kurtin and Pete Singh. Both are paid a basic rate per hour for a 35-hour week with two overtime rates: time-and-a-third for weekdays (rate 1), and time-and-a-half for week-ends (rate 2). In addition, a production bonus is paid of 25p per 1,000 copies printed.

Details for last week are as follows:

	Steve Kurtin	Pete Singh
Basic rate per hour	£5.50	£6.50
Total hours worked	39	42
Overtime: rate 1	4	3
rate 2	–	4
Number of copies printed	45,000	57,000

You are to

• calculate the gross wages earned by each employee for last week

• calculate the piecework rate per 1,000 copies printed that would be equal to the gross wages earned by Steve Kurtin for the week, assuming the same output level of 45,000 copies.

3.5 Wyvern Fabrication Company has two departments – moulding and finishing. Data relating to labour for a four-week period is given on the labour cost sheet below.

The company uses a bonus scheme whereby employees receive 50 per cent of the standard hours saved in each department, paid at the actual labour rate per hour. This is not included in the actual wages cost, which shows actual hours multiplied by the actual wage rate.

LABOUR COST SHEET		
for the four weeks ended 26 February 2004		
	MOULDING	FINISHING
Actual wages cost (£)	31,160	36,450
Standard hours	4,000	5,000
Actual hours	4,100	4,500
Standard hours saved		
Bonus (£)		
Total labour cost (£)		

You are to calculate the total labour cost for each department.

3.6 The direct workers of Haven Limited are paid a basic wage of £6.20 per hour. For time worked above 40 hours per week, they receive overtime pay at time-and-a-half. For two particular weeks, we have the following information for a team of 10 direct workers:

Week 1: Total hours worked = 450 hours, including 50 hours of overtime.

Week 2: Total hours worked = 400 hours, including 20 hours of non-production work, clearing up and re-organising a section of the factory during a machine breakdown.

For each of the two given weeks you are to:

• calculate the gross earnings in total for the team of 10 employees.

• state how much of the gross earnings would normally be treated as an indirect labour cost.

3.7 Last week the wages control account of Annabel's Bakery had three credit entries:

• work-in-progress   £2,100

• production overheads   £ 900

• non-production overheads £ 700

TOTAL PAYROLL FOR THE WEEK   £3,700

You are to explain the purpose of the three entries, and the total payroll for the week.

3.8 Breeden Bakery Limited makes 'homestyle' cakes which are sold to supermarket chains. The payroll for the week ended 26 March 2004 has been completed, with the following amounts to pay:

	£
• net wages to be paid to employees	7,500
• income tax and National Insurance Contributions (NIC) to be paid to the Inland Revenue	1,450
• pension contributions to be paid to the pension fund	750
TOTAL PAYROLL FOR THE WEEK	9,700

The total payroll for the week is analysed as:

	£
• direct labour costs	6,500
• indirect labour costs	2,700
• administration labour costs	500
	9,700

As an accounts assistant at Breedon Bakery you have been given the following tasks:

Task 1

Prepare wages control account for the week ended 26 March 2004:

Dr	Wages Control Account	Cr
£		£

Task 2

All of the direct labour costs are for the manufacture of fruit cakes. The following cost accounting codes are in use to record labour costs:

code number	description
3300	work-in-progress – fruit cakes
3500	production overheads
3700	non-production overheads – administration
5200	wages control

Complete the table below to show how the total cost of the payroll is split between the various cost centres of the business.

2004	Code	Debit	Credit
26 March	3300		
26 March	5200		
26 March	3500		
26 March	5200		
26 March	3700		
26 March	5200		

3.9 Icod Limited manufactures golf clubs. The following data relates to the production of its 'Mulligan' brand of clubs for October 2004:

Total direct labour hours worked	16,000 hours
Normal time hours	14,400 hours
Overtime hours	1,600 hours
Normal time rate per hour	£8 per hour
Overtime premium per hour	£4 per hour

In the company's cost book-keeping system all direct labour overtime payments are included in direct costs.

The following cost accounting codes are in use to record labour costs:

code number	description
1500	work-in-progress – 'Mulligan' clubs
5000	wages control

You are to:

• calculate the total cost of direct labour for October

• show the cost book-keeping entries, together with account codes, in order to transfer the direct labour costs to work-in-progress

4 Expenses

this chapter covers . . .

In this chapter we examine:

- expenses as an element of cost
- the distinction between capital expenditure and revenue expenditure
- the distinction between direct expenses and indirect expenses
- the book-keeping entries for expenses
- the nature and behaviour of fixed, semi-variable and variable costs

NVQ PERFORMANCE CRITERIA COVERED

unit 6: RECORDING AND EVALUATING COSTS AND REVENUES
element 6.1
record and analyse information relating to direct costs and revenues

A identify direct costs in accordance with the organisation's costing procedures

B record and analyse information relating to direct costs

C calculate direct costs in accordance with the organisation's policies and procedures

E resolve or refer queries to the appropriate person

EXPENSES – AN ELEMENT OF COST

The third main element of cost is that of expenses, ie any cost that cannot be classified as materials or labour. Expenses include items such as rent, rates, telephone, lighting, heating, royalties paid to the designer of a product, special items bought in for a particular product, etc.

It is important that expenses are categorised correctly in order that costs can be calculated accurately and accounting statements can show a true representation of the state of the business. To achieve this, as shown by the diagram below, we need to distinguish between:

- capital expenditure and revenue expenditure
- direct expenses and indirect expenses
- fixed costs and variable costs

Note that both direct and indirect expenses can be either fixed or variable in nature – see page 100.

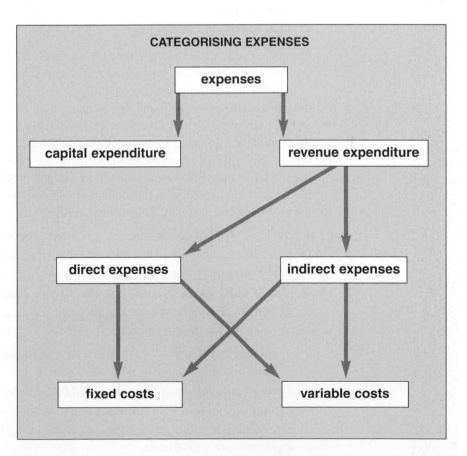

CAPITAL EXPENDITURE AND REVENUE EXPENDITURE

Capital expenditure can be defined as *expenditure incurred on the purchase, alteration or improvement of fixed assets.* For example, the purchase of a car for use in the business is capital expenditure. Included in capital expenditure are costs such as:

- delivery of fixed assets
- installation of fixed assets
- improvement (but not repair) of fixed assets
- legal costs of buying property

Revenue expenditure is *expenditure incurred on running costs.* For example, the cost of petrol or diesel for the car (above) is revenue expenditure. Included in revenue expenditure are the running costs of:

- maintenance and repair of fixed assets
- making, selling and distributing the goods or products in which the business trades
- administration of the business

Capital expenditure is shown in the balance sheet, while revenue expenditure is a cost in the profit and loss account. It is important to classify these types of expenditure correctly in the accounting system. For example, if the cost of the car was shown in profit and loss account, then costs would be overstated and the net profit would be reduced considerably, or a net loss recorded; meanwhile, the balance sheet would not show the car as a fixed asset – clearly this is incorrect as the business owns the asset. Note, however, that there is a link between capital expenditure and the profit and loss account: as fixed assets are depreciated, the amount of depreciation is shown as a cost in the profit and loss account. Thus depreciation relates to the time period over which the fixed asset is used.

In some circumstances we must take care to distinguish between capital and revenue expenditure. For example:

- ***cost of building an extension to the factory £30,000, which includes £1,000 for repairs to the existing factory***
  - capital expenditure, £29,000
  - revenue expenditure, £1,000 (because it is for repairs to an existing fixed asset)
- ***a plot of land has been bought for £20,000, the legal costs are £750***
  Capital expenditure £20,750 (the legal costs are included in the capital expenditure, because they are the cost of acquiring the fixed asset, ie the legal costs are capitalised).

- *own employees used to install a new air conditioning system: direct labour £1,000, materials £1,500*

  Capital expenditure £2,500 (an addition to the property). Note that, in cases such as this, revenue expenditure, ie direct labour and materials purchases, will need to be reduced to allow for the transfer to capital expenditure.

- *own employees used to repair and redecorate the premises: direct labour £500, materials £750*

  Revenue expenditure £1,250 (repairs and redecoration are running expenses).

- *purchase of a new machine £10,000, payment for installation and setting up £250*

  Capital expenditure £10,250 (costs of installation and setting up of a fixed asset are capitalised).

Only by allocating capital expenditure and revenue expenditure correctly can costs be ascertained properly and the profit and loss account and balance sheet reflect accurately the financial state of the business. It is especially important to identify revenue expenditure in the costing of output; a product that is costed wrongly (for example at too high a price) may not sell well because the selling price is too expensive for buyers. Identification of capital expenditure is important for knowing the assets owned by a business, which are shown on the balance sheet. If you, as an accounts assistant, are unsure about the allocation of costs between capital and revenue, you should always refer queries to the accounts supervisor.

DIRECT EXPENSES AND INDIRECT EXPENSES

For cost accounting purposes, revenue expenditure needs to be identified as either a direct expense or an indirect expense:

- direct expenses – those expenses which can be attributed to particular units of output
- indirect expenses – other expenses which cannot be attributed directly to particular units of output

The correct identification of these expenses will enable us to obtain a more accurate costing of each unit of output of the business or organisation.

direct expenses

Examples of direct expenses include:

- royalties payable to the designer of a product
- special items bought in for a particular product or job
- hire of specialist machinery/equipment for a particular product or job
- consultant's fees related to a particular product or job
- power costs of running machinery (provided that the machinery is separately metered and is used for a particular product or job)
- depreciation methods linked directly to output, eg units of output (or service) method

units of output depreciation

The units of output (or service) method of depreciation estimates:

- the number of units to be produced by a machine, or
- the number of hours of operation of a machine, or
- the number of miles/kilometres expected from a vehicle

over its expected life. Depreciation for a given year is calculated by reference to the number of units/hours/miles for that year.

For example, a machine costs £1,000. The total number of units of output to be produced by the machine over its life is expected to be 100,000. Therefore, each year's depreciation will be calculated at £100 for every 10,000 units produced (£1,000 ÷ 100,000 units). If year 1 production is 30,000 units, then depreciation of the machine will be £300 for the year. Over the machine's life of, say, four years, output and depreciation are as follows:

	output	depreciation
year 1	30,000 units	£300
year 2	25,000 units	£250
year 3	20,000 units	£200
year 4	25,000 units	£250
total	100,000 units	£1,000

indirect expenses

Examples of indirect expenses include:

- factory and office rent and rates
- telephone costs
- power costs of running machinery (where machinery is used for a variety of products or jobs, or where power consumption is low and it is not worthwhile for the costing system to analyse the amount of the direct expense)

- heating and lighting
- insurance
- cost of running motor vehicles
- depreciation methods not linked directly to output, eg straight-line and reducing balance methods

straight-line depreciation

A fixed percentage is written off the original cost of the asset each year, calculated by reference to the useful economic life of the asset as follows:

$$\frac{\text{cost of asset} - \text{estimated residual (scrap or salvage) sale proceeds}}{\text{number of years' expected use of the asset}}$$

For example, a machine costs £2,000, has an estimated life of four years, and an estimated scrap value at the end of four years of £400. The depreciation amount will be:

$$\frac{£2,000 - £400}{4 \text{ years}} = £400 \text{ per year (ie 20\% per year on cost)}$$

reducing balance depreciation

A fixed percentage is written off the reduced balance of the asset each year. The reduced balance is the cost of the asset less the provision for depreciation. For example, the machine seen earlier (which cost £2,000, has an estimated life of four years, and an estimated scrap value at the end of four years of £400) is to be depreciated by 33.3% (one-third) each year, using the reducing balance method. The depreciation amounts for the four years of ownership are:

	£
Original cost	2,000
Year 1 depreciation: 33.3% of £2,000	667
Value at end of year 1	1,333
Year 2 depreciation: 33.3% of £1,333	444
Value at end of year 2	889
Year 3 depreciation: 33.3% of £889	296
Value at end of year 3	593
Year 4 depreciation: 33.3% of £593	193
Value at end of year 4	400

Note: the figures have been rounded to the nearest £, and year 4 depreciation has been adjusted by £5 to leave a residual value of £400.

The formula to calculate the percentage of reducing balance depreciation is:

$$r = 1 - \sqrt[n]{\frac{s}{c}}$$

where:

r = percentage rate of depreciation

n = number of years

s = salvage (residual) value

c = cost of asset

In the example above the 33.3% is calculated as:

$$r = 1 - \sqrt[4]{\frac{400}{2,000}}$$

$$r = 1 - \sqrt[4]{0.2}$$ (to find the fourth root press the square root key on the calculator twice)

$$r = 1 - 0.669$$

r = 0.331 or 33.1% (which is close to the 33.3% used above)

BOOK-KEEPING FOR EXPENSES

The cost book-keeping entries to record expenses – the transfer of expenses to work-in-progress and to overheads – form part of the book-keeping system for costing.

The cost of direct expenses – which is attributable to output – is charged to work-in-progress. The cost of indirect expenses is charged to overheads and split between:

• production overheads

• non-production overheads, such as

– selling and distribution

– administration

– finance

The cost book-keeping entries are:

- **transfer of direct expenses to work-in-progress**
  - debit work-in-progress account
  - credit expense account
- **transfer of indirect expenses to production overheads**
  - debit production overheads account
  - credit expense account
- **transfer of indirect expenses to non-production overheads**
  - debit non-production overheads account, eg selling and distribution, administration, finance
  - credit expense account

These cost book-keeping entries are shown diagrammatically as follows:

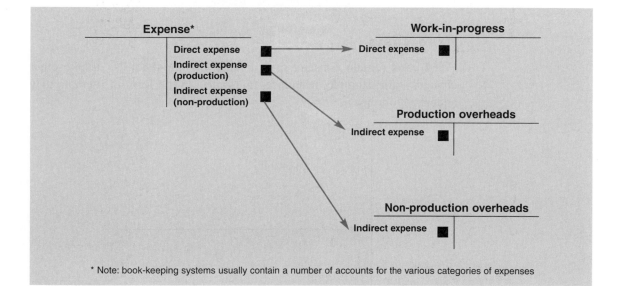

* Note: book-keeping systems usually contain a number of accounts for the various categories of expenses

Direct expenses are included with the costs of direct materials and direct labour to give a total of direct costs (prime cost). Indirect expenses are included in the total of indirect costs (overheads) of a business. For a service business, a major proportion of the costs are likely to be in the form of indirect costs; by contrast, a manufacturing business is likely to have a greater proportion of direct costs.

We shall be looking at the layout of the manufacturing account and the integrated book-keeping system for costing in Chapter 7.

FIXED AND VARIABLE COSTS

It is important in costing to appreciate the *nature of costs* – in particular to realise that not all costs increase or decrease in line with increases or decreases in output. As seen in Chapter 1 (page 21), 'Classification of costs by nature', all costs are:

• fixed, or

• semi-variable, or

• variable

We shall be studying the relationship between fixed and variable costs in detail later in the book (Chapter 8). In particular, we will be looking at the technique of break-even analysis – the point at which costs are exactly equal to income.

fixed costs

Fixed costs remain constant over a range of output levels, despite other changes – for example, insurance, rent, rates. In the form of a graph, they appear as follows:

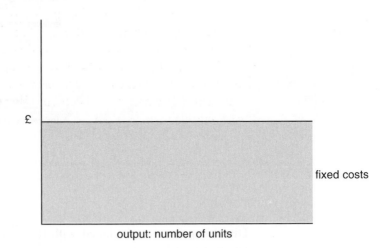

Note that money amounts are shown on the vertical axis and units of output on the horizontal axis.

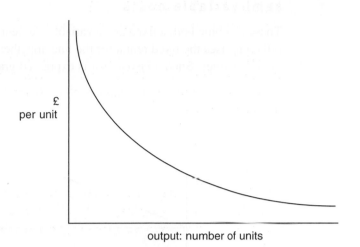

output: number of units

For fixed costs, the *cost per unit* falls as output increases, as follows:

For example, with rent of £40,000 per year:

• at output of 4,000 units, equals £10 per unit
• at output of 10,000 units, equals £4 per unit

Whilst it is sensible to seek to achieve maximum output in order to reduce the cost per unit, fixed costs do not remain fixed at all levels of production. For example, a decision to double production is likely to increase the fixed costs – an increase in factory rent, for example, because an additional factory may need to be rented. Fixed costs are often described as *stepped fixed costs,* because they increase by a large amount all at once; graphically, the cost behaviour is shown as a step:

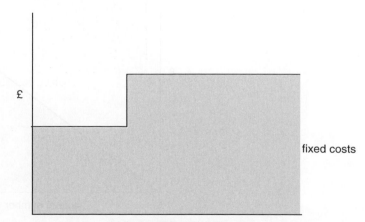

output: number of units

semi-variable costs

These combine both a fixed and a variable element. For example, a telephone
bill comprises the fixed rental for the line, together with the variable element
of call charges. Such a *mixed cost* is expressed graphically as:

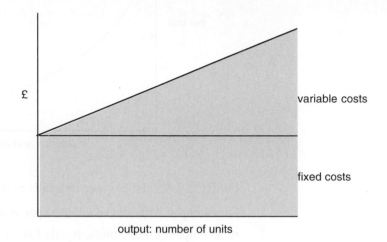

variable costs

Variable costs alter directly with changes in output levels, ie as activity
increases, then the cost increases. Examples include direct materials, direct
labour, direct expenses such as royalties. Graphically, variable costs appear
as follows:

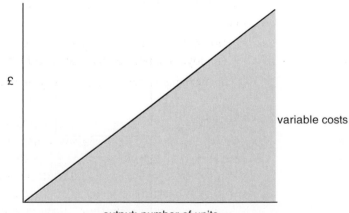

For example, a record company paying a royalty of £1 for each compact disc (CD) produced:

- at output of 1,000 CDs, equals variable cost of £1,000
- at output of 10,000 CDs, equals variable cost of £10,000

The cost per unit remains constant at all levels of output, as follows:

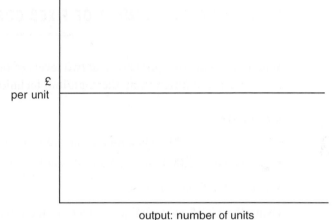

FIXED AND VARIABLE COSTS IN DECISION-MAKING

Identifying costs as being fixed, semi-variable or variable helps with decision-making – the business might be able to alter the balance between fixed and variable costs in order to increase profits. A product could be made:

- either, by using a labour-intensive process, with a large number of employees supported by basic machinery
- or, by using expensive machinery in an automated process with very few employees

In the first case, the cost structure will be high variable costs (direct labour) and low fixed costs (depreciation of machinery – assuming that straight-line or reducing balance depreciation methods are used). In the second case, there will be low variable costs, and high fixed costs. Management will need to examine the relationship between the costs – together with the likely sales figures, and the availability of finance with which to buy the machinery – before making a decision.

More specifically, a knowledge of the nature of costs can be used to help management to:

- identify the element of fixed costs within total costs
- prepare schedules of budgeted production costs
- identify the point at which costs are exactly equal to income – known as the break-even point (covered in Chapter 8)

IDENTIFYING THE ELEMENT OF FIXED COSTS

Where the total costs are known at two levels of output, the element of fixed costs can be identified using the 'high/low' technique.

example

- at output of 1,000 units, total costs are £7,000
- at output of 2,000 units, total costs are £9,000

What are the fixed costs?

Using the 'high/low' technique to identify the fixed costs:

- The high output and costs are deducted from the low output and costs, as follows:

	high output	2,000 units	£9,000
less	low output	1,000 units	£7,000
equals	difference	1,000 units	£2,000

- The amount of the variable cost per unit is now calculated as:

$$\frac{\text{change in cost}}{\text{change in units}} \quad = \quad \frac{£2,000}{1,000} \quad = \quad £2 \text{ variable cost per unit}$$

- Therefore, at 1,000 units of output the cost structure is:

	total cost		£7,000
less	variable costs (1,000 units x £2 per unit)		£2,000
equals	fixed costs		£5,000

- Check this now at 2,000 units of output when the cost structure is:

	variable costs (2,000 units x £2 per unit)	£4,000
add	fixed costs (as above)	£5,000
equals	total costs	£9,000

Note that the 'high/low' technique can only be used when variable costs increase by the same money amount for each extra unit of output (ie there is a linear relationship), and where there are no stepped fixed costs.

SCHEDULES OF BUDGETED PRODUCTION COSTS

Where fixed and variable costs are known for the three elements of costs – materials, labour and expenses – at a particular level of output, it is relatively simple to calculate what the costs will be at changed levels of output. For example, if variable materials costs at an output of 1,000 units are £2,000 then, at an output of 1,100 units, they will be £2,200 (ie a 10 per cent increase in both output and cost). By contrast, the fixed expense of factory rent of, say, £5,000 will be unchanged if output increases by 10 per cent. (Note that such calculations assume a linear relationship for variable costs and that there are no stepped fixed costs.)

Such changes in costs can be incorporated, as part of a business' planning process, into a formal schedule of *budgeted production costs*. This calculates total production cost and the cost per unit at changed (either increased or decreased) levels of output, as shown in the Case Study which follows.

Case Study

SPEEDPEN LTD: BUDGETED PRODUCTION COSTS

situation

Speedpen Limited, which manufactures quality rollerball pens, has budgeted its production costs for 2005 on the basis of an output of 100,000 units as follows:

			£
•	variable costs	– materials	75,000
		– labour	50,000
		– expenses	10,000
•	fixed costs	– labour	22,500
		– overheads	33,500

The sales department thinks that demand for the product is more likely to be 110,000 units, or could be as high as 125,000 units.

You have been asked to prepare a budgeted cost schedule based on outputs of 100,000 units, 110,000 units and 125,000 units. The cost schedule is to show total production cost and the cost per unit at each level of output.

solution

2005	BUDGETED PRODUCTION COSTS		
UNITS	100,000	110,000	125,000
COSTS	£	£	£
Variable costs			
Materials	75,000	82,500	93,750
Labour	50,000	55,000	62,500
Expenses	10,000	11,000	12,500
	135,000	148,500	168,750
Fixed costs			
Labour	22,500	22,500	22,500
Overheads	33,500	33,500	33,500
	56,000	56,000	56,000
TOTAL PRODUCTION COST	191,000	204,500	224,750
COST PER UNIT	£1.91	£1.86	£1.80

Notes:

- Variable costs per unit are: materials, £0.75 (ie £75,000 ÷ 100,000 units); labour, £0.50; expenses, £0.10
- At the higher levels of output simply multiply the unit costs by 110,000 and 125,000
- Fixed costs remain fixed at the higher levels of output
- Total production cost is total variable costs plus total fixed costs
- Cost per unit is total production cost divided by output (note that cost per unit has been rounded to the nearest penny)
- The costs at higher levels of output assume that:
  - there is a linear relationship for variable costs
  - there are no stepped fixed costs
- The fall in cost per unit as output increases occurs because the fixed costs are being spread over a greater number of units, ie the fixed cost per unit falls

Chapter Summary

- Expenses, together with materials and labour, form the three main elements of cost.

- Expenses are categorised between:
  - capital expenditure and revenue expenditure
  - direct expenses and indirect expenses
  - fixed costs and variable costs

- Identification of revenue expenditure is important in the costing of output; identification of capital expenditure is important for knowing the assets owned by a business.

- Direct expenses are charged to work-in-progress.

- Indirect expenses are charged to overheads and split between:
  - production overheads
  - non-production overheads, such as selling and distribution, administration, finance

- The nature of costs means that not all costs increase or decrease in line with increases or decreases in output; all costs, by nature, are:
  - fixed, or
  - semi-variable, or
  - variable

- A knowledge of the nature of costs enables:
  - identification of the element of fixed costs within total costs
  - preparation of a schedule of budgeted production costs
  - identification of the break-even point

Key Terms

capital expenditure expenditure incurred on the purchase, alteration or improvement of fixed assets

revenue expenditure expenditure incurred on running costs

direct expenses those expenses that are attributable to particular units of output

indirect expenses all other expenses which are not attributable directly to particular units of output

overheads	the indirect costs of materials, labour and expenses
fixed costs	costs which remain fixed over a range of output levels
semi-variable costs	costs which combine a fixed and variable element
variable costs	costs which vary directly with output
'high/low' technique	method used to identify the element of fixed costs within total costs
budgeted production costs	schedule which shows the calculation of total production cost and cost per unit at particular levels of output

Student Activities

4.1 Define:

(a) capital expenditure

(b) revenue expenditure

Give two examples of each.

4.2 Define:

(a) direct expenses

(b) indirect expenses

Give two examples of each.

4.3 Fred Jarvis normally works as a production-line employee of Wyevale Plastics. However, for the past four weeks he has been building an extension to the company's warehouse.

How should his wages for this period be dealt with in the accounts? Why is this?

4.4   Explain the nature of the costs, as shown by the following graphs:

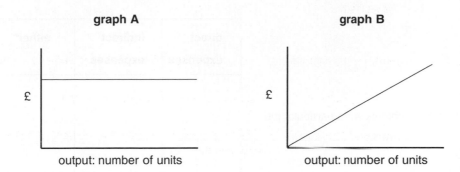

Graph (a) shows the cost of the rent of a factory.

Graph (b) shows the wages of production-line employees who are paid on a piecework basis.

4.5   Classify the following costs (tick the appropriate column):

		capital expenditure	revenue expenditure
(a)	purchase of motor vehicles		
(b)	depreciation of motor vehicles		
(c)	payment of office rent		
(d)	salaries of office staff		
(e)	legal fees relating to the purchase of property		
(f)	re-decoration of office		
(g)	installation of air-conditioning in office		
(h)	wages of own employees used to build extension to the stockroom		
(i)	installation and setting up of a new machine		

4.6 Classify the following costs (tick the appropriate column):

		direct expenses	indirect expenses	either*
(a)	hire of machinery for a particular job			
(b)	office rent			
(c)	cleaning materials			
(d)	power costs			
(e)	royalty paid to designer for each unit of output			
(f)	sales staff car expenses			
(g)	depreciation of production machinery			
(h)	consultant's fees relating to a particular job			
(i)	heating and lighting			

*explain your reasons for classifying costs in this column

4.7 Classify the following costs (tick the appropriate column):

		fixed	semi-fixed	variable
(a)	rates of business premises			
(b)	royalty paid to designer for each unit of output			
(c)	car hire with fixed rental and charge per mile			
(d)	employees paid on piecework basis			
(e)	straight-line depreciation			
(f)	units of output depreciation			
(g)	direct materials			
(h)	telephone bill with fixed rental and charge per unit			
(i)	office salaries			

4.8 Eveshore Pottery Limited manufactures a range of 'souvenir' mugs, cups and saucers, plates, etc, which sell well to visitors from abroad who are seeking a memento of 'Olde England'. A number of different costs have been incurred during the last month, and you are asked to classify them into:

- direct materials
- indirect materials
- direct labour
- indirect labour
- direct expenses
- indirect expenses

The costs are:

(a) cleaning materials for the machines

(b) wages of factory supervisor

(c) clay from which the 'pots' are made

(d) 10p royalties payable to the designer for each 'Eveshore Plate' made

(e) salary of office assistant

(f) electricity used to heat the kilns

(g) rates of factory

(h) depreciation of office equipment

(i) wages of production-line workers

(j) salesperson's salary

(k) interest charged on bank overdraft

If you believe alternative classifications exist, argue the case and state if you need further information from the company.

Of the overhead costs, ie indirect materials, indirect labour and indirect expenses, you are to indicate which would be classified as:

- production overheads
- selling and distribution overheads
- administration overheads
- finance overheads

4.9 Bodytone Limited manufactures two types of exercise equipment – a treadmill and an exercise cycle. The general expenses account for the month ended 30 June 2004 has a debit balance of £28,250. This balance is analysed as:

		£
•	direct expenses – treadmills	5,450
•	direct expenses – exercise cycles	3,170
•	production overheads	12,950
•	non-production overheads – selling and distribution	3,860
•	non-production overheads – administration	2,820
		28,250

The following cost accounting codes are in use to record expenses:

code number	description
2100	work-in-progress: treadmills
2200	work-in-progress: exercise cycles
3500	production overheads
4200	non-production overheads: selling and distribution
4400	non-production overheads: administration
5150	general expenses

As an accounts assistant at Bodytone Limited you have been given the following tasks:

Task 1

Prepare general expenses account for the month ended 30 June 2004:

Dr		General Expenses Account (5150)		Cr
2004		£	2004	£
30 June	Balance b/d	28,250		

Task 2

Complete the following table to show how the total cost of general expenses is split between work-in-progress, production overheads and non-production overheads.

2004	Code	Debit	Credit
30 June	2100		
30 June	5150		
30 June	2200		
30 June	5150		
30 June	3500		
30 June	5150		
30 June	4200		
30 June	5150		
30 June	4400		
30 June	5150		

4.10 The accounts supervisor of Nerca Manufacturing Limited has provided you with the following information:

- at 10,000 units of output, total costs are £50,000
- at 15,000 units of output, total costs are £65,000

You are to use the 'high/low' technique to identify the element of fixed costs. The supervisor tells you that variable costs have a linear relationship, and that there are no stepped fixed costs.

4.11   Monica Manufacturing has budgeted the production costs for 2005 on the basis of an output of 250,000 units as follows:

		£
variable costs	– materials	400,000
	– labour	325,000
	– expenses	100,000
fixed costs	– labour	96,500
	– overheads	107,500

The sales department thinks that demand for the product is more likely to be 300,000 units, or could be as high as 350,000 units.

You are to prepare a schedule of budgeted production costs based on outputs of 250,000 units, 300,000 units and 350,000 units. The schedule is to show total production cost and the cost per unit at each level of output. (Note: you may assume that there is a linear relationship for variable costs, and that there are no stepped fixed costs.)

Briefly describe and explain the trend in costs per unit for the three budgeted levels of production.

5 Overheads

- the need to recover the cost of overheads through units of output
- the process of allocating and apportioning the cost of overheads into the units of output
- the different bases of apportionment of overheads
- apportionment of service department costs
- the commonly-used overhead absorption rates and their relative merits in given circumstances
- the book-keeping entries for overheads

NVQ PERFORMANCE CRITERIA COVERED

unit 6: RECORDING AND EVALUATING COSTS AND REVENUES

element 6.2

record and analyse information relating to the allocation, apportionment and absorption of overhead costs

A identify overhead costs in accordance with the organisation's procedures

B attribute overhead costs to production and service cost centres in accordance with agreed bases of allocation and apportionment

C calculate overhead absorption rates in accordance with the agreed bases of absorption

D record and analyse information relating to overhead costs in accordance with the organisation's procedures

E make adjustments for under and over recovered overhead costs in accordance with established procedures

F review methods of allocation, apportionment and absorption at regular intervals in discussions with senior staff and ensure agreed changes to methods are implemented

G consult staff working in operational departments to resolve any queries in overhead cost data

OVERHEADS

In Chapter 1 'An Introduction to Cost Accounting' we saw that costs could be classified as follows:

	DIRECT MATERIALS		INDIRECT MATERIALS
+	DIRECT LABOUR	+	INDIRECT LABOUR
+	DIRECT EXPENSES	+	INDIRECT EXPENSES
=	TOTAL DIRECT COSTS	=	TOTAL OVERHEADS
	(PRIME COST)		

Direct costs can be identified directly with each unit of output, but indirect costs (overheads) cannot be identified directly with each unit of output.

Overheads do not relate to particular units of output but must, instead, be shared amongst all the cost units (units of output to which costs can be charged) to which they relate. For example, the cost of the factory rent must be included in the cost of the firm's output.

The important point to remember is that all the overheads of a business, together with the direct costs (materials, labour and expenses) must be covered by money flowing in from the firm's output – the sales of products or services. This point is demonstrated in the Case Study which follows.

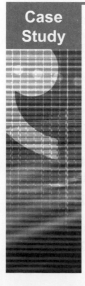

Case Study

COOLHEADS: A HAIRDRESSING BUSINESS

situation

CoolHeads is a new hairdressing business, being set up by Nathan and Morgan in a rented shop.

Nathan and Morgan are preparing their price list. They must set the prices sufficiently high to cover all their costs and to give them a profit.

They have details of the costs of all the materials they need (shampoos, colourings and so on) from a specialist supplier. Nathan and Morgan have decided the rate to charge to the business for their own work and they do not intend to employ anyone else for the time being.

But there are other costs which they will also incur – their overheads – and they are not so sure how they will work these into their pricing structure. Nathan asks:

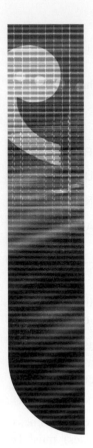

'What about the shop rent and the business rates we have to pay? What about the electricity, the insurance, the telephone bill and all the advertising we have to do? How are we going to cover these costs?'

'How much will it cost us in total to deal with each customer?'

'How do we make sure that we are going to make a profit?'

solution

For pricing purposes, Nathan and Morgan need to include overheads in the cost of each item on their price list.

In a small business like this, the whole business could be a single cost centre. All the overheads could be allowed for in a single rate to charge for a hair cut.

Suppose Nathan and Morgan estimate that their total overheads for the first year of trading will be £27,000. They expect to be working on hairstyling for 1,500 hours each during the year, ie a total of 3,000 hours between them.

Therefore, they could decide in advance that each hour of their work should be charged £27,000 ÷ 3,000 = £9 for overheads. A job that takes two hours to complete would then be charged 2 x £9 = £18 for overheads.

Notice that in a service business such as hairdressing, direct materials costs are likely to be relatively small in comparison with the cost of direct labour and overheads. It is essential for Nathan and Morgan to consider the cost of overheads when they are setting their prices and the hourly rate is one possible way of doing this. This is called an 'overhead absorption rate' and we will look in more detail at this idea later in this chapter (page 128).

In larger businesses and organisations, overheads are usually classified by function under headings such as:

- factory or production, eg factory rent and rates, indirect factory labour, indirect factory materials, heating and lighting of factory

- selling and distribution, eg salaries of sales staff, vehicle costs, delivery costs

- administration, eg office rent and rates, office salaries, heating and lighting of office, indirect office materials

- finance, eg bank interest

Each of these functions or sections of the business is likely to be what is known as a cost centre, a term which was defined in Chapter 1 as follows:

Cost centres are sections of a business to which costs can be charged.

In order to deal with the overheads we need to know how the whole organisation is split into cost centres. This will depend on the size of the business and the way in which the work is organised.

COLLECTING OVERHEADS IN COST CENTRES

allocation of overheads

Some overheads belong entirely to one particular cost centre, for example:

* the salary of a supervisor who works in only one cost centre

* the rent of a separate building in which there is only one cost centre

* the cost of indirect materials that have been issued to one particular cost centre

Overheads like these can therefore be allocated to the cost centre to which they belong.

Allocation of overheads is the charging to a particular cost centre of overheads that are incurred entirely by that cost centre.

apportionment of overheads

Overheads that cannot be allocated to a particular cost centre have to be shared or **apportioned** between two or more cost centres.

Apportionment of overheads is the sharing of overheads over a number of cost centres to which they relate. Each cost centre is charged with a proportion of the overhead cost.

For example, a department which is a cost centre within a factory will be charged a proportion of the factory rent and rates. Another example is where a supervisor works within two departments, both of which are separate cost centres: the indirect labour cost of employing the supervisor is shared between the two cost centres.

With apportionment, a suitable **basis** – or method – must be found to apportion overheads between cost centres; the basis selected should be related to the type of cost. Different methods might be used for each overhead.

Look at the example on the next page.

OVERHEAD	BASIS OF APPORTIONMENT
rent, rates	floor area (or volume of space) of cost centres
heating, lighting	floor area (or volume of space) of cost centres
buildings insurance	floor area (or volume of space) of cost centres
buildings depreciation	floor area (or volume of space) of cost centres
machinery insurance	cost or net book value of machinery and equipment
machinery depreciation	value of machinery; or machine usage (hours)
canteen	number of employees in each cost centre
supervisory costs	number of employees in each cost centre, or labour hours worked by supervisors in each cost centre

It must be stressed that apportionment is used for those overheads that cannot be allocated to a particular cost centre. For example, if a college's Business Studies Department occupies a building in another part of town from the main college building, the rates for the building can clearly be allocated to the Business Studies cost centre. By contrast, the rates for the main college building must be apportioned amongst the cost centres on the main campus.

review of allocation and apportionment

It is important that the allocation and apportionment of overheads are reviewed at regular intervals to ensure that the methods being used are still valid. For example:

* *allocation*

    The role of a supervisor may have changed – whereas previously the supervisor worked in one department only, he or she might now be working in two departments

* *apportionment*

    Building work may have expanded the floor area of a department, so that the apportionment basis needs to be reworked

Any proposed changes to allocation and apportionment must be discussed with senior staff and their agreement obtained before any changes to methods are implemented. Accounting staff will often have to consult with staff (such as managers and supervisors) working in operational departments, to discuss how overheads are charged to their departments, and to resolve any queries.

apportionment and ratios

It is important to understand the method of apportionment of overheads using ratios. For example, overheads relating to buildings are often shared in the ratio of the floor area used by the cost centres.

Now read through the Worked Example and the Case Study which follow.

WORKED EXAMPLE: APPORTIONMENT USING RATIOS

A business has four cost centres: two production departments, A and B, and two non-production cost centres, stores and maintenance. The total rent per year for the business premises is £12,000. This is to be apportioned on the basis of floor area, given as:

	production dept A	production dept B	stores	maintenance
Floor area (square metres)	400	550	350	200

Step 1
Calculate the total floor area: 400 + 550 + 350 + 200 = 1,500 square metres

Step 2
Divide the total rent by the total floor area: £12,000 ÷ 1,500 = £8
This gives a rate of £8 per square metre.

Step 3
Multiply the floor area in each cost centre by the rate per square metre. This gives the share of rent for each cost centre. For example, in Production Department A, the share of rent is 400 x £8 = £3,200. The results are shown in the table:

	production dept A	production dept B	stores	maintenance
Floor area (square metres)	400	550	350	200
Rent apportioned	£3,200	£4,400	£2,800	£1,600

Step 4
Check that the apportioned amounts agree with the total rent:
£3,200 + £4,400 + £ 2,800 + £1,600 = £12,000.

PILOT ENGINEERING LIMITED:
OVERHEAD ALLOCATION AND APPORTIONMENT

situation

Pilot Engineering Limited, which makes car engine components, uses some of the latest laser equipment in one department, while another section of the business continues to use traditional machinery. Details of the factory are as follows:

Department X is a 'hi-tech' machine shop equipped with laser-controlled machinery which cost £80,000. This department has 400 square metres of floor area. There are three machine operators: the supervisor spends one-third of the time in this department.

Department Y is a 'low-tech' part of the factory equipped with machinery which cost £20,000. The floor area is 600 square metres. There are two workers who spend all their time in this department: the supervisor spends two-thirds of the time in this department.

The overheads to be allocated or apportioned are as follows:

1	Factory rates	£12,000
2	Wages of the supervisor	£21,000
3	Factory heating and lighting	£2,500
4	Depreciation of machinery	£20,000
5	Buildings insurance	£2,000
6	Insurance of machinery	£1,500
7	Specialist materials for the laser equipment	£2,500

How should each of these be allocated or apportioned to each department?

solution

The recommendations are:

1   Factory rates – apportioned on the basis of floor area.

2   Supervisor's wages – apportioned on the basis of time spent, ie one-third to Department X, and two-thirds to Department Y. If the time spent was not known, an alternative basis could be established, based on the number of employees.

3   Factory heating and lighting – apportioned on the basis of floor area.

4   Depreciation of machinery – apportioned on the basis of machine value.

5   Buildings insurance – apportioned on the basis of floor area.

6   Insurance of machinery – apportioned on the basis of machine value.

7   Specialist materials for the laser equipment – allocated to Department X because this cost belongs entirely to Department X.

It is important to note that there are no fixed rules for the apportionment of overheads – the only proviso is that a fair proportion of the overhead is charged to each department which has some responsibility for the cost being incurred. Methods of apportionment will need to be reviewed at regular intervals to ensure that they are still valid; changes can only be implemented with the agreement of senior staff.

The apportionment of overheads for Pilot Engineering Limited is as follows (sample workings are shown below the table):

overhead	basis of apportionment	total	dept X	dept Y
		£	£	£
Factory rates	Floor area	12,000	4,800	7,200
Wages of supervisor	Time spent	21,000	7,000	14,000
Heating and lighting	Floor area	2,500	1,000	1,500
Dep'n of machinery	Machine value	20,000	16,000	4,000
Buildings insurance	Floor area	2,000	800	1,200
Machinery insurance	Machine value	1,500	1,200	300
Specialist materials	Allocation	2,500	2,500	–
		61,500	33,300	28,200

workings

For example, the floor areas of the two departments are:

Dept X	400	square metres
Dept Y	600	square metres
Total	1,000	square metres

Factory rates are apportioned as follows:

$$\frac{£12,000}{1,000} = £12 \text{ per square metre}$$

Dept X rates:	£12 x 400 =	£4,800
Dept Y rates	£12 x 600 =	£7,200
Total (check)		£12,000

Note that overhead apportionment is often, in practice, calculated using a computer spreadsheet.

SERVICE DEPARTMENTS

Many businesses have departments which provide services within the business; for example, maintenance, transport, stores or stationery. Each service department is likely to be a cost centre, to which a proportion of overheads is charged. As service departments do not themselves have any cost units to which their overheads may be charged, the costs of each service department must be re-apportioned to the production departments (which do have cost units to which overheads can be charged). A suitable basis of re-allocation must be used, for example:

*   the overheads of a maintenance department might be re-apportioned to production departments on the basis of value of machinery or equipment, or on the basis of time spent in each production department

*   the overheads of a stores or stationery department could be re-apportioned on the basis of value of goods issued to production departments

*   the overheads of a subsidised canteen could be re-apportioned on the basis of the number of employees

Re-apportionment of service department overheads is considered in the next section.

RE-APPORTIONMENT OF SERVICE DEPARTMENT OVERHEADS

The overheads of service departments are charged to production cost centres using one of the following techniques:

*   **direct apportionment** is used where service departments provide services to production departments only

*   the **step-down method** is used where service departments provide services to production departments and to some other service departments

To illustrate re-apportionment, we will apply these techniques to a business with two production departments, A and B, and two service departments, stores and maintenance. After allocation and apportionment of production overheads, the totals are:

	total	production dept A	production dept B	stores	maintenance
	£	£	£	£	£
Overheads	20,400	10,000	5,000	2,400	3,000

direct apportionment

Here the service departments do not provide services to one another. Their costs are directly apportioned to production departments using a suitable basis. In the example on the previous page:

- stores overheads are re-apportioned on the basis of the number of stores requisitions – department A has made 150 requisitions; department B has made 50
- maintenance overheads are re-apportioned on the value of machinery – department A has machinery with a net book value of £20,000, department B's machinery has a value of £10,000

Using direct apportionment, the overheads of the service departments are re-apportioned as shown in the table below. The method of calculation using ratios is the same as we used for apportionment.

Notice that the total is taken out of the service cost centre column when it is shared between the production cost centres.

	total	production dept A	production dept B	stores	maintenance
	£	£	£	£	£
Overheads	20,400	10,000	5,000	2,400	3,000
Stores	–	1,800	600	(2,400)	–
Maintenance	–	2,000	1,000	–	(3,000)
	20,400	13,800	6,600	–	–

Thus all the overheads have now been charged to the production departments where they can be 'absorbed' into the cost units which form the output of each department. We will see how the absorption is carried out later in this chapter.

step-down method

This is used where, as well as to production departments, one service department provides services to another. Using the example, the stores department deals with requisitions from the maintenance department, but no maintenance work is carried out in the stores department. Under the step-down method we re-apportion firstly the overheads of the stores department (because it does not receive any services from the maintenance department), and secondly the overheads of the maintenance department:

- stores requisitions
  - department A   150
  - department B   50
  - maintenance   50
- value of machinery
  - department A   £20,000
  - department B   £10,000

The re-apportionment of the production overheads of the service departments, using the step-down method, is as follows:

	total	production dept A	production dept B	stores	maintenance
	£	£	£	£	£
Overheads	20,400	10,000	5,000	2,400	3,000
Stores	–	1,440	480	(2,400)	480
					– *3,480
Maintenance	–	2,320	1,160	–	(3,480)
	20,400	13,760	6,640	–	–

* Note that a new total is calculated for the maintenance department before it is re-apportioned. £480 from stores is added to the original £3,000 overheads in the maintenance department.

All the overheads have now been charged to the production departments.

ALLOCATION AND APPORTIONMENT – A SUMMARY

The diagram on the next page summarises the allocation and apportionment of overheads that we have seen in this chapter. It shows:

- allocation of overheads directly to cost centres
- apportionment of overheads on an equitable basis to cost centres
- re-apportionment of service department costs to production cost centres

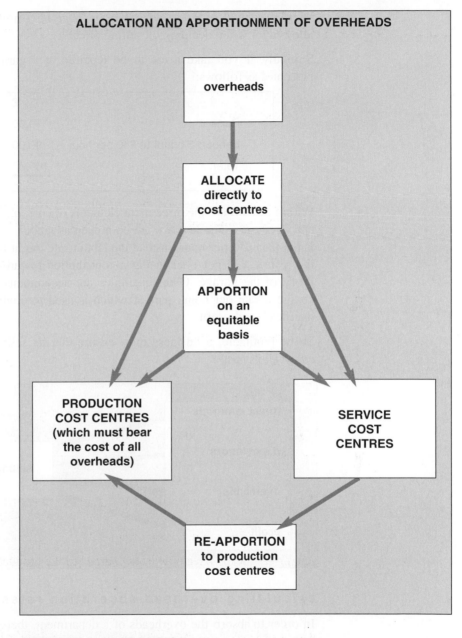

ALLOCATION AND APPORTIONMENT OF OVERHEADS

overheads

ALLOCATE
directly to
cost centres

APPORTION
on an
equitable
basis

PRODUCTION
COST CENTRES
(which must bear
the cost of all
overheads)

SERVICE
COST
CENTRES

RE-APPORTION
to production
cost centres

OVERHEAD ABSORPTION

Once overheads have been allocated or apportioned to production cost
centres, the final step is to ensure that the overheads are charged to cost units.
In the language of cost accounting this is known as 'absorption' or
'recovery', ie the cost of overheads is charged to the cost units which pass
through that particular production department.

We saw in the Case Study of CoolHeads (page 117), how overheads could be allowed for when deciding on selling prices.

Similarly, if you take a car to be repaired at a garage, the bill may be presented as follows:

	£
Parts	70.00
Labour: 3 hours at £30 per hour	90.00
Total	160.00

Within this bill are the three main elements of cost: materials (parts), labour and overheads. The last two are combined as labour – the garage mechanic is not paid £30 per hour; instead the labour rate might be £10 per hour, with the rest, ie £20 per hour, being a contribution towards the overheads and profit of the garage. Other examples are accountants and solicitors, who charge a 'rate per hour', part of which is used to contribute to the cost of overheads and profit.

To be profitable, a business must ensure that its selling prices more than cover all its costs:

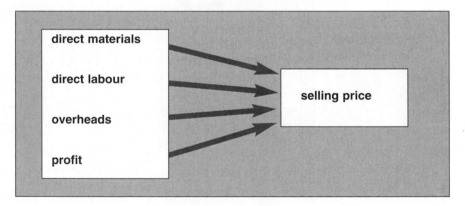

calculating overhead absorption rates

In order to absorb the overheads of a department, there are two steps to be followed:

1 calculation of the overhead absorption rate (OAR)

2 application of this rate to actual work done

The overhead absorption rate is calculated using estimated or budgeted figures as follows, for a given time period:

$$OAR = \frac{total\ budgeted\ cost\ centre\ overheads}{total\ planned\ work\ in\ the\ cost\ centre}$$

The amount of work must be measured in a suitable way, usually:

- direct labour hours, or
- machine hours

These methods are illustrated below.

direct labour hour method of calculation

With this method, production overhead is absorbed on the basis of the number of direct labour hours worked.

1 Calculation of the overhead absorption rate, using budgeted (expected) figures:

$$\frac{\textit{total cost centre overheads}}{\textit{total direct labour hours (in cost centre)}} = \textit{cost per direct labour hour}$$

2 Application of the rate:

direct labour hours worked x overhead absorption rate

= overhead absorbed

Example

Department A   total budgeted cost centre overheads for year   £40,000

expected direct labour hours for year   5,000

actual direct labour hours in March   450

1   Overhead absorption rate:

$$\frac{£40,000}{5,000 \text{ hours}} = £8 \text{ per direct labour hour}$$

2   Application of the rate:

450 hours x £8 = £3,600 of overhead absorbed in March

machine hour method of calculation

Here the production overhead is absorbed on the basis of machine hours.

1 Calculation of the overhead absorption rate, using budgeted (expected) figures:

$$\frac{\textit{total cost centre overheads}}{\textit{total machine hours (in cost centre)}} = \textit{cost per machine hour}$$

2 Application of the rate:

machine hours worked x overhead absorption rate

= overhead absorbed

Example

Department B   total budgeted cost centre overheads for year   £216,000

expected machine hours for year   36,000

actual machine hours in March   3,500

1   Overhead absorption rate:

$$\frac{£216,000}{36,000 \text{ hours}} = £6 \text{ per machine hour}$$

2   Application of the rate:

3,500 hours x £6 = £21,000 of overhead absorbed in March

---

which method to use?

Only one overhead absorption rate will be used in a particular department, and the method selected must relate to the reason why the costs are incurred. For example, a cost centre which is machine based, where most of the overheads incurred relate to machinery, will use a machine hour basis.

The direct labour hour method is a very popular method (eg the garage mentioned earlier) because overheads are absorbed on a time basis. Thus the cost unit that requires twice the direct labour of another cost unit will be charged twice the overhead. However this method will be inappropriate where some units are worked on by hand while others quickly pass through a machinery process and require little direct labour time.

A machine hour rate is particularly appropriate where expensive machinery is used in the department. However, it would be unsuitable where not all products pass through the machine but some are worked on by hand: in the latter case, no overheads would be charged to the cost units.

It is important to select the best method of overhead absorption for the particular business, otherwise wrong decisions will be made on the basis of the costing information. The particular absorption method selected for a department will need to be reviewed at regular intervals to ensure that it is still valid. For example, the direct labour hour method is unlikely to continue to be appropriate where a machine has been brought in to automate processes that were previously carried out by hand. Any proposed changes must be discussed with senior staff and their agreement obtained before any changes to methods are implemented. The changes will need to be discussed with staff (such as managers and supervisors) working in operational departments to explain how overheads will be charged to their departments in the future, and any queries will need to be resolved.

In this chapter, we have calculated overhead absorption rates based on:

• direct labour hours

• machine hours

There are other possible bases which could be used. For example, overheads could be charged as a percentage of:

• direct material cost

• direct labour cost

• prime cost

The principles are the same for any method of absorption:

• the rate to use is calculated in advance using estimates

• the rate is applied to the actual work done

For example, if the estimates showed that it would be necessary to add 20% on to prime cost for overheads, then a job having a prime cost of £6,000 would absorb £6,000 x 20% = £1,200 of overheads, making a total of £7,200.

using a pre-determined rate

Most businesses and organisations calculate a pre-determined overhead absorption rate for each department. This is then applied to all production passing through that department.

The OAR is calculated in advance using estimates – this avoids having to calculate the rate regularly, which may result in changes over quite short time periods. Instead the rate is smoothed out over fluctuations in cost and activity over a longer accounting period.

OVER- OR UNDER-ABSORPTION OF OVERHEADS

In the Case Study of CoolHeads (page 117) we saw that Nathan and Morgan estimated that their total overheads for the first year of trading would be £27,000. They expected to be working on hairstyling for 1,500 hours each during the year, ie a total of 3,000 hours between them.

Therefore, they could have decided in advance that each hour of their work should be charged £27,000/3,000 = £9 for overheads. A job taking two hours to complete would then be charged 2 x £9 = £18 for overheads. This is a simple example of the absorption of overheads using a pre-determined rate. (The word 'recovery' is sometimes used instead of 'absorption' – it means the same.)

At the end of CoolHeads' first year, it is most unlikely that Nathan and Morgan will find that everything went exactly according to plan. They may have spent more or less on the overheads than £27,000. They may have worked on styling for more or less than 3,000 hours in total.

They will find, therefore, that the amount of overheads they have absorbed into the cost of their actual work during the year is not the same as the amount they have spent. If the amount absorbed is the greater, the difference is called 'over-absorption' or 'over-recovery' of overheads. If the amount absorbed is less than the amount spent, the difference is called 'under-absorption' or 'under-recovery'.

Over-absorption or under-absorption (recovery) is the difference between the total amount of overheads absorbed (recovered) in a given period and the total amount spent on overheads.

The following worked example shows the calculation when the overhead absorption rate is based on direct labour hours.

Example
Department C

overhead absorption rate (based on direct labour hours)	£6.00 per labour hour
actual labour hours in year	6,300 hours
actual overheads for year	£36,000

- actual overheads for the department are £36,000
- actual overhead absorbed: 6,300 hours x £6.00 per hour = £37,800
- over-absorption of overhead: £37,800 – £36,000 = £1,800

At the end of the financial year, an adjustment is made to profit and loss account for the total over-absorbed or under-absorbed overhead.

On first impressions, over-absorption of overheads seems to be a 'bonus' for a business – profits will be higher; however, it should be remembered that the overhead rate may have been set too high. As a consequence, sales might have been lost because the selling price has been too high. The OAR will need to be reviewed if over-absorption continues on a regular basis.

In the next section we see the book-keeping entries to record the over-absorption or under-absorption of overheads.

BOOK-KEEPING ENTRIES FOR OVERHEADS

In this section we look at the cost book-keeping entries to record the transfer of the cost of overheads to work-in-progress, together with the entries for over- or under-absorption of overheads (which are transferred to profit and loss account). These entries form part of the book-keeping system for costing; Chapter 7 looks in detail at an integrated book-keeping system.

A production overheads account is used to:

- transfer production overheads to work-in-progress
- credit the amount of over-absorbed overheads to profit and loss account
- charge the amount of under-absorbed overheads to profit and loss account

The cost book-keeping entries are:

- **transfer production overheads to work-in-progress**
  - debit work-in-progress account
  - credit production overheads account

- **credit over-absorbed overheads to profit and loss account**
  - debit production overheads account
  - credit profit and loss account

  Here, the amount of over-absorbed overheads reduces the total cost of production, and so increases profits.

- **charge under-absorbed overheads to profit and loss account**
  - debit profit and loss account
  - credit production overheads account

  Here the amount of under-absorbed overheads adds to the total cost of production, and so reduces profits.

These cost book-keeping entries are shown diagrammatically as shown on the next page.

book-keeping entries for overheads

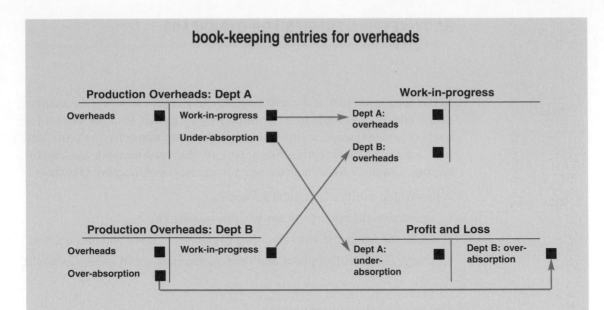

Note: Instead of transferring the over- or under-absorption of overheads direct to profit and loss account, an alternative is to use a holding account for the amounts. At the end of the financial year, the balance of this account is then transferred to profit and loss account – as either a debit or a credit entry, depending on the balance.

Case Study

BOXIT LIMITED: BOOK-KEEPING FOR OVERHEADS

situation

Boxit Limited manufactures and sells cardboard boxes which are used for packaging and storage. The boxes pass through two departments – cutting and assembly. Details of overheads for the departments for the four weeks ended 24 March 2004 are as follows:

Cutting Department

- overhead absorption rate is £10.00 per machine hour
- machine hours worked were 1,000
- actual cost of production overhead was £11,000

Assembly Department

- overhead absorption rate is £4.00 per direct labour hour
- direct labour hours worked were 2,000
- actual cost of production overhead was £7,500

The following cost accounting codes are in use to record overheads:

code number	description
2200	work-in-progress
2500	production overheads: cutting department
2600	production overheads: assembly department
5500	profit and loss account

As an accounts assistant at Boxit Limited, you are asked to prepare the two production overheads accounts and to fill in the table below to account for the overheads and the over- and under-absorption of overheads.

2004	Code	Debit	Credit
24 March	2200		
24 March	2500		
24 March	2200		
24 March	2600		
24 March	5500		
24 March	2500		
24 March	2600		
24 March	5500		

solution

The production overheads accounts are prepared as follows:

Dr	Production Overheads Account: Cutting Department		Cr
	£		£
Bank (overheads incurred)	11,000	Work-in-progress	10,000
		Profit and loss (under-absorption)	1,000
	11,000		11,000

Dr	Production Overheads Account: Assembly Department		Cr
	£		£
Bank (overheads incurred)	7,500	Work-in-progress	8,000
Profit and loss (over-absorption)	500		
	8,000		8,000

The cost book-keeping entries are:

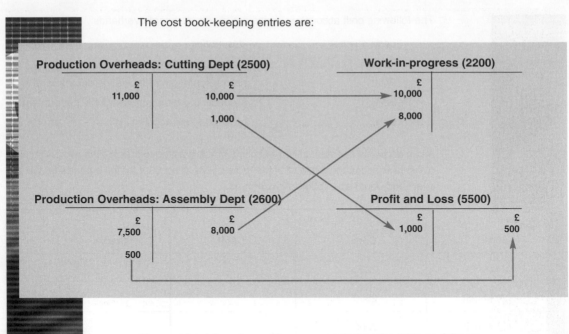

The cost book-keeping entries are recorded on the table as follows:

2004	Code	Debit	Credit
24 March	2200	£10,000	
24 March	2500		£10,000
24 March	2200	£8,000	
24 March	2600		£8,000
24 March	5500	£1,000	
24 March	2500		£1,000
24 March	2600	£500	
24 March	5500		£500

In this way, the cost of the pre-determined overhead rates is charged to work-in-progress, while the amount of over- or under-absorption of overheads is transferred to profit and loss account.

Chapter Summary

- Direct costs can be charged directly to cost units.

- Indirect costs (overheads) cannot be charged to cost units immediately.

- Overheads are:
  - allocated to a specific cost centre, if they belong entirely to that cost centre
  - apportioned between cost centres, if they are shared

- Apportionment is done on a suitable basis, using ratios of floor area, numbers of employees and so on.

- Methods of allocation and apportionment should be reviewed regularly.

- The total overheads allocated and apportioned to the service cost centres are then re-apportioned to the production cost centres.

- After re-apportionment of the service cost centre overheads, the total overheads in each production cost centre can be calculated.

- All the above steps can be carried out using expected or budgeted overhead amounts.

- Overhead absorption rates are calculated using the total expected or budgeted overheads in each cost centre.

- An overhead absorption rate is calculated as follows:

$$\text{overhead absorption rate} = \frac{\text{total budgeted cost centre overheads}}{\text{total planned work in cost centre}}$$

where the planned amount of work may be measured, often in terms of direct labour hours or machine hours.

- Overhead absorption rates are applied to the actual work carried out. A direct labour hour absorption rate is applied as follows, for example:

$$\textit{Direct labour hours worked x overhead absorption rate}$$
$$= \textit{overhead absorbed}$$

- At the end of a given period, the amount of overhead absorbed may differ from the amount actually spent on the overheads. The difference is either an over-absorption (when the amount absorbed is greater than the amount spent) or an under-absorption (when the amount absorbed is less than the amount spent).

- Cost book-keeping entries are made to record:
  - the transfer of overheads to work-in-progress
  - the transfer of over- or under-absorption of overheads to profit and loss account

Key Terms	
overheads	indirect costs, made up of
	indirect materials + indirect labour + indirect expenses
cost centres	sections of a business to which costs can be charged
allocation of overheads	the charging to a particular cost centre of overheads that are incurred entirely by that cost centre
apportionment of overheads	the sharing of overheads over a number of cost centres to which they relate – each cost centre is charged with a proportion of the overhead cost
service department	a non-production cost centre that provides services to other cost centres in the business
re-apportionment of service department overheads	the sharing of the total overheads from a service department, a proportion being charged to each cost centre it serves; after all re-apportionment has been carried out, the overheads will be charged to production cost centres only
absorption (recovery) of overheads	the charging of overheads to cost units (units of output)
overhead absorption rate (OAR)	the rate used to charge overheads to cost units – calculated in advance, as:
	budgeted total overhead ÷ planned amount of work
basis of absorption	the measurement of work used to calculate the overhead absorption rate, for example:
	• direct labour hours
	• machine hours
over- or under-absorption (recovery)	the difference between the total amount of overheads absorbed (recovered) in a given period and the total amount spent on overheads

Student Activities

5.1 Distinguish between:
- allocation of overheads
- apportionment of overheads

5.2 Wyvern Fabrication Company has two production departments – moulding and finishing.

The company charges overheads on the basis of machine hours and the following overhead analysis information is available to you (note that service department overheads have already been apportioned to production departments):

OVERHEAD ANALYSIS SHEET		
	MOULDING	FINISHING
Budgeted total overheads (£)	9,338	3,298
Budgeted machine hours	1,450	680
Budgeted overhead absorption rate (£)		

Details of a particular job of work are as follows:

JOB OVERHEAD ANALYSIS SHEET		
	MOULDING	FINISHING
Job machine hours	412	154
Budgeted overhead absorption rate (£)		
Overhead absorbed by job (£)		

You are to:

(a) Calculate the overhead absorption rate for each of the two departments and complete the overhead analysis sheet.

(b) Calculate the production overhead absorbed by the job and complete the job overhead analysis sheet.

(c) Suggest two other overhead absorption rates that the company might use and comment on the circumstances that would make them appropriate.

5.3 ABC Limited is a manufacturing business with three cost centres: Departments A, B and C. The following are the expected factory overheads for the forthcoming year:

Rent and rates	£7,210
Depreciation of machinery	£10,800
Supervisor's salary	£12,750
Insurance of machinery	£750

Departmental information is:

	Dept A	Dept B	Dept C
Floor area (sq m)	300	150	250
Value of machinery	£25,000	£15,000	£10,000
Number of production-line employees	8	4	3

You are to:

(a) Apportion the overheads to the cost centres, stating the basis of apportionment.

(b) Calculate the overhead absorption rate (to two decimal places) of each department, based on direct labour hours. Note that the factory works a 37 hour week for 48 weeks in a year.

5.4 Wye Engineering Limited offers specialist engineering services to the car industry. It has two production departments – machining and finishing – and a service department which maintains the machinery of both departments. Expected production overheads for the forthcoming year are:

	£
Rent and rates	5,520
Buildings insurance	1,320
Insurance of machinery	1,650
Lighting and heating	3,720
Depreciation of machinery	11,000
Supervisory salaries	30,000
Maintenance department salary	16,000
Factory cleaning	4,800

The following information is available:

	Machining	Finishing	Maintenance
Floor area (square metres)	300	200	100
Number of employees	6	3	1
Value of machinery	£40,000	£15,000	–

The factory works a 35 hour week for 47 weeks each year.

You are to:

(a) Prepare an analysis of production overheads showing the basis of allocation and apportionment to the three departments of the business.

(b) Re-apportion the service department overheads to production departments on the basis of value of machinery.

(c) Calculate an overhead absorption rate based on direct labour hours for each of the two production departments.

(d) Discuss alternative overhead absorption rates that the company could use.

5.5 Mercia Tutorial College has two teaching departments – business studies and general studies – and two service departments – administration and technical support. The overheads of each department are as follows:

	£
• business studies	40,000
• general studies	20,000
• administration	9,600
• technical support	12,000

The basis for re-apportioning the overheads of the service departments is:

• technical support, on the value of equipment in each department – business studies, £50,000; general studies, £25,000; administration, £25,000

• administration, on the number of students in the teaching departments – business studies, 500; general studies, 250

You are to use the step-down method to re-apportion the two service department overheads to the two teaching departments.

5.6 Rossiter and Rossiter is a firm of chartered accountants, with two partners. Overhead costs for next year are estimated to be:

	£
Office rent	10,000
Office salaries	30,000
Rates	4,800
Heating and lighting	2,400
Stationery	2,000
Postage and telephone	5,100
Car expenses	5,600

The two partners plan to work for 47 weeks next year. They will each be in the office for 40 hours per week, but will be working on behalf of their clients for 35 hours per week.

(a)   What is the overhead absorption rate per partner hour?

(b)   If each partner wishes to earn a salary of £30,000 per year, what is the combined hourly rate per partner, which includes overheads and their salaries?

(c)   If both partners actually work on their clients' behalf for 37 hours per week, what will be the total over-absorption of overheads for the year?

5.7   A friend of yours is about to start in business making garden seats. She plans to make two different qualities – 'Standard' and 'De Luxe'. Costs per unit for direct materials and labour are expected to be:

	Standard	De Luxe
	£	£
Direct materials	12.50	20.00
Direct labour:		
3 hours at £8.00 per hour	24.00	–
3.5 hours at £10.00 per hour	–	35.00
	36.50	55.00
Machine hours	1	2.5

Production overheads are expected to be £1,000 per month.

Production is expected to be 80 'Standard' seats and 40 'De Luxe' seats per month.

(a)   Suggest two different methods by which overheads can be absorbed.

(b)   Calculate the production cost of each of the two qualities of garden seats using the two different methods of overhead absorption.

(c)   Compare the results of your calculations and suggest to your friend the most appropriate method of overhead absorption for this business.

5.8   Durning Limited manufactures and sells household furniture. The company's operations are organised by departments, as follows:

•   Warehouse

•   Manufacturing

•   Sales

•   Administration

The budgeted and actual fixed overheads of the company for November 2004 were as follows:

	£
Depreciation of fixed assets	9,150
Rent	11,000
Other property overheads	6,200
Administration overheads	13,450
Staff costs:	
− warehouse	3,600
− indirect manufacturing	9,180
− sales	8,650
− administration	5,940
Total budgeted and actual fixed overheads	67,170

The following information is also relevant:

Department	% of floor space occupied	Net book value of fixed assets £000
Warehouse	15%	120
Manufacturing	60%	400
Sales	10%	20
Administration	15%	60
	100%	600

Overheads are allocated and apportioned between departments using the most appropriate basis.

Task 1

Please see next page.

Task 2

Manufacturing fixed overheads are absorbed on the basis of budgeted machine hours. The budgeted number of machine hours for November 2004 was 10,000 hours.

You are to calculate the budgeted fixed overhead absorption rate for the manufacturing department for November 2004.

Task 1

Complete the following table showing the allocation and apportionment of fixed overheads between the four departments.

Fixed overheads for November 2004	Basis	Total £	Warehouse £	Manufacturing £	Sales £	Administration £
Depreciation		9,150				
Rent		11,000				
Other property overheads		6,200				
Administration overheads		13,450				
Staff costs		27,370				
		67,170				

5.9 You work as an accounts assistant at the Trevaunance Hotel which is part of a group of hotels. Each month it is one of your tasks to record and report cost information to head office.

The Trevaunance Hotel has fifty bedrooms and its operations are organised into five departments, as follows:

- Accommodation
- Restaurant
- Bar
- Kitchen
- Administration

The budgeted and actual fixed overheads for the Trevaunance Hotel for August 2004 were as follows:

	£
Bedroom repairs	3,200
Electricity	1,700
Rent	9,000
Kitchen repairs	1,025
Staff costs:	
– accommodation	4,550
– restaurant	6,740
– bar	3,045
– kitchen	2,310
– administration	6,950
Other property overheads	4,000
Total budgeted and actual fixed overheads	42,520

The following information is also relevant:

Department	% of floor space occupied	Metered electricity costs £
Accommodation	65%	550
Restaurant	15%	250
Bar	10%	150
Kitchen	5%	700
Administration	5%	50
	100%	1,700

Overheads are allocated and apportioned to the five departments using the most appropriate basis. The total administration overheads are then re-apportioned to the other four departments using the following percentages:

- Accommodation 60%
- Restaurant 20%
- Bar 10%
- Kitchen 10%

Task 1

Complete the following table showing the allocation and apportionment of fixed overheads between the five departments.

Fixed overheads for August 2004	Basis	Total £	Accommodation £	Restaurant £	Bar £	Kitchen £	Administration £
Bedroom repairs		3,200					
Electricity		1,700					
Rent		9,000					
Kitchen repairs		1,025					
Staff costs		23,595					
Other property overheads		4,000					
		42,520					( )
Administration		42,520					( )

Task 2

Kitchen fixed overheads are absorbed on the basis of budgeted labour hours. The budgeted number of labour hours for the kitchen during August 2004 was 1,000 hours.

You are to calculate the budgeted fixed overhead absorption rate per labour hour for the kitchen for August 2004.

5.10 AggieSurf Limited manufactures and sells surfboards. The boards pass through two departments – moulding and finishing. Details of overheads for the departments for the four weeks ended 26 May 2004 are as follows:

Moulding Department

- overhead absorption rate is £8.00 per machine hour
- machine hours worked were 600
- actual cost of production overhead was £5,000

Finishing Department

- overhead absorption rate is £5.00 per direct labour hour
- direct labour hours worked were 1,500
- actual cost of production overhead was £7,000

The following cost accounting codes are in use to record overheads:

code number	description
3000	work-in-progress
3400	production overheads: moulding department
3500	production overheads: finishing department
6000	profit and loss account

As an accounts assistant at AggieSurf Limited, you are asked to prepare the two production overheads accounts and to fill in the following table to account for the overheads and the over- and under-absorption of overheads.

2004	Code	Debit	Credit
26 May	3000		
26 May	3400		
26 May	3000		
26 May	3500		
26 May	6000		
26 May	3400		
26 May	3500		
26 May	6000		

6 Methods of costing

this chapter covers . . .

In this chapter we examine:

- *the principles of unit costing*

- *the methods of costing used for separate jobs: job costing, batch costing and contract costing*

- *the methods of costing used when the work is continuous: service costing and process costing*

- *the method of costing that would be used in various types of business*

- *the calculation of job or batch costs and selling prices from given data*

- *the calculation of average costs per cost unit in service costing and in process costing*

- *the book-keeping entries for process costing*

NVQ PERFORMANCE CRITERIA COVERED

unit 6: RECORDING AND EVALUATING COSTS AND REVENUES

element 6.1

record and analyse information relating to direct costs and revenues

C   calculate direct costs in accordance with the organisation's policies and procedures

element 6.2

record and analyse information relating to the allocation, apportionment and absorption of overhead costs

B   attribute overhead costs to production and service cost centres in accordance with agreed bases of allocation and apportionment

element 6.3

prepare and evaluate estimates of costs and revenues

A   identify information relevant to estimating current and future revenues and costs

UNIT COSTING

One of the main aims of costing is to establish the cost of one **cost unit** of work, whatever kind of work it is.

The cost unit must be a suitable way of measuring the work of an organisation – examples include:

- for a manufacturing business, per item manufactured

- for a chemical business, per kilo or litre of output

- for a transport company, per passenger mile/kilometre

- for a nursing home, per day for each resident

- for a hospital, per day per patient, or per operation

The principles of unit costing are the same whatever method of costing is used by the business or organisation. The unit cost of production or output is always calculated as:

$$\frac{\textit{total cost of production/output}}{\textit{number of cost units}} \quad = \quad \textit{unit cost}$$

The total cost of production comprises:

direct costs

- – direct materials

- – direct labour

- – direct expenses

indirect costs

- – production overheads

Non-production overheads – such as administration, selling and distribution – can also be added to give a figure for total cost.

Study the worked example set out on the next page.

WORKED EXAMPLE – unit costing

A toy manufacturer makes a popular type of doll. During the four-week period which has just ended 10,000 dolls were produced, with the following costs:

Product: Vita doll	
Direct costs	
Direct materials	£16,500
Direct labour	£17,500
Direct expenses	£5,000
Indirect costs	
Production overheads	£15,000
Total cost of production	£54,000
Number of Vita dolls produced	10,000
Unit cost of production	£5.40

The unit cost was calculated as

$$\frac{\text{total cost of production}}{\text{number of dolls produced}} = \frac{£54,000}{10,000} = £5.40 \text{ per doll}$$

The addition of non-production overheads – such as administration, selling and distribution – gives a figure for total cost, which can be marked-up with the company's profit percentage. To continue with the production of Vita dolls:

Total cost of production (see above)	£54,000
Non-production overheads	£15,000
Total cost	£69,000
Profit mark-up of 30% on £69,000	£20,700
Selling price	£89,700
Number of Vita dolls produced	10,000
Unit cost (including profit)	£8.97

In this chapter we will be looking at a number of different costing methods and will see that most calculate a unit cost of production.

We look firstly at costing methods for specific orders, and secondly at costing methods for continuous work (page 157).

COSTING METHODS FOR SPECIFIC ORDERS

Specific order costing is where customers order what they want, before it is made. Thus, the customer places the specific order, and agrees to buy the product before the work is done.

Many service businesses also carry out work to customers' requirements, for example, accountants and solicitors. Each piece of work is different and is kept separate from the others.

Costing methods which are used by business to collect costs and to calculate the total cost of their output include:

- job costing
- batch costing
- contract costing

Each of these is used in conjunction with absorption costing to recover the cost of overheads. Remember that businesses must recover their overheads in the total price charged to their customers – this applies both to manufacturing businesses and to service industries, such as banks, shops and transport companies.

Case Study

RACERS LIMITED: MANUFACTURING RACING BIKES

situation

Otto Kranz, a former cycling champion, is setting up a company to manufacture racing bikes. The business is to be called Racers Limited.

Otto is aware that he has two very distinct markets into which to sell his bikes:

- Some of his bikes will be produced to the specific requirements of individual customers for international level competition racing – this is the area which really interests Otto. He can charge a premium price for these custom-built designs.

- He also has to sell to the mass-market for quality racing bikes which will be made in batches of 20 to standard designs. These will sold in specialist shops and are cheaper, both to manufacture and in terms of selling price.

But Otto is confused about how he is going to cost out these two different methods of production – the 'one-off' and the standard design. He says:

'I can record the costs of the direct materials and labour hours used to make the 'one-off' bike and the batches of 20. But what about the overheads? Will I need more than one costing system here?'

solution

Racers Limited is likely to use two different methods of costing, depending on the kind of work being done:

- job costing – for the one-off designs
- batch costing – for the mass-market bikes

JOB COSTING

Job costing is used where each job can be separately identified from other jobs and costs are charged to the job.

The job becomes the cost unit to which costs are charged.

Examples of job costing include engineering firms that produce 'one-offs' to the customer's specifications, printing businesses, vehicle repairs, jobbing builders, painters and decorators.

The diagram below shows the main steps involved in job costing.

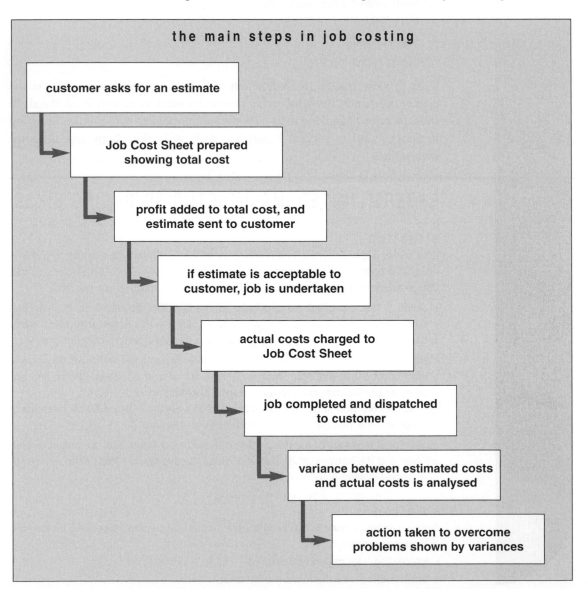

the main steps in job costing

customer asks for an estimate

Job Cost Sheet prepared showing total cost

profit added to total cost, and estimate sent to customer

if estimate is acceptable to customer, job is undertaken

actual costs charged to Job Cost Sheet

job completed and dispatched to customer

variance between estimated costs and actual costs is analysed

action taken to overcome problems shown by variances

The important points to note from the diagram are:

- each job is given a number, in order to identify it

- a separate job cost sheet is prepared for each job, listing the estimates of direct materials, direct labour, direct expenses and overheads (most businesses nowadays use a computer system to help with their costing and, in practice, the job cost sheet is held as a computer record on a database)

- the actual costs incurred are compared with the estimated costs, and the differences (called 'variances') between the two are analysed; action can then be taken to correct the variances, which will help when preparing future estimates

Case Study

FASHION AID:
JOB COSTING A CHARITY PROGRAMME

situation

The youth group at a local church has decided to organise an evening fashion show, to be called 'FashionAid'. The objective of the show is to raise money to send to a children's charity working in Central Africa. One of the organisers has asked for your help in arranging the printing a programme for the evening's events. You approach Pearshore Printers for an estimate of the cost of printing 750 copies of a sixteen page programme.

solution

Pearshore Printers allocate a reference number to the job. They prepare a Job Cost Sheet on their computer database as follows:

JOB NO. 6789 'FashionAid' Programme: 750 copies	
	£
Direct Materials	
Paper for text: white glossart paper code 135	82.00
Paper for cover: coated board code 235	55.00
Printing plates	15.00
Direct Labour	
Printing: 5 hours at £10.00 per hour	50.00
Finishing: 2 hours at £9.00 per hour	18.00
Overheads (based on direct labour hours)	
7 hours at £20.00 per hour	140.00
TOTAL COST	360.00
Profit (40% of total cost)	144.00
SELLING PRICE	504.00

These estimated costs will be obtained as follows:

- *direct materials,* from the stores ledger records for materials already in stock, and from the firm's Purchasing Department for items that need to be bought in especially for this job

- *direct labour,* from the payroll records of the different grades of labour to be employed on this job

- *overheads,* from the pre-determined overhead absorption rate based, for this job, on direct labour hours

Assuming that the price is acceptable to the customer, the job will go ahead and Pearshore Printers will record the actual costs of the job. These can then be compared with the estimated costs, and any differences or 'variances' between the two can be investigated. For example, it might be that actual labour costs are much higher than was estimated – this could mean that the employees took longer to do the job than was expected, or that pay rates had increased, or that more skilled staff – earning higher rates of pay – were used to do the job. This type of analysis, called 'variance analysis', will be studied in detail at NVQ Level 4 Accounting.

BATCH COSTING

Batch costing is used where the output consists of a number of identical items which are produced together as a batch.

Examples of batch costing include a bakery producing a batch of standard white loaves, and then a batch of croissants; or a clothing factory producing a batch of jackets, and then a batch of trousers. Each batch is the cost unit to which the costs are charged. Once the batch has been produced, the cost per unit is calculated as follows:

$$\frac{total\ batch\ cost}{number\ of\ units\ of\ output} = cost\ per\ unit$$

In essence, batch costing is very similar to job costing, but in a batch a number of identical units are produced. The batch is costed as a job during manufacture and the costs are collected together. Upon completion of the batch, the cost per unit can be calculated.

Batch numbers are frequently used to identify the output of a particular time – examples include paint colours, wallpaper production. The reason for identifying batches in this way is that there might be slight production variations – for example, in the quantities of raw materials used.

<table>
<tr><td>**Case Study**</td></tr>
</table>

AMBER LIMITED:
BATCH COSTING FOR CHILDREN'S CLOTHES

situation

Amber Limited is a company that designs and manufactures children's clothes. The company's products are noted for their design flair, and the use of fabrics that appeal to children and also wear well. The clothes sell through specialist shops and department stores.

This week, Amber Limited is making a batch of 1,000 sequin dresses for a department store. The costs of the batch are expected to be:

- direct materials, £3,500
- direct labour: cutting, 100 hours at £6 per hour

  sewing, 200 hours at £7 per hour

  finishing, 100 hours at £8 per hour
- the overhead absorption rate is £4 per direct labour hour
- a profit mark-up of 40% is added to the total cost

The accounts supervisor asks you, an accounts assistant, to calculate the cost of producing the batch of sequin dresses, and to add the profit mark-up. She also asks you to calculate the company's cost per dress and the selling price per dress.

solution

Batch cost: 1,000 sequin dresses

	£	£
Direct materials		3,500
Direct labour:		
cutting, 100 hours at £6 per hour	600	
sewing, 200 hours at £7 per hour	1,400	
finishing, 100 hours at £8 per hour	800	
		2,800
Overheads: 400 direct labour hours at £4 per hour		1,600
TOTAL COST	7,900	
Profit (40% x £7,900)		3,160
SELLING PRICE		11,060

- cost per unit = $\frac{\text{total batch cost}}{\text{number of units of output}}$ = $\frac{£7,900}{1,000}$ = £7.90

- selling price = $\dfrac{\text{total batch cost} + \text{profit}}{\text{number of units of output}}$ = $\dfrac{£11{,}060}{1{,}000}$ = £11.06

As with most types of costing, the estimated costs above will need to be compared with the actual costs of making the batch. Any significant differences or 'variances' will need to be investigated.

CONTRACT COSTING

Contract costing is used by the construction industry and major engineering companies to cost large, complex projects which last for a long period of time (usually more than a year).

The principles followed are those of job costing but the length and complexity of contract work causes financial differences:

- A large contract will often itself comprise a considerable number of smaller jobs (some of which may be sub-contracted) to be costed.

- Invariably, building contracts are based at the construction site – this means that many costs that would otherwise be indirect become direct costs, eg supervisors' wages, site power and telephones, fuel for vehicles, depreciation of equipment.

- As many contracts run for longer than one year, there is a need to calculate the profit or loss on the contract at the end of the financial year of the construction company, and to value the contract for balance sheet purposes. The contract is valued as follows:

  – if an overall **profit** is expected, the value equals costs to date plus attributable profit (depending on the stage reached in the contract)

  – if an overall **loss** is expected, the value equals costs to date, less the whole of the expected loss

Clearly the costing of a contract is a major task and one which can go spectacularly wrong, as a number of companies have found in the past.

SUMMARY – SPECIFIC ORDER COSTING

The diagram on the next page summarises the costing methods for specific orders.

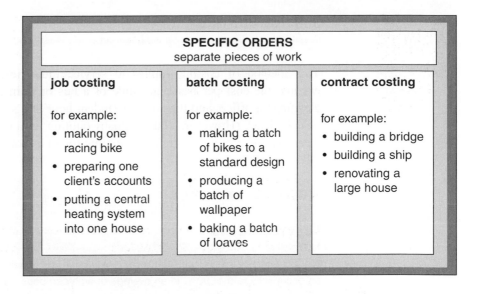

COSTING METHODS FOR CONTINUOUS WORK

In both manufacturing and service industries, work may be done continuously rather than in separate jobs. This requires specific costing methods appropriate to those types of business. For example:

- a bus company runs a continuous service of buses, available for customers to use and customers pay for their use of the service – the business will be costed using the **service costing** method

- in the manufacture of chocolate bars, production is a continuous process and the chocolate bars are available for customers to come along and choose to buy them, after they are made – the business will be costed using the **process costing** method

These two methods are summarised as follows:

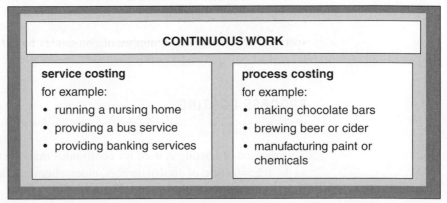

We will now look at these two methods in turn.

SERVICE COSTING

This method of costing applies to service industries. By using service costing, the cost per passenger mile of a bus or train service, the cost of cleaning an office, and the cost per student hour at a school or college, can be calculated. (However, a bus company quoting for a trip to the seaside for a pensioners' group, or a college tendering for an in-house course, would use job costing.)

WORKED EXAMPLE

service costs

A nursing home has capacity for twenty residents at any one time. The home achieves an occupancy rate of 90%, ie an average of eighteen beds are occupied at any one time. Costs for last year were:

	£
direct costs	
food and other supplies	27,290
nursing and medical staff	116,340
other support services	22,650
indirect costs	
overheads	29,410
	195,690

The cost per day of each resident is calculated as follows:

- The occupancy in days is (20 residents x 365 days) x 90% = 6,570 days

- Cost per day per resident is:

$$\frac{\text{total cost}}{\text{number of days}} = \frac{£195,690}{6,570} = £29.79 \text{ per resident}$$

- This is the unit cost for this organisation

PROCESS COSTING

This method of costing is used for continuous manufacturing processes, such as the manufacture of chocolate bars, cider, chemicals and so on. The process continually produces identical units of output.

The total costs of the process for a given time period are collected together. To obtain an average cost per unit of output, the total cost is divided by the number of units of output in the period.

cost per cost unit = $\dfrac{\textit{total costs of continuous work for the period}}{\textit{total cost units for the period}}$

WORKED EXAMPLE

process costing

Chox Limited manufactures chocolate bars in a continuous process. In a given time period 1,600,000 bars are made and the costs of the process are as follows:

	£
Direct materials (ingredients)	40,000
Direct labour (machine operators)	24,000
Production overheads	32,000
Total costs of production for period	96,000

Unit cost of production = $\dfrac{£96,000}{1,600,000}$ = £0.06 per bar

Many products pass through more than one separate process before they are completed. For example, the unleaded petrol with which you fill the tank of your car started the production process as crude oil – this is passed through a number of refining processes before it is suitable to use in cars. Similarly, the production of chemicals starts with raw materials which pass through various processes – often with further chemicals being added – before the finished product is completed.

In process costing we need to know the costs of each process in order to find out the total cost of the finished goods, and also the cost per unit.

WORKED EXAMPLE

costing two processes

Greengrass Limited manufactures 'Weed 'n Feed' – a combined lawn weedkiller and fertiliser. The product is made in two separate processes, with direct materials being added at each process.

In a given time period 20,000 kilos are made and the costs of the processes are as follows:

	£	£
Direct materials	5,000	
Direct labour	4,000	
Production overheads	4,000	
Total costs of process 1		13,000
(passed to process 2)		

PROCESS 1

	£	£
Direct materials	2,000	
Direct labour	3,000	
Production overheads	5,000	
Total costs of process 2		10,000

PROCESS 2

Total cost of production   23,000

Cost per unit:

$$\frac{\text{total cost of production}}{\text{no. of units produced}} = \frac{£23,000}{20,000 \text{ kilos}} = £1.15 \text{ per kilo}$$

Finished goods

The book-keeping entries for process costing are explained on pages 162-174.

PROCESS COSTING AND WORK-IN-PROGRESS

Process costing is straightforward if all the items on the production line are completed at the end of the day. In a more complex environment there will be items that have been started but not completed. This is known as **part-finished goods** or **work-in-progress** – see also Chapter 2 (page 38).

For example, the production line at a car factory will always have cars which vary from being only just started, to those nearing the end of the line which are almost complete.

In calculating the cost per unit, it is necessary to take into account the degree of completeness of the part-finished goods. This is done by making equivalent unit calculations:

number of units in progress x percentage of completeness   =   equivalent units

Thus, 100 units which are exactly 40% complete are equal to 40 completed units.

The formula for calculating the cost per unit now becomes:

$$\frac{\text{total cost of production}}{\text{number of units of output + equivalent units-in-progress}} = \text{cost per unit}$$

WORKED EXAMPLE

work-in-progress

Cradley Cider Company brews a popular local cider at its cider house in rural Herefordshire. The figures for the first month of the new season's production of its award-winning 'Triple X' variety are:

total cost of production	£8,500
units completed	800 barrels
units in progress	100 barrels

The units in progress are exactly half-finished. The equivalent units in progress, and the cost per barrel, for the month are as follows:

completed units		=	800 barrels
equivalent units	100 x 50%	=	50 barrels
cost per unit	$\frac{£8,500}{800 + 50}$	=	£10 per barrel

Although, in the example above, it was assumed that the work-in-progress was exactly half-finished, this may well not be the case for all the elements of cost. For example, while direct materials might be 100% complete, direct labour, and overheads might be 50% complete. Allowance has to be made for these differences in the calculation of the valuation of work-in-progress, and the layout used in the example below is one way in which the calculations can be made.

WORKED EXAMPLE

work-in-progress

The Toy Manufacturing Company makes a plastic toy called a 'Humber-Wumber'. The figures for the first month's production are:

direct materials	£6,600
direct labour	£3,500
production overheads	£4,000
units completed	900
units in progress	200

The units in progress are complete as regards materials, but are 50% complete for direct labour and overheads.

Cost element	Costs	Completed Units	Work-in-progress			Total Equivalent Units	Cost per Unit	WIP value
			Units	% complete	Equivalent Units			
	A	B	C	D	E	F	G	H
					C x D	B + E	A ÷ F	E x G
	£			%			£	£
Direct materials	6,600	900	200	100	200	1,100	6.00	1,200
Direct labour	3,500	900	200	50	100	1,000	3.50	350
Production overheads	4,000	900	200	50	100	1,000	4.00	400
Total	14,100						13.50	1,950

Note: columns are lettered to show how calculations are made.

Using an average cost basis, the cost per unit of the first month's production, and the month-end valuation figure for work-in-progress (WIP) is as follows:

900 completed units at £13.50 each	=	£12,150
work-in-progress valuation	=	£1,950
total costs for month	=	£14,100

BOOK-KEEPING ENTRIES FOR PROCESS COSTING

In this section we look at the cost book-keeping entries to record process costing transactions. The account to be used is a *process account*, which carries out a similar function to the work-in-progress account that we have used previously.

The basic layout of a process account, which has inputs on the debit side and outputs on the credit side, is shown at the top of the next page.

Dr				Process Account			Cr
	Quantity	Unit cost £	Total £		Quantity	Unit cost £	Total £
Inputs to the process: • transfer from previous process • direct materials • direct labour • direct expenses • production overheads				Outputs from the process: • transfer to next process, or • transfer to finished goods			

Note:

- there are columns for the quantity of goods (eg kilos, litres) input to, and output from, the process

- there are money columns for the unit cost (eg cost per kilo, cost per litre), and for the total

- inputs to the process can include a transfer from a previous process (if any), and any direct costs and production overheads that are added to this stage of the process

- outputs from the process are either a transfer to the next process or, if this is the last or only process, to finished goods stock

- where there is more than one process involved in production, each will have a separate account, eg 'Process 1 Account', 'Process 2 Account'

aspects of process costing

An important feature of process costing is that you don't always get out what you put in to the process. This is illustrated by the example of ordering a steak in a restaurant; the menu will say '250g fillet steak' (explaining that this is the uncooked weight); what comes on the plate will weigh rather less because, when the steak is grilled, fat and liquids are cooked away. Thus, in the 'process' of cooking a steak, the output is less than the input. This is unlike other costing, where the input always equals the output, for example, input the materials for 100 cars, and the output will be 100 cars.

The aspect of process costing where you don't get out what you put in is mainly described as a *normal loss*. This is an unavoidable loss arising from the production process. For example, the normal loss on a 250g steak might be 50g. Normal losses, which occur as a result of factors such as evaporation, breakage, sampling and testing, are included as part of the cost of the output.

Once a standard of normal loss has been established for a process, this then forms the expectation for future processing. Any variation from this normal loss is treated separately in the book-keeping and will be either:

- *abnormal loss*, where the loss is greater than normal, or
- *abnormal gain*, where the loss is less than normal

If any of the losses can be sold as *scrap sales*, the amount of money so received is treated as a reduction in the total costs of the process. Examples include: wood chippings and shavings sold off from wood processing, scrap metal from an engineering company.

With normal loss, abnormal loss, abnormal gain, and scrap sales to consider, there are seven possible outcomes from process costing. These are shown in the following diagram:

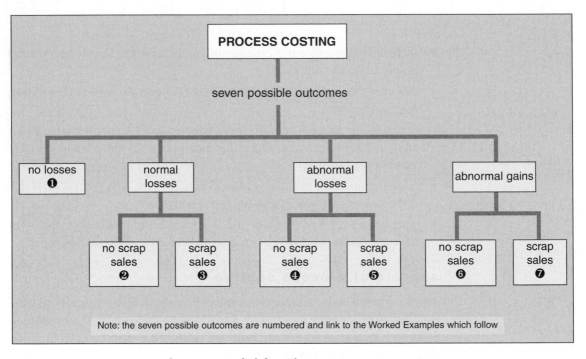

Note: the seven possible outcomes are numbered and link to the Worked Examples which follow

no losses within the process

Here the process account is debited with inputs and credited with the output, which is transferred either to the next process or to finished goods stock.

The cost book-keeping entries are:

- **transfer inputs to the process account**
  - – debit process account
  - – credit materials, labour, production overhead accounts
- **transfer outputs to the next process or to finished goods stock**
  - – debit next process account, or finished goods account
  - – credit process account

The cost book-keeping entries are shown diagrammatically as follows:

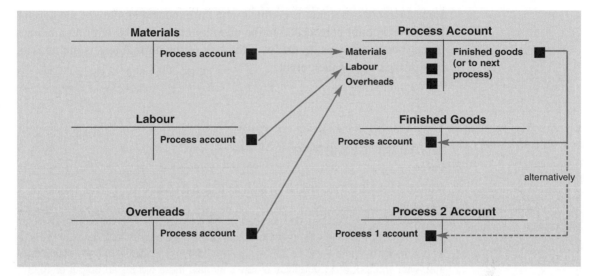

WORKED EXAMPLE 1

no losses within the process

Garden Eezee Limited manufactures granular fertiliser for use on flowers and vegetables. The fertiliser is made in one production process.

For the four weeks ended 30 January 2004 the company input 11,000 kilos of direct materials and had an output of 11,000 kilos. The input costs were; materials £6,600, labour £3,300, overheads £1,100. There was no opening or closing stock at the beginning and end of the process; all output was complete.

The process cost account for the period is prepared as follows:

Dr				Process Account			Cr
	Quantity	Unit cost	Total		Quantity	Unit cost	Total
	(kilos)	£	£		(kilos)	£	£
Materials	11,000	0.60	6,600	Finished goods	11,000	1.00	11,000
Labour		0.30	3,300	(or to next process)			
Overheads		0.10	1,100				
	11,000		11,000		11,000		11,000

Note:
- here the inputs of materials, labour and overheads total £1.00 (60p + 30p + 10p) – this figure will be used in subsequent Worked Examples
- inputs could also include the costs of a previous process

normal losses, with no scrap sales

Here the process account is credited with the expected amount of the normal loss. The amount is recorded in the quantity column only, with no amounts in the money columns. In this way, the cost of the normal loss is included as part of the costs of the output.

WORKED EXAMPLE 2

normal losses, with no scrap sales

Garden Eezee Limited has had to change the chemical composition of its granular fertiliser in order to meet with new European Union regulations. As a result of this, not all of the output can be sold to gardeners. The company's scientists have established that, with an input of 11,000 kilos of raw materials there will be an output of 10,000 kilos and a normal loss of 1,000 kilos.

For the four weeks ended 27 February 2004, the process account is prepared as follows (with the same input costs from Worked Example 1):

Dr				Process Account			Cr
	Quantity	Unit cost	Total		Quantity	Unit cost	Total
	(kilos)	£	£		(kilos)	£	£
Inputs (see	11,000	1.00	11,000	Normal loss	1,000	–	–
Worked Example 1)				Finished goods	10,000	1.10	11,000
				(or to next process)			
	11,000		11,000		11,000		11,000

The cost of the normal losses is included as part of the costs of the output, so the cost per unit is:

$$\frac{\text{input cost}}{\text{expected output}} = \frac{£11,000}{10,000 \text{ kilos}} = £1.10 \text{ per kilo}$$

The cost of the output is transferred to finished goods stock (or to the next process).

normal losses, with scrap sales

If any of the normal losses from a process can be sold – called 'scrap sales' – the process account is credited with the money received. The amount of such sales is recorded in the money column against the normal loss. In this way, the receipts from scrap sales reduce the cost of the output.

WORKED EXAMPLE 3

normal losses, with scrap sales

Garden Eezee Limited is now able to sell its normal losses to a specialist reprocessing company. The price it receives for the scrap sales is 50p per kilo.

For the four weeks ended 26 March 2004 the process account is prepared as follows (with the same input costs and normal loss as Worked Example 2):

Dr	Quantity (kilos)	Unit cost £	Total £	**Process Account**	Quantity (kilos)	Unit cost £	Total Cr £
Inputs	11,000	1.00	11,000	Normal loss (scrap sales)	1,000	–	500
				Finished goods (or to next process)	10,000	1.05	10,500
	11,000		11,000		11,000		11,000

The value of the scrap sales reduces the cost per unit of the expected output to:

$$\frac{\text{input cost} - \text{scrap value of normal loss}}{\text{expected output}} \quad = \quad \frac{£11,000 - £500}{10,000 \text{ kilos}}$$

$$= £1.05 \text{ per kilo}$$

Normal loss account is debited with £500 by transfer from the process account. The receipts from scrap sales are then credited to this account and debited to either bank account (cash received), or debtor's account (sold on credit terms). Normal loss account then appears as:

Dr	£	**Normal Loss Account**	Cr £
Process account	500	Bank/debtors	500

abnormal losses, with no scrap sales

An abnormal loss is, as we have seen, where output is lower than after a normal loss. For example:

	kilos
inputs	11,000
less normal loss	1,000
expected output	10,000
actual output	9,400
abnormal loss	600

Clearly, if there are recurring abnormal losses, the managers will wish to investigate the causes and to take corrective action. Causes of abnormal losses can include poor quality raw materials, wastage and spillages caused by poor handling, faults in the process.

For cost book-keeping, the value of the abnormal loss is credited to the process account at the same cost per unit as the expected output; the value is debited to a separate *abnormal loss account*. These cost book-keeping entries are shown diagrammatically as follows:

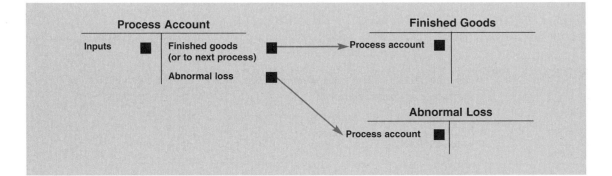

WORKED EXAMPLE 4

abnormal losses, with no scrap sales

For the four weeks ended 23 April 2004, Garden Eezee Limited inputs 11,000 kilos of direct materials. Output transferred to finished goods is 9,400 kilos – the difference of 1,600 kilos being made up of a normal loss of 1,000 kilos and an abnormal loss of 600 kilos. For technical reasons, none of the losses was able to be sold as scrap.

The process account is prepared as follows (with the same input costs as Worked Example 1):

Dr				**Process Account**			Cr
	Quantity (kilos)	Unit cost £	Total £		Quantity (kilos)	Unit cost £	Total £
Inputs	11,000	1.00	11,000	Normal loss	1,000	–	–
				Finished goods (or to next process)	9,400	1.10	10,340
				Abnormal loss	600	1.10	660
	11,000		11,000		11,000		11,000

Both the transfer to finished goods (or to the next process) and the abnormal loss are valued at the cost per unit of the expected output, ie

$$\frac{\text{input cost}}{\text{expected output}} = \frac{£11,000}{10,000 \text{ kilos}} = £1.10 \text{ per kilo}$$

The amount of abnormal loss is debited to abnormal loss account:

Dr		**Abnormal Loss Account**		Cr
	£			£
Process account	660			

At the end of the financial year, the balance of abnormal loss account is debited to profit and loss account. In this way, abnormal losses are treated as a period cost instead of being included with the closing stock valuation.

abnormal losses, with scrap sales

Where there are receipts from scrap sales for both normal losses and abnormal losses, we must be careful to distinguish between the two amounts:

- receipts for scrap sales from normal losses are credited to the process account (where they reduce the cost of the output – including the abnormal loss)

- receipts for scrap sales from abnormal losses are credited to abnormal loss account (where they reduce the amount of the abnormal loss and, at the end of the financial year, the amount debited to profit and loss account)

WORKED EXAMPLE 5

abnormal losses, with scrap sales

Here the details are the same as Worked Example 4, except that all losses – both normal and abnormal – are sold to a specialist reprocessing company at a price of 50p per kilo.
For the four weeks ended 21 May 2004, the process account and abnormal loss account are prepared as follows (with the same input costs and normal and abnormal loss as Worked Example 4):

Dr				Process Account			Cr
	Quantity	Unit cost	Total		Quantity	Unit cost	Total
	(kilos)	£	£		(kilos)	£	£
Inputs	11,000	1.00	11,000	Normal loss	1,000	–	500
				Finished goods	9,400	1.05	9,870
				(or to next process)			
				Abnormal loss	600	1.05	630
	11,000		11,000		11,000		11,000

Both the transfer to finished goods (or to the next process) and the abnormal loss are valued at the cost per unit of the expected output, ie

$$\frac{\text{input cost} - \text{scrap value of normal loss}}{\text{expected output}} = \frac{£11,000 - £500}{10,000 \text{ kilos}} = £1.05 \text{ per kilo}$$

The amount of abnormal loss (600 kilos x £1.05 per kilo = £630) is debited to abnormal loss account; the receipts for scrap sales from either bank or debtors are then credited to abnormal loss account.

Dr		Abnormal Loss Account	Cr
	£		£
Process account	630	Bank/debtors (600 kilos x 50p)	300

If there are no more abnormal losses, the balance of this account (£630 – £300 = £330) will be debited as an expense to profit and loss account at the end of the company's financial year.
Normal loss account is debited with £500 by transfer from the process account; receipts from scrap sales are credited to the account (as in Worked Example 3):

Dr		Normal Loss Account			Cr
	£				£
Process account	500	Bank/debtors			500

abnormal gains, with no scrap sales

An abnormal gain is, as we have seen, where output is higher than after a normal loss. For example:

	kilos
inputs	11,000
less normal loss	1,000
expected output	10,000
actual output	10,200
abnormal gain	200

If there are recurring abnormal gains, the managers will wish to investigate the causes with a view to reducing the amount of the normal loss. Causes of abnormal gains can include good quality raw materials, less wastage and spillage caused by improved handling techniques, improved processing caused by the introduction of better machinery.

For cost book-keeping, the value of the abnormal gain is debited to the process account at the same cost per unit as the expected output; the value is credited to a separate *abnormal gain account*. The cost book-keeping entries are shown diagrammatically as follows:

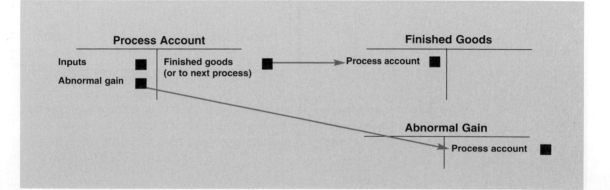

WORKED EXAMPLE 6

abnormal gains, with no scrap sales

For the four weeks ended 18 June 2004, Garden Eezee Limited inputs 11,000 kilos of direct materials. Output transferred to finished goods is 10,200 kilos – the difference of 800 kilos being made up of a normal loss of 1,000 kilos and an abnormal gain of 200 kilos. For technical reasons, none of the losses was able to be sold as scrap.

The process account is prepared as follows (with the same input costs as Worked Example 1)

Dr				Process Account				Cr
	Quantity	Unit cost	Total		Quantity	Unit cost	Total	
	(kilos)	£	£		(kilos)	£	£	
Inputs	11,000	1.00	11,000	Normal loss	1,000	–	–	
Abnormal gain	200	1.10	220	Finished goods	10,200	1.10	11,220	
				(or to next process)				
	11,200		11,220		11,200		11,220	

Both the transfer to finished goods (or to next process) and the abnormal gain are valued at the cost per unit of the expected output, ie

$$\frac{\text{input cost}}{\text{expected output}} = \frac{\pounds 11,000}{10,000 \text{ kilos}} = \pounds 1.10 \text{ per kilo}$$

The amount of the abnormal gain is credited to abnormal gain account:

Dr		Abnormal Gain Account		Cr
	£			£
		Process account		220

At the end of the financial year, the balance of abnormal gain account is credited to profit and loss account. In this way, abnormal gains are treated as a period gain instead of being included with the closing stock valuation.

abnormal gains, with scrap sales

Where there are normal losses (with a scrap sales value) and abnormal gains, we must be careful to distinguish between the two amounts:

- the value of the full amount of normal losses is credited to the process account (notwithstanding the fact that normal losses are reduced because of the abnormal gains)

- the value of abnormal gains is debited to the process account and credited to abnormal gains account (at the cost per unit of the expected output)

WORKED EXAMPLE 7

abnormal gains, with scrap sales

Here the details are the same as Worked Example 6, except that normal losses have a scrap value of 50p per kilo.

For the four weeks ended 16 July 2004, the process account and abnormal gain account are prepared as follows (with the same input costs and abnormal gain as Worked Example 6):

Dr			Process Account				Cr
	Quantity	Unit cost	Total		Quantity	Unit cost	Total
	(kilos)	£	£		(kilos)	£	£
Inputs	11,000	1.00	11,000	Normal loss	1,000	–	500
Abnormal gain	200	1.05	210	Finished goods	10,200	1.05	10,710
				(or to next process)			
	11,200		11,210		11,200		11,210

Both the transfer to finished goods (or to next process) and the abnormal gain are valued at the cost per unit of the expected output, ie

$$\frac{\text{input cost} - \text{scrap value of normal loss}}{\text{expected output}} = \frac{£11,000 - £500}{10,000 \text{ kilos}} = £1.05 \text{ per kilo}$$

Dr	Abnormal Gain Account		Cr
	£		£
Normal loss account	100	Process account	210

If there are no more abnormal gains, the balance of this account (£210 – £100 = £110) will be credited as income to profit and loss account at the end of the company's financial year

The transactions on abnormal gain account are:

	Quantity (kilos)	Unit cost £	Total £
• credit (transfer from process account)	200	1.05	210
• debit (transfer to normal loss account)	200	0.50	100
• balance		0.55	110

The reason for the transfer of £100 to normal loss account is to leave only the amount of the abnormal gain, £110. This is 55p per kilo, which is left after deducting the value of normal losses of 50p from the cost per unit of expected output of £1.05. By doing this, we highlight the value of abnormal gains above the normal efficiency of the process.

At the end of the financial year, the balance of abnormal gain account is credited to profit and loss account.

Dr		Normal Loss Account		Cr
	£			£
Process account	500	Bank/debtors		400
		Abnormal gain account		100
	500			500

Here, normal loss account is debited with £500 by transfer from the process account. Credits to the account come from two sources:

• receipts of £400 (ie 800 kilos sold at 50p per kilo) from bank or debtors

• transfer of £100 (ie 200 kilos at 50p per kilo) from abnormal gain account

Tutorial note: A Case Study illustrating normal losses, abnormal losses and abnormal gains using the example of a two-process company is given on pages 196-198

Chapter Summary

• The method chosen for cost accounting within a business depends on the kind of work being done.

• In manufacturing and in service industries, work may consist of separately identifiable jobs or it may be continuous.

• Separately identifiable jobs are usually done to a customer's specific order.

• Costs are calculated for each separately identifiable job.

• The costing method to be used for specific orders (separate jobs) is:

   – job costing for a single unit of work

   – batch costing for a batch of identical units

   – contract costing for a long-term contract

- The costing method to be used for continuous work is:
  - process costing for continuous manufacturing processes
  - service costing for continuous services
- To obtain a cost per cost unit for continuous work, the total costs for a time period are first collected together, then divided by the number of cost units produced or provided in the time period, ie

  cost per cost unit = $\dfrac{\text{total costs of continuous work for the period}}{\text{total cost units for the period}}$

- If there is work-in-progress at the end of the period, the number of equivalent complete units is calculated, for example 500 units that are 50% complete are equivalent to 500 x 50% = 250 completed units.
- Book-keeping for process costing uses a process account to calculate the cost per unit of expected output. Possible outcomes of process costing to be recorded in the accounts are:
  - no losses within the process
  - normal losses, with or without scrap sales
  - abnormal losses, with or without scrap sales
  - abnormal gains, with or without scrap sales

  At the end of a financial year, the balance of abnormal loss account is debited to profit and loss account, while the balance of abnormal gain account is credited.

Key Terms

costing method	a technique used to collect costs and to calculate the total cost of output
job/batch/contract costing	a form of specific order costing which applies costs to jobs/batches/contracts
service costing	a form of costing for service industries; costs are averaged to find the cost per unit
job cost sheet	sheet (or record on a computer database) which shows the estimated and actual direct and indirect costs for a particular job
variance	the difference between an estimated cost and an actual cost
process costing	method of costing applied to continuous manufacturing processes
work-in-progress (WIP)	part-finished goods at a particular time
equivalent units	number of units in progress x percentage of completeness

cost per unit	$\dfrac{total\ costs}{number\ of\ units\ (including\ equivalent\ units)}$
process account	book-keeping account used in process costing to calculate the cost per unit of expected output
normal loss	an unavoidable loss arising from the production process
abnormal loss	where the loss in a process is greater than the normal loss
abnormal gain	where the loss in a process is less than the normal loss

Student Activities

6.1 State, with reasons, the method of costing you think would be appropriate for:

- an accountant
- a bus company
- a baker
- a sports centre
- a hotel
- a construction company

6.2 A clothing manufacturer has been asked to give a quotation for the supply of a batch of uniforms for a band. Materials for the uniforms will be:

- 100 metres of cloth at £7.50 per metre
- 75 metres of braiding at £4.00 per metre

It is estimated that the job will take the machinists a total of 35 hours.

They are paid at the rate of £6.00 per hour.

The overhead absorption rate is £8.50 per direct labour hour.

You are to:

(a) calculate the cost of the job

(b) calculate the selling price if the company is to make a profit of 20% on the cost price

6.3 Rowcester Engineering Limited is asked to quote for the supply of a replacement cylinder head for a large stationary engine installed in a local factory.

The item will need to be cast in the foundry and then passed to the finishing shop for machining to specification.

Materials needed will be a 100 kg ingot of high-strength steel, which costs £10 per kg.

Direct labour will be 10 hours in the foundry, and 15 hours in the finishing shop, of which 12 hours will be machine hours.

Foundry workers are paid £10 per hour, while machine operators in the finishing shop are paid £12 per hour.

Overheads are charged on the basis of 80% of direct labour cost in the foundry, and on the basis of £20 per machine hour in the finishing shop.

Profit is to be 25% of cost price.

You are to prepare a Job Cost Sheet which shows the estimated cost of the job, and the selling price.

6.4 City Transit plc is a small train operating company which runs passenger rail services on a commuter line in a large city. The line links the docks area, which has been redeveloped with flats and houses, with the city centre, and then runs on through the suburbs. An intensive service is operated from early morning to late at night carrying people to and from work, schoolchildren, shoppers and leisure travellers.

The tracks that City Transit uses are leased from the track owner, Railnet plc.

The modern fleet of six diesel trains is owned and maintained by City Transit.

The following information is available in respect of last year's operations:

	cost	estimated life
Diesel trains	£650,000 each	20 years

Depreciation is on a straight-line basis, assuming a residual value of £50,000 for each train.

Leasing charges for track	£500,000 pa
Maintenance charges for trains	£455,000 pa
Fuel for trains	£105,000 pa
Wages of drivers and conductors	£240,000 pa
Administration	£260,000 pa

There were 2.5 million passenger journeys last year with an average distance travelled of five miles.

You are to calculate the cost per passenger mile of operating the railway for last year.

6.5   A manufacturer of plastic toys has the following information concerning the first month of production:

Direct materials	£11,500
Direct labour	£9,000
Production overheads	£18,000
Toys completed	20,000
Toys in progress	5,000

The work-in-progress is complete as regards materials, but is 50% complete as regards direct labour and production overheads.

You are to:

(a)   Calculate the cost per toy of the first month's production

(b)   Calculate the month-end valuation for work-in-progress

6.6   Agro Chemicals Limited produces a chemical, which is made in one production process.

For the four weeks ended 27 February 2004, the company input 22,000 litres of direct materials, had an output of 20,000 litres and a normal loss of 2,000 litres. The input costs were: materials £5,500, labour £3,300, overheads £2,200. Normal losses were sold to a specialist reprocessing company for 20p per litre.

There was no opening or closing stock at the beginning and end of the process; all output was complete.

As an accounts assistant, you are to prepare the process account and the normal loss account for the four weeks ended 27 February 2004.

6.7   GrowFast Limited produces a granular lawn fertiliser, which is made in one production process.

For the four weeks ended 21 May 2004, the company input 42,000 kilos of direct materials, had an output of 39,500 kilos – the difference of 2,500 kilos was made up of a normal loss of 2,000 kilos and an abnormal loss of 500 kilos.

The input costs were: materials £10,500, labour £4,200, overheads £2,100. All losses were sold to a specialist reprocessing company for 20p per kilo.

There was no opening or closing stock at the beginning and end of the process; all output was complete.

As an accounts assistant, you are to prepare the process account, the abnormal loss account, and the normal loss account for the four weeks ended 21 May 2004.

6.8   RP Industries Limited produces a liquid furniture polish called 'EasyShine'. The product is made in two production processes before completion and transfer to finished goods stock.

For the four weeks ended 26 November 2004, details of production of 'EasyShine' were as follows:

	Process 1	Process 2
Direct materials (10,000 litres)	£5,000	–
Labour	£4,000	£1,800
Overhead	£2,000	£1,350
Normal loss in process	10% of input	5% of input
Output	9,000 litres	8,300 litres
Scrap value of all losses	£0.40 per litre	£0.50 per litre

There was no opening or closing stock at the beginning and end of either process; all output was complete.

As an accounts assistant, you are to prepare the process 1 account, process 2 account, normal loss account, and abnormal loss account for the four weeks ended 26 November 2004. Note: calculate costs per unit of expected output to the nearest penny.

6.9 Zelah Chemicals Limited produces an insect repellant called 'BuzzOff', which is made in one production process.

For the four weeks ended 16 July 2004, the company input 11,000 litres of direct materials, and had an output of 10,200 litres – the difference of 800 litres was made up of a normal loss of 1,000 litres and an abnormal gain of 200 litres.

The input costs were: materials £5,500, labour £3,850, overheads £2,750. All losses were sold to a specialist reprocessing company for 30p per litre.

There was no opening or closing stock at the beginning and end of the process; all output was complete.

As an accounts assistant, you are to prepare the process account, abnormal gain account, and normal loss account for the four weeks ended 16 July 2004.

7 Book-keeping for costing

this chapter covers . . .

This chapter explains:

- the use of
  - a manufacturing account to show production cost
  - a profit and loss account to show net profit
- the importance of identification and coding of costs
- how an integrated book-keeping system incorporates the accounts for both costing and financial accounting
- the book-keeping to record under-absorption and over-absorption of overheads
- the book-keeping entries for process costing

NVQ PERFORMANCE CRITERIA COVERED

unit 6: RECORDING AND EVALUATING COSTS AND REVENUES

element 6.1

record and analyse information relating to direct costs and revenues

A   identify direct costs in accordance with the organisation's costing procedures

B   record and analyse information relating to direct costs

C   calculate direct costs in accordance with the organisation's policies and procedures

element 6.2

record and analyse information relating to the allocation, apportionment and

absorption of overhead costs

D   record and analyse information relating to overhead costs in accordance with the organisation's procedures

E   make adjustments for under and over recovered overhead costs in accordance with established procedures

THE USE OF A MANUFACTURING ACCOUNT

As we saw in Chapter 1, a business brings together all of the costs involved in producing its output in the form of a *total cost statement:*

		£
	Direct materials	x
add	Direct labour	x
add	Direct expenses	x
equals	PRIME COST	x
add	Production overheads	x
equals	PRODUCTION COST	x
add	Non-production overheads, eg	
	• selling and distribution expenses	x
	• administration expenses	x
	• finance expenses	x
equals	TOTAL COST	x

A total cost statement can be prepared on the basis of a single cost unit, or a batch, or a whole production unit such as a factory. However, overall, a business needs to have an accounting system that records its costs and its sales for all its output, and then shows the profit or loss that has been made for the accounting period. For a business such as a retailer that buys and sells goods, without carrying out any production processes, the accounting system is relatively simple – the figure for sales is deducted from the amount of purchases (after allowing for changes in the value of opening and closing stock) and the amount of overheads; a profit is made when sales exceed the total costs. For a manufacturer, though, the costs are more complex as they comprise the direct and indirect costs of materials, labour and expenses; also, a manufacturer will invariably have opening and closing stock in three different forms – direct materials, work-in-progress and finished goods.

In its year-end (or final) accounts a manufacturer uses the layout of the total cost statement and prepares:

- a manufacturing account, which shows production cost
- a profit and loss account, which shows net profit for the accounting period

The final accounts use the following outline:

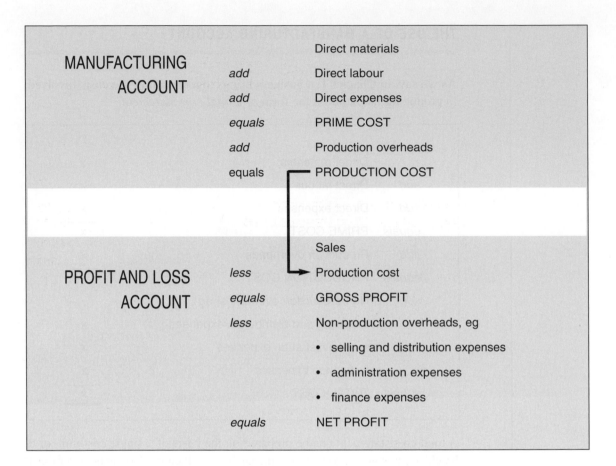

MANUFACTURING ACCOUNT		Direct materials
	add	Direct labour
	add	Direct expenses
	equals	PRIME COST
	add	Production overheads
	equals	PRODUCTION COST
		Sales
PROFIT AND LOSS ACCOUNT	*less*	Production cost
	equals	GROSS PROFIT
	less	Non-production overheads, eg
		• selling and distribution expenses
		• administration expenses
		• finance expenses
	equals	NET PROFIT

notes

- Adjustments have to be made to allow for changes in the value of stock at the start of the accounting period (opening stock) and at the end of the accounting period (closing stock) for:
  - direct materials, in the manufacturing account
  - work-in-progress (or partly manufactured goods), in the manufacturing account
  - finished goods, in the profit and loss account
- The profit and loss account shows two levels of profit:
  - gross profit, the difference between selling price and production cost (after allowing for changes in the value of opening and closing stock)
  - net profit, the profit after all costs have been deducted and which belongs to the owner(s) of the business
- Certain expenses might be apportioned on an appropriate basis between the manufacturing account and the profit and loss account – for example, rent and rates might be apportioned 75 per cent to the factory (production overheads) and 25 per cent to the office (non-production overheads)

An example of a manufacturing and profit and loss account is shown below:

ALPHA MANUFACTURING COMPANY
MANUFACTURING AND PROFIT AND LOSS ACCOUNT
for the year ended 31 December 2004

	£	£
Opening stock of direct materials		5,000
Add Purchases of direct materials		50,000
		55,000
Less Closing stock of direct materials		6,000
COST OF DIRECT MATERIALS USED		49,000
Direct labour		26,000
Direct expenses		2,500
PRIME COST		77,500
Add Production (factory) overheads:		
Indirect materials	2,000	
Indirect labour	16,000	
Indirect expenses:		
Rent of factory	5,000	
Depreciation of factory machinery	10,000	
Factory light and heat	4,000	
		37,000
		114,500
Add Opening stock of work-in-progress		4,000
		118,500
Less Closing stock of work-in-progress		3,000
PRODUCTION COST OF GOODS COMPLETED		115,500
Sales		195,500
Opening stock of finished goods	6,500	
Production cost of goods completed	115,500	
	122,000	
Less Closing stock of finished goods	7,500	
COST OF SALES		114,500
Gross profit		81,000
Less Non-production overheads:		
Selling and distribution expenses	38,500	
Administration expenses	32,000	
Finance expenses	3,500	
		74,000
Net profit		7,000

IDENTIFICATION AND CODING OF COSTS

In order to be able to prepare the final accounts of manufacturing account and profit and loss account, a business must use a detailed book-keeping system which enables accurate information to be extracted. For the book-keeping system to be accurate, as costs are incurred they must be charged to the correct account in the system. This is achieved by a system of:

• identification of the cost unit or cost centre to which the cost is to be charged

• coding the cost so that it is charged to the correct book-keeping account of the cost unit or cost centre

Systems of coding have been discussed earlier (page 14). Here we are concerned with the place of the coding system as a part of the book-keeping process. This is illustrated as follows:

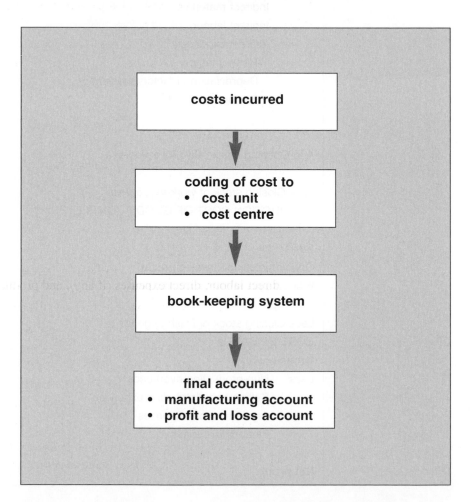

INTEGRATED BOOK-KEEPING SYSTEM

This section brings together the double-entry accounts which record transactions about the cost of a product or service, and the sales revenues. Such an *integrated book-keeping system* incorporates the accounts of the business for both costing and financial accounting, ie the book-keeping for the two types of accounting is combined together in one ledger rather than being kept in separate, non-integrated, ledgers. We have already seen the book-keeping entries for various aspects of the costing system:

- for materials, Chapter 2 (pages 61-65)
- for labour, Chapter 3 (pages 82-85)
- for expenses, Chapter 4 (pages 98-99)
- for overheads, Chapter 5 (pages 133-136)

Here we look at how these are integrated into the book-keeping system. Always remember the principles of double-entry book-keeping that are to be followed:

- a debit entry records a gain in value, an asset or an expense
- a credit entry records the giving of value, a liability or an income item

We will see how an integrated book-keeping system is used by considering three separate stages:

stage 1 – manufacturing costs and profit and loss account

stage 2 – direct and indirect costs

stage 3 – receipts and payments

Using the diagram on the next page, we will focus on each of the three stages.

stage 1 – manufacturing costs and profit and loss account (on the right-hand side of the diagram)

- this stage incorporates the manufacturing costs of direct materials, direct labour, direct expenses (if any), and production overheads
- these costs are debited to work-in-progress account
- from work-in-progress account the cost of those goods that are completed is transferred to finished goods account
- cost of sales is the manufacturing cost of those goods that have been sold
- profit and loss account incorporates the non-production overheads
- profit is sales minus cost of sales and non-production overheads
- transfers out of materials, work-in-progress and finished goods are for the amount taken to the next stage of production; for example, with

continued on page 187

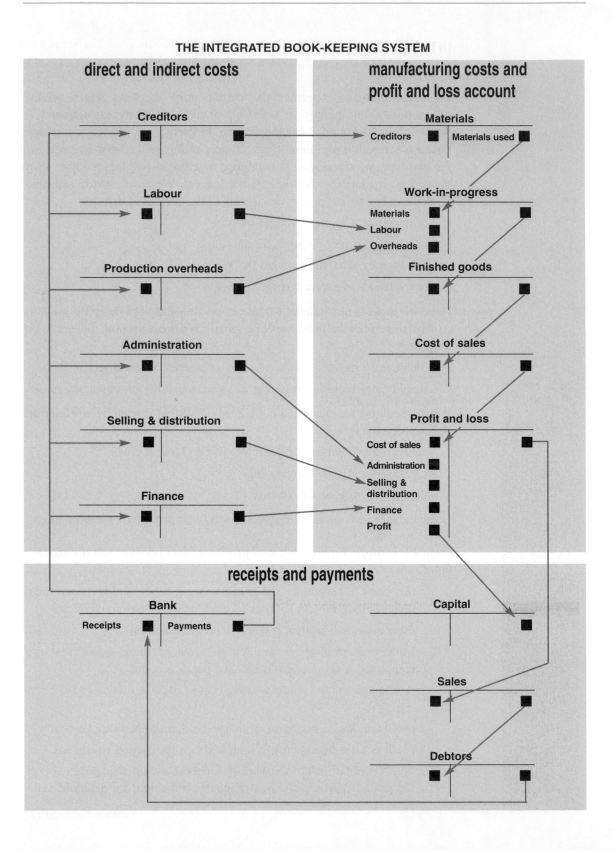

THE INTEGRATED BOOK-KEEPING SYSTEM

materials, only those materials used in production will be transferred to work-in-progress – any balance remaining on materials account represents the stock held at the end of the accounting period

stage 2 – direct and indirect costs (on the left-hand side of the diagram)
  - this shows how the direct and indirect costs are built up on the debit side of each account
  - amounts are then transferred to manufacturing costs and profit and loss account

stage 3 – receipts and payments (at the bottom of the diagram)
  - here profit for the accounting period is transferred to capital
  - the sales account is linked to profit and loss account and to the debtors' accounts
  - receipts from debtors are debited in bank account
  - payments are made from bank account to settle creditors and the direct and indirect costs of the business, so completing the book-keeping 'loop'

Case Study

MARTLEY MANUFACTURING: INTEGRATED BOOK-KEEPING SYSTEM

situation
Martley Manufacturing started in business making wooden toys on 1 January 2004. During January the following transactions took place:

	£
Opening capital paid in to bank	10,000
Direct materials bought on credit	5,000
Direct labour costs paid by cheque	6,000
Production overheads paid by cheque	3,000
Non-production overheads paid by cheque	2,000
Credit sales	15,000
Receipts from debtors	12,000
Payments to creditors	3,500
Direct materials transferred to work-in-progress	4,000
Work-in-progress transferred to finished goods	11,000
Finished goods transferred to cost of sales	10,000

The above transactions are to be recorded in the integrated book-keeping system of Martley Manufacturing. Note that:

- the full cost of direct labour is to be transferred to work-in-progress
- there are no direct expenses
- the full cost of production overheads is to be transferred to work-in-progress

solution

It is suggested that you 'audit' the month's transactions to the double-entry accounts; in particular, ensure that you can understand the debit and credit entry for each transaction.

STAGE 1: MANUFACTURING COSTS AND PROFIT AND LOSS ACCOUNT

Dr		**Materials Account**		Cr
	£			£
Creditors	5,000	Work-in-progress		4,000
		Balance c/d		1,000
	5,000			5,000
Balance b/d	1,000			

Dr		**Work-in-Progress Account**		Cr
	£			£
Direct materials	4,000	Finished goods		11,000
Direct labour	6,000	Balance c/d		2,000
Production overhead	3,000			
	13,000			13,000
Balance b/d	2,000			

Dr		**Finished Goods Account**		Cr
	£			£
Work-in-progress	11,000	Cost of sales		10,000
		Balance c/d		1,000
	11,000			11,000
Balance b/d	1,000			

Dr		**Cost of Sales Account**		Cr
	£			£
Finished goods	10,000	Profit and loss		10,000

Dr	**Profit and Loss Account**		Cr
	£		£
Cost of sales	10,000	Sales	15,000
Non-production overhead	2,000		
Net profit (to capital account)	3,000		
	15,000		15,000

STAGE 2: DIRECT AND INDIRECT COSTS

Dr	**Creditors' Account**		Cr
	£		£
Bank	3,500	Materials	5,000
Balance c/d	1,500		
	5,000		5,000
		Balance b/d	1,500

Dr	**Labour Costs Account**		Cr
	£		£
Bank	6,000	Work-in-progress	6,000

Dr	**Production Overheads Account**		Cr
	£		£
Bank	3,000	Work-in-progress	3,000

Dr	**Non-Production Overheads Account**		Cr
	£		£
Bank	2,000	Profit and loss	2,000

STAGE 3: RECEIPTS AND PAYMENTS

Dr		Capital Account		Cr
	£			£
Balance c/d	13,000	Bank		10,000
		Profit and loss		3,000
	13,000			13,000
		Balance b/d		13,000

Dr		Sales Account		Cr
	£			£
Profit and loss	15,000	Debtors		15,000

Dr		Debtors Account		Cr
	£			£
Sales	15,000	Bank		12,000
		Balance c/d		3,000
	15,000			15,000
Balance b/d	3,000			

Dr		Bank Account		Cr
	£			£
Capital	10,000	Creditors		3,500
Debtors	12,000	Labour		6,000
		Production overheads		3,000
		Non-production overheads		2,000
		Balance c/d		7,500
	22,000			22,000
Balance b/d	7,500			

In bank account the transactions have been listed in the order in which they appear in the book-keeping, and are not necessarily in chronological order.

Note the following points:
• At the end of January the book-keeping system balances, as shown by the following trial balance:

	Dr	Cr
	£	£
Materials	1,000	
Work-in-progress	2,000	
Finished goods	1,000	
Creditors		1,500
Capital		13,000
Debtors	3,000	
Bank	7,500	
	14,500	14,500

- As the business has stocks of materials, work-in-progress and raw materials at the end of the month, transfers from the accounts to the next stage of production are reduced; the balance remaining on each account shows the value of the stock at the end of the month.

- For simplicity, control accounts have not been used. An example of a wages control account is shown in Chapter 3, page 85.

OVERHEADS: UNDER-ABSORPTION AND OVER-ABSORPTION

In Chapter 5, we saw that businesses and other organisations often set pre-determined overhead rates for production overheads. Differences may occur between the pre-determined rate and the actual amount of overhead absorbed into the cost units because of a combination of:

- actual output differing from expected output

- actual costs incurred differing from expected costs

Thus it is common for overhead to be either under-absorbed, or over-absorbed:

- with under-absorption the overheads absorbed into the cost units are less than the overheads actually incurred

- with over-absorption the overheads absorbed into the cost units are more than the overheads actually incurred

Under-absorbed overhead is debited to profit and loss account, where it adds to costs and reduces profit; over-absorbed overhead is credited to profit and loss account, where it increases profit. Remember that neither excessive under- or over-absorption of overheads is desirable; they are an indication that the product has been costed inaccurately, which is likely to mean that the selling price has been calculated either too low (under-absorption) or too high (over-absorption).

For non-production overheads, there are no under-absorption or over-absorption amounts. This is because non-production overheads are not part of production cost; instead their costs are debited directly to profit and loss account.

The Case Study which follows summarises the book-keeping entries for overheads. These are also covered in Chapter 5 (pages 133-136).

Case Study

UNDER-ABSORPTION AND OVER-ABSORPTION OF OVERHEADS: DEPARTMENTS A AND B

DEPARTMENT A

situation

- overhead absorption rate is £2.00 per direct labour hour
- direct labour hours worked in March were 2,000
- actual cost of production overhead in March was £4,500

solution

overhead absorbed by cost units £2.00 x 2,000 hours	=	£4,000
actual cost of production overhead	=	£4,500
under-absorption of overhead	=	£500

The work-in-progress account is charged with production overheads of £4,000; however, this will leave a debit balance of £500 on production overheads account. This amount is transferred to profit and loss account as follows:

- debit profit and loss account
- credit production overheads account

Production overheads account appears as follows:

Dr	**Production Overheads Account: Department A**		Cr
	£		£
Bank (overheads incurred)	4,500	Work-in-progress	4,000
		Profit and loss (under-absorption)	500
	4,500		4,500

The amount of under-absorbed overhead adds to the total costs of the business, and so reduces profits.

DEPARTMENT B

situation

- overhead absorption rate is £5.00 per machine hour
- machine hours worked in March were 5,000
- actual cost of production overhead in March was £23,000

solution

- overhead absorbed by cost units £5.00 x 5,000 hours = £25,000
- actual cost of production overhead = £23,000
- over-absorption of overhead = £ 2,000

The work-in-progress account is charged with production overheads of £25,000; however, this will leave a credit balance of £2,000 on production overheads account. This amount is transferred to profit and loss account as follows:

- debit production overheads account
- credit profit and loss account

Production overheads account appears as follows:

Dr	**Production Overheads Account: Department B**		Cr
	£		£
Bank (overheads incurred)	23,000	Work-in-progress	25,000
Profit and loss (over-absorption)	2,000		
	25,000		25,000

The amount of over-absorbed overhead adds to profits; however, it should be remembered that the overhead recovery rate may have been set too high and, as a consequence, sales might have been lost because the selling price has been set too high.

Instead of transferring the over- or under-absorption of overheads direct to profit and loss account, an alternative is to use a holding or suspense account for the amounts. At the end of the financial year, the balance of this account is then transferred to profit and loss account – as either a debit or a credit entry, depending on the balance.

PROCESS COSTING

Process costing has been discussed already in Chapter 6. In this section we will summarise the book-keeping entries to account for:

- no losses within the process
- normal losses
- abnormal losses
- abnormal gains

The diagram on the next page illustrates the book-keeping entries for process costing.

no losses within the process

the book-keeping entries are:

- **transfer inputs to the process account**
  - debit process account
  - credit materials, labour, direct expenses (if any), production overhead accounts
- **transfer outputs to the next process or to finished goods stock**
  - debit next process account, or finished goods account
  - credit process account

normal losses

If there are normal losses with no scrap sales, the book-keeping entries are as above; however, as the unit cost of output of the process is affected, the amount of normal losses is recorded in the 'quantity' column on the credit side of the process account – no money amount is recorded.

If there are scrap sales, the book-keeping entries are as above, together with the following transfer to normal loss account:

- debit normal loss account
- credit process account

Receipts from scrap sales are credited to normal loss account, and debited to either bank account (cash received), or debtor's account (sold on credit terms).

abnormal losses

Where there are abnormal losses, as well as normal losses, the additional book-keeping entry is:

- debit abnormal loss account
- credit process account

Note that the value of the abnormal loss is made at the cost per unit value of the expected output.

Receipts from scrap sales relating to abnormal losses are credited to abnormal loss account and debited to either bank account (cash received), or debtor's account (sold on credit terms).

At the end of a company's financial year, the debit balance on abnormal loss account is charged as an expense to profit and loss account.

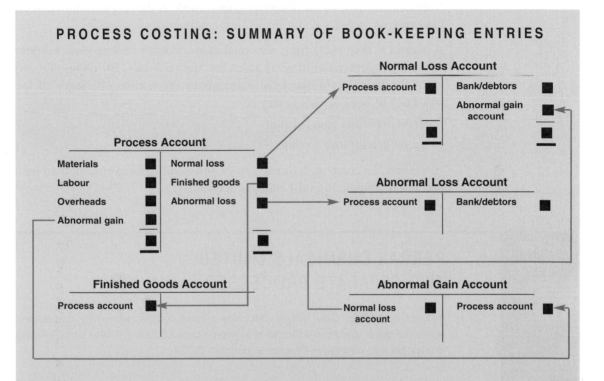

Note:

- accounts not shown are materials, labour, overheads, bank, debtors

- receipts from scrap sales (bank or debtors) are credited to normal loss account and/or abnormal loss account, as appropriate

- the transfer from abnormal gain account to normal loss account is made at the value of scrap sales for normal losses

- transfers from process account to abnormal loss account and abnormal gain account are made at the cost per unit value of expected output

- at the end of the financial year:

  - the balance of abnormal loss account is debited to profit and loss account

  - the balance of abnormal gain account is credited to profit and loss account

abnormal gains

Where there are abnormal gains, as well as normal losses, the additional book-keeping entry is

- debit process account
- credit abnormal gain account

Note that the value of the abnormal gain is made at the cost per unit value of the expected output.

A transfer is then made from abnormal gain account to normal loss account at the equivalent value of scrap sales for normal losses. By doing this, we highlight the value of abnormal gains above the normal efficiency of the process. The book-keeping entry is:

- debit abnormal gain account
- credit normal loss account

At the end of a company's financial year, the credit balance on abnormal gain account is credited to profit and loss account.

Case Study

PERRAN CHEMICALS LIMITED: TWO SEPARATE PROCESSES

Tutorial note: This Case Study illustrates normal losses, abnormal losses and abnormal gains using the example of a two-process company. These book-keeping entries are also covered in Chapter 6 (pages 162-174).

situation

Perran Chemicals Limited manufactures a product, Xenova, within two separate processes. For the week ended 14 May 2004 the details were:

- *Process 1*
  - materials input, 2,000 kilos at £4 per kilo
  - labour, £720
  - overheads, £1,440
- *Process 2*
  - materials input, 3,100 kilos at £6 per kilo
  - labour, £960
  - overheads, £480

Normal outputs are:

- Process 1, 80% of input
- Process 2, 90% of input

All losses are sold at a scrap value of £1 per kilo to a specialist reprocessing company.

There was no work-in-progress at either the beginning or end of the week.

Output during the week was 1,400 kilos from Process 1 and 4,200 kilos from Process 2.

As an accounts assistant at Perran Chemicals Limited you are asked to prepare the process 1 account, process 2 account, normal loss account, abnormal loss account, and abnormal gain account for the week ended 14 May 2004. Note: calculate costs per unit of expected output to the nearest penny.

solution

Dr			Process 1 Account				Cr
	Quantity (kilos)	Unit cost £	Total £		Quantity (kilos)	Unit cost £	Total £
Materials	2,000	4.00	8,000	Normal loss (20%)	400	–	400
Labour			720	Transfer to process 2	1,400	6.10	8,540
Overheads			1,440	Abnormal loss	200	6.10	1,220
	2,000		10,160		2,000		10,160

Dr			Process 2 Account				Cr
	Quantity (kilos)	Unit cost £	Total £		Quantity (kilos)	Unit cost £	Total £
Transfer from process 1	1,400	6.10	8,540	Normal loss (10%)	450	–	450
Materials	3,100	6.00	18,600	Finished goods	4,200	6.95	29,172
Labour			960				
Overheads			480				
	4,500		28,580				
Abnormal gain	150	6.95	1,042				
	4,650		29,622		4,650		29,622

Dr	Normal Loss Account		Cr
	£		£
Process 1 account	400	Bank/debtors	400
Process 2 account	450	Abnormal gain account	*150
		Bank/debtors	300
	850		850

* see abnormal gain account

Dr		Abnormal Loss Account		Cr
	£			£
Process 1 account	1,220	Bank/debtors (200 kilos x £1.00)		200

Dr		Abnormal Gain Account		Cr
	£			£
Normal loss account	*150	Process 2 account		1,042
* 150 kilos x £1.00 per kilo				

Tutorial notes:

- In process 1, the cost per unit of expected output is:

$$\frac{£10,160 - £400}{1,600 \text{ kilos*}} = £6.10 \text{ per kilo}$$

  * ie 2,000 kilos x 80%

- In process 2, the cost per unit of expected output is:

$$\frac{£28,580 - £450}{4,050 \text{ kilos**}} = £6.95 \text{ per kilo}$$

  ** ie 4,500 kilos x 90%

- At the end of the financial year:

  – the balance of abnormal loss account, here £1,020 (ie £1,220 - £200), is debited to profit and loss account

  – the balance of abnormal gain account, here £892 (ie £1,042 - £150), is credited to profit and loss account

Chapter Summary

- A manufacturing account shows prime cost and production cost.

- Profit and loss account shows non-production overheads and the net profit of the business.

- Correct identification and coding of costs is important in the preparation of accurate final accounts.

- An integrated book-keeping system incorporates the accounts of the business for both costing and financial accounting.

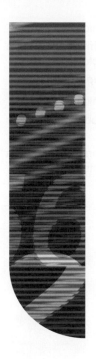

- Under- or over-absorption of overheads affects profit:
  - under-absorbed overhead is debited to profit and loss account, so reducing profit
  - over-absorbed overhead is credited to profit and loss account, so increasing profit
- Book-keeping for process costing uses a process account to calculate the cost per unit of expected output. Possible outcomes of process costing to be recorded in the accounts are:
  - no losses within the process
  - normal losses, with or without scrap sales
  - abnormal losses, with or without scrap sales
  - abnormal gains, with or without scrap sales

  At the end of a financial year, the balance of abnormal loss account is debited to profit and loss account, while the balance of abnormal gain account is credited

Key Terms

manufacturing account	double-entry account which brings together all the elements of cost that make up production cost
integrated book-keeping	combines the accounts for costing and financial accounting
under-absorption of overheads	where overheads absorbed into the cost units are less than the overheads actually incurred; profit is reduced
over-absorption of overheads	where overheads absorbed into the cost units are more than the overheads actually incurred; profit is increased
process account	account which is used to calculate the cost per unit of expected output; it is: – debited with the cost of inputs (materials, labour and overheads) – credited with the transfer to the next process or to finished goods
normal loss account	account used in process costing which is – debited with the scrap sales value of normal losses – credited with receipts from scrap sales

abnormal loss account   account used in process costing which is

    – debited with the value of abnormal losses (at a cost per unit value of the expected output)

    – credited with receipts from scrap sales

abnormal gain account   account used in process costing which is

    – debited with the equivalent value of scrap sales for normal losses

    – credited with the value of abnormal gains (at a cost per unit value of the expected output)

Student Activities

7.1   Which one of the following does not appear in a manufacturing account?

    (a)   depreciation of factory machinery

    (b)   indirect labour

    (c)   depreciation of office equipment

    (d)   factory light and heat

Answer (a) or (b) or (c) or (d)

7.2   For a manufacturing business, which type of stock is recorded in the profit and loss account?

    (a)   raw materials

    (b)   work-in-progress

    (c)   partly manufactured goods

    (d)   finished goods

Answer (a) or (b) or (c) or (d)

7.3 Allocate the following costs to:

- manufacturing account
- profit and loss account

(a)   factory rent

(b)   production supervisors' wages

(c)   insurance of factory buildings

(d)   depreciation of office equipment

(e)   sales commission

(f)   raw materials purchased

(g)   advertising

7.4 The following figures relate to the accounts of Crown Heath Manufacturing Company for the year ended 31 December 2004:

	£
Stocks at 1 January 2004:	
Raw materials	10,500
Finished goods	4,300
Stocks at 31 December 2004:	
Raw materials	10,200
Finished goods	3,200
Expenditure during year:	
Purchases of raw materials	27,200
Factory wages – direct	12,600
Factory wages – indirect	3,900
Factory rent and rates	1,200
Factory power	2,000
Depreciation of factory machinery	900
Repairs to factory buildings	300
Sundry factory expenses	900
Non-production overheads	6,500
Sales during year	60,400

You are to prepare the year end:

- manufacturing account
- profit and loss account

7.5 The following figures relate to the accounts of Barbara Francis, who runs a furniture manufacturing business, for the year ended 31 December 2004:

	£
Stocks of raw materials at 1 January 2004	31,860
Stocks of raw materials, 31 December 2004	44,790
Stocks of finished goods, 1 January 2004	42,640
Stocks of finished goods, 31 December 2004	96,510
Purchases of raw materials	237,660
Sale of finished goods	796,950
Rent and rates	32,920
Manufacturing wages	234,630
Manufacturing power	7,650
Manufacturing heat and light	2,370
Manufacturing expenses and maintenance	8,190
Salaries	138,700
Advertising	22,170
Office expenses	7,860
Depreciation of plant and machinery	7,450

Rent and rates are to be apportioned 75 per cent to manufacturing and 25 per cent to administration.

You are to prepare the year end:
- manufacturing account
- profit and loss account

7.6   P & A Manufacturing started in business on 1 July 2004. During July the following transactions took place:

	£
Opening capital paid into bank	50,000
Bought machinery, paying by cheque	20,000
Direct materials bought on credit	7,500
Direct labour costs paid by cheque	10,000
Production overheads paid by cheque	5,000
Non-production overheads paid by cheque	4,000
Credit sales	37,000
Receipts from debtors	25,000
Paid to creditors	7,000
Direct materials transferred to work-in-progress	6,000
Work-in-progress transferred to finished goods	19,000
Finished goods transferred to cost of sales	16,000

You are to:

(a) Record the above transactions in the integrated book-keeping system of P & A Manufacturing and show the net profit for the month. (Note that the full cost of direct labour and production overheads is to be transferred to work-in-progress.)

(b) Show the the trial balance at 31 July 2004, *after* preparing the profit and loss account.

7.7   A company's wages account for last week had two credit entries:

- work-in-progress account   £16,500
- production overheads account   £5,900

Explain the purpose of these two entries.

7.8   Production overheads of £125 have been under-absorbed in the machining department of Mereford Limited. Identify the double-entry book-keeping to record this in the accounts.

7.9   Last month the overheads of the finishing department of Eveshore Packers were over-absorbed.

- What is the accounting treatment for this?
- What will be the effect on profit for the period?

7.10 The following information is available about two departments of Mac Manufacturing for the month of April 2004:

DEPARTMENT A

- overhead absorption rate is £3.00 per direct labour hour
- direct labour hours work in April were 1,240
- actual cost of production overhead in April was £3,800

DEPARTMENT B

- overhead absorption rate is £6.00 per machine hour
- machine hours worked in April were 1,660
- actual cost of production overhead in April was £9,040

You are to show for each department:

- the under- or over-absorption of overhead
- the production overheads account, including any transfer to profit and loss account

7.11 Lanner Industries Limited produces a liquid soap called 'Cleanall' which is made in one production process.

For the four weeks ended 19 November 2004, the company input 22,000 litres of direct materials, and had an output of 20,300 litres – the difference of 1,700 litres was made up of a normal loss of 1,800 litres and an abnormal gain of 100 litres.

The input costs were: materials £15,400, labour £6,600, overheads £4,150. All losses were sold to a specialist reprocessing company for 50p per litre.

There was no opening or closing stock at the beginning and end of the process; all output was complete.

As an accounts assistant, you are to prepare the process account, abnormal gain account and normal loss account for the four weeks ended 19 November 2004.

7.12   Bissoe Chemicals Limited manufactures a product, Zenner, within two separate processes. For the week ended 24 September 2004 the details were:

- *Process 1*
- – materials input, 4,000 kilos at £3 per kilo
- – labour, £1,840
- – overheads, £2,150

- *Process 2*
- – materials input, 2,200 kilos at £4 per kilo
- – labour, £1,420
- – overheads, £1,050

Normal outputs are:

- Process 1, 90% of input
- Process 2, 80% of input

All losses have a scrap value of £0.50 per kilo.

There was no work-in-progress at either the beginning or end of the week.

Output during the week was 3,700 kilos from Process 1 and 4,600 kilos from Process 2.

As an accounts assistant at Bissoe Chemicals Limited you are asked to prepare the process 1 account, process 2 account, normal loss account, abnormal gain account, and abnormal loss account for the week ended 24 September 2004. Note: calculate costs per unit of expected output to the nearest penny.

this chapter covers . . .

In this chapter we see how cost accounting information is used to help a business or organisation to make short-term decisions. The techniques we will look at include:

- *break-even analysis*
- *margin of safety*
- *target profit*
- *profit volume ratio*
- *limiting factors*

We also look at the technique of marginal costing – seeing how it can be used to help with short-term decision-making, and how it differs from absorption costing.

NVQ PERFORMANCE CRITERIA COVERED

unit 6: RECORDING AND EVALUATING COSTS AND REVENUES

element 3

prepare and evaluate estimates of costs and revenues

A   *identify information relevant to estimating current and future revenues and costs*

B   *prepare estimates of future income and costs*

C   *calculate the effects of variations in capacity on product costs*

D   *analyse critical factors affecting costs and revenues using appropriate accounting techniques and draw clear conclusions from the analysis*

E   *state any assumptions used when evaluating future costs and revenues*

F   *identify and evaluate options and solutions for their contribution to organisational goals*

G   *present recommendations to appropriate people in a clear and concise way and supported by a clear rationale*

SHORT-TERM DECISIONS

what is meant by short-term decisions?

By short-term decisions we mean those actions which will affect the costs and revenues of a business or organisation over the next few weeks and months, up to a maximum of one year ahead. Long-term decisions – see Chapter 9 – affect the costs and revenues of future years. For example, an ice-cream manufacturer might make the following decisions:

• *short-term* – 'we have to increase production over the summer months in order to meet higher sales'

• *long-term* – 'we need to build a production line so that we can make the new Veneto range of ice creams that we are developing.'

types of short-term decisions

The decisions that we will be looking at include:

• Break-even analysis, where the break-even point is the output level (units manufactured or services provided) at which the income from sales is just enough to cover all the costs. Break-even analysis answers questions such as:

– what output do we need in order to break-even?

– at current levels of output we are above break-even, but how safe are we?

– we have to make a profit of £1,000 per week; what level of output do we need to achieve this?

– what is the effect on profit if we sell more or less than we think?

• Limiting factors, where there is a shortage which affects output. Limiting factors include a shortage of materials, skilled labour, machine hours, etc. Once the limiting factor has been identified, the effect of the constraint on output can be minimised in order to achieve the best results for the business or organisation. A knowledge of limiting factors answers questions such as:

– there is a shortage of materials this week – shall we produce Product Exe or Product Wye?

– until we complete the training programme we have a shortage of skilled labour; how best can we use the skilled labour that we have available?

– one of the machines has broken down; both of our products need machine hours – which product takes priority?

• Marginal costing identifies the fixed and variable costs that are required to make a product or to provide a service. Once these are known questions about pricing can be answered:

- if we increase prices, sales are expected to fall but how will our profit be affected?
- if we decrease prices, sales are expected to increase but how will our profit be affected?
- a potential customer wants to buy our product but at a lower price than we usually charge; how will our profit be affected?

what information is needed?

Decision-making, both in the short-term and long-term, is concerned with the future and always involves making a choice between alternatives. To help with decision-making it is important to identify the *relevant costs*.

Relevant costs are those costs that are appropriate to a particular decision.

In order to make a decision, information is needed about costs and revenues:

- future costs and revenues
  - it is the expected future costs and revenues that are important
  - past costs and revenues are only useful in so far as they provide a guide to the future
  - costs already spent (called *sunk costs*) are irrelevant to decision-making
- differential costs and revenues
  - only those costs which alter as a result of decision-making are relevant
  - where costs are the same for each alternative, they are irrelevant
  - thus any cost that changes when a decision is made is a relevant cost

In the short-term, a business or organisation always attempts to make the best use of existing resources. This involves focusing on what will change as a result of a decision being made, such as:

- selling prices
- variable costs
- contribution per unit of output, which is selling price minus variable cost
- marginal cost, which is the cost of producing one extra unit of output

Typically, fixed costs do not alter in short-term decision-making, eg the rent of a car factory is most likely to be the same when 11,000 cars are produced each year instead of 10,000 previously.

reporting decisions

With decision-making – both short- and long-term – the costing information has to be reported to managers, or other appropriate people, in a clear and concise way. The information should include recommendations which are supported by well-presented reasoning. The decisions will not be taken by the person who has prepared the information, but the decision-makers will be influenced by the recommendations of the report. Remember that managers, and other appropriate people, do not always have an accounting background, so any form of presentation must be set out clearly and must use as little technical accounting terminology as possible.

Methods of presentation include:

• verbal presentations
• written reports/memorandums

Both of these require a similar amount of preparation; the steps are:

– plan the report
– check that the plan deals with the tasks set
– be aware of the context in which the report is written
– make sure all work is legible
– express the report, verbal or written, in clear and concise English

written reports

The written report should include:

– an introduction, which sets out the task or the problem
– the content of the report, which explains the steps towards a solution and may include accounting calculations
– a conclusion, which includes a recommendation of the decision to be taken
– an appendix, which can be used to explain fully the accounting calculations, and to detail any sources of reference consulted

In this chapter we will see two written reports on short-term decisions which make recommendations – see pages 224 and 232. The next chapter includes an example of a report for a long-term decision. Unit 7 of NVQ Level 3 Accounting, 'Preparing Reports and Returns', covers the preparation of reports in more detail, and for more information on methods of presentation please see Chapter 13 of this book.

verbal presentations

A verbal presentation requires the same preparation and content as a written report and is probably the more difficult to present. Accordingly, verbal presentations often include support material in the form of handouts, overhead projector transparencies, or computer displays linked to an overhead projector. Such material can be used to explain accounting data and to make key points and recommendations.

FIXED AND VARIABLE COSTS

Before we can look at short-term decision-making techniques, it is important to understand that costs behave in different ways as the volume of output or activity changes. We have already seen (Chapter 4, pages 100-103) that there are three ways in which costs can behave within a range of output levels. These are summarised as follows:

variable costs   These are the costs where the cost varies in proportion to the level of output. For example, if a car manufacturer makes more cars it will use more sheet metal – a variable cost.

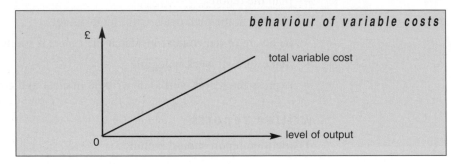

fixed costs   These are costs that do not normally change when the level of output changes. The cost of insuring a car factory against business risks will not vary in line with the number of cars produced – it is a fixed cost.

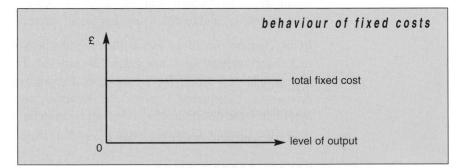

Remember that increases in output may produce a stepped fixed cost, eg an increase in factory rent because an additional factory is needed for the increase in output. The nature of stepped fixed costs is illustrated on page 101.

semi-variable costs   These are costs where a part of the cost acts as a variable cost, and a part acts as a fixed cost. Some fuel bills are semi-variable: there is a fixed 'standing charge' and a variable 'unit charge'.

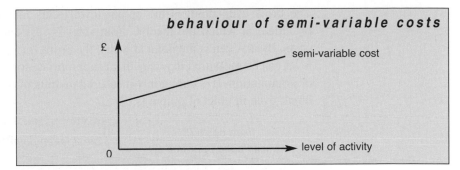

costs, contribution and profit

To help with decision-making, costs are classifed as either variable costs or fixed costs (semi-variable costs are divided into their fixed and variable components). For example, a car manufacturer will need to identify:

• the variable costs of each car

• the total fixed costs of running the business over a period of time

When the manufacturer sells a car it receives the selling price, which covers the variable costs of the car. As the selling price is greater than the variable costs there will also be money available to pay off the fixed costs incurred. This amount of money is known as the **contribution**. The formula is:

selling price per unit *less* variable cost per unit = contribution per unit

It follows that the difference between the sales income and the variable costs of the units sold in a period is the **total contribution** that the sales of all the units in the period make towards the fixed costs of the organisation.

A business can work out its profit for any given period from the total contribution and fixed costs figures:

total contribution *less* total fixed costs = profit

A profit statement can be prepared in the following format:

	sales revenue
less	variable costs
equals	contribution
less	fixed costs
equals	profit

BREAK-EVEN

Break-even is the point at which neither a profit nor a loss is made.

The break-even point is the output level (units manufactured or services provided) at which the income from sales is just enough to cover all the costs. Break-even is the point at which the profit (or loss) is zero. The output level can be measured in a way that is appropriate for the particular business or organisation. It is commonly measured in units of output. The formula for break-even in units of output is:

$$\frac{fixed\ costs\ (£)}{contribution\ per\ unit\ (£)} \quad = \quad break\text{-}even\ point\ (in\ units\ of\ output)$$

In order to use break-even analysis, we need to know:

- selling price (per unit)
- costs of the product
    - variable costs (such as materials, labour) per unit
    - overhead costs, and whether these are fixed or variable
- limitations, such as maximum production capacity, maximum sales

The Case Study of Fluffy Toys Limited which follows shows how the break-even point can be worked out.

Case Study

FLUFFY TOYS LIMITED: BREAK-EVEN

situation

Fluffy Toys Limited manufactures soft toys, and is able to sell all that can be produced. The variable costs (materials and direct labour) for producing each toy are £10 and the selling price is £20 each. The fixed costs of running the business are £5,000 per month. How many toys need to be produced and sold each month for the business to cover its costs, ie to break-even?

solution

This problem can be solved by calculation, by constructing a table, or by means of a graph. Which method is used depends on the purpose for which the information is required:

- the *calculation method* is quick to use and is convenient for seeing the effect of different cost structures on break-even point
- the *table method* shows the amounts of fixed and variable costs, sales revenue, and profit at different levels of production

- the *graph method* is used for making presentations – for example, to the directors of a company – because it shows in a visual form the relationship between costs and sales revenue, and the amount of profit or loss at different levels of production

Often the calculation or table methods are used before drawing a graph. By doing this, the break-even point is known and suitable scales can be selected for the axes of the graph in order to give a good visual presentation.

calculation method

The contribution per unit is:

	selling price per unit	£20
less	variable costs per unit	£10
equals	contribution per unit	£10

Each toy sold gives a contribution (selling price, less variable costs) of £10. This contributes towards the fixed costs and, in order to break-even, the business must have sufficient £10 'lots' to meet the fixed costs. Thus, with fixed costs of £5,000 per month, the break-even calculation is:

$$\frac{fixed\ costs\ (£)}{contribution\ per\ unit\ (£)} = \frac{£5,000}{£10} = 500\ toys\ each\ month$$

The break-even point (in units of output) is 500 toys each month.

table method

units of output	fixed costs	variable costs	total cost	sales revenue	profit/(loss)
	A	B	C	D	
			A + B		D – C
	£	£	£	£	£
100	5,000	1,000	6,000	2,000	(4,000)
200	5,000	2,000	7,000	4,000	(3,000)
300	5,000	3,000	8,000	6,000	(2 000)
400	5,000	4,000	9,000	8,000	(1,000)
500	5,000	5,000	10,000	10,000	nil
600	5,000	6,000	11,000	12,000	1,000
700	5,000	7,000	12,000	14,000	2,000

graph method

A graphical presentation uses money amounts as the common denominator between fixed costs, variable costs, and sales revenue.

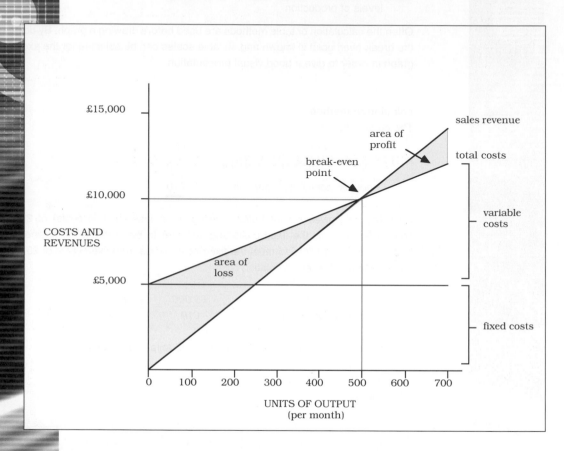

notes to the graph

- With a break-even graph, it is usual for the vertical axis to show money amounts; the horizontal axis shows units of output/sales.

- The fixed costs are unchanged at all levels of output, in this case they are £5,000.

- The variable costs commence, on the vertical axis, *from the fixed costs amount*, not from 'zero'. This is because the cost of producing zero units is the fixed costs.

- The fixed costs *and* the variable costs form the *total costs line*.

- The point at which the total costs and sales revenue lines cross is the break-even point.

- From the graph we can read off the break-even point both in terms of units of output, 500 units on the horizontal axis, and in sales value, £10,000 on the vertical axis.

- The 'proof' of the break-even chart is:

		£
	sales revenue (500 units at £20 each)	10,000
less	variable costs (500 units at £10 each)	5,000
equals	contribution	5,000
less	fixed costs	5,000
equals	profit/loss	nil

HINTS FOR DRAWING A BREAK-EVEN GRAPH

> **Tutorial note**: It is unlikely that you will be asked to draw a break-even graph in a Skills Test or Examination for *Recording and Evaluating Costs and Revenues*. Nevertheless, it is good practice and illustrates well the relationship between costs and revenues.

- In most break-even charts *all lines are straight.* This means that only two points need be plotted for each line; for example, with sales, choose a number that is fairly near to the maximum expected, multiply by the selling price per unit, and this is the point to be marked on the graph. As the sales line always passes through zero, there are now two points along which to draw a straight line.

- When drawing a break-even graph it is often difficult to know what total value to show on each axis, ie how many units, and/or how much in costs and revenues. As a guide, look for a maximum output or sales level that will not be exceeded: this will give the horizontal axis. Multiply the maximum sales, if known, by the unit selling price to give the maximum sales revenue for the vertical axis. If the figure for maximum sales is not known, it is recommended that the break-even point is calculated before drawing the graph so that the extent of the graph can be established.

- A common error is to start the variable costs from the zero point instead of the fixed costs line.

- Although fixed costs are likely to be unchanged within a fairly narrow range of outputs, watch out for *stepped fixed costs* (see page 101). For example, a major expansion of output may require that additional premises are rented: thus the fixed cost of rent will increase at a particular point (and is shown graphically as a step). Such a stepped fixed cost has a direct effect on total costs.

INTERPRETATION OF BREAK-EVEN

When interpreting break-even, it is all too easy to concentrate solely on the break-even point. The graph, for example, tells us much more than this: it also shows the profit or loss at any level of output/sales contained within the graph. To find this, simply measure the gap between sales revenue and total costs at a chosen number of units, and read the money amounts off on the vertical axis (above break-even point it is a profit; below, it is a loss). For example, the graph in the Case Study above shows a profit or loss at:

- 650 units = £1,500 profit
- 600 units = £1,000 profit
- 400 units = £1,000 loss

Break-even analysis, whether by calculation, by table, or by graph, can be used by all types of businesses and organisations. For example, a shop will wish to know the sales it has to make each week to meet costs; a sports centre will wish to know the ticket sales that have to be made to meet costs; a club or society might wish to know how many raffle tickets it needs to sell to meet the costs of prizes and of printing tickets.

Once the break-even point has been reached, the *additional* contribution forms the profit. For example, if the business considered in the Case Study above was selling 650 toys each month, it would have a total contribution of 650 x £10 = £6,500; of this the first £5,000 will be used to meet fixed costs, and the remaining £1,500 represents the profit (which can be read off the break-even graph). This can be shown by means of a profit statement as follows:

		£
	sales revenue (650 units at £20 each)	13,000
less	variable costs (650 units at £10 each)	6,500
equals	contribution (to fixed costs and profit)	6,500
less	monthly fixed costs	5,000
equals	profit for month	1,500

LIMITATIONS OF BREAK-EVEN ANALYSIS

The problem of break-even analysis is the assumption that the relationship between sales revenue, variable costs and fixed costs, remains the same at all levels of production. This is a rather simplistic view because, for example, in order to increase sales, a business will often need to offer bulk discounts, so reducing the sales revenue per unit at higher levels. The limitations of break-even analysis can be summarised as follows:

*   The assumption is made that all output is sold. There is no point in preparing the cost data, calculating the break-even point, and estimating the profits to be made if the product will not sell in sufficient quantities. However, break-even analysis is useful for a new business in order to establish the level of sales that must be achieved to reach break-even point. The feasibility of reaching that level of sales must then be considered by the owners.

*   All costs and revenues are expressed in terms of straight lines. However, this relationship is not always so. As indicated above selling prices may vary at different quantities sold; in a similar way, as we have seen earlier in the chapter, variable costs alter at different levels as advantage is taken of the lower prices to be gained from bulk buying, and/or more efficient production methods.

*   Fixed costs do not remain fixed at all levels of production; instead, as we have seen, there may be stepped fixed costs.

*   It is not possible to *extrapolate* the graph or calculation; by extrapolation is meant extending the lines on the graph beyond the limits of the activity on which the graph is based. For example, in the Case Study, the graph cannot be extended to, say, 1,000 units of output and the profit read off at this point. The relationship between sales revenues and costs will be different at much higher levels of output – different methods of production might be used, for example.

*   The profit or loss shown by the graph or calculations is probably only true for figures close to current output levels – the further away from current figures, the less accurate will be the expected profit or loss.

*   A further disadvantage of break-even analysis is that it concentrates too much attention on the break-even point. While this aspect is important, other considerations such as ensuring that the output is produced as efficiently as possible, and that costs are kept under review, are just as important.

BREAK-EVEN: MARGIN OF SAFETY

The margin of safety is the amount by which sales exceed the break-even point. Margin of safety can be expressed as:

*   a number of units
*   a sales revenue amount

- a percentage, using the following formula

$$\frac{current\ output - break\text{-}even\ output}{current\ output} \times \frac{100}{1} = percentage\ margin\ of\ safety$$

WORKED EXAMPLE

margin of safety

In the Case Study earlier in this chapter, Fluffy Toys Limited, (pp. 212-215), if current output is 700 units, while the break-even point is 500 units, the margin of safety is:

- 200 units (ie 700 − 500)

- £4,000 of sales revenue (ie 200 units at £20 each)

- 29 per cent, ie $\frac{700 - 500}{700} \times \frac{100}{1}$

In interpreting this margin of safety we can say that production/sales can fall by these values before the business reaches break-even point and ceases to make a profit.

Margin of safety is especially important in times of recession as it expresses to management the amount of the 'cushion' which current production/sales gives beyond the break-even point. Where there is a comparison to be made between two or more products, each with different margins of safety, the product with the highest margin of safety is looked on favourably; however, margin of safety is only one factor in decision-making.

BREAK-EVEN: TARGET PROFIT

A further analysis of break-even is to calculate the output that needs to be sold in order to give a certain amount of profit – the *target profit*. This is calculated as follows:

$$\frac{fixed\ costs\ (\pounds) + target\ profit\ (\pounds)}{contribution\ per\ unit\ (\pounds)} = number\ of\ units\ of\ output$$

Thus, if Fluffy Toys Limited (see the Case Study on pages 212-215) required a profit of £2,000 per month, the calculation is:

$$\frac{\pounds5,000 + \pounds2,000}{\pounds10} = 700\ units,\ with\ a\ sales\ value\ of\ \pounds14,000^*$$

* 700 units at £20 each = £14,000

This target profit can then be shown by means of a profit statement as follows:

		£
	sales revenue (700 units at £20 each)	14,000
less	variable costs (700 units at £10 each)	7,000
equals	contribution (to fixed costs and profit)	7,000
less	monthly fixed costs	5,000
equals	target profit for month	2,000

Target profit can also be calculated by making use of the profit volume ratio (see below).

PROFIT VOLUME RATIO

The profit volume (PV) ratio – also known as the contribution sales (CS) ratio – expresses the amount of contribution in relation to the amount of the selling price:

$$\frac{\text{contribution (£)}}{\text{selling price (£)}} = \text{contribution to sales ratio}$$

The ratio, or percentage, can be calculated on the basis of a single unit of production or for the whole business.

In break-even analysis, if fixed costs are known, we can use the PV ratio to find the sales value at which the business breaks-even, or the sales value to give a target amount of profit.

WORKED EXAMPLE

profit volume ratio
Referring back to the Case Study (Fluffy Toys Limited), the PV ratio (on a per unit basis) is:

$$\frac{\text{contribution (£)}}{\text{selling price (£)}} = \frac{£10^*}{£20} = 0.5 \text{ or } 50\%$$

* selling price (£20) – variable costs (£10) = contribution £10

Fixed costs are £5,000 per month, so the sales revenue needed to break-even is:

$$\frac{\text{fixed costs (£)}}{\text{PV ratio}} = \frac{£5,000}{0.5 \text{ (see above)}} = £10,000$$

As the selling price is £20 per toy, we can get back to the break-even in units of output as follows: £10,000 ÷ £20 = 500 units

If the directors of Fluffy Toys Limited wish to know the sales revenue that must be made to achieve a target profit of £2,000 per month, the PV ratio is used as follows:

$$\frac{\text{fixed costs + target profit}}{\text{PV ratio}} \quad = \quad \text{required level of sales}$$

$$\frac{\text{£5,000 + £2,000}}{0.5} \quad = \quad \underline{\text{£14,000}}$$

As the selling price is £20 per toy, we can get to the units of output as follows:

£14,000 ÷ £20 = 700 units to achieve a target profit of £2,000.

WHEN TO USE BREAK-EVEN ANALYSIS

Break-even analysis is often used:

before starting a new business

The calculation of break-even point is important in order to see the level of sales needed by the new business in order to cover costs, or to make a particular level of profit. The feasibility of achieving the level can then be considered by the owner of the business, and other parties such as the bank manager.

when making changes

The costs of a major change will need to be considered by the owners and/or managers. For example, a large increase in production will, most likely, affect the balance between fixed and variable costs. Break-even analysis will be used as part of the planning process to ensure that the business remains profitable.

to measure profits and losses

Within the limitations of break-even analysis, profits and losses can be estimated at different levels of output from current production. (Remember that this can be done only where the new output is close to current levels and where there is no major change to the structure of costs – ie it is not possible to extrapolate.)

to answer 'what if?' questions

Questions such as 'what if sales fall by 10 per cent?' and 'what if fixed costs increase by £1,000?' can be answered – in part at least – by break-even analysis. The effect on the profitability of the business can be seen, subject to the limitations noted earlier. A question such as 'what if sales increase by 300 per cent?' is such a fundamental change that it can only be answered by examining the effect on the nature of the fixed and variable costs and then re-calculating the break-even point.

to evaluate alternative viewpoints

There are often different ways of production; this is particularly true of a manufacturing business. For example, a product could be made:

* either, by using a labour-intensive process, with a large number of employees supported by basic machinery

* or, by using expensive machinery in an automated process with very few employees.

In the first case, the cost structure will be high variable costs (labour) and low fixed costs (depreciation of machinery). In the second case, there will be low variable costs and high fixed costs. Break-even analysis can be used to examine the relationship between the costs which are likely to show a low break-even point in the first case, and a high break-even point in the second. In this way, the management of the business is guided by break-even analysis; management will also need to know the likely sales figures, and the availability of money with which to buy the machinery.

LIMITING FACTORS

Limiting factors (or scarce resources) are those aspects of a business which affect output. Examples of limiting factors include:

* availability of materials

* availability of skilled labour

* availability of machine hours

* finance

* the quantity of the output which can be sold – whether a manufactured product or a service

At any one time there is usually one main limiting factor. It is essential to minimise its effect by optimising resources and maximising profit. After one limiting factor has been dealt with, another one then affects the business – for example, once a shortage of materials has been resolved, the limiting factor might well become a lack of skilled labour.

Where a business sells more than one product, under normal circumstances it will be best to switch output to the product that gives the highest contribution in relation to sales (the profit volume ratio). For example, a company makes two products, X and Y, with the following costs and revenues:

	Product	X £	Y £
	Selling price per unit	100	200
less	Unit variable costs	60	140
equals	Contribution per unit	40	60

With no limiting factors, the company should concentrate on making and selling product X. The reason for this is that the profit volume ratio is 40 per cent (£40 ÷ £100) when compared with product Y, where it is 30 per cent (£60 ÷ £200).

Where there is a limiting factor, for example the availability of skilled labour, a business will switch production to the product which gives the highest contribution from each unit of the limiting factor (eg contribution per direct labour hour). Thus the key to dealing with limiting factors is to:

maximise the contribution per unit of limiting factor

Following this rule will always maximise profits. Where there is a maximum level of output for the selected product, this product should be produced to the full if possible, and any units of limiting factors which remain unused should be 'spilled over' to the next best product. This is illustrated in the Case Study which follows.

Case Study

SOUND SYSTEMS LIMITED: LIMITING FACTORS

situation

Sound Systems Limited is a small company which makes reproduction radios to 1930s' designs (but with year 21st century sound quality!). Two models are made – the 'Windsor' and the 'Buckingham'. Both products require skilled direct labour which cannot be increased in the short term. Demand for the company's products is increasing rapidly and, while the company is taking steps to train new employees, the managing director is unsure of the 'mix' of products that should be produced each week.

Costs and revenues are as follows:

	Product	Windsor £	Buckingham £
	Selling price per unit	50	100
less	Unit variable costs	30	70
equals	Contribution per unit	20	30

- each radio takes two direct labour hours to make
- the number of direct labour hours each week is 260
- the weekly fixed overheads of the business are £2,000
- demand for the Windsor model is currently 100 radios per week, and for the Buckingham it is 80 radios per week

As an accounts assistant, prepare a report for the managing director which gives your recommendations for next week's production. Support your views with a forecast profit statement.

solution

Tutorial notes:

Ignoring, for the moment, the limiting factor of direct labour, the better model for the company to produce is the Windsor, because this gives a higher profit volume ratio:

- Windsor: £20 contribution on £50 of sales = PV ratio of 40 per cent
- Buckingham: £30 contribution on £100 of sales = PV ratio of 30 per cent

However, as direct labour is the limiting factor, the company should maximise the contribution from each hour of direct labour:

- Windsor: contribution per direct labour hour £20 ÷ 2 hours = £10
- Buckingham: contribution per direct labour hour £30 ÷ 2 hours = £15

To make best use of the limiting factor, the company should produce all of the Buckingham model that can be sold, ie 80 per week. This will utilise 160 direct labour hours (80 units x 2 hours per unit). The remaining 100 direct labour hours (260 hours less 160 hours) will be used to produce 50 of the Windsor model (50 units x 2 hours per week).

Report for managing director:

REPORT

To: Managing Director

From: Accounts Assistant

Date: Today

Production of Windsor and Buckingham models

Introduction

- You asked for my recommendations for next week's production.

- Until we have completed the training of new employees, the company has insufficient skilled labour to enable us to manufacture both models to meet customer demand. We therefore need to use our skilled labour to the best advantage of the company.

Report

- With insufficient skilled labour we have a limiting factor (or a scarce resource). To make best use of this limiting factor to produce profits for the company, we must maximise the contribution (selling price – variable costs) from each hour of skilled labour.

- The contribution from producing each Windsor radio is £20. As this product requires two hours of skilled labour, the contribution per hour is £20 ÷ 2 hours = £10.

- The contribution from producing each Buckingham radio is £30. As this product also requires two hours of skilled labour, the contribution per hour is £30 ÷ 2 hours = £15.

- To make best use of the limiting factor of skilled labour, the company should produce all of the Buckingham model that can be sold, ie 80 per week. This will take 160 hours of skilled labour (80 radios x 2 hours each) and will leave 100 hours available to produce 50 of the Windsor model (50 radios x 2 hours each).

- Please note that, if this production plan is followed, insufficient Windsor models will be produced to meet demand. This may make it difficult to re-establish the Windsor in the market when full production of this model can be resumed following the completion of training of new employees.

Conclusion

- Based on the concept of maximising the contribution from each hour of skilled labour (the limiting factor), I recommend that the production for next week should be:

    80 Buckingham radios

    50 Windsor radios

continued on next page

- This will give a forecast profit statement for next week as follows:

		Windsor £	Buckingham £	Total £
	Sales revenue:			
	50 Windsor at £50 per unit	2,500		2,500
	80 Buckingham at £100 per unit		8,000	8,000
		2,500	8,000	10,500
less	Variable costs:			
	50 Windsor at £30 per unit	1,500		1,500
	80 Buckingham at £70 per unit		5,600	5,600
equals	Contribution	1,000	2,400	3,400
less	Fixed overheads			2,000
equals	Profit			1,400

Summary:

The procedures for decision-making with limiting factors are:

- calculate the *contribution per unit of limiting factor* to make the decision as to which product to manufacture – the one with the higher contribution per unit of limiting factor will maximise profits

- calculate the profit statement using the *number of units of output* (and not the number of units of limiting factor)

- where there is a maximum level of output for the selected product, use as much of the limiting factor as possible, and then 'spill over' any unused limiting factor to the next best product (as in the Case Study)

Note that, where there are limiting factors, fewer of one or more products will be produced causing a shortfall in the market. It may be difficult to re-establish these products when full production can be resumed after the limiting factor has been resolved. The problem is that often customers want availability of all products and, if one isn't fully available, they won't buy the others (think of a store closing its carpet department and the effect on sales in the furniture department).

MARGINAL COSTING

In this chapter we have already applied the techniques of marginal costing to break-even analysis and the use of limiting factors.

Marginal cost is the cost of producing one extra unit of output.

Marginal cost is often – but not always – the total of the variable costs of producing a unit of output. For most purposes, marginal costing is not concerned with fixed costs (such as the rent of a factory); instead it is concerned with variable costs – direct materials, direct labour, direct expenses, and variable production overheads – which increase as output increases. For most decision-making, the marginal cost of a unit of output is, therefore, the variable cost of producing one more unit.

Knowing the marginal cost of a unit of output enables the management of a business or organisation to focus their attention on the *contribution* provided by each unit. As we have seen earlier, the contribution is the amount of money coming in from sales after marginal/variable costs have been paid. We usually express the calculation of contribution as:

selling price – variable cost = contribution

It can be calculated on a per unit basis, or for a batch of output (eg 1,000 units), or for a whole business or organisation.

The contribution, as its name implies, contributes to the cost of the overheads – once these are covered, the remainder of the contribution is profit. This has been seen already in break-even analysis where, after break-even point is reached, the contribution from additional sales adds to profit. Knowing the marginal cost of production helps with decision-making and, in the next section, we will see how it is used in making pricing decisions for 'special orders' and in the calculation of profit, and the valuation of closing stock.

Case Study

WYVERN BIKE COMPANY: MARGINAL COSTS

situation

The Wyvern Bike Company produces 100 bikes a week, and sells them for £200 each. Its costs are as follows:

weekly costs for producing 100 bikes	£
direct materials (£40 per bike)	4,000
direct labour (£50 per bike)	5,000
production overheads (fixed)	5,000
total cost	14,000

The factory has the capacity to produce 200 bikes a week, with no increase in production overheads.

As an accounts assistant at the Wyvern Bike Company, you are asked to:

• calculate the marginal cost of producing one bike
• calculate the contribution per bike
• prepare a weekly profit statement
• calculate the absorption cost of producing one bike
• give advice to the owner as to the price to be charged to a friend who wants a bike making next week – this will be extra to normal production and the owner wants to "cover the costs" but not make a profit

solution

• The marginal cost of producing one bike is:

	£
direct materials	40
direct labour	50
marginal cost per unit	90

The marginal cost is, here, the same as the variable cost (because production overheads are a fixed cost).

• The contribution per bike is:

selling price – variable costs = contribution
£200 – £90 = £110

• The weekly profit statement for 100 bikes is:

	£	£
sales (£200 per bike)		20,000
less direct materials (£40 per bike)	4,000	
direct labour (£50 per bike)	5,000	
		9,000
equals contribution		11,000
less fixed costs (production overheads)		5,000
equals profit		6,000

• The absorption cost of producing one bike is:

	£
direct materials	40
direct labour	50
production overheads (£5,000 ÷ 100 bikes)	50
absorption cost per bike	140

- The friend will be charged £90, ie the variable cost, rather than the absorption cost of £140. (If you think the friend should pay £140, try reworking the profit statement, based on 101 bikes, and see if the owner has covered the costs or has made a profit.)

'SPECIAL ORDER' PRICING

'Special order' pricing is where a business uses spare capacity to make extra sales of its product at a lower price than its normal selling price. Such pricing is normally used once the business is profitable at its current level of output, ie it has reached break-even. Additional sales – at 'special order' prices – can be made at a selling price above marginal cost, but below absorption cost. In this way, profits can be increased, provided that the additional sales are spare capacity. The key to increasing profit from additional sales is to ensure that a contribution to profit is made from the special order: the Case Study (below) illustrates this principle.

Case Study

WYVERN BIKE COMPANY: SPECIAL ORDERS

situation

The Wyvern Bike Company produces 100 bikes a week, and sells them for £200 each. Its costs are as follows:

weekly costs for producing 100 bikes

	£
direct materials (£40 per bike)	4,000
direct labour (£50 per bike)	5,000
production overheads (fixed)	5,000
total cost	14,000

The owner of the company has been approached by a mail order warehouse which wishes to buy:

- *either* 50 bikes each week at a price of £120 per bike
- *or* 100 bikes each week at a price of £80 per bike

The bikes can be produced in addition to existing production, with no increase in overheads. The special order is not expected to affect the company's existing sales. How would you advise the owner?

solution

The *absorption cost* of producing one bike is £140 (£14,000 ÷ 100 bikes). The mail order warehouse is offering either £120 or £80 per bike. On the face of it, with an absorption cost of £140, both orders should be rejected. However, as there will be no increase in production overheads, we can use *marginal costing* to help with decision-making.

The *marginal cost* per bike is £90 (direct materials £40 + direct labour £50), and so any contribution, ie selling price less marginal cost, will be profit:

- **50 bikes at £120 each**

  Although below absorption cost, the offer price of £120 is above the marginal cost of £90 and increases profit by the amount of the £30 extra contribution, ie (£120 – £90) x 50 bikes = £1,500 extra profit.

- **100 bikes at £80 each**

  This offer price is below absorption cost of £140 and marginal cost of £90; therefore there will be a fall in profit if this order is undertaken of (£80 – £90) x 100 bikes = £1,000 reduced profit.

weekly profit statements

	Existing production of 100 units	Existing production + 50 units @ £120 each	Existing production + 100 units @ £80 each
	£	£	£
Sales revenue (per week):			
100 bikes at £200 each	20,000	20,000	20,000
50 bikes at £120 each	–	6,000	–
100 bikes at £80 each	–	–	8,000
	20,000	26,000	28,000
Less production costs:			
Direct materials (£40 per unit)	4,000	6,000	8,000
Direct labour (£50 per unit)	5,000	7,500	10,000
Production overheads (fixed)	5,000	5,000	5,000
PROFIT	6,000	7,500	5,000

The conclusion is that the first special order from the mail order warehouse should be accepted, and the second declined. The general rule is that, once the fixed overheads have been recovered (ie break-even has been reached), provided additional units can be sold at a price above marginal cost, then profits will increase.

COST AND REVENUE PLANNING

The techniques of marginal costing can also be used to establish the effect of changes in costs and revenues on the profit of the business. Such changes include

- a reduction in selling prices in order to sell a greater number of units of output and to increase profits

- an increase in selling prices (which may cause a reduction in the number of units sold) in order to increase profits

Any change in selling prices and output will have an effect on revenues and the variable costs; there may also be an effect on fixed costs. The best way to show such changes is to use a columnar layout which shows costs and revenues as they are at present and then – in further columns – how they will be affected by any proposed changes. This method is used in the Case Study which follows.

Case Study

BROOKES AND COMPANY: COST AND REVENUE PLANNING

situation

Brookes and Company produces tool kits for bikes. The company produces 100,000 tool kits each year and the costs per unit of output are:

	£
direct materials	2.20
direct labour	2.00
variable production overheads	0.80
fixed production overheads	0.40
fixed non-production overheads	0.60
	6.00

The selling price per tool kit is £10.00

The managing director of the business, John Brookes, has been thinking about how to increase profits for next year. He has asked you, as an accounts assistant, to look at the following two proposals from a cost accounting viewpoint.

Proposal 1

To reduce the selling price of each tool kit to £9.00. This is expected to increase sales by 20,000 kits each year to a total of 120,000 kits. Apart from changes in variable costs, there would be no change in fixed costs.

Proposal 2

To increase the selling price of each tool kit to £12.00. This is expected to reduce sales by 20,000 kits each year to a total of 80,000 kits. Apart from changes in variable costs, there would be a reduction of £5,000 in fixed production overheads.

You are to write a memorandum to John Brookes stating your advice, giving reasons and workings. Each of the two proposals is to be considered on its own merits without reference to the other proposal.

solution

The following calculations, presented in columnar format, will form an appendix to the memorandum to John Brookes. Note that the three money columns deal with the existing production level, and then the two proposals.

BROOKES AND COMPANY

Cost and revenue planning for next year

	existing output (100,000 units) £	proposal 1 (120,000 units) £	proposal 2 (80,000 units) £
Sales:			
100,000 units at £10.00 per unit	1,000,000		
120,000 units at £9.00 per unit		1,080,000	
80,000 units at £12.00 per unit			960,000
TOTAL REVENUE	1,000,000	1,080,000	960,000
Direct materials at £2.20 per unit	220,000	264,000	176,000
Direct labour at £2.00 per unit	200,000	240,000	160,000
Variable production overhead at £0.80 per unit	80,000	96,000	64,000
Fixed production overhead	40,000	40,000	35,000
Fixed non-production overhead	60,000	60,000	60,000
TOTAL COSTS	600,000	700,000	495,000
PROFIT	400,000	380,000	465,000

Tutorial notes:
- fixed production overheads: 100,000 units at £0.40 per unit (note £5,000 reduction under proposal 2)
- fixed non-production overheads: 100,000 units at £0.60 per unit

MEMORANDUM

To:	Managing Director
From:	Accounts Assistant
Date:	Today

Cost and revenue plans for next year

Introduction

- You asked for my comments on the proposals for next year's production.

- I have looked at the expected profits if

  - we continue to sell 100,000 units each year at a selling price of £10.00 each

  - selling price is reduced to £9.00 per unit, with sales volume expected to increase to 120,000 units each year

  - selling price is increased to £12.00 per unit, with sales volume expected to decrease to 80,000 units each year

Report

- Please refer to the calculations sheet.

- At existing levels of production, the contribution (selling price – variable costs) per unit is:

    £10.00 – (£2.20 + £2.00 + £0.80) = £5.00 per unit x 100,000 units = £500,000

    Fixed costs total £100,000.

    Therefore profit is £400,000.

- For proposal 1, the contribution per unit is:

    £9.00 – (£2.20 + £2.00 + £0.80) = £4.00 per unit x 120,000 units = £480,000

    Fixed costs total £100,000.

    Therefore profit is £380,000.

- For proposal 2, the contribution per unit is:

    £12.00 – (£2.20 + £2.00 + £0.80) = £7.00 per unit x 80,000 units = £560,000

    Fixed costs total £95,000.

    Therefore profit is £465,000.

Conclusion

- Proposal 2 maximises the contribution from each unit of output.

- Although we expect to sell fewer units, the total contribution is greater.

- There is a small reduction in fixed costs under this proposal.

- Before proposal 2 is adopted, we would need to be sure of the accuracy of the expected fall in sales volume.

MARGINAL COSTING: OTHER POINTS

We have seen how marginal costing techniques can be useful in decision-making. Nevertheless, there are a number of points that must be borne in mind:

- *fixed costs must be covered*

  A balance needs to be struck between the output that is sold at above marginal cost and the output that is sold at absorption cost. The overall contribution from output must cover the fixed costs of the business and provide a profit. Overall output should be sold at a high enough price to provide a contribution to fixed costs.

- *separate markets for marginal cost*

  It is sensible business practice to separate out the markets where marginal cost is used. For example, a business would not quote a price based on absorption cost to retailer A and a price based on marginal cost to retailer B, when A and B are both in the same town! It would be better to seek new markets – perhaps abroad – with prices based on marginal cost.

- *effect on customers*

  One of the problems of using marginal cost pricing to attract new business is that it is difficult to persuade the customer to pay closer to, or above, absorption cost later on. Thus one of the dangers of using marginal cost is that profits can be squeezed quite dramatically if the technique is used too widely.

- *problems of product launch on marginal cost basis*

  There is great temptation to launch a new product at the keenest possible price – below absorption cost (but above marginal cost). If the product is highly successful, it could well alter the cost structure of the business. However, it could also lead to the collapse of sales of older products so that most sales are derived from output priced on the marginal cost basis – it may then be difficult to increase up prices to above absorption cost levels.

- *special edition products*

  Many businesses use marginal costing techniques to sell off older products at a keen price. For example, car manufacturers with a new model due in a few months' time will package the old model with 'special edition' bodywork and sell it at a low price (but above marginal cost).

MARGINAL COSTING AND ABSORPTION COSTING

In this chapter we have used marginal costing techniques in short-term decision-making. Nevertheless, we must always remember that one of the objectives of the costing system is to ensure that all the costs of a business or organisation are recovered by being charged to production. This is achieved by means of absorption costing (see Chapter 5). We will now make a comparison between the two methods of costing.

- *marginal costing*

    As we have seen in this chapter, the technique of marginal costing recognises that fixed costs vary with time rather than activity, and attempts to identify the cost of producing one extra unit. For example, the rent of a factory relates to a certain time period, eg one month, and remains unchanged whether 100 units of output are made or whether 500 units are made (always assuming that the capacity of the factory is at least 500 units); by contrast, the production of one extra unit will incur an increase in variable costs, ie direct materials, direct labour and direct expenses (if any) – this increase is the *marginal cost*.

- *absorption costing*

    This technique absorbs all production costs into each unit of output (see Chapter 5). Thus each unit of output in a factory making 100 units will bear a greater proportion of the factory rent than will each unit when 500 units are made in the same time period.

The diagram below demonstrates how the terms in marginal costing relate to the same production costs as those categorised under absorption costing terms. As noted above, when using marginal costing it is the behaviour of the cost – fixed or variable – that is important, not the origin of the cost.

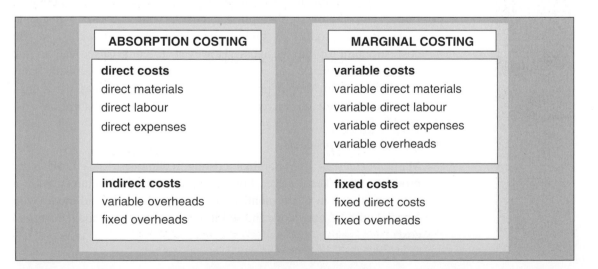

ABSORPTION COSTING	MARGINAL COSTING
direct costs direct materials direct labour direct expenses	**variable costs** variable direct materials variable direct labour variable direct expenses variable overheads
indirect costs variable overheads fixed overheads	**fixed costs** fixed direct costs fixed overheads

marginal costing and absorption costing: profit comparisons

Because of the different ways in which marginal costing and absorption costing treat fixed costs, the two techniques produce different levels of profit when there is a closing stock figure. This is because, under marginal costing, the closing stock is valued at variable production cost; by contrast, absorption cost includes a share of fixed production costs in the closing stock valuation. This is illustrated in the Case Study which follows, looking at the effect of using marginal costing and absorption costing on the profit statement of a manufacturing business.

Note that the marginal cost approach is used to help with the decision-making process – as we have seen in this chapter with break-even, limiting factors, 'special order' pricing, and cost and revenue planning. However, for financial accounting, absorption costing must be used for stock valuation purposes in order to comply with SSAP 9 (see page 58). Under SSAP 9, the closing stock valuation is based on the costs of direct materials, direct labour, direct expenses (if any), and production overheads. Note that non-production overheads are not included, as they are charged in full to the profit statement in the year to which they relate.

Case Study

CHAIRS LIMITED:
MARGINAL AND ABSORPTION COSTING

situation

Chairs Limited commenced business on 1 January 2004. It manufactures a special type of chair designed to alleviate back pain. Information on the first year's trading is as follows:

number of chairs manufactured	5,000
number of chairs sold	4,500
selling price	£110 per chair
direct materials	£30 per chair
direct labour	£40 per chair
fixed production overheads	£100,000

The directors ask for your help in producing profit statements using the marginal costing and absorption costing techniques. They say that they will use 'the one that shows the higher profit' to the company's bank manager.

solution

CHAIRS LIMITED
Profit statement for the year ended 31 December 2004

	MARGINAL COSTING		ABSORPTION COSTING	
	£	£	£	£
Sales at £110 each		495,000		495,000
Variable costs				
Direct materials at £30 each	150,000		150,000	
Direct labour at £40 each	200,000		200,000	
	350,000			
Less Closing stock (marginal cost)				
500 chairs at £70 each	35,000			
	315,000			
Fixed production overheads	100,000		100,000	
			450,000	
Less Closing stock (absorption cost)				
500 chairs at £90 each			45,000	
Less Cost of goods sold		415,000		405,000
PROFIT		80,000		90,000

Tutorial notes:

- Closing stock is always calculated on the basis of this year's costs:

  marginal costing, variable costs only, ie £30 + £40 = £70 per chair

  absorption costing, variable and fixed costs, ie £450,000 ÷ 5,000 chairs = £90 per chair

- The difference in the profit figures is caused only by the closing stock figures: £35,000 under marginal costing and £45,000 under absorption costing – the same costs have been used, but fixed production overheads have been treated differently.

- Only fixed production overheads are dealt with differently using the techniques of marginal and absorption costing – both methods charge non-production overheads *in full* to the profit statement in the year to which they relate.

With marginal costing, the full amount of the fixed production overheads has been charged in this year's profit statement; by contrast, with absorption costing, part of the fixed production overheads (here, £10,000) has been carried forward in the stock valuation.

With regard to the directors' statement that they will use 'the one that shows the higher profit', two points should be borne in mind:

- A higher profit does *not* mean more money in the bank.

- The two techniques simply treat fixed production overheads differently and, in a year when there is no closing stock, total profits *to date* are exactly the same – but they occur differently over the years.

Chapter Summary

- Short-term decisions are those actions which will affect the costs and revenues over the next few weeks and months.

- Break-even analysis distinguishes between fixed costs and variable costs.

- The relationship between sales revenue, fixed costs and variable costs is used to ascertain the break-even point, by means of a calculation, a table, or a graph.

- Break-even analysis can show:
  - break-even point in units of production
  - break-even point in value of sales
  - profit or loss at a given level of output/sales

- Break-even analysis has its limitations. Care needs to be taken to make sure that is is applied appropriately.

- Limiting factors (or scarce resources) are those aspects of a business which affect output, eg availability of materials, skilled labour, machine hours. The key to dealing with limiting factors is to *maximise the contribution per unit of limiting factor.*

- 'Special order' pricing is where a business uses spare capacity to make extra sales of its product at a lower price than normal. In order to increase profits the special order selling price must be above marginal cost.

- Marginal costing techniques are used in short-term decision-making for break-even, limiting factors, and 'special order' pricing.

- The use of marginal costing instead of absorption costing will have an effect on profit. This is because, under marginal costing, fixed costs are excluded from the closing stock valuation.

Key Terms

relevant costs	those costs that are appropriate to a particular decision
sunk costs	past costs which are irrelevant to decision-making
cost behaviour	the way in which costs behave in different ways as the volume of output or activity changes

contribution	selling price less variable cost
break even	the point at which neither a profit nor a loss is made, calculated in units of output as follows:

$$\frac{fixed\ costs\ (£)}{contribution\ per\ unit\ (£)}$$

margin of safety	the amount by which sales exceed the break-even point; calculated as a percentage as follows:

$$\frac{current\ output - break\text{-}even\ output}{current\ output} \quad x \quad \frac{100}{1}$$

target profit	the output that needs to be sold to give a certain amount of profit, calculated in number of units of output as follows:

$$\frac{fixed\ costs\ (£) + target\ profit\ (£)}{contribution\ per\ unit}$$

profit volume (PV) ratio	ratio which expresses the amount of contribution in relation to the amount of the selling price:

$$\frac{contribution\ (£)}{selling\ price\ (£)}$$

PV ratio is used to calculate the sales revenue needed to break-even as follows:

$$\frac{fixed\ costs\ (£)}{PV\quad ratio}$$

marginal cost	the cost of producing one extra unit of output
marginal costing	costing system which categorises costs according to their cost behaviour, and divides them into variable and fixed costs; the cost of units of output is based on the variable (or 'marginal') costs – all fixed costs are regarded as varying with time rather than activity

Student Activities

8.1   Bright Limited estimates that costs and revenue for next month will be:

selling price	£10 per unit
variable cost	£5 per unit
fixed costs for the month	£7,500

Maximum output is 3,000 units per month

As an accounts assistant, you are to complete the following table:

units of output	fixed costs	variable costs	total cost	sales revenue	profit/(loss)
	£	£	£	£	£
0					
500					
1,000					
1,500					
2,000					
2,500					
3,000					

8.2 Cuddly Toys Limited manufactures a popular children's teddy bear. At present production is limited by the capacity of the factory to 50 bears each week. The following information is available:

Selling price per teddy bear	£20
Materials per teddy bear	£4
Direct labour per teddy bear	£5
Weekly fixed expenses	
• factory rent and rates	£100
• fuel and power	£20
• other costs	£34

You are to find the weekly break-even point by the graphical method, and to check your answer by calculation.

8.3 Mike Etherton, a manufacturer of cricket bats, has the following monthly costs:

Material cost	£8 per bat
Labour cost	£12 per bat
Selling price	£35 per bat
Overheads (fixed)	£12,000

You are to:

(a) Prepare a table showing costs, sales revenue, and profit or loss for production of bats in multiples of 100 up to 1,200.

(b) Draw a graph showing the break-even point.

(c) Prove your answer by calculation.

(d) Read off the graph the profit or loss if 200 bats, and 1,200 bats are sold each month: prove the answer by calculation.

(e) If production is currently 1,000 bats per month, what is the margin of safety, expressed as a percentage and in units?

8.4 Riley Limited has made the following estimates for next month:

Selling price	£25 per unit
Variable cost	£10 per unit
Fixed costs for the month	£300,000
Forecast output	30,000 units
Maximum output	40,000 units

As an accounts assistant, you are to carry out the following tasks:

Task 1

Calculate:

- the profit volume ratio
- the break-even point in units
- the break-even point in sales revenue
- the margin of safety at the forecast output
- the number of units to generate a profit of £100,000

Task 2

Calculate the profit at:

- the forecast output
- the maximum output

Task 3

One of the managers has suggested that, if the selling price were reduced to £20 per unit, then sales would be increased to the maximum output.

- For this new strategy, you are to calculate:
    - the profit volume ratio
    - the break-even point in units
    - the break-even point in sales revenue
    - the margin of safety
    - the forecast profit
- Write a report to the general manager advising whether you believe that the new strategy should be implemented. (Use a copy of the report form in the Appendix.)

8.5 Sesame Shoes Limited manufactures shoes at its factory in Wyvern. It has three shoe ranges – the 'Madrid', the 'Paris', and the 'Rome'. The expected monthly costs and sales information for each range is as follows:

Product	'Madrid'	'Paris'	'Rome'
Sales and production units*	5,000	3,000	500
Machine hours per month	2,500	1,200	375
Total sales revenue	£150,000	£120,000	£30,000
Total direct materials	£50,000	£45,000	£10,000
Total direct labour	£25,000	£24,000	£6,000
Total variable overheads	£10,000	£9,000	£1,250

* note: a unit is a pair of shoes

The total expected monthly fixed costs relating to the production of all shoes are £72,800.

As an accounts assistant at Sesame Shoes Limited, you are to carry out the following tasks.

Task 1

Complete the table below to show for each product range the expected contribution per unit.

Product	'Madrid' £	'Paris' £	'Rome' £
Selling price per unit			
Less: Unit variable costs			
Direct materials			
Direct labour			
Variable overheads			
Contribution per unit			

Task 2

If the company only manufactures the 'Madrid' range, calculate the number of units it would need to make and sell each month to cover the fixed costs of £72,800.

Task 3

The breakdown of a machine used in the manufacture of shoes has reduced available machine time from 4,075 to 3,000 hours. The finance director asks you to calculate the contribution of each unit (pair of shoes) per machine hour.

Using the data from Task 1, complete the table below.

Product	'Madrid'	'Paris'	'Rome'
Contribution per unit			
Machine hours per unit			
Contribution per machine hour			

Task 4

Using the data from Task 3, calculate how many units of each of product ranges 'Madrid', 'Paris', and 'Rome' the company should make and sell in order to maximise its profits using 3,000 machine hours.

8.6   Dean Limited makes two products – A and B. Both products are made from the same type of direct materials. These materials are currently in short supply. At present the company can obtain only 500 kilos of the direct materials each week. The production manager seeks your guidance as to the 'mix' of products that should be produced each week. The information available is:

Product		A	B
	Selling price per unit	£150	£200
less	Unit variable costs	£120	£150
equals	Contribution per unit	£30	£50
	Kilos of direct materials per unit	2	4
	Demand per week (in units)	200	150

The weekly fixed overheads of the business are £4,000.

As an accounts assistant, you are to write a report to the production manager giving your recommendations for next week's production. Support your views with a forecast profit statement. (Use a copy of the report form in the Appendix.)

8.7   You are an accounts assistant at Durning Foods Limited. The company produces ready meals which are sold in supermarkets and convenience stores. You have just received the following memorandum from the general manager:

MEMORANDUM

To: Accounts Assistant

From: General Manager

Date: 8 October 2004

Production line of Indian meals

Please prepare a cost and revenue plan for the Indian meals production line for November.

We plan to sell 36,000 meals in November and will base our projection on the cost and revenue behaviour patterns experienced during July to September.

The cost accounting records show the following for July, August and September:

DURNING FOODS LIMITED: Production line for Indian meals

Actual results for July to September 2004

	July	August	September
Number of meals sold	33,500	31,000	34,700
	£	£	£
Direct materials	25,125	23,250	26,025
Direct labour	15,075	13,950	15,615
Direct expenses	6,700	6,200	6,940
Overheads for Indian meals production line	12,525	12,150	12,705
Other production overheads	4,000	4,000	4,000
Total cost	63,425	59,550	65,285
Sales revenue	67,000	62,000	69,400
Profit	3,575	2,450	4,115

Task 1

- Use the above information to identify the cost and revenue projections to be used in your projections.

- Use the identified cost and revenue behaviour patterns to complete the projection for November 2004.

Task 2

After you have completed Task 1, the general manager sends you the following memorandum:

MEMORANDUM

To: Accounts Assistant

From: General Manager

Date: 14 October 2004

Production line of Indian meals

Thank you for your work on the cost and revenue projections for November.

Our Buying Department has found an alternative supplier of materials – meat, rice and sauces. The buyers say that the quality is better than we use at the moment and the price is 20 per cent cheaper. However, we will need to buy in larger quantities to get such good prices. To allow for this, I would like to increase production and sales to 40,000 meals in November.

Could you please recalculate the cost and revenue projections for November 2004 based on the increased activity and taking advantage of the cheaper prices?

Also, please calculate the break-even point in terms of the number of meals to be sold in November if we make this change. Please include a note of the margin of safety we will have.

- Use your identified cost and revenue behaviour patterns to adjust for the change in material costs and to prepare a revised projection for November 2004 based on sales of 40,000 meals.

- Calculate the break-even point in terms of meals to be sold in November if the lower priced materials are used.

- Calculate the margin of safety, expressed as a percentage of the increased planned activity for November.

8.8   Westfield Limited makes 2,000 units of product Exe each month. The company's costs are:

monthly costs for making 2,000 units of Exe

	£
direct materials	6,000
direct labour	4,000
production overheads (fixed)	8,000
total cost	18,000

Each unit of Exe is sold for £12.

The management of the company has been approached by a buyer who wishes to purchase:

- *either* 200 units of Exe each month at a price of £6 per unit

- *or* 500 units of Exe each month at a price of £4 per unit

The extra units can be produced in addition to existing production, with no increase in overheads. The special order is not expected to affect the company's existing sales. How would you advise the management?

8.9 Popcan Limited manufactures and sells a soft drink which the company sells at 25p per can. Currently output is 150,000 cans per month, which represents 75 per cent of production capacity. The company has an opportunity to use the spare capacity by producing the product for a supermarket chain which will sell it under their own label. The supermarket chain is willing to pay 18p per can.

Use the following information to advise the management of Popcan Limited if the offer from the supermarket should be accepted:

POPCAN LIMITED

Costs per can

	pence
Direct materials	5
Direct labour	5
Production overheads (variable)	4
Production overheads (*fixed)	6

* fixed production overheads are apportioned on the basis of current output

8.10 Maxxa Limited manufactures one product, the Maxx. For the month of January 2004 the following information is available:

number of units manufactured	4,000
number of units sold	3,000
selling price	£8 per unit
direct materials for month	£5,000
direct labour for month	£9,000
fixed production overheads for month	£6,000

There was no finished goods stock at the start of the month. Both direct materials and direct labour behave as variable costs.

As an accounts assistant, the directors ask for your help in producing profit statements using the marginal costing and absorption costing techniques.

9 Long-term decisions

In this chapter we see how cost accounting information is used to help a business or organisation to make long-term decisions. In particular, we focus on capital investment projects – for example, if we need a new photocopier for the office, shall we buy a Toshiba or a Canon model?

The main methods of capital investment appraisal are:

- *payback period*
- *discounted cash flow*

We look at what capital investment appraisal involves, and then study these two methods by means of a Case Study, and make comparisons between them. Towards the end of the chapter, we look briefly at a further capital investment appraisal method called internal rate of return.

NVQ PERFORMANCE CRITERIA COVERED

unit 6: RECORDING AND EVALUATING COSTS AND REVENUES

element 3

prepare and evaluate estimates of costs and revenues

A   *identify information relevant to estimating current and future revenues and costs*

B   *prepare estimates of future income and costs*

C   *calculate the effects of variations in capacity on product costs*

D   *analyse critical factors affecting costs and revenues using appropriate accounting techniques and draw clear conclusions from the analysis*

E   *state any assumptions used when evaluating future costs and revenues*

F   *identify and evaluate options and solutions for their contribution to organisational goals*

G   *present recommendations to appropriate people in a clear and concise way and supported by a clear rationale*

WHAT IS CAPITAL INVESTMENT APPRAISAL?

You will readily appreciate that, whether at home or at work, resources are limited in supply and, as a result, there is a need to use them in such a way as to obtain the maximum benefits from them. To do this it is necessary to choose between various financial alternatives available; for example, on a personal level, we have to make decisions such as:

Should I save my spare cash in a bank or in a building society?

Should I save up for a car, or should I buy on hire purchase?

Which make of car, within my price range, should I buy?

Should I rent a house or should I buy, taking out a mortgage?

While these decisions are personal choices, the management of businesses of all sizes are faced with making choices, as are other organisations such as local authorities and central government.

The management of any business is constantly having to make decisions on *what* goods or services to produce, *where* to produce, *how* to produce, and *how much* to produce. For each major choice to be made, some method of appraisal has to be applied to ensure that, whatever decisions are taken, they are consistent with the objectives of the organisation. This means that it is necessary to look at all the alternatives available and to choose the one that is going to give the most benefit. For example, a business may have to decide whether to replace its existing machinery with new, more up-to-date machinery. If it decides on new machinery, it then has to choose between different makes of machine and different models, each having a different cost and each capable of affecting output in a different way. At the same time a decision has to be made whether to pay cash outright, to buy on hire purchase, or to lease.

The objective of capital investment appraisal is to enable a business or organisation to decide whether or not to invest in a particular capital investment project and, where there are a number of viable alternatives, to decide in which of them to invest.

WHAT IS A CAPITAL INVESTMENT PROJECT?

A capital investment project is the spending of money now in order to receive benefits (or reduce costs) in future years; it is illustrated in the diagram on the next page.

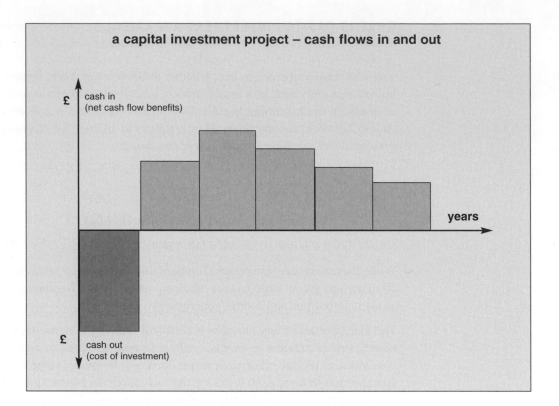

Here, the cost of the investment, or capital expenditure, is being spent at the start – either at the very beginning of the project (often stated as 'year 0'), or during the first year. The difference between these two is illustrated by the following:

• bought a new photocopier is a cash outflow at the beginning of the project

• the installation of a new production line may well incur cash outflows during the first year

The cost of the investment brings benefits (or reduced costs) in future years for as long as the project lasts. Businesses and organisations need to apply capital investment appraisal methods to ensure that the long-term decisions they make are the correct choices.

INVESTMENT APPRAISAL IN CONTEXT

As well as the cash flows in and out for a capital investment project, a number of other factors need to be considered before a long-term decision is made. These factors include:

- *Source of finance.* Where is the money coming from to finance the project? Is it from a cash surplus, an existing or new bank overdraft, loans? A large project may warrant a share or debenture (loan) issue to raise specific finance. Assets such as machinery, equipment and vehicles are often financed using hire purchase and leasing.

- *Cost of capital.* All finance has a cost – invariably expressed as a rate of return. The rate of return will be different for each source of finance – from the interest foregone on cash surpluses, to that which must be paid on bank overdrafts and loans. With ordinary shares, the cost of capital is the dividend that shareholders expect to receive. Hire purchase and leasing payments include the interest cost. Note that, with variable interest rates, cost of capital may well vary during the life of a project.

- *Total estimated cost of project.* It is important to forecast accurately the total capital expenditure cost of projects. Historically, the cost of large-scale projects has often been under-estimated and the final actual cost has been much higher than anticipated, leading to financial difficulties.

- *Taxation implications.* A project will usually include both tax allowances and payments. The allowances occur when new assets – such as machinery, equipment and vehicles – are purchased; called writing down allowances, these reduce the amount of tax to be paid. However, the cost savings or increasing profits of the investment project will increase overall profitability of the business and will lead to more tax being paid. Note that in AAT Skills Tests and Examinations for *Recording and Evaluating Costs and Revenues* you will not be assessed on the taxation implications of long-term decisions.

- *Working capital requirements.* Most projects will also require an investment in working capital – stock, debtors and creditors. Thus an amount of working capital is needed at the start, and throughout the project's life. It will only be disinvested at the end of the project.

- *Audit of project.* It is important to keep a regular check on costs to ensure that they are in line with the estimates. There are three separate phases that should be audited:

  – costs of bringing the project into commission

  – operational costs

  – decommissioning costs

- *Other considerations*

  Economic climate – recession or period of growth.

  Political implications – a possible change of government may affect investment decisions.

  Commissioning – the length of time that it will take for the project to be up and running.

Training – the costs and implications of staff training.

Location – where the project is to be located, and subsequent effects on the culture of the organisation.

Capacity – effect on overall output of the organisation.

Product life cycle – the implications on the project of the stage of the company's output in the product life cycle.

Case Study

AYE OR BEE: WHICH PROJECT?
MAKING THE DECISION

situation

A business is investing in a new project and has to make the choice between Project Aye and Project Bee. The initial cost and the net cash flow (income, less expenses but not depreciation) to the business have been calculated over five years for each project as follows:

	PROJECT AYE	PROJECT BEE
Initial cost at the beginning of the project	£20,000	£28,000
Net cash inflow:		
Year 1	£8,000	£10,000
Year 2	£12,000	£10,000
Year 3	£5,000	£8,000
Year 4	£4,000	£9,000
Year 5	£2,000	£9,000

- At the end of year 5, both projects will have a scrap value of £1,000; this amount is already included in the year 5 cash inflows.

- Only one project can be undertaken.

- The business requires an annual rate of return of 10 per cent on new projects.

Which project should be chosen?

solution

The two methods commonly used to appraise a capital investment project such as this are:

- payback period

- discounted cash flow

These methods will be considered in this chapter in order to help the business to make its decision. At the end of the chapter we will also look at how the internal rate of return (or discounted cash flow yield) is used in order to make a direct comparison between projects which have different amounts of capital investment at the start.

PAYBACK PERIOD

This method, as its name implies, shows how long it takes for the initial outlay to be repaid by the net cash flow coming in. The cash flows and the cumulative cash flows (ie net cash flows to date) are shown in the table below. From this information it can be seen that project Aye costs £20,000 (paid out at the beginning of the project) and it is expected that the net cash flow over the first two years will equal the cost. The payback period for Project Aye is, therefore, two years, while that for Project Bee is three years. So, using payback, Project Aye is preferable.

	PROJECT AYE		PROJECT BEE	
Year	Cash Flow	Cumulative Cash Flow	Cash Flow	Cumulative Cash Flow
	£	£	£	£
0	(20,000)	(20,000)	(28,000)	(28,000)
1	8,000	(12,000)	10,000	(18,000)
2	12,000	–	10,000	(8,000)
3	5,000	5,000	8,000	–
4	4,000	9,000	9,000	9,000
5	2,000	11,000	9,000	18,000

The payback period is indicated by the shading

Although these payback periods work out to exact years, they rarely do so in practice. Be prepared to calculate part years in Skills Tests and Examination. For example, if Project Aye had an initial cost of £22,000, the payback would require £2,000 of the £5,000 cash flow in year 3. The payback period would then be 2 years + (£2,000/£5,000 x 12 months) = 2 years and 5 months (taken to the nearest month). Note that, in calculating part years, we are making the assumption that cash flows occur at an even rate throughout the year – this may not be the case for all projects – sales (and costs) may be higher at certain times: for example, retailers are likely to have high sales in the pre-Christmas shopping period.

The shorter the payback period the better, particularly where high technology or fashion projects are concerned – they may be out-of-date before they reach the end of their useful lives. Earlier cash flows are likely to prove more accurate estimates than later cash flows. Thus, if two projects have the same payback, the one with the greater cash flow in the early years is preferred.

For example, consider two projects with a payback period of two years from the following cash flows:

	Wye	Zed
Year 1	£8,000	£12,000
Year 2	£12,000	£8,000

While both projects have the same payback period of two years, Zed is the preferred project under the payback method because of earlier cash flows.

advantages of payback

- it is easy to calculate
- it is easy to understand
- it places emphasis on the earlier cash flows, which are more likely to be accurate than later cash flows
- an ideal capital investment appraisal method for high technology projects

disadvantages of payback

- all cash flows after the payback period are ignored
- within the payback period it fails to take into account the timing of net cash flows, eg Project Aye would still have had a payback of two years even if the cash flows for years one and two had been reversed (as noted above, greater cash flows in earlier years are to be preferred)

DISCOUNTED CASH FLOW

Discounted cash flow (DCF) is a capital investment appraisal method which recognises that money has a time value. For example, supposing that today a friend asks you to lend her £1 and offers to repay you either tomorrow, or in one year's time, which will you choose? The answer is clear: you would want the money back sooner rather than later because, if you don't intend to spend it, you can always save it in a bank or building society, where it will earn interest. Thus the rate of interest represents the time value of money.

Using £1 as an example, if it is invested with a bank or building society at an interest rate of 10 per cent per year, it will increase as follows:

original investment	£1.00
interest at 10% on £1	£0.10
value at end of first year	£1.10
interest at 10% on £1.10	£0.11
value at end of second year	£1.21

This uses the technique of compound interest. So, with interest rates of 10 per cent per year, we can say that the future value of £1 will be £1.10 at the end of year one, £1.21 at the end of year two, and so on; thus £1 set aside now will gain in value so that, at some time in the future, we will have access to a larger sum of money. However, supposing that we were to receive £1 at the end of year one, what is it worth to us now? To find the answer to this, we need to carry out the following calculation:

$$£1 \quad \times \quad \frac{100}{110*} \quad = \quad £0.91$$

* 100 per cent, plus the rate of interest (in this example, 10 per cent).

Therefore, if we had £0.91 now and invested it at 10 per cent per year, we would have £1 at the end of year one. We can say that the *present value* of £1 receivable in one year's time is £0.91. In the same way, £1 receivable in two years' time is £0.83, calculated as follows:

$$£1 \quad \times \quad \frac{100}{110} \times \frac{100}{110} \quad = \quad £0.83$$

We can build up a *table of factors* (for 10 per cent interest rate) as shown below:

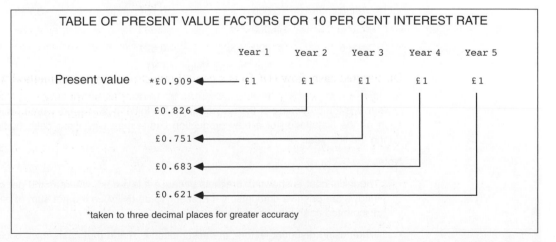

TABLE OF PRESENT VALUE FACTORS FOR 10 PER CENT INTEREST RATE

	Year 1	Year 2	Year 3	Year 4	Year 5
Present value	*£0.909 ← £1	£1	£1	£1	£1
	£0.826 ←				
	£0.751 ←				
	£0.683 ←				
	£0.621 ←				

*taken to three decimal places for greater accuracy

Note that there is no need to learn how to calculate present value factors – the correct factors will always be given to you in Skills Tests and Examinations.

The table of factors reminds us of the basic principle that *money has a time value* and, from this, the further into the future that we expect to receive money, then the lower is its *present value*. Thus the present value (or discount) factors relate to interest rates which represent the cost of capital (ie the rate of return that the business or organisation expects on its money, or the rate of interest it has to pay when borrowing).

Let us now return to the problem of the business which has to choose between Projects Aye and Bee. We will look at this assuming, firstly, a cost of capital – or rate of return – of 10 per cent. For each project, the expected net cash flows are multiplied by the relevant factor to give the *discounted cash flow*; the difference between total discounted cash flow and the initial cost is the *net present value* of the project.

WORKED EXAMPLE

Project Aye calculations

	Cash Flow		Discount Factor		Discounted Cash Flow
	£				£
Year 0*	(20,000)	x	1.000	=	(20,000)
Year 1	8,000	x	0.909	=	7,272
Year 2	12,000	x	0.826	=	9,912
Year 3	5,000	x	0.751	=	3,755
Year 4	4,000	x	0.683	=	2,732
Year 5	2,000	x	0.621	=	1,242
	Net Present Value (NPV)			=	4,913

* Year 0 is the beginning of the project when the initial cost is paid. Some projects such as the installation of a new production line – may well incur cash outflows during the first year.

Notes:

• The initial cost is shown in brackets because it is a cost, whereas the net cash inflows are positive amounts. Net Present Value (NPV) is the net sum of all the discounted cash inflows and outflows.

• When using discount factors, the assumption is made that cash flows occur at the end of each year – apart, that is, from the Year 0 initial cash flow.

Project Bee calculations

	Cash Flow		Discount Factor		Discounted Cash Flow
	£				£
Year 0	(28,000)	x	1.000	=	(28,000)
Year 1	10,000	x	0.909	=	9,090
Year 2	10,000	x	0.826	=	8,260
Year 3	8,000	x	0.751	=	6,008
Year 4	9,000	x	0.683	=	6,147
Year 5	9,000	x	0.621	=	5,589
	Net Present Value (NPV)			=	7,094

Here, with a cost of capital – or rate of return – of 10 per cent, Project Bee is better, producing a considerably higher net present value than Aye. Note that both projects give a positive net present value at 10 per cent: this means that either project will be of benefit to the organisation but Bee is preferable; a negative NPV would indicate that a project should not go ahead.

Thus, using a discounted cash flow method, future cash flows are brought to their value now; this means that, the further on in time that cash flows are receivable, the lower is the net present value.

advantages of discounted cash flow

- all cash flows are used
- the timing of cash flows is taken into account
- using a table of factors the calculations are easy to make

disadvantages of discounted cash flow:

- the cost of capital rate – or rate of return – is, in practice, difficult to ascertain and may also vary over the life of the project
- the meaning of net present value is not always clear to users of the information
- the project with the higher net present value does not always represent the better project for the business or organisation

CAPITAL INVESTMENT APPRAISAL: COMPARISON

It is unlikely that a business will rely on one investment appraisal method only; instead both methods might need to be satisfied before a capital project is given the go-ahead. Supposing, for example, that the organisation, having to choose between Projects Aye and Bee, applied the following criteria: "projects must have a payback period not exceeding two-and-a-half years, and must have a positive net present value at a 10 per cent rate of return." How do the two projects compare?

	Project Aye	*Project Bee*
Payback period	2 years	3 years
NPV at 10 per cent	£4,913	£7,094

Under the criteria that the organisation has laid down, Aye would be chosen. However, Bee seems a better project on the net present value basis and is only rejected because it does not meet the payback period requirement. However, the capital expenditure required for Bee is £8,000 greater than Aye – £28,000 compared with £20,000; this is something which NPV does not take fully into account. To obtain a better analysis, we need to use the method of *internal rate of return*.

INTERNAL RATE OF RETURN

The principles of discounted cash flow can be developed further in order to calculate the capital investment appraisal method of *internal rate of return* (IRR) – this method is also known as *DCF (Discounted Cash Flow) yield*.

The internal rate of return is the rate of cost of capital at which the present value of the cash inflows exactly balances the initial investment. In other words, it shows the cost of capital, or rate of return, percentage at which the investment 'breaks-even', ie income equals expenditure, but still applying discounted cash flow principles.

You will not be required to calculate the internal rate of return in Skills, Tests and Examinations. However, you should know what it means and be able to comment upon it.

We will look at two ways in which IRR can be illustrated:
- tabulation
- graphically

tabulation

To illustrate IRR by tabulation we start with a cost of capital which gives a positive net present value – for example, 10 per cent cost of capital for Project Aye gives a NPV of £4,913 (as we saw on page 254). We increase the cost of capital by one or two percentage points each time, and repeat the NPV calculation (workings not shown here) until, eventually, it becomes negative. This is shown as follows (note that net present value is calculated from column A minus column B):

PROJECT AYE			
Cost of Capital*	Present Value of Cash Flow	Capital Investment	Net Present Value
	£	£	£
	A	B	A – B
10%	24,913	(20,000)	4,913
12%	23,946	(20,000)	3,946
14%	23,025	(20,000)	3,025
16%	22,177	(20,000)	2,177
18%	21,375	(20,000)	1,375
20%	20,619	(20,000)	619
22%	19,915	(20,000)	(85)
24%	19,242	(20,000)	(758)

* or rate of return

The net present value that balances the present value of cash flow with the initial investment lies between 20% and 22% – closer to 22% than 20%, so we can call it approximately 22% (an answer to the nearest one or two percentage points is acceptable for most long-term decisions).

graphically

Internal rate of return can be found by means of a graph, as shown on the next page. The horizontal axis of the graph is the cost of capital percentage; the vertical axis shows the net present value – both positive and negative amounts.

Two points have been plotted on the graph:

* a low cost of capital percentage which gives a positive net present value figure (here £4,913 positive, at 10%, taken from the table above)

* a high cost of capital percentage which gives a negative net present value figure (here £758 negative, at 24%, taken from the table above)

The two points have been joined in a straight line, and then the internal rate of return can be read from the horizontal axis. Here the graph shows that IRR is approximately 22%.

Technical note: Whilst the graph shows a straight line, if more than two points were plotted, the line would be slightly curved and to the left of that shown. This has the effect of very slightly reducing the reading of internal rate of return from the graph: in practice the difference is unlikely to affect investment appraisal decisions.

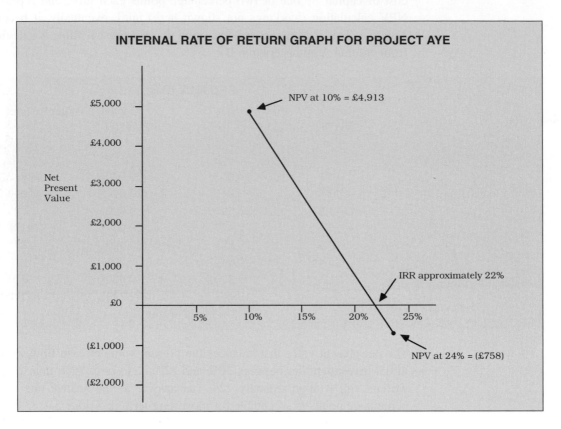

INTERNAL RATE OF RETURN GRAPH FOR PROJECT AYE

NPV at 10% = £4,913

IRR approximately 22%

NPV at 24% = (£758)

conclusion

Returning to the two projects, Aye and Bee, the IRR for Aye is approximately 22%. Although not shown here, the calculations for Bee are found to be approximately 20%. Thus, Aye gives a higher IRR and is the preferred capital investment. The reason for this is that Aye requires a lower capital expenditure than Bee, and the timing of its cash flows is weighted towards the earlier years.

The decision-making criteria when using IRR is to:

• accept the higher IRR, where there is a choice between different capital investments

• accept projects with an IRR greater than either the cost of borrowing (the cost of capital), or the rate of return specified by the business or organisation

Thus, while IRR can be compared between two (or more) different capital investments, it can also be applied to cost of capital. In the example we have followed in this chapter, the cost of capital is 10%. The organisation could have gone ahead with either investment. However, if the cost of capital had been 20%, project Bee would have been rejected and Project Aye accepted – although the 2% margin above the cost of capital is very tight.

OTHER CONSIDERATIONS

As well as the numerical techniques that can be used for capital investment appraisal, an organisation must consider a number of other factors before making the final decision. These include:

- *Total implications*. The effect of the project on the organisation as a whole will include implications for
    - sales, with possible increases in output
    - output, with changes in techniques, eg a switch from labour-intensive to machine-intensive output
    - staff, with possible redundancies, training needs, pay structure
    - working capital required for the project
    - needs, such as premises, transport, materials

- *Cost of finance*. Possible changes in the cost of capital will have a direct effect on the viability of the project. For example, an increase in the general level of interest rates will reduce the project's overall profitability. Projects are often financed through fixed interest rate loans, or through hire purchase and leasing, thus establishing some part of the finance at fixed rates; however, invariably working capital is at variable rates.

- *Taxation considerations*. The project will include the implications of both tax allowances and charges. However, a change in the level of taxation – including 'one-off' charges – will affect the viability of the project.

- *Forecasting techniques*. These can be used to answer 'what if?' questions: for example, "what if sales increase by 25 per cent?" or "what if materials costs fall by 5 per cent?" In this way, a business or organisation can use *sensitivity analysis* to see how the project is affected by changes to any of the data used in the appraisal.

REPORTING DECISIONS

As we saw in the last chapter, with decision-making the costing information has to be reported to managers, or other appropriate people, in a clear and concise way. The information should include recommendations which are supported by well-presented reasoning. Please refer back to pages 208-209 for the methods of presentation and the format of reports.

To conclude, we include a written report addressed to the General Manager on Projects Aye and Bee, which we have looked at in this chapter. The company has the following criteria: "projects must have a payback period not exceeding two-and-a-half years, and must have a positive net present value at a 10 per cent rate of return."

REPORT

To:	General Manager
From:	Accounts Assistant
Date:	Today

Projects Aye and Bee

Introduction

• You asked me to apply capital investment appraisal methods to these two projects.

• In my appraisal, I have used the cash inflows and outflows that you supplied.

Report

• Please refer to the calculation sheet *(tutorial note: see page 251 and pages 254-255).*

• Both projects are acceptable from a financial viewpoint because they each return a positive net present value (NPV) at a discount rate of 10%, as follows: Project Aye £4,913; Project B £7,094. These calculations assume that net cash inflows occur at the end of each year.

• The payback periods are: Project Aye, 2 years; Project B, 3 years.

• The internal rates of return (IRR) for the projects are: Project Aye, 22%; Project B, 20%. Both of these are well above the required rate of return of 10 per cent.

Conclusion

• Project A meets both the company requirements of payback within two-and-a-half years, and a positive NPV at a 10 per cent rate of return. It also has a higher IRR than Project B.

• Project B does not meet the payback requirement, but does have a positive NPV at a 10 per cent rate of return. It has a lower IRR than Project A.

- Project A has a lower NPV than Project B – this is because of a lower initial cost. This imbalance of initial cost is neutralised by the IRR calculation, which shows Project A to be superior.

- On balance, Project A is recommended:

  - lower initial cost

  - high cash inflows in the first two years

  - quick payback

  - positive NPV

  - higher IRR in relation to the company's required rate of return

---

Chapter Summary	
	• Capital investment appraisal uses a number of methods to help in management decision-making.
	• The main methods are payback period and discounted cash flow.
	• Businesses often use a combination of appraisal methods before making long-term decisions about major projects.
	• Internal rate of return (also known as DCF yield) is used to rank projects, while still applying the principles of discounted cash flow.
	• Before authorising a capital project, other considerations include:
	– total implications for the organisation
	– cost of finance, and effect of changes
	– taxation
	– forecasting techniques to answer 'what if?' questions

Key Terms		
	capital investment appraisal	enables a business or organisation to make long-term decisions whether or not to invest in a particular capital investment project and, where there are alternatives, to help to decide in which to invest
	cost of capital	The percentage cost of financing an investment – either the rate of return that the business expects on its money, or the rate of interest it has to pay when borrowing
	payback period	time period for the initial outlay to be repaid by the net cash inflow
	discounted cash flow	capital investment appraisal technique that uses cash flows and recognises the time value of money

net present value (NPV) the value of cash outflows and inflows for a project discounted to present-day amounts

internal rate of return (IRR) the rate of return at which the net present value of cash inflows equals the cost of the initial investment

Student Activities

TABLE OF DISCOUNTED CASH FLOW FACTORS

Cost of capital/ rate of return	10%	12%	14%	16%	18%	20%	22%	24%
Year 1	0.909	0.893	0.877	0.862	0.847	0.833	0.820	0.806
Year 2	0.826	0.797	0.769	0.743	0.718	0.694	0.672	0.650
Year 3	0.751	0.712	0.675	0.641	0.609	0.579	0.551	0.524
Year 4	0.683	0.636	0.592	0.552	0.516	0.482	0.451	0.423
Year 5	0.621	0.567	0.519	0.476	0.437	0.402	0.370	0.341
Year 6	0.564	0.507	0.456	0.410	0.370	0.335	0.303	0.275

Tutorial note: In Skills Tests and Examinations you will always be given the appropriate factors.

9.1 Robert Smith is considering two major capital investment projects for his business. Only one project can be chosen and the following information is available:

	Project Exe	Project Wye
	£	£
Initial cost at the beginning of the project	80,000	100,000
Net cash inflows, year: 1	40,000	20,000
2	40,000	30,000
3	20,000	50,000
4	10,000	50,000
5	10,000	40,000

The initial cost occurs at the beginning of the project and you may assume that the net cash inflows will arise at the end of each year. Smith requires an annual rate of return of 12 per cent. Neither project will have any residual value at the end of five years.

To help Robert Smith make his decision, as accounts assistant you are to:

- produce numerical assessments of the two projects based on the following capital investment appraisal methods:

  (a) the payback period

  (b) the net present value

- write a report to Robert Smith on the relative merits of the project appraisal methods, and advise him which capital Investment, if either, should be undertaken.

9.2 Sesame Shoes Limited manufactures shoes at its factory in Wyvern. The company requires an annual rate of return of 10% on any new project. The Managing Director has asked you to appraise the financial effects of developing a new range of shoes. You are given the following information relating to this project.

	Year 0 £000	Year 1 £000	Year 2 £000	Year 3 £000	Year 4 £000	Year 5 £000
Design costs	–	95	–	–	–	–
Sales revenue	–	–	60	80	100	50
Variable costs	–	–	30	40	50	25
10% Present value factor	1.000	0.909	0.826	0.751	0.683	0.621

Task 1

Calculate for the new project:

(a) the payback period

(b) the net present value

Task 2

A few days after submitting your calculations to the Managing Director, she says to you:

"I have calculated the internal rate of return on the new project to be almost 20 per cent. What I don't understand is whether this is good or bad in relation to the 10 per cent return we require on new projects."

Explain the significance of the internal rate of return in relation to the return required on new projects. (There is no need to show how IRR is calculated.)

9.3 You are an accounts assistant at Durning Foods Limited. The company produces ready meals which are sold in supermarkets and convenience stores. You have just received the following memorandum from the general manager:

MEMORANDUM

To: Accounts Assistant

From: General Manager

Date: 10 November 2004

Purchase of delivery vehicles

We are considering the purchase and operation of our own fleet of delivery vehicles at the end of this year.

The distribution manager tells me that we will be able to cancel our current delivery contract and, as a result, there will be cash savings of £28,300 each year from 2005 onwards, after taking account of the vehicle operating costs.

The vehicles will cost us £80,000 and will have a resale value of £10,000 when they are sold at the end of 2008.

Please appraise this proposal from a financial viewpoint. I need to know the payback period and the net present value. As you know, the maximum required payback period is three years and, for net present value, we require a return of 12 per cent.

Task 1

Use the working paper on the next page to calculate the net present value and the payback period of the proposed investment. Ignore inflation and calculate all money amounts to the nearest £.

Task 2

Write a report, dated 12 November 2004, to the General Manager evaluating the proposal from a financial viewpoint. State any assumptions you have made in your analysis. (Use a copy of the report form in the Appendix.)

DURNING FOODS LIMITED

Working paper for the financial appraisal of purchase of delivery vehicles

DISCOUNTED CASH FLOW

Year	Cash Flow	Discount Factor at 12%	Discounted Cash Flow
	£		£
2004	_____	1.000	_____
2005	_____	0.893	_____
2006	_____	0.797	_____
2007	_____	0.712	_____
2008	_____	0.636	_____
Net Present Value (NPV)			_____

PAYBACK PERIOD

Year	Cash Flow	Cumulative Cash Flow
	£	£
2004	_____	_____
2005	_____	_____
2006	_____	_____
2007	_____	_____
2008	_____	_____
Payback period =	_____	

9.4 The Wyvern Bike Company is planning to introduce a new range of bikes in addition to its existing range. The company requires an annual rate of return of 12 per cent on any new project. The Managing Director has asked you, the accounts assistant, to appraise the financial effects of introducing the new range. You are given the following information relating to this project (see next page).

	Year 0 £000	Year 1 £000	Year 2 £000	Year 3 £000	Year 4 £000	Year 5 £000
Development costs	40	60	–	–	–	–
Sales revenue	–	–	75	90	150	100
Variable costs	–	–	30	36	60	40
12% Present value factor	1.000	0.893	0.797	0.712	0.636	0.567

Task 1

Calculate for the new project:

(a)   the payback period

(b)   the net present value

Task 2

Use the data from Task 1 to prepare a report to the Managing Director on the new bike project. Your report should be based on the format shown in this chapter and will:

(a)   identify *two* additional items of information relevant to appraising this project

(b)   make a recommendation to accept or reject the project based on its net present value

9.5   Ken Jones needs some equipment for his printing firm. He has to choose between the following methods of acquisition:

•   purchase of the equipment for cash

•   purchase under a hire purchase contract, involving an initial deposit and two annual payments

•   leasing the equipment

The following information is available:

– cash price of equipment	£10,000
– period of use in Jones' firm	5 years
– scrap value at end of use	£1,000
– initial deposit under hire purchase contract	£4,000
– two annual hire purchase payments due at end of first year and end of second year	£4,000 each
– leasing equipment, five annual hire charge payments due at end of each year	£2,500 each

Ken Jones requires a rate of return over the five year period of 10 per cent per annum.

To assist Ken Jones make his decision, you are asked to:

•   produce numerical appraisals of the three methods of acquisition using the net present value method

•   advise Ken Jones of the best method of acquisition

Unit 7

Preparing reports and returns

In this chapter we take a practical look at the types of financial and non-financial information used by management. We look at:

- *external information, such as government statistics*
- *the different types of internal financial information – related to costs and revenue – that will be recorded*
- *non-financial internal information such as the number of units of output*
- *the different types of organisations and their structure*
- *the need for financial information at different levels within the organisation*

In the next chapter we examine the way in which performance – eg profitability – can be measured by the use of performance indicators.

NVQ PERFORMANCE CRITERIA COVERED

unit 7: PREPARING REPORTS AND RETURNS

element 7.1

prepare and present periodic performance reports

A   consolidate information derived from different units of the organisation into the appropriate form

B   reconcile information derived from different information systems within the organisation

THE NEED FOR INFORMATION

There are many different types of organisation that an accountant may deal with, ranging from the sole trader business to the public limited company or major charity.   People who run organisations need a wide variety of information – financial data and other forms of information – in order to make management decisions. Information can either be *external* or *internal.*

EXTERNAL INFORMATION

External information includes:

• the way individual competitors are performing

• the way the industry is performing

• the way the economy is performing

• what is required by legislation

This type of information can be gathered by studying Government statistics (economic reports), trade and Chamber of Commerce publications and by subscribing to commercially available industry and company reports.

government statistics

Government statistical publications, available in reference libraries and on websites such as www.statistics.gov.uk, can be very useful to businesses in the planning process, showing patterns of change in population, income, and economic well-being in the UK. These publications include:

Social Trends   This book of statistics presents a interesting picture of the UK's social make-up, providing details about population, income, transport and leisure interests.

Economic Trends This provides data about the economic performance within the UK

Censuses   The government regularly publishes data relating to population and production in the regions.

Other useful publications include the *Annual Abstract of Statistics, Monthly Digest of Statistics, Business Monitor, National Income Statistics, Import and Export Statistics.*

commercial organisations and Trade Associations

Much useful information can be gathered from organisations which cater for the needs of businesses and particular trades and professions. These include the Confederation of British Industry (CBI), Chambers of Commerce – local and national, Business Clubs and Trade Associations.

the relevance of external statistics

You may well ask what relevance these publications have for Accounting Technicians. Your studies do not require you to be familiar with the details of all these sources, but their relevance is the point that no business can afford to 'bury its head in the sand' – an awareness of external information will enable it to make sensible decisions. For example, the fact that people have more leisure time than previously and that there are more retired people with money to spend than ever before means that a business developing up-market holidays is likely to be profitable – because the statistics are in its favour.

Another area in which these statistics are relevant is in their compilation. As we will see in Chapter 15 you may be required to provide financial and other information to government agencies and other bodies that are collecting data.

INTERNAL INFORMATION

Internal information can be financial or non-financial.

Financial internal information required by an organisation includes:

- *costs* – eg wages, the price of supplies, overheads, and
- *revenues* – the sales of products and services

Non-financial information includes items such as units of output, the numbers of employees and the number of items in stock.

The information collected may well cover a wide time period:

- *past* performance – eg previous years' costs and revenues
- *present* performance – up-to-date reports
- *future* performance – eg what is forecast to happen in the next 12 months

The way this information is gathered and presented forms the material for the remainder of this book. An organisation which successfully gathers and summarises this information is in a position to make informed decisions.

The problem is that some organisations are in a better position to carry out this process than others. Organisations with 'flat' structures (these are often the smaller organisations) have fewer problems with communication than the 'hierarchical' organisations which have more levels through which the information has to pass.

ORGANISATIONAL STRUCTURES

flat organisational structure

The sole trader business will have a 'flat' organisational structure. The example shown below shows the simple structure of a sole trader shop which employs four assistants: three in the shop and one in the stock room.

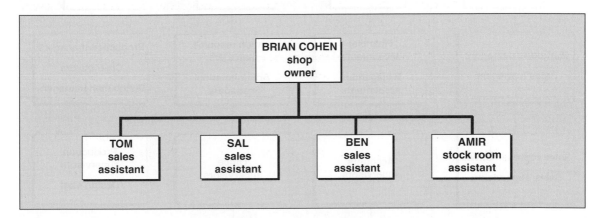

The information that the owner needs will be simple and readily available: sales figures from the shop tills and stock levels from the stockroom. Financial control is straightforward: sales can be monitored easily and decisions about what to stock and what not to stock taken on a day-to-day basis. Flat structures are also typical of modern larger organisations which have had layers of middle management 'stripped out'.

hierarchical organisational structure

Many organisations, however, are far more complex in structure, and reporting has to take place through a series of different levels. Such an organisation has a *hierarchical* structure such as the one illustrated on the next page. This is a traditional structure, typified by a limited company business. It is also known as a *pyramid* or *tall* structure. The main features of this type of structure are:

- a hierarchy – a series of levels, each responsible to and controlled by the level above

- as you move up the levels, the number of people or units decreases – hence the 'pyramid' effect

- at the top of the pyramid is the managing director (or equivalent) who is ultimately responsible for all decision-making, including financial decisions based on information passed up through the company

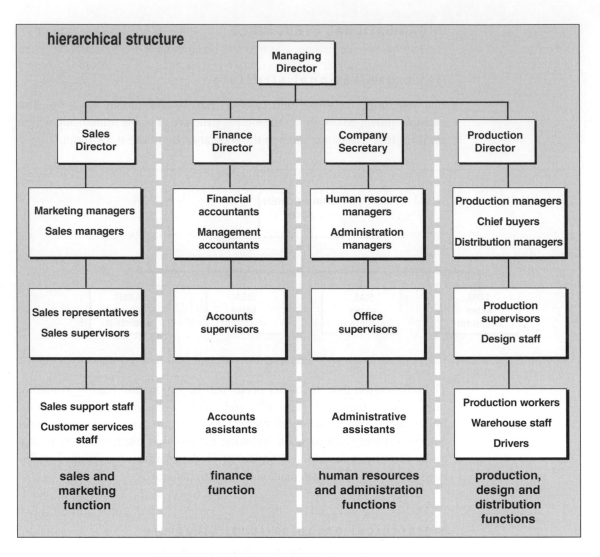

hierarchical structure

(Managing Director → Sales Director, Finance Director, Company Secretary, Production Director)

- **Sales Director**
  - Marketing managers / Sales managers
  - Sales representatives / Sales supervisors
  - Sales support staff / Customer services staff
  - **sales and marketing function**

- **Finance Director**
  - Financial accountants / Management accountants
  - Accounts supervisors
  - Accounts assistants
  - **finance function**

- **Company Secretary**
  - Human resource managers / Administration managers
  - Office supervisors
  - Administrative assistants
  - **human resources and administration functions**

- **Production Director**
  - Production managers / Chief buyers / Distribution managers
  - Production supervisors / Design staff
  - Production workers / Warehouse staff / Drivers
  - **production, design and distribution functions**

REPORTING INFORMATION

reporting at different levels

It should be noted at this point that the *amount* of detail reported at each level varies according to the *needs* of the person for whom the report is prepared. *Labour cost*, for example, is often a significant item. What type of reporting is necessary at the different levels of a manufacturing business?

- *production-line workers* will complete time sheets or clock cards
- *line management* will obtain labour costings for various product areas and compare against budget and take decisions relating to efficiency and work practices

- *senior management* will obtain an overall report of the labour cost of all the areas of the business and take strategic decisions – what products to develop, what products to scrap, which departments to expand and where to look for redundancies

In other words, as the reporting process goes up through the hierarchy (the management levels), there is *less depth of detail at each level* but more of an overall picture of what is going on in the organisation.

what is recorded and reported?

So far we have referred to labour hours in a manufacturing business, but it is important to appreciate that the recording and reporting process is common to all organisations and covers a wide variety of *costs* and *revenues* and other statistics. The table on the next page shows in more detail what might be recorded and used in the reporting process in manufacturing and service industries. You will see that in addition to costs and revenues other factors such as floor area and occupancy rates are recorded in order to provide information about the efficiency and profitability of the organisation.

quality reporting

It is obvious that if the reporting process is to be valid and efficient, the data brought together must be in a *appropriate* format. It must:

- *be consistent* – the same forms and counting systems must be used throughout the organisation; for example there is no point in comparing Shop A and Shop B if floor areas are measured in square metres and square feet respectively

- *relate to the same time period* – if the reporting period is a week, it must be the same week and all data must cover the same hours

- *be reported promptly* – if data is late in coming in, it may miss the deadline for a report; this may invalidate the whole process

- *be accurate* – if inaccurate information is provided, not only will the reporting process be flawed but a wrong decision may result; as an extreme example management might decide to discontinue a product

reconciling information from different sources

The internal checking procedures within an organisation should ensure that information collected centrally for reporting purposes should be reconciled. For example:

- the total labour hours recorded for all employees on the payroll analysis should agree with the total of the hours charged out to the departments

- the total unit sales of a chain of shops – normally recorded on the shops' electronic tills – should agree with the records of stock movements

A MANUFACTURER

- sales revenue from each product

- the cost of producing each product

- administration and finance costs

- the number of units of each product manufactured

These statistics enable the management to calculate the cost and the profitability of manufacturing each product.

A SUPERMARKET CHAIN

- the sales of each shop

- the staffing and overhead cost of each shop

- the selling area of each shop (square metres)

- the number of customers per shop

These statistics enable the management to calculate how busy each shop is, how much customers spend and how profitable each shop is per square metre.

A GROUP OF HOTELS

- the revenue from each hotel

- the running costs of each hotel

- the number of rooms per hotel

- the number of rooms occupied each night

These statistics enable the management to calculate how full each hotel is, and how profitable it is.

A HOSPITAL TRUST

- the revenue from each hospital

- the running costs of each hospital

- the number of beds per hospital

- the number of patients treated

These statistics enable the management to calculate the efficiency and profitability of each hospital.

manufacturing and service industries: reporting of information

- Organisations need accurate information to help them make management decisions. This information can be internal or externally sourced. It can relate to past, present or future time periods.

- Externally-sourced information includes data from government published statistics, Chambers of Commerce and Trade Associations.

- Internal financial information that will be particularly useful involves both revenues and costs – money in and money out.

- Non-financial information which will be used includes items such as: units produced, hours worked, number of employees, floor areas.

- The ability for information to pass within an organisation will depend to some extent on its structure; traditionally, communication has been better in a 'flat' structure than in a hierarchical structure with a number of management levels.

- The amount of detail in reporting will vary according to the level for which the report is prepared: a senior management report will comprise an overall picture with summarised information; a lower level report will contain more operational detail and less of a 'global' picture.

- Valid reported information must be consistent, prompt, accurate and relate to a specific time period.

- Information gathered within an organisation must be reconciled with the internal records of the organisation in order to ensure that it is accurate and consistent.

financial information	information which is measured in money terms, eg revenues and costs
non-financial information	information which is not measured in money terms but relates to other areas of business activity such as the level of output and the number of employees
flat structure	an organisational structure which has few 'layers' of management – it is typical of a small business or a modern organisation which has had its middle layers 'stripped out'
hierarchical structure	an organisational structure which has a number of different layers of management through which communication and information has to pass

Student Activities

10.1 (a)   State four reasons why an organisation needs external information.

(b)   What are the main *sources* of external statistics?

(c)   Why should *Social Trends* prove useful?

10.2 What are the *two* main types of internal financial data used in the information gathering process of an organisation?

10.3 The flow of information through a hierarchical structure is likely to be more efficient than the flow through a flat structure.

True or false? Give reasons for your answer.

10.4 What data is likely to be included in

(a)   a labour performance report for a supervisor?

(b)   a labour performance report presented to a managing director?

Explain the reasons why the two reports are likely to be different.

10.5 What types of internal information are likely to be used in performance reports for the following organisations:

(a)   a hospital

(b)   a firm of accountants

(c)   a manufacturer of computer games

(d)   a company owning a gym in three different towns

Important note to students

The remaining two Activities in this chapter are designed to help you develop your analytical and communication skills. An important requirement of this Unit is the analysis of data and writing of a Report. These are skills that need constant practice, which should start now.

Be flexible! These remaining Activities do not necessarily have to be carried out individually. You will often find that carrying out Activities in small groups can be very helpful and certainly add to the interest of the subject.

10.6 Many sources of external information can now be found on the internet. Try www.statistics.gov.uk to start with. The screen shown below was taken from this site.

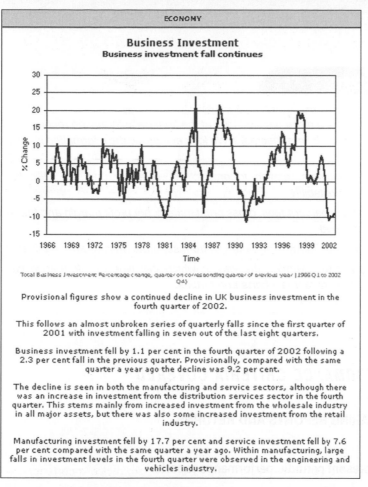

Someone who is thinking of investing money in the business sector is worried about the trends in the economy. Write two paragraphs in simple plain English, each answering a question:

(a) the first question is 'What is the trend in business investment shown in the above report?'

(b) the second question is 'What type of business do you think I ought to invest in?'

10.7 Locate a short report about the performance of a well-known company or organisation, eg after the announcement of financial results. Possible sources include the financial press or the company's or organisation's website (look on the site for 'press releases' or 'News' items).

Individually, or in small groups, discuss the main points of the article, and note them down in simple terms.

Then individually write (or word process) a paragraph or two in plain simple English, stating what the article has said. If you are working in a group compare and discuss the text you have produced. Is it in plain English? Does it cover all the main points? Has this exercise helped?

In this chapter we take a more detailed look at the financial information recorded within organisations and used by management. We look at the way the information is reported in the form of:

- performance indicators relating to productivity, cost per unit, the utilisation of resources and profitability

- specific ratios and percentages: gross profit margin, net profit margin and the return on capital employed

- the consolidation of information received from separate units of an organisation

In the next chapter we examine the way in which this type of information can be presented in the form of tables, charts and graphs.

NVQ PERFORMANCE CRITERIA COVERED

unit 7: PREPARING REPORTS AND RETURNS

element 7.1

prepare and present periodic performance reports

A   consolidate information derived from different units of the organisation into the appropriate form

B   reconcile information derived from different information systems within the organisation

D   account for transactions between separate units of the organisation in accordance with the organisation's procedures

E   calculate ratios and performance indicators in accordance with the organisation's procedures

PERFORMANCE INDICATORS

In simple terms a *performance indicator* is a method of expressing by way of a formula how well a business is performing in certain areas:

- *productivity* – how well it is using its available resources
- *cost per unit* – how much it costs to produce each item it makes
- *resource utilisation* – how well it is making use of its workforce and equipment
- *profitability* – how great a return it is making on its sales and capital employed

Remember that more businesses are now in the service sector than in manufacturing: the terms 'product' or 'item sold' apply equally to holidays, audits carried out, sessions in the gym, as to manufactured goods such as cars and packets of crisps.

Before we explain these performance indicators in more detail, we will first explain *percentages,* as they are often used – and not always understood.

USING PERCENTAGES

a quantity as a percentage of another quantity

A percentage is a proportion of a whole where the whole equates to the number 100 as a basis for comparison.

If you eat half a pizza you have eaten 50% because the whole pizza is equated to 100 and the part you have eaten is 50 'parts' of that 100.

When dealing with numbers you will often need to make comparisons. A *fraction* is often the starting point. For example there may be two accounting classes studying at the same level. One class (Class A) has 20 students and the other (Class B) has 16 students. The classes could be analysed as follows:

	Class A	Class B
students	20	16
females	12	8
students who pass	18	12

If you ask what proportion of students in each class are female, you could use a fraction. The numbers used in the fraction show that proportion:

$$\text{Class A: } \frac{12}{20} \qquad\qquad \text{Class B: } \frac{8}{16}$$

But this still does not give you a clear comparison of the proportion of females in each class. You can achieve this by turning each fraction into a percentage which will relate both classes to a base number 100:

$$\text{percentage} = \frac{\text{top number in the fraction x 100}}{\text{bottom number in the fraction}}$$

This works out as:

Class A:

$$\frac{12 \times 100}{20} = 60\%$$

Class B:

$$\frac{8 \times 100}{16} = 50\%$$

The situation is now clear: Class A is 60% female, Class B is 50% female.

If you now turn again to the table on the previous page, you will be able to work out the percentage pass rate of each class:

Class A: $\frac{18}{20}$ students pass
student total

Class B: $\frac{12}{16}$ students pass
student total

You can then convert this to a percentage:

Class A:

$$\frac{18 \times 100}{20} = 90\%$$

Class B:

$$\frac{12 \times 100}{16} = 75\%$$

The next question, of course, is whether there is any connection between the number of females in the class and the pass rate!

We will now look at some more formulas using percentages.

finding a percentage of an amount

Suppose that you earn £19,500 a year and are given a 5% pay rise. What extra money will you be awarded (ignoring what the tax man will take)?

The formula for working out a percentage of an amount is:

$$\frac{\text{amount x percentage}}{100}$$

The calculation is:

$$\frac{£19,500 \times 5}{100} = £975 \text{ (before tax!)}$$

This formula is useful for calculating VAT or interest. You can, of course, use your percentage button on your calculator to perform this calculation.

increasing an amount by a given percentage

Suppose that your sales figures for this year are £925,000. Your finance director wants to see an 8% increase in sales next year. What will your sales have to be next year to meet this target?

The formula for this calculation is:

$$\frac{\text{amount} \times (100 \ + \ \text{percentage increase})}{100}$$

The calculation is: $\dfrac{£925,000 \times (100 + 8)}{100} = £999,000 \text{ sales}$

An easy way of doing this is £925,000 × 1.08 = £999,000 sales

decreasing an amount by a given percentage

The formula here is similar to the one above. Suppose the finance director also wants to cut the annual wages bill of £450,000 by 5%. The formula is:

$$\frac{\text{amount} \times (100 \ - \ \text{percentage decrease})}{100}$$

The calculation is: $\dfrac{£450,000 \times (100 - 5)}{100} = £427,500 \text{ wages bill}$

An easy way of doing this is £450,000 × 0.95 = £427,500.

We will now look in detail at performance indicators, a number of which are expressed as percentages.

PRODUCTIVITY

If you say that you have had a 'productive' day you mean that you have achieved a great deal despite all the circumstances. For a business or organisation which manufactures a product or provides a service 'productivity' measures

the level of output (goods manufactured or services provided) in relation to the cost of producing the product or service

labour productivity

Labour productivity is normally measured by dividing the output (the number of items produced or services provided) over a given period (eg week, year) by the number of employees. Take, for example, a travel agency business which employs 4 staff and aims to arrange 500 holidays in a week.

The productivity (the output per employee per* week) is calculated as follows:

$$\text{output per* employee} = \frac{\text{output (500 holidays)}}{\text{number of employees (4)}} = \frac{500}{4} = 125$$

*Note here the use of the word 'per' which compares the output to something else such a time value – in the same way that one refers to 'kilometres per hour' for speed or 'units per week' for car production.

It is common practice to compare *actual* output against the benchmark of *expected* output. For example, the travel agency may have set 125 holidays per week as the expected level of productivity per employee, but over a four week period with 4 staff it achieves the results shown below. The right-hand column shows productivity per employee.

period	holidays booked	productivity
Week 1	520	130
Week 2	600	150
Week 3	440	110
Week 4	580	145

A further method of measuring labour productivity, which is useful when there is a variety of products and a fluctuating number of employees is to compare output in money terms (eg the sales figure) and the number of hours worked over a given period:

$$\text{labour productivity (sales per hour)} \quad = \quad \frac{\text{output (£) over a given period}}{\text{hours worked over a given period}}$$

efficiency

The efficiency of an organisation – expressed as a percentage – is calculated by comparing actual output (in units) with expected (standard) output:

$$\text{efficiency \%} \quad = \quad \frac{\text{actual output (units)} \ \times \ 100}{\text{expected/standard output (units)}}$$

In the case of the travel agency on the previous page, the efficiency percentage in week 1 in which 520 holidays have been booked (against the expected 500) is:

$$\text{efficiency \%} \quad = \quad \frac{520 \text{ (actual output)} \ \times \ 100}{500 \text{ (expected output)}} \quad = \quad 104\%$$

It is then a simple calculator operation (dividing actual output by expected output) to see that the efficiency in the other weeks was: 120% in week 2, 88% in week 3 and 116% in week 4.

other productivity measures

Organisations often find it useful to compare output over a given period with factors other than labour. Examples in the manufacturing sector include:

machine productivity   = $\dfrac{\text{sales (£) over a given period}}{\text{machine hours for the period}}$

capital productivity   = $\dfrac{\text{sales (£) over a given period}}{\text{capital employed (see page 289)}}$

Examples in the services industries include:

in a supermarket (sales per employee): $\dfrac{\text{sales (£) over a given period}}{\text{employees}}$

at a college (contact hours per lecturer): $\dfrac{\text{total student contact hours}}{\text{lecturers employed}}$

cost per unit

Another performance indicator is the cost per unit.

cost per unit is the cost of producing each unit

This is calculated using the formula

cost per unit   = $\dfrac{\text{cost of production over a given period}}{\text{number of units produced over a given period}}$

This performance indicator provides useful information because costs can be compared over different time periods. It must be remembered that the 'unit' ('cost unit') referred to can be produced by a service industry as well as in a manufacturing process. Costs can be worked out for:

'producer'	*unit*
BMW	car produced
Kelloggs	packet of cereal produced
police force	offence dealt with
fire service	incident dealt with

Further detail can be extracted by relating the number of units produced to different cost classifications of cost, eg advertising cost per unit, labour cost per unit, distribution cost per unit. These all assist management in monitoring performance and identifying problem areas.

resource utilisation

The major resources of any organisation – whether in the manufacturing or in the services sector – are *labour* and *equipment.* The ideally efficient organisation will ensure that its employees and its equipment are working 'flat out' all the time. Resource utilisation in this case will obviously be 100% and there is no *idle time* or *slack time*:

• *idle time* – hours in the working day spent by employees *not* working, not through any fault of their own, but because of factors such as computer/machine breakdown, power cuts, or simply because the work in hand is finished and no other task has been allocated

• *slack time* – hours in the working day during which machinery and equipment is not in productive use, eg a printing press switched off because there are no books or catalogues to print

Resource utilisation – for labour and for equipment – can be measured as a percentage. Clearly the higher the percentage, the better:

$$\text{resource utilisation \%} = \frac{\text{actual hours worked} \times 100}{\text{hours available for working}}$$

Monitoring of resource utilisation will highlight any problem areas and enable management to take decisions, eg to reduce the contracted hours of the workforce, to lay off staff, to sell or replace machinery. Of course the management also has a major responsibility in operations management to plan for efficient working of staff and machine utilisation.

profitability

One of the principal objectives of any business is to make a profit which will benefit the owners, employees and customers. This objective also extends to other organisations such as charities and public sector services, but the motives are different – a charity helps a good cause and a public service aims to be efficient, given the resources that are available.

There are a number of ways of measuring profit performance, normally expressed as *percentages,* but traditionally and perhaps misleadingly called *ratios.* We will deal with some of these in the next section. Before examining the ways in which profit is measured it is important to appreciate the way in which profit is *calculated.* As you will know from your studies, a business (or its accountants) will normally draw up a *profit and loss account* from the accounting records. Now study the notes and refer to the profit and loss account illustrated on the next page.

sales	this figure represents the sales for the period (often a year); it may be sales of a product or it may be sales of a service (eg fees for a management consultant)
cost of sales	this figure is what it has cost the business to acquire what has *actually been sold* during the period, eg raw materials for a manufacturer or stock bought from wholesalers in the case of a shop (cost of sales is also often known as 'cost of goods sold')
gross profit	*sales minus cost of sales* – this gives an indicator of the 'mark-up' of a business, eg a shop buying jeans in at £15 a pair and selling them at £35 – the gross profit on the jeans will be £20, ie £35 minus £15
overheads	these are expenses which have to be paid, such as insurance, advertising, rates, power bills; they are not normally directly related to the level of sales; they are deducted from gross profit
net profit	*gross profit minus overheads* – this is essentially sales minus all costs, and represents the final profit figure the business has achieved for the period

---

PROFIT AND LOSS ACCOUNT

		£	£
	Sales		600,000
less	**Cost of sales**		360,000
equals	**Gross profit**		240,000
less	**Overheads**:		
	Administration/labour	85,000	
	Selling and distribution	50,000	
	Finance costs	15,000	
			150,000
equals	**Net profit**		90,000

RATIO ANALYSIS

We will now explain the performance indicators relating to profitability:

- gross profit margin
- net profit margin
- return on capital employed

As noted earlier, these indicators are often known as accounting *ratios:* although they express a relationship between two figures, they are often quoted as *percentages.*

gross profit margin

gross profit margin %   = $\dfrac{\text{gross profit} \times 100}{\text{sales}}$

This percentage shows the proporetion of gross profit (sales less cost of sales) to the sales figure for the period. In the example profit and loss account shown on the previous page the calculation is:

gross profit margin %   = $\dfrac{£240{,}000 \times 100}{£600{,}000}$ = 40%

In other words, for every £100 of sales, gross profit is £40. An organisation should expect to see this percentage stay fairly constant from year-to-year, and to be similar to the gross profit margin of other organisations in the same line of business. Gross profit margins in different types of business will vary widely: a jeweller will have a high margin and a food supermarket a low margin, reflecting the length of time it takes to sell the stock.

a note on mark-up and margin

In your study of incomplete records you will encounter the use of *mark-up* and *margin* – these sometimes cause confusion. It is the *margin* which is generally used in ratio analysis. Using the profit and loss account on page 285:

the *margin* is based (as seen above) on the selling price:

$\dfrac{\text{gross profit} \times 100}{\text{sales}}$ = $\dfrac{£240{,}000 \times 100}{£600{,}000}$ =   40%

the *mark-up* is based on cost price (cost of sales):

$\dfrac{\text{gross profit} \times 100}{\text{cost of sales}}$ = $\dfrac{£240{,}000 \times 100}{£360{,}000}$ =   67%

net profit margin

In the same way, *net profit margin* relates net profit to sales.

net profit margin % $\quad = \quad \dfrac{\text{net profit} \times 100}{\text{sales}}$

This percentage relates net profit (gross profit less overheads) to the sales figure for the period. In the example profit and loss account shown on the previous page the calculation is:

net profit margin % $\quad = \quad \dfrac{\text{£90,000} \times 100}{\text{£600,000}} = 15\%$

The business is making £15 overall profit on every £100 of sales. Ideally an organisation would hope to see this percentage increase from year-to-year, as this profit figure represents funds which can be used in expanding the business. If the percentage falls over time the management will be concerned: sales may be falling or expenses may be increasing (or both).

return on capital employed (ROCE)

return on capital employed % $\quad = \quad \dfrac{\text{net profit} \times 100}{\text{capital}}$

Here 'capital' is the investment in the business made by the owner(s) plus profits. Capital is not found in the profit and loss account but at the bottom of the balance sheet – the statement of what the business owns and owes. The return on capital employed is exactly what it says it is – it is the percentage return made on the owner's investment.

This ratio involves a closer look at the balance sheet of a business. An example of a sole trader balance sheet is shown on the next page. It is essentially an equation based on a 'snapshot' of a business at a particular moment in time:

assets (items owned by the business) – shown in the top half

minus

liabilities (items owed by the business) – shown half-way down

equals

capital (capital and profit) – shown at the bottom

Net assets are total assets less total liabilities. They are equal to the owner's stake or investment in the business.

SOLE TRADER BALANCE SHEET

Fixed assets

Premises		250,000
Machinery		18,000
Vehicle		15,000
		283,000

assets

Current assets

Stock	24,000	
Debtors	15,000	
Bank	13,500	
	52,500	

less

Less **Current liabilities**

Creditors	25,500	
Working capital		27,000
		310,000

liabilities

Less **Long-term liabilities**

Bank loan		10,000
NET ASSETS		300,000

equals

FINANCED BY

Capital		240,000
Add Profit		90,000
Less drawings		30,000
		300,000

capital

balance sheet format

definitions of return on capital employed

It must be stressed that the *return on capital employed* formula already quoted (and shown below) is not the only way of calculating return on capital employed. The terms 'return' and 'capital employed' may mean different things to different types of business. For example, in some circumstances, the term 'capital employed' can include long-term liabilities such as fixed bank loans (see the balance sheet illustrated on the previous page).

The sole trader business shown here is the simplest form of business; a limited company, on the other hand, may have a complex capital structure made up of different types of shares and other forms of funding; the profit and loss account, too, will be more complex. These, however, are subject areas covered in NVQ Level 4 Accounting, and you do not need to study them at this stage.

In this text we will adopt the formula:

return on capital employed %   = $\dfrac{\text{net profit} \times 100}{\text{capital}}$

If we then apply this to the balance sheet shown on the previous page:

return on capital employed %   = $\dfrac{£90,000 \times 100}{£300,000}$ =   30%

This sole trader is clearly running a very profitable enterprise: he or she is achieving a 30% return on the money tied up in the business – better than any bank account. Note, however, that profit does *not* equal cash which can be drawn out of the business. The profit earned will have been ploughed back into the business and will be represented by the assets on the balance sheet, eg the bank balance, stocks, machinery and so on.

PERFORMANCE INDICATORS AND PERFORMANCE REPORTING

The performance indicators and ratios explained so far are commonly used in periodic performance reports prepared by businesses. They enable the owner(s) of the business and other interested parties such as lenders and the Inland Revenue to monitor the financial 'health' of the business. Performance indicators also help the owner(s) of the business to assess *quality* as it relates to the business: not only production, but aspects such as customer service and supplier deliveries. Constant improvement can be implemented as feedback is received.

In the Case Study which follows we analyse the performance of Citro Plc, a soft drinks manufacturer, and provide comments which can be used in the reporting process (see Chapter 13).

Case Study

CITRO PLC: PERFORMANCE INDICATORS

situation

Citro Plc is a company which manufactures soft drinks. It operates three separate production divisions in the UK: Citro North, Citro South and Citro West. Performance figures for the last three months have just been made available. What do they say about the performance of the company's three divisions and about the company as a whole?

	Citro North £000s	Citro South £000s	Citro West £000s	Total £000s
profit and loss data				
Sales	400	600	500	1,500
Cost of sales	250	375	375	1,000
Gross profit	150	225	125	500
Overheads	85	150	100	335
Net profit	65	75	25	165
balance sheet data				
Capital employed	1,300	1,250	1,250	3,800
other data				
Employees	120	130	135	385
Total labour hours available	55,200	63,000	75,000	193,200
Total hours worked	54,720	62,400	69,660	186,780
Units produced and sold	320,000	400,000	325,000	1,045,000
Target unit production	300,000	360,000	375,000	1,035,000

You have been asked to calculate performance indicators and ratios for the three month period (as far as the data allows) and to comment on your findings. The areas you are looking at are:

• **productivity** – how well Citro is using its available resources

• **cost per unit** – how much it costs to produce each item sold

• **resource utilisation** – how well Citro is making use of resources, eg its workforce

• **profitability** – what return Citro is making on its sales and its capital employed

You first draw up the table of results shown on the next page, and then you add your comments under the four headings listed above.

	Citro North	Citro South	Citro West	Total
PRODUCTIVITY				
labour productivity				
units/employees	2667	3077	2407	2714
sales (£)/hours	£7.30	£9.60	£7.20	£8.00
capital productivity				
sales (£)/				
capital employed	£0.30	£0.50	£0.40	£0.40
efficiency %				
actual output/target output	107%	111%	87%	101%
COST PER UNIT				
production cost*/units sold	£0.78	£0.94	£1.15	£0.96
•cost, in this case = Cost of Sales				
RESOURCE UTILISATION				
labour utilisation%				
actual hours/available hours	99%	99%	93%	97%
PROFITABILITY				
Gross profit margin %				
gross profit/sales	37.5%	37.5%	25%	33.3%
Net profit margin %				
Net profit/sales	16.3%	12.5%	5.0%	11.0%
Return on capital employed %				
net profit/capital employed	5.0%	6.0%	2.0%	4.3%

comments on productivity

There are two measures of *labour productivity*. They link

- the number of employees to units produced

- hours worked to the sales income from the units sold

The *labour productivity* of the three divisions follows the same pattern over the three month period: Citro North and Citro South have higher labour productivity (2,667 and 3,077 units per employee, whereas Citro West is the least productive (2,407 units per employee).

Citro West is also the least *efficient:* 87% against 107% (Citro North) and 111% (Citro South). The *capital productivity* of the three divisions is reasonably consistent.

The overall conclusion is that the productivity of Citro West needs investigating.

comments on cost per unit

These figures are not strictly comparable because each division manufactures a different range of products, each of which will have different levels of cost. The figures that will need to be compared are the three-monthly results for *each division* over a period of time to pick up any trend.

comments on resource utilisation

Citro North and Citro South are performing very well with 99% of available hours worked. Again Citro West is the weakest division with labour utilisition of only 93%. This will need investigating.

comments on profitability

Gross profit margin is consistent at 37.5% at Citro North and Citro South; Citro West is less profitable at 25%. This pattern is repeated for net profit margin and return on capital employed. Citro West's overheads need investigating.

overall conclusion

All companies are profitable and achieving a reasonable level of productivity. Citro West is the weakest performer. Management may need to investigate this division, and look particularly at:

- working practices – to improve labour utilisation and efficiency
- containing costs – to improve profitability

Management will also need to look at the figures for the other financial periods so that trends over time can be established and analysed.

a note on formal reports . . .

As this Case Study shows, once the figures have been extracted, some skill is needed in reporting the information and in presenting it in a meaningful way. But the stage we have reached here is only a 'halfway house' in this respect – in Chapter 13 we continue the Case Study, having looked at the format of the report and the ways in which information can be presented in the form of graphs and charts.

Case Study

CITRO PLC: PERFORMANCE REPORTING USING A COMPUTER SPREADSHEET

situation

You have been asked to set up a spreadsheet to produce the figures in the Citro Performance Report.

You first set up the spreadsheet headings and then enter the formulas. These are shown on the screen below.

🗋 Citro

	A	B	C	D	E	
1		North	South	West	Total	
2		£'000s	£'000s	£'000s	£'000s	
3	Profit and Loss Account Data					
4	Sales				=SUM(B4:D4)	
5	Cost of sales				=SUM(B5:D5)	
6	Gross profit	=B4-B5	=C4-C5	=D4-D5	=E4-E5	
7	Overheads				=SUM(B7:D7)	
8	Net Profit	=B6-B7	=C6-C7	=D6-D7	=E6-E7	
9						
10	Balance Sheet Data					
11	Capital employed				=SUM(B11:D11)	
12						
13	Other Data					
14	Employees				=SUM(B14:D14)	
15	Total Hours Available				=SUM(B15:D15)	
16	Total Hours Worked				=SUM(B16:D16)	
17	Units Produced and Sold				=SUM(B17:D17)	
18	Target Production				=SUM(B18:D18)	
19						
20	PERFORMANCE INDICATORS AND RATIOS					
21	*Productivity*					
22	Labour Productivity					
23	Output per worker	=B17/B14	=C17/C14	=D17/D14	=E17/E14	
24	Sales revenue per hour worked	=B4*1000/B16	=C4*1000/C16	=D4*1000/D16	=E4*1000/E16	
25	Capital Productivity					
26	Sales revenue per £ capital employed	=B4/B11	=C4/C11	=D4/D11	=E4/E11	
27	Efficiency%					
28	Actual output/target output	=B17/B18	=C17/C18	=D17/D18	=E17/E18	
29	COST PER UNIT					
30	cost of sales / units sold	=B5*1000/B17	=C5*1000/C17	=D5*1000/D17	=E5*1000/E17	
31	RESOURCE UTILISATION					
32	labour utilisation%					
33	actual hours /available hours	=B16/B15	=C16/C15	=D16/D15	=E16/E15	
34	PROFITABILITY					
35	Gross profit margin%					
36	Gross profit/sales	=B6/B4	=C6/C4	=D6/D4	=E6/E4	
37	Net profit %					
38	Net profit/sales	=B8/B4	=C8/C4	=D8/D4	=E8/E4	
39	Return on Capital Employed%					
40	Net profit/capital employed	=B8/B11	=C8/C11	=D8/D11	=E8/E11	
41						
42						

Your next task is to enter the financial data in the appropriate cells. This then automatically calculates the performance indicators, as shown in the screen below.

	A	B	C	D	E
1		North	South	West	Total
2		£'000s	£'000s	£'000s	£'000s
3	Profit and Loss Account Data				
4	Sales	400	600	500	1500
5	Cost of sales	250	375	375	1000
6	Gross profit	150	225	125	500
7	Overheads	85	150	100	335
8	Net Profit	65	75	25	165
9					
10	Balance Sheet Data				
11	Capital employed	1300	1250	1250	3800
12					
13	Other Data				
14	Employees	120	130	135	385
15	Total Hours Available	55200	63000	75000	193200
16	Total Hours Worked	54720	62400	69660	186780
17	Units Produced and Sold	320000	400000	325000	1045000
18	Target Production	300000	360000	375000	1035000
19					
20	PERFORMANCE INDICATORS AND RATIOS				
21	PRODUCTIVITY				
22	Labour Productivity				
23	Output per worker	2667	3077	2407	2714
24	Sales revenue per hour worked	£7.30	£9.62	£7.18	£8.03
25	Capital Productivity				
26	Sales revenue per £ capital employed	£0.31	£0.48	£0.40	£0.39
27	Efficiency %				
28	Actual output/target output	107%	111%	87%	101%
29	COST PER UNIT				
30	cost of sales / units sold	£0.78	£0.94	£1.15	£0.96
31	RESOURCE UTILISATION				
32	labour utilisation %				
33	actual hours /available hours	99%	99%	93%	97%
34	PROFITABILITY				
35	Gross profit margin %				
36	Gross profit/sales	37.5%	37.5%	25.0%	33.3%
37	Net profit %				
38	Net profit/sales	16.3%	12.5%	5.0%	11.0%
39	Return on Capital Employed %				
40	Net profit/capital employed	5.0%	6.0%	2.0%	4.3%
41					

When you have studied the figures and made notes about what you are going to say in your report, you will then extract spreadsheet charts which you can paste into your word-processed report.

You are particularly worried about the performance of Citro West and decide to extact comparative bar charts for the three Citro divisions, which show

• efficiency percentages

• the Return on Capital Employed percentages

These charts are shown in the continuation of this Case Study on page 339.

Chapter Summary	• Performance within a business is measured by means of formulas, percentages and ratios – known as performance indicators. These cover:

- productivity – how well the business is using its available resources
- cost per unit – how much it costs the business to produce each item it makes
- resource utilisation – how well the business is making use of its workforce and equipment
- profitability – how great a return the business is making on its sales

These performance indicators are covered in the Key Terms section set out below.

• An important skill, once the performance indicators have been extracted, is to comment and report on them.

• Spreadsheets are often used by organisations to calculate performance indicators.

Key Terms

percentage
A percentage is a proportion of a whole where the whole equates to the number 100 for comparison

productivity
the level of output (goods manufactured or services provided) in relation to the cost of producing the product or service

labour productivity
$$\frac{\text{output (units)}}{\text{number of employees}} \quad or \ldots$$

$$\frac{\text{output (sales £)}}{\text{hours worked}}$$

capital productivity
$$\frac{\text{output (sales £)}}{\text{capital employed}}$$

efficiency %
$$\frac{\text{output (units) x 100}}{\text{expected (standard) units}}$$

cost per unit
$$\frac{\text{cost of production over a given period}}{\text{number of units produced over a given period}}$$

resource utilisation %
$$\frac{\text{actual hours worked x 100}}{\text{hours available for working}}$$
note: this can apply to both labour hours and machine hours

gross profit margin %
$$\frac{\text{gross profit x 100}}{\text{sales}}$$

net profit margin %
$$\frac{\text{net profit x 100}}{\text{sales}}$$

return on capital employed %
$$\frac{\text{net profit x 100}}{\text{capital employed}}$$

Student Activities

11.1 Helicon Limited is a holiday company, specialising in holidays on the Adriatic coast. It operates two independent offices, one in Cardiff, the other in Newcastle. A breakdown of the costs of the two offices is as follows:

	Cardiff	Newcastle
	£000	£000
Holiday (cost of sales)	428	310
Marketing	96	40
Staffing	120	76
Financial Costs	24	14
General Office costs	48	26
Total costs	716	466

The following questions ask you to work out percentages. Round your answers to the nearest whole unit percentage.

(a) What percentage of the combined cost of the two offices is represented by the costs incurred by the Cardiff office?

(b) What percentage of the total staff costs is borne by the Newcastle office?

(c) What percentage of the Cardiff office's total costs is represented by its staff costs?

(d) The sales manager in Newcastle is predicting a 12% rise in holiday sales next year. What would the Newcastle holiday cost of sales be if they rose by 10%?

(e) The Cardiff accounts manager wants to see a 15% reduction in staffing costs next year. What would this cost be?

(f) Helicon Limited has to pay for most of its holiday costs in Euros. At the beginning of the year 1 Euro cost GB£0.65. During the year the pound fell in value by 10% against the Euro.

How much would 1 Euro cost in GB£ at the end of the year?

How do you think this would affect Helicon Limited's profits, bearing in mind that holiday prices are fixed at the beginning of the year?

11.2 Severn Car Insurance Brokers employ five sales staff. They record between them the following number of new policies arranged each month of the year:

January	600	July	890
February	545	August	675
March	655	September	465
April	680	October	750
May	550	November	670
June	615	December	560

The expected average monthly number of policies is 625

You are to calculate:

(a)   the monthly labour productivity (output per employee)

(b)   the monthly efficiency percentage (to the nearest %)

(c)   the average monthly labour productivity (a) and average efficiency (b) over the year

Set out your results in a table and comment on the figures. If you are not sure about how to calculate averages, please see page 309.

11.3 Sentinel Security installs domestic alarm systems. During the year it records the following figures for systems installed and total costs incurred:

month	units	costs	month	units	costs
January	20	£4,000	July	20	£4,000
February	25	£4,800	August	21	£4,200
March	22	£4,400	September	26	£4,900
April	30	£5,500	October	28	£5,000
May	32	£5,600	November	30	£5,600
June	28	£5,200	December	26	£5,000

You are to calculate

(a)   the monthly cost per unit (to the nearest £)

(b)   the average annual cost per unit

Set out your results in a table comparing units sold, costs and unit costs. Comment on the figures. If you are not sure about how to calculate averages, please see page 309.

11.4 Cool Designs provides a computer graphic design service. The business employs eight staff who all work a seven hour day, five days a week. During the course of a week their timesheets record the total daily hours worked: Monday 56, Tuesday 50, Wednesday 28, Thursday 56, Friday 48.

You are to calculate:

(a)   the labour utilisation percentage for each day (to the nearest %)

(b)   the labour utilisation percentage for the week

State why you think idle time may have occurred and how it might reflect on working practices.

11.5 Trend Toys plc is a UK manufacturer planning to capture the Christmas market with its new 'RoboZapper' toy which has been heavily advertised in the pre-Christmas period. In the month of November the marketing campaign proves very successful, demand takes off and orders flood in. In order to cope with this increased demand, extra staff are taken on and overtime is worked in the factory and in the despatch department. Extra raw materials have to be purchased from new suppliers, and the price negotiated for these materials is higher than Trend Toys normally pays.

The following figures are reported for the four weeks of November.

Production figures for the Trend RoboZapper:				
	Week 1	*Week 2*	*Week 3*	*Week 4*
Sales (£)	240,000	300,000	330,000	360,000
Units produced and sold	16,000	20,000	22,000	24,000
Expected output (units)	15,500	19,000	20,000	21,000
Cost of production (£)	120,000	150,000	190,000	210,000
Hours worked	4,000	4,700	4,850	5,150
Capital employed (£)	1,500,000	1,500,000	1,500,000	1,500,000

You are to calculate for each week:

(a)   labour productivity (sales [£] per hour worked) – to the nearest £

(b)   capital productivity (sales per £1 of capital employed) – to the nearest p

(c)   efficiency percentage – to the nearest %

(d)   cost per unit

Set out your results in the form of a table and comment on the trends shown.

11.6 The accounts office of Witley Agricultural Machines Limited has brought together the sales and costs figures for the four quarters of the financial year (which ends on 31 December):

	Jan-March	April-June	July-Sept	Oct-Dec
Sales	280,000	350,000	375,000	210,000
Cost of sales	168,000	217,000	221,250	128,100
Overheads	70,000	77,000	80,000	65,000

You are to calculate for each quarter *and* for the whole financial year:

(a)   the gross profit and the gross profit percentage (to the nearest %)

(b)   the net profit and the net profit percentage (to the nearest %)

and for the financial *year* only:

(c)   return on capital employed of £1.25 million

Set out your results in the form of a table and comment on them.

You could use a spreadsheet to set out and calculate the data. A suggested format is shown below.

	Jan-March	April-June	July-Sept	Oct-Dec	Total
Sales (£)					
Cost of sales (£)					
Gross profit (£)					
Gross profit %					
Overheads (£)					
Net profit (£)					
Net profit %					
ROCE %					

12 Charts, averages and indices

this chapter covers . . .

In this chapter we examine the techniques used in presenting the performance indicators in the form of tables, charts and graphs:

- *the construction of tables and the use of 'time series' data*
- *visual presentation of this data in the form of:*
  - *line graphs*
  - *bar charts*
  - *pie charts*

We also explain the technique of indexing numbers when comparing figures over a period of time in order to allow for changing price levels

We conclude by describing how averages work and how they can be used to forecast future data trends.

NVQ PERFORMANCE CRITERIA COVERED

unit 7: PREPARING REPORTS AND RETURNS

element 7.1

prepare periodic performance reports

C   *compare results over time using an appropriate method that allows for changing price levels*

F   *prepare reports in the appropriate form and present them to management within the required timescales*

TIME SERIES ANALYSIS

a definition

Time series analysis is a phrase which means

'comparing figures recorded over a period of time.'

In an accounting context time series analysis can include, for example, annual, quarterly, monthly or weekly comparison of figures for

- sales
- cost of sales
- overhead costs
- gross and net profits

In short, 'time series analysis' is a technical term for the commonly-used technique of comparing the results of different accounting periods.

constructing a time series table

In many of the Assessments and Student Activities that you will be doing, the data is already set out in a table. If you are processing the figures at work you may have to construct a table; alternatively the table may be in 'pro-forma' form (ready made) or it may be output from a computer information system, or be completed as a computer spreadsheet. Look at the example shown below, and read the notes that follow.

Sphere Paints PLC Summary Profit Statement				
	Year 1 *£000s*	**Year 2** *£000s*	**Year 3** *£000s*	**Year 4** *£000s*
Sales	500	970	1,430	1,912
Cost of sales	250	505	750	985
Gross profit	250	465	680	927
Overheads	185	370	548	780
Net profit	65	95	132	147

- the title clearly sets out the subject matter of the data
- each time period is allocated a vertical column
- each time period is clearly headed up (it could be a year, a month or a week)

- the units are stated below the time period – here £000s are chosen to prevent the table being cluttered up with unnecessary zeros
- the variables (ie sales, costs, profits) are set out in the left-hand column
- lines are added to clarify the table – it is not necessary in this case to draw a line under each variable as the columns can easily be read across; if, however, there was a large number of columns, lines would be helpful

presenting a time series – graphs and charts

Figures set out in a table can be interpreted: upward and downward trends can be detected by reading across the rows of figures, in other words by *interpreting the time series*. A much clearer idea of trends can be obtained by presenting the time series in the form of a graph or chart which will provide a very visual concept of each trend. This process can be carried out manually or by using a computer spreadsheet or charting package. The graphs and charts which follow in the next few pages were produced by a simple spreadsheet program into which the figures above had been input.

LINE GRAPH

The simplest form of visual representation of a time series is the *line graph*.

A line graph – which can be in a straight line or a curve – shows the relationship between two variables. One variable will always depend on the other. They are kown as:

- the *independent variable* – the measurement that is at a fixed interval
- the *dependent variable* – the figure that will depend on the independent variable

A common independent variable is time, and a common dependent variable is money but as you will see from the table shown below, it is not the only fixed measurement.

independent variable	dependent variable
time (years)	sales (£)
units produced	costs of production (£)
income level (£)	number of holidays per year
working out in gym (hours)	calories burned up

Now study the diagram shown on the next page and read the notes which follow.

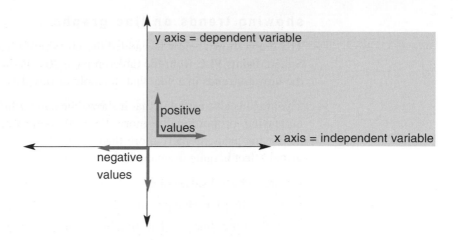

- the *independent variable* (eg years) is set out on the *horizontal* 'x' axis
- the *dependent variable* (eg sales) is set out on the *vertical* 'y' axis
- the line graph can show negative figures as well as positive figures (eg a company showing a loss over a period of years), but the most common format shows the area shaded in grey – ie both variables being positive; it is this format which is illustrated below

Now study the graph shown below and note the points made in grey text.

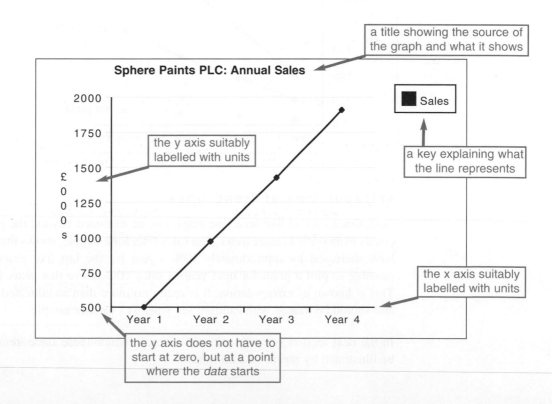

showing trends on line graphs

The graph shown below has added the gross profit and net profit figures for Sphere Paints PLC from the table on page 301. It shows simply and clearly the upward trends in a way that the table of raw data is unable to do.

The graph is also useful in that it shows the *comparative* trends – ie sales are increasing proportionally more than gross profit, and gross profit is increasing proportionally more than net profit – as you would expect. The visual effect is quite dramatic in its impact.

On the technical side, note:

- the scaling has changed on the 'y' axis – it now goes down to zero
- each of the lines is identified by a label (or a key could be used)
- the title has changed

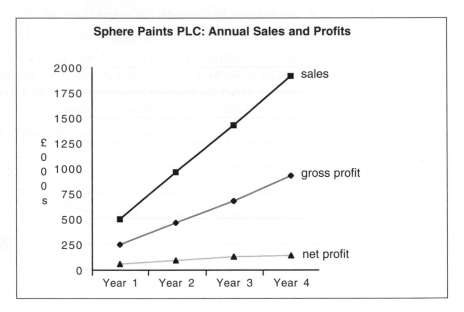

extrapolation of trend lines

Sometimes a trend line on a line graph can be extended beyond the plotted points to *forecast* a future trend. If a sales line, for example, shows that sales have increased by approximately 10% a year for the last five years, it is possible to plot a point for next years's sales 10% above this years figure. This is known as *extrapolation.* It is really no more than an educated guess and should be treated with caution; see page 312 for an example.

In the next section we will look at the way in which these same trends can be illustrated by means of a *bar chart.*

BAR CHARTS

A bar chart is a chart which sets out a series of bars, the height of which indicates the extent of the dependent variable. It is normal to set out a bar chart along the horizontal 'x' axis (so that they look like high-rise buildings) but the practice can be varied so that they stretch left to right from the 'y' axis.

Bar charts can be simple, compound or component, depending on what data comparisons need to be made.

simple bar chart

The simple bar chart is the most common type. It works on the same basis as a line graph and illustrates a trend. Set out below is a simple bar chart which uses the sales figures for Sphere Paints PLC from the table on page 301. Compare it with the line graph on page 303.

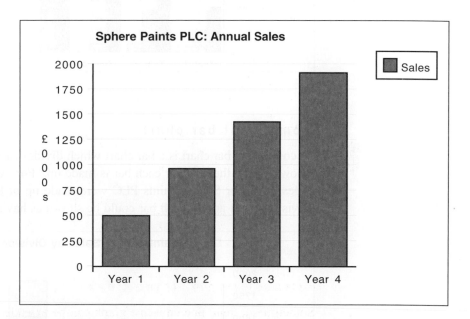

Note that:

- the labelling conventions are the same as for a line graph – here the bars are given a shading identity
- the 'y' axis goes down to zero – the whole length of the bar is needed (this is different from the line graph scaling)
- the bars are separated – this is common, but not essential – they can be drawn so that their sides touch

compound bar chart

Just as it is possible to draw a line graph with more than one line, it is also possible to construct a bar chart with more than one set of data for each independent variable – eg sales and profits for each year. This is known as a *compound bar chart*. An example, constructed from the table of data on page 301 is shown below.

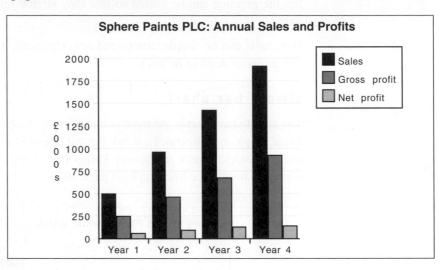

component bar chart

A component bar chart is a bar chart which divides each bar into segments, showing how the total for each bar is made up. For example, if the annual sales totals for Sphere Paints PLC were made up of totals for three sales divisions A, B and C, each bar could be shown as having three segments.

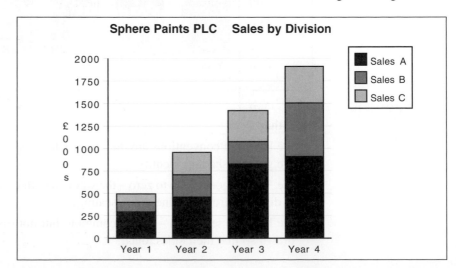

percentage component bar chart

Another way of presenting the sales data is to express the divisional sales figures as *percentages* of the annual sales total in a percentage component bar chart. Each bar is then the same height, ie 100%, and the subdivisions show the trends of divisional sales over the four years. In this case you can see that the performance of Division A *as a percentage of total sales* fluctuates substantially each year, a trend that is not shown on the ordinary component chart (previous page) which indicates a steady increase. This is the type of trend that the management might be advised to investigate.

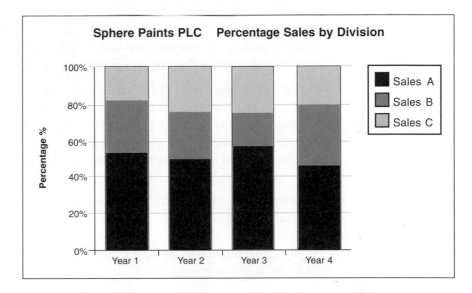

These divisional trends could also be presented in the form of a line graph:

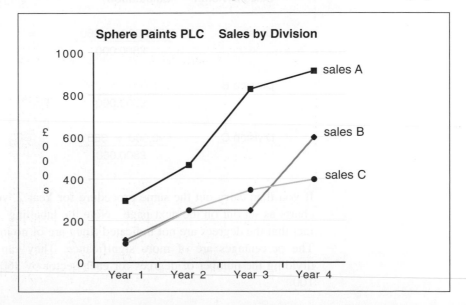

PIE CHARTS

A *pie chart* is a circle divided into sectors to represent in the correct proportions the parts of a whole. It is called a pie chart because, like a meat or fruit pie, it can be cut into 'slices'.

Line graphs and bar charts are suitable for the presentation of *time series* data – data which varies from time period to time period. Pie charts, on the other hand, are useful in showing the breakdown of a whole into its constituent parts at a particular moment in time.

Pie charts can be constructed by hand, or by using a computer spreadsheet or charting package. If you are constructing a pie chart by hand you will need a calculator, accurate drawing equipment and a protractor.

If you take Sphere Paints PLC's sales figures for Year 1 you will equate the total sales of £500,000 with the whole pie circle. This will be divided into segments, each of which will proportionally represent a divisional sales figure. As the angle at the centre of a circle is 360° it is necessary to work out the angle for each segment individually. The formula is as follows:

$$\frac{\text{Divisional sales figure} \times 360°}{\text{Total sales figure}} = \text{the angle at the centre for the segment (°)}$$

Applying the formula to the Year 1 divisional sales figures for Sphere Paints PLC, the calculation is:

Sales Division	Calculation		Angle of segment (°)
Division A	$\frac{£300,000 \times 360°}{£500,000}$	=	216
Division B	$\frac{£110,000 \times 360°}{£500,000}$	=	79.2
Division C	$\frac{£90,000 \times 360°}{£500,000}$	=	64.8

If you then carry out the same procedure for Year 2, you can construct pie charts as set out on the next page. Note the labelling and shading, and the fact that the degrees are not indicated (they are of no interest to the reader). The percentages are of more significance. They can be worked out by dividing the number of degrees for each sector by 360 and multiplying by 100.

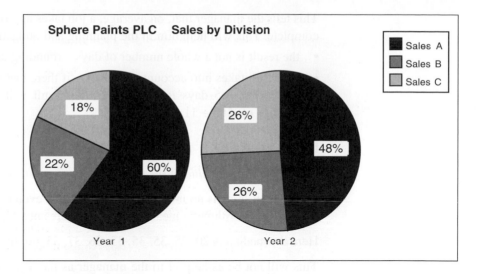

Sphere Paints PLC   Sales by Division

Sales A
Sales B
Sales C

Year 1: 18%, 22%, 60%

Year 2: 26%, 26%, 48%

USING AVERAGES

A statistical technique which is useful when reporting on a series of performance figures is the use of *averages*. There are three commonly-used types of average: the mean, the median and the mode.

which average?

Suppose the finance manager of a kitchen installation business wanted to know for budgeting purposes the average job completion time in days, from initial enquiry through to final installation. He has just received the figures for the jobs completed last month. The figures are (in days):

20, 25, 35, 35, 35, 36, 37, 55, 60, 65, 65

What is the average job completion time? We will look in turn at the mean, median and mode averages.

the mean

The arithmetic mean is probably the most commonly used and statistically reliable form of average.

The arithmetic mean is the sum of all the figures divided by the number of figures.

The sum of 20, 25, 35, 35, 35, 36, 37, 55, 60, 65, 65 = 468

The arithmetic mean   = $\frac{468}{11}$ =   42.6 days

This tells the manager that, on average, a job takes approximately 43 days to complete. This will help him in the planning and budgeting process. Note:

- the result is not a whole number of days – rounding up to 43 is necessary
- the result takes into account all values – if there had been an exceptional job taking 165 days instead of 65, the result will have been a mean average of $568 \div 11 = 51.6$ days

the median

The median is the value of the middle figure in a series of figures.

Note that if there is no middle figure, as with an even number of values, the median is the arithmetic mean of the two figures nearest to the middle.

Here the median is 20, 25, 35, 35, 35, **36**, 37, 55, 60, 65, 65 = 36 days.

This will not be as helpful to the manager as the mean in this context; it is useful because it is not distorted by extreme values (eg 165 days) – the mean, however, is more reliable because an equal weighting is given to each value.

the mode

The mode is the value that occurs most often in a series.

In this case the most common period is 35 days (3 jobs), followed closely by 65 days (2 jobs). Note that these two time periods are very widely dispersed. This would suggest that this type of average is not as helpful in the planning process. The mode is more useful in areas such as market research in answering questions such as

"How much do people on average spend on a meal?"

"What is the most commonly occurring size of shirt?"

USING AVERAGES IN FORECASTING

Forecasts in the reporting process are based on information about the way in which trends have established themselves in the past and are showing themselves in the present. It is then assumed that these trends will continue into the future. If one takes a profits trend, for example, established in the past, it is possible to predict a trend for the future by using a number of techniques, including the *moving average.*

The use of moving averages is the technique of repeatedly calculating a series of different arithmetic mean values for a dependent variable along a time series to produce a trend graph.

A moving average will move forward in time (the independent variable), step by step along the trend line, calculating a new average from the given data at each step, removing in the averaging process data which is literally "out of line" with the trend. Some data will be above the line, some below it; in the averaging process these fluctuations will offset each other to produce a smoother line. The following example, assuming we are in the future – in 2015 – shows the profit figures of a company, Arco Plc, over 15 years.

Year	annual profit £M	5 Year Moving Average £M
2001	10	
2002	4	
2003	8	64 ÷ 5 =12.8
2004	18	17.6
2005	24	20.8
2006	34	21.6
2007	20	23.2
2008	12	26.4
2009	26	26.8
2010	40	26.4
2011	36	30.4
2012	18	34.0
2013	32	34.0
2014	44	
2015	40	

This table has been produced as follows:
- the profit figures were plotted on a line graph (see next page)
- a five-yearly fluctuating cycle was noted
- the profit figures for the first five years were added and divided by five to find the first of the moving averages:

  $(10 + 4 + 8 + 18 + 24 = 64; 64 \div 5 = 12.8)$

- the next arithmetic mean is calculated over the five years 2002 to 2006, ie the average moves forward a year:

  $(4 + 8 + 18 + 24 + 34 = 88; 88 \div 5 = 17.6)$

- the process is repeated for the following years until the data is exhausted
- the moving average line is plotted on the same axes as the annual profit

This line graph shows that the moving average smooths out the fluctuations, plotting a profit trend line which could be extended to provide an estimate of profit in, say, 2017, as on the graph on the next page.

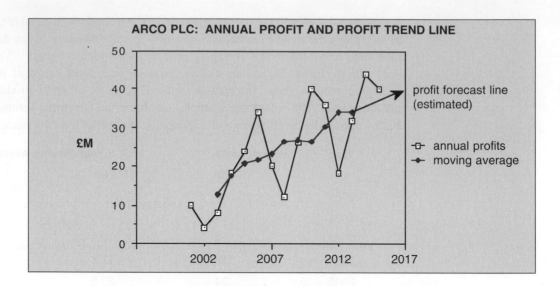

ARCO PLC: ANNUAL PROFIT AND PROFIT TREND LINE

forecasting using the incremental method

The profit forecast line to 2017 on the graph shown above is merely a guess based on the trend shown by the moving average. It is possible, however, to plot this forecast line on the graph by working out the average increase ('increment') in the moving averages (the trend). In the case shown here this will be the *average annual increase in profits*. This average increase can then be applied to subsequent years for forecasting purposes.

The arithmetic is as follows.

1   Calculate the moving averages (see previous page) and set the results out in a table (see next page)

2   Calculate the increments (increases) in the annual moving average, starting in 2004 by deducting £12.8M from £17.6M = £4.8M.

3   Repeat this process as far as you are able for each year. If the result is negative, show it in brackets. For example, the increment in 2010 is £26.4M minus £26.8M, which produces a minus figure, written as (£0.4M).

4   Add up all the increments, making sure to deduct any minus figures in the process. Here the total is £21.2M.

5   Divide the total of the increments by the number of increments to produce an average annual increment. The calculation is £21.2M ÷ 10 = £2.12M

Another way of calculating an average annual increment is by using a formula. This is normally quicker than working out each increment individually. The formula applied to this example is:

$$\frac{\text{(Last moving average} - \text{First moving average)}}{\text{(Number of moving averages} - 1)} = \frac{(£34.0M - £12.8M)}{10} = £2.12M$$

We can now use this average annual increment of £2.12M to produce a profit forecast beyond 2015, which is the last year for which we have data.

The arithmetic is as follows (see also the graph on the next page):

1   Decide how far in the future you want the forecast to extend. Here it is the year 2017.

2   Extend the moving average line on the graph (it goes up to 2013), increasing the profit by £2.12M a year. If you want the profit forecast to go up to 2017, this will involve plotting another *four* points, ie 2014, 2015, 2016, 2017, with the increment of £2.12M each time.

From this you can see that the *forecast* profit for 2017 will be:

£34M (the moving average for 2013) + £8.48M (ie 4 x £2.12M)

= £42.48M

calculation of increments in an annual moving average			
Year	**annual profit**	**moving average**	**annual increment**
	£M	*£M*	*£M*
2001	10		
2002	4		
2003	8	12.8	
2004	18	17.6	4.8
2005	24	20.8	3.2
2006	34	21.6	0.8
2007	20	23.2	1.6
2008	12	26.4	3.2
2009	26	26.8	0.4
2010	40	26.4	(0.4)
2011	36	30.4	4.0
2012	18	34.0	3.6
2013	32	34.0	0.0
2014	44		
2015	40		

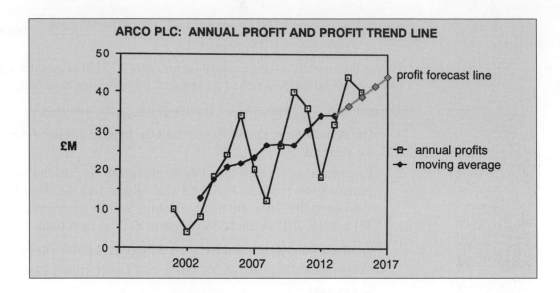

ARCO PLC: ANNUAL PROFIT AND PROFIT TREND LINE

SEASONAL VARIATIONS AND CENTRED MOVING AVERAGES

The moving averages calculated on the last few pages have been used to plot a trend line (see the graph above) which can then be extended to forecast future performance. This can be used for a variety of performance indicators: for example sales, profit, numbers of visitors to a theme park, holidays sold. The trend line – the average – can also be compared with the actual recorded data to calculate **seasonal variations** – ie the fluctuation from the average. This can be useful in forecasting because businesses such as ice cream sellers and ski wear manufacturers are greatly affected by seasonal variations. You should note that 'seasonal variations' in statistical terms can also apply to periods of time other than spring, summer, autumn and winter. It can apply to distinctions such as weekends and weekdays, night and daytime.

In the example we have dealt with so far, the trend was calculated by using a five point moving average. This was because using five points (years) provides an average centred at its middle figure – the third point. If there are four 'seasons' we need to use a four-point moving average. But a problem arises because the average falls *in between the two middle figures,* and does not 'tie up' with an actual period of time. Because of this you cannot compare it with actual data such as a seasonal variation.

This problem can be overcome by a further stage involving *the averaging of each pair of moving averages.* This gives figures that can be used as a trend because the figures produced will then fall in line with actual periods of time, such as the seasons. The additional averages produced in this way are called **centred moving averages** and are dealt with in the Case Study that follows. It may sound rather complex, but it is in fact straightforward!

Case Study

SKIWARE PLC:
MOVING AVERAGES AND FORECAST TRENDS

situation

SkiWare PLC sells a wide variety of ski equipment: clothing, boots, skis, and snowboards. The quarterly management accounts for recent quarters show that the following numbers of ski boots were sold in the four quarters (seasons) of the year:

	Quarter 1	Quarter 2	Quarter 3	Quarter 4
2000	4,000	1,600	2,200	4,800
2001	4,400	2,000	2,500	5,200
2002	4,800	2,400	3,100	5,600
2003	5,200	2,800	3,400	6,000

You are an accounts assistant and have been asked to use moving averages to analyse the data to show the trend and identify the seasonal variations from the trend.

You have also been asked to use this data to forecast the sales for each quarter of next year, ie 2004.

solution

calculating the trend and seasonal variations

1   The first thing to do is to set out the data (sales of pairs of boots) into a single column with spaces in between each of the figures, to the right of the date column (see the table on the next page). This is the 'quarter' column.

2   Calculate the 4 point moving averages for the quarters of the year. This is the average of each group of four figures, starting with 2000 quarters 1 to 4, followed by 2000 quarter 2 to 2001 quarter 1, and so on. Place each 4 point moving average in the next column to the right, alongside the centre point of the figures from which it was calculated. We are using a 4-point average because there are 4 quarters in our data. Note for the first calculation of the series that the average falls in a gap between quarter 2 and quarter 3 – it does not tie up with a quarter. This pattern repeats itself for the subsequent calculations. Note that the dotted lines and arrows are drawn here for illustration only – to show where the figures come from.

3   Calculate the average of each adjacent pair of moving averages in the next column to the right (headed 'Step 3'). These are also known as 'centred moving averages'. This is carried out so that these figures can be placed alongside the centre of each pair, and will therefore fall in line with the original quarterly data (see shaded arrow). We have now calculated the trend figures. Notice that the first trend calculated is in quarter 3 of the first year, and the last one is in quarter 2 of the last year, so in fact we do not have trend data for the last two quarters of 2003. This is part of the averaging process, and cannot be avoided.

4   Calculate the seasonal variations, and insert them into the last column. These are
the amounts by which the actual quarter figures (left hand column) are greater or
smaller than the trend figures. Be careful to use the correct + or − sign. The
shaded arrows show the figures used, here 2,200 *minus* 3,200 = − 1,000

Year	Quarter	Step 1 Historical Sales Data	Step 2 4-point Moving Average	Step 3 Averaged Pairs (Trend)	Step 4 Seasonal Variation
2000	1	4,000			
	2	1,600			
			3,150		
	3	2,200		3,200	−1,000
			3,250		
	4	4,800		3,300	+1,500
			3,350		
2001	1	4,400		3,387.5	+1,012.5
			3,425		
	2	2,000		3,475	−1,475
			3,525		
	3	2,500		3,575	−1,075
			3,625		
	4	5,200		3,675	+1,525
			3,725		
2002	1	4,800		3,800	+1,000
			3,875		
	2	2,400		3,925	−1,525
			3,975		
	3	3,100		4,025	− 925
			4,075		
	4	5,600		4,125	+ 1,475
			4,175		
2003	1	5,200		4,212.5	+ 987.5
			4,250		
	2	2,800		4,300	−1,500
			4,350		
	3	3,400			
	4	6,000			

forecasting the sales for each quarter of 2004

In order to work out the forecast we will need to calculate some averages:

1   the average quarterly increment – ie the number of extra pairs of boots, on
average, the business will sell each quarter, according to the moving averages
calculated (the trend line)

2   the average seasonal variation – ie the amount on average the seasonal figure will
differ from the trend line – sales will normally be higher in autumn and winter, and
lower in spring and summer

the average quarterly increment

A quick and easy formula for working out the average quarterly increment is:

$$\frac{(Last\ known\ trend - First\ known\ trend)}{(Number\ of\ Quarterly\ trends - 1)} = \frac{(4,300 - 3,200)}{11} = + 100$$

In other words, the increase in sales of pairs of boots each quarter is, *on average,* 100
pairs of boots.

average seasonal variations can be calculated as follows:

	Quarter 1	Quarter 2	Quarter 3	Quarter 4
2000			− 1,000	+ 1,500
2001	+ 1,012.5	− 1,475	− 1,075	+ 1,525
2002	+ 1,000	− 1,525	− 925	+ 1,475
2003	+ 987.5	− 1,500		
Totals	+ 3,000	− 4,500	− 3,000	+ 4,500
Averages	+ 1,000	− 1,500	− 1,000	+ 1,500

The data relating to the average quarterly increment of 100 and the average seasonal variations can then be brought together. Note that an addition of 200 (ie 2 x 100) units has to be built into the forecast trend to take account of the last two quarters of 2003 where there are no centred moving averages.

		Forecast Trend		Seasonal Variations	Forecast
2004	Qtr 1	4,300 + (3 x 100)	= 4,600	+ 1,000	5,600
	Qtr 2	4,300 + (4 x 100)	= 4,700	− 1,500	3,200
	Qtr 3	4,300 + (5 x 100)	= 4,800	− 1,000	3,800
	Qtr 4	4,300 + (6 x 100)	= 4,900	+ 1,500	6,400

All this data – actual and forecast – is then plotted on the graph shown below.

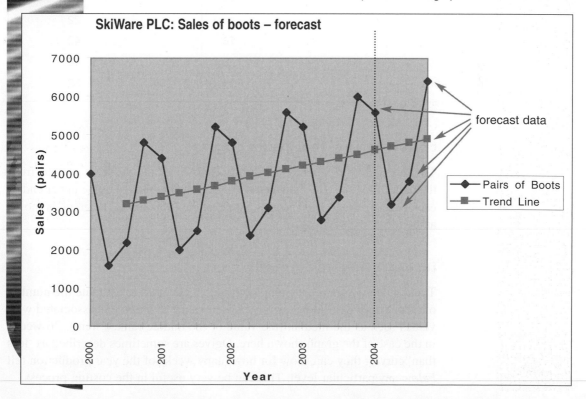

CUMULATIVE FREQUENCY GRAPHS (OGIVES)

Line graphs are sometimes used to show the *frequency* of certain results. This concept is best explained by looking at an example: a car factory will want to know the number of cars produced each week over, say, a year. All this data will be useful for management of any business for planning and costing purposes. It will be particularly useful if the data can be displayed so that management can see for how many weeks of the year production (or sales) will be *below* certain levels.

The starting point for this exercise is a table of data. The first column shows the weekly production levels in 'bands' of 100. The second column sets out the number of weeks each level is achieved; ie the number of times (the 'frequency'). The third column adds up the frequencies from the second column; ie 10 + 12 = 22 then 22 + 18 = 40 then 40 + 8 = 48, and so on.

weekly production of cars	number of weeks with production at this level (frequency)	cumulative frequency
0 to 1,000	10	10
1,001 to 1,100	12	22
1,101 to 1,200	18	40
1,201 to 1,300	8	48
1,301 to 1,400	4	52

constructing the graph (ogive)

The cumulative frequency graph, also known as the *ogive*, is plotted from thistable. The units are shown on the x axis and are plotted at the upper end of each band, eg the 0–1000 band is plotted at the 1000 point. The graph is shown at the top of the next page.

interpreting the graph

The cumulative frequency graph (ogive) can be used to estimate the number of frequencies that lie below any chosen value. The ogive is associated with values such as the median (the value of the middle ranked item): 26 weeks in the case of the graph shown here. Ogives are sometimes described as 'less than' curves: they can show for how many weeks of the year production fell *below* any particular level. This can be very useful in the costing process.

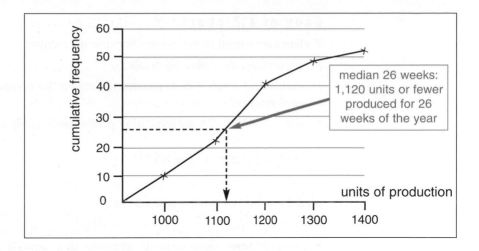

median 26 weeks:
1,120 units or fewer
produced for 26
weeks of the year

Z CHARTS

The Z chart is so-called because it combines three separate lines in the shape
of the letter Z. The lines are:

1 any variable such as sales figures plotted over a time period (eg a year)

2 the cumulative total of that variable, plotted over the same period

3 the annual total to date of that variable (usually incorporating data from
the previous year)

A simplified Z chart for sales figures looks like this:

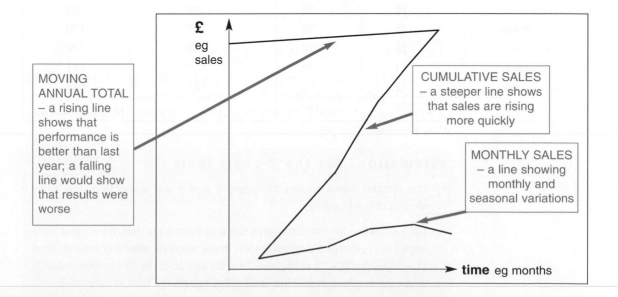

MOVING
ANNUAL TOTAL
– a rising line
shows that
performance is
better than last
year; a falling
line would show
that results were
worse

CUMULATIVE SALES
– a steeper line shows
that sales are rising
more quickly

MONTHLY SALES
– a line showing
monthly and
seasonal variations

uses of a Z chart

Z charts are useful to businesses because they show:

- *present trends* – monthly totals
- *cumulative totals* – performance to date can be compared with budgeted performance
- *a moving annual total* indicating performance compared with last year

constructing a Z chart

The first step is to construct a *table* for the data. The example below is based on the sales of a business and sets out:

- monthly sales figures for this year (B) and a cumulative total (C)
- monthly sales figures for the previous time period (A) – ie last year – required for calculating the moving annual total (D)

The calculations on the table are explained in the text that follows it.

month	sales (£000) A year 1	sales (£000) B year 2	cumulative sales (£000) C year 2	moving annual D total (£000)
January	10	11	11	163
February	11	12	23	164
March	12	13	36	165
April	12	14	50	167
May	15	16	66	168
June	15	17	83	170
July	15	18	101	173
August	16	18	119	175
September	15	18	137	178
October	15	16	153	179
November	14	16	169	181
December	12	15	184	184
	162	184		

calculations for the Z chart table

- The monthly sales figures for years 1 and 2 are taken from the sales records of the business.

- The calculation for the *cumulative sales* (column C) is that of the ogive (see page 318) – they are a running total of the monthly figures in column B: ie 11 + 12 = 23, 23 + 13 = 36, 36 + 14 = 50 and so on to 184 in December. A useful cross check is that this total (184) equals the total of column B.

- The *moving annual total* for any month (column D) is the sales total for the last twelve months, including the figure for that month. To calculate the moving annual total you start at month 1 (January):

  total sales for previous year <u>less</u> sales for month 1 in the previous year <u>plus</u> sales for month 1 in the current year

- The calculation here is £162,000 (total sales for Year 1) less £10,000 (sales for January, Year 1) plus £11,000 (sales for January Year 2) = £163,000

- The calculation for the next month takes this total of £163,000 as the starting point and performs the same process with the February sales figures in columns A and B: £163,000 − £11,000 + £12,000 = £164,000.

- This process continues until December when the moving annual total is, of course, the sales total for Year 2, ie £184,000. If it is not, you will need to check your arithmetic!

Once the table is complete you can then chart the graph (shown below):

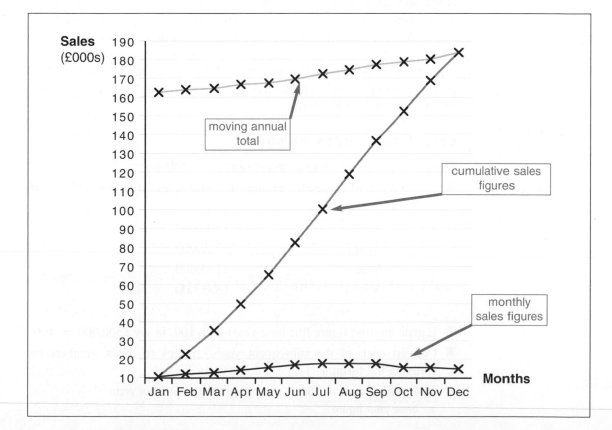

ALLOWING FOR CHANGES IN PRICES: INDEX NUMBERS

performance figures as index numbers

A further method of presenting a numeric trend over a time series is converting the figures in question into a series of *index numbers.*

An index is a sequence of values where one base value is equated to 100 and the other values are proportionally related to 100.

The object of using an index system is to simplify comparison of complex values by replacing the complicated figures with simple ones, all related to a base of 100.

It is therefore possible to convert periodic performance figures such as sales and profits to index numbers in order to analyse trends much more easily. The procedure for doing this is explained at the bottom of the page.

RPI: price levels as index numbers

Another form of index is the Retail Price Index (RPI) which regularly looks at the price of a defined 'shopping basket' of products in the UK economy and gives them an index number related to a base year. This index charts the rise in the level of prices. This is important to businesses because if prices are rising sharply, a true comparison of performance figures becomes difficult. There is no point in saying that sales in money terms have increased by 10% when the level of prices has risen by 15% – in this case the volume of sales may have gone down.

calculating index numbers

The procedure for creating an index series is as follows:

■ Take a series of values, for example the total sales for Osborne PLC over four years:

Year 1	£500,000
Year 2	£520,000
Year 3	£525,000
Year 4	£535,000

■ Equate the first figure (the base year) with 100, ie say £500,000 = 100
■ Convert each of the subsequent years' figures to index numbers by applying the formula:

$$\frac{\text{other year's figure} \times 100}{\text{base year figure}} = \text{index number of other year}$$

The calculation for the index for the sales of Osborne PLC is therefore:

Year 1	£500,000 (base year figure)	=	100
Year 2	£520,000 x 100 £500,000	=	104
Year 3	£525,000 x 100 £500,000	=	105
Year 4	£535,000 x 100 £500,000	=	107

The indices (index numbers) for the four years are therefore: 100, 104, 105 and 107. There would seem to be a modest upward trend in sales. Or is there? Suppose that for the four years in question the prices of goods and services in the economy had been rising sharply – in other words in real terms the value of money had been declining. It follows that sales *in real terms* may also have been declining. Using index numbers it is possible to compare the sales trend with inflation. The table below shows the RPI (Retail Price Index) as quoted for the four years in question:

	RPI index	Osborne sales index
Year 1	150	100
Year 2	160	104
Year 3	170	105
Year 4	182	107

It is clear from this exercise that sales are increasing at a slower rate than the level of prices: the RPI index figures are increasing at a higher rate. In the next section we will see how these sales figures can be adjusted to *sales in real terms* by using the RPI index figures.

converting figures to adjust for price changes

The following formula is used to present the sales trend in the light of the rise in the price level as shown by the RPI:

Sales figure for year in question x RPI index for Year 1 = Adjusted sales figure

RPI index for year in question

For Year 2, therefore, the calculation is:

£520,000 x 150 = Adjusted sales figure of £487,500

160

For Year 3 the calculation is:

$$\frac{£525,000 \times 150}{170} = \text{Adjusted sales figure of } £463,235$$

For Year 4, therefore, the calculation is:

$$\frac{£535,000 \times 150}{182} = \text{Adjusted sales figure of } £440,934$$

The sales figures can then be presented in a table as follows:

Year	Actual sales figures £	Sales figures adjusted by RPI index £
Year 1	500,000	500,000
Year 2	520,000	487,500
Year 3	525,000	463,235
Year 4	535,000	440,934

It is clear from these adjusted figures that sales *in real terms* are on a serious decline: although the actual figure for Year 4 is £535,00, when adjusted for the change in price levels as measured by the RPI, it is only £440,934.

Chapter Summary

- Performance reports contain the presentation of figures – money amounts, units produced hours – over a period of time. This is known as *time series analysis*.

- Time series analysis normally starts with the presentation of the figures in a table; these are the raw data from which can be constructed a variety of graphs and charts, either on paper or on a computer.

- A line graph is a simple and effective way of showing trends over time. More than one line can be displayed on a line graph.

- A bar chart also illustrates trends and can be in simple form (one variable charted) or compound (a number of variables charted separately) or component (showing the make-up of a figure in a single bar).

- A pie chart – a circular 'pie' divided into slices – shows the proportional make-up of a single figure. A pie chart is not so helpful in showing trends as it is limited to a single time period.

- When analysing periodic performance figures it is important to be able to use averages. There are three types of average: the mean (the most common), the median (the middle figure in a series) and the mode (the most common figure). All types have their particular uses (see Key Terms below).

- The use of moving averages enables a trend to be established when the figures in the time series vary widely; this technique also enables a future trend to be forecast.

- A cumulative frequency graph shows how frequently a range of results is achieved.

- A Z chart is a graph showing three separate lines: a set of variables , the cumulative total of that data and the moving annual total of that data. The lines form a shape like the letter Z.

- A series of index numbers enables a set of complex time series values (eg sales over five years) to be related to a base figure of 100. This makes comparison of the values much simpler.

- The Retail Price Index (RPI) charts changes in price levels in the UK economy over time. It is useful – particularly when prices are rising rapidly – to adjust a set of time series figures (eg sales) to the RPI index. This will show the *actual* trend of the time series figures.

Key Terms

time series analysis	the comparison of a set of figures recorded over a period of time
line graph	a visual representation of a time series
independent variable	the measurement on a line graph which is set at fixed intervals – this is often time, eg months, years
dependent variable	the measurement on a line graph which *depends* on the independent variable, eg sales, profit, over time
simple bar chart	a chart which sets out a series of bars, the height of which indicates the extent of the independent variable
compound bar chart	a bar chart which displays more than one set of data (and more than one bar) for each independent variable
component bar chart	a bar chart which divides each bar into segments which shows how the total for each bar is made up
percentage component bar chart	a component bar chart where all the bars are the same height and shows the segments as percentages of each bar
pie chart	a circle divided into sectors to represent in the correct proportion the parts of a whole – like a pie divided into 'slices'

arithmetic mean	an average worked out as the sum of all the figures in a series divided by the number of figures
median	an average which is the value of a middle figure in a series of figures
mode	an average which is the value that occurs most often in a series
moving average	the technique of repeatedly calculating a series of different arithmetic mean values for a dependent variable along a time series to produce a trend graph
incremental forecasting	producing a trend line by working out the average increase in trend figures and using the average increase as a basis for forecasting
seasonal variation	the difference between a trend figure and the actual recorded data for that period
centred moving average	the production of additional moving averages from pairs of moving averages where the original trend figure falls between two sets of data; this process enables a further 'centred' trend figure to be produced which then falls in line with the data
cumulative frequency graph	a graph showing the frequency of certain results over a time period – it is also known as an *ogive*
Z chart	a chart presenting three line graphs in the shape of a letter Z. The three lines show – a set of dependent variables – a cumulative total of those figures – an annual moving total
index	a sequence of values where one base value is equated to 100 and the other values are proportionally related to 100
Retail Price Index (RPI)	an index which represents the price of a 'shopping basket' of products in the UK economy over time – it measures the price level and is an indicator of inflation

Student Activities

Note: graphs and charts may be drawn by hand (pencil and graph paper are recommended) or produced using a computer spreadsheet. If a computer is used, care must be taken with specification of labels, keys, axes, etc.

12.1   A colleague hands you the following table which is to be used in a performance report. What is wrong with it? Redraft it as you think it should appear and construct a line graph to illustrate sales and profitability. Note: the figures for sales, cost of sales and overheads are known to be correct.

Gemini PLC				
	Year 1	**Year 2**	**Year 3**	**Year 3**
Sales	1,000	1,250	1,300	1,450
Cost of sales	500	650	650	700
Gross profit	500	600	640	750
Overheads	350	350	380	400
Net profit	250	300	260	350

12.2   The table below shows the divisional sales figures for Newbury Products PLC.

Newbury Products PLC Sales by Division				
	Year 1 *£000s*	**Year 2** *£000s*	**Year 3** *£000s*	**Year 4** *£000s*
Sales Division A	400	500	550	600
Sales Division B	100	250	350	400
Sales Division C	350	300	250	300
Total Sales	850	1,050	1,150	1,300

You are to:

(a)   Construct a compound bar chart showing the sales for all three divisions over the four years. Make brief comments on the trends shown. Is this the best form of chart to use to show these trends?

(b)   Construct a component bar chart using the same data. Comment on the differences between the charts in (a) and (b) and state in what circumstances you would use them.

(c)   Construct pie charts for Year 1 and Year 4 and comment on what they do and do not show.

12.3 Calculate the average (mean, median and mode) hourly rate of shopfloor workers pay from the following figures:

£5.50, £5.75, £5.80, £5.85, £5.90, £8.00, £10.00, £10.00, £35.00.

Which average figure are you likely to use if you are compiling a report on wage costs, and why?

12.4 The following figures represent the number of unit sales (measured in millions) of a highly successful new computer game 'Final Frontier' over the last 12 weeks, following a worldwide advertising campaign promoting the product.

3, 5, 10, 5, 7, 12, 7, 9, 17, 8,10,18

(a) Set up a table to work out a moving average on these figures, using a three point moving average as a basis for your calculation. Calculate to the nearest decimal place.

(b) Calculate the average increment of the moving averages (to the nearest decimal place).

(c) Plot the original figures and the moving average figures on a line graph. Include a forecast for the next three weeks using the average increment you have calculated. (Note: you need to allow for 15 weeks on your graph).

12.5 The following figures represent the quarterly unit sales of a range of swimwear by BigSplash PLC over the last 4 years.

	Quarter 1	Quarter 2	Quarter 3	Quarter 4
2001	2,000	4,500	6,000	2,000
2002	3,000	5,000	7,500	3,000
2003	4,000	6,500	8,500	4,000
2004	5,000	8,000	10,000	5,000

(a) Set up a table to work out a moving average on these figures, using a four point moving average as a basis for your calculation.

(b) Calculate centred averages to obtain trend figures and the seasonal variations.

(c) Calculate the average quarterly increment in the trend (to the nearest unit).

(d) Plot the original data and the trend line on a graph. Include a forecast for the four quarters of 2005, using the average increment you have calculated.

Optional task (e): calculate average seasonal variations (to the nearest decimal place) and plot forecast seasonal variations on the graph to the end of 2005.

12.6 Oakwood PLC manufactures sets of dining tables and chairs. Production figures for last year are:

weekly production of dining sets	number of weeks at this level of production
0 to 100	4
101 to 110	12
111 to 120	21
121 to 130	12
131 to 140	3

You are to:

(a) calculate the cumulative frequency of the data

(b) draw up a cumulative frequency graph

(c) identify where the graph is at its steepest and explain what this indicates

12.7 The comparative sales figures for the first six months of this year and last year for Monarch Products are shown below.

month	sales (£M) year 1	sales (£M) year 2
January	6	8
February	7	9
March	9	10
April	10	12
May	11	12
June	10	11

You are to:

(a) Draw up a table in the format used on page 320, but showing only six months' figures.

(b) Calculate the six-monthly total for both years.

(c) Calculate the monthly cumulative sales figure for Year 2 (third column of figures). Check that the June cumulative total is the same as the total in the second column of figures.

(d) Calculate the moving half-year total for Year 2 (the calculation is carried out on the same basis as an annual moving total). Check that the June moving total is the same as June cumulative total.

(e) Draw up a Z chart using the data from your table. What trends does it show?

12.8 The following table shows the sales and net profit figures for Pilot Design Consultancy for the last five years, together with the Retail Price Index for those years.

Pilot Design Consultancy: sales and profitability			
	Sales (£)	Net profit (£)	RPI
Year 1	350,000	45,000	155
Year 2	355,000	46,000	163
Year 3	365,000	48,000	169
Year 4	380,000	48,500	176
Year 5	390,000	49,000	189

You are to:

(a) Convert the sales and net profit figures into index numbers, using year one as the base. Comment on the trends shown.

(b) Adjust (to the nearest £) the sales and net profit figures for the changing price levels shown by the RPI indices. Comment on the trends shown.

13 Report writing

In this chapter we examine written reports:

- *the context in which reports are written*
- *the report format*
- *interpreting data for use in reports*
- *techniques used in report writing*
- *the importance of keeping to deadlines*

NVQ PERFORMANCE CRITERIA COVERED

unit 7: PREPARING REPORTS AND RETURNS

element 7.1

prepare periodic performance reports

F   *prepare reports in the appropriate form and present them to management within the required timescales*

REPORT WRITING

the report in context

Reports are written in a wide variety of contexts; they may be very long or they may be very short. Examples of extended reports include the report to shareholders produced by quoted public limited companies, or Government reports on areas such as Higher Education or Prisons. The shortest reports are probably school reports! They are all essentially the same: performance is reported, commented on and recommendations normally made. The important point about a report is that it should set out information clearly and concisely and come to a firm conclusion. It should also be submitted within the given timescale.

In the context of your accounting studies a report is often a relatively short document – maybe one or two pages – setting out financial data and analysis, normally for the benefit of management, and suggesting a specific course of action or investigation. This type of report is often known as the 'short formal report'.

report format

Report writing may at first appear difficult and complex, but it is in fact a very straightforward process.

Reports normally fall into a series of sections. These sections can be given a formal heading, eg 'introduction', or they can be left as a series of self-contained paragraphs. For the purposes of your studies, it is suggested that you use the headings – they help to concentrate the mind and they do make the document look clearer and more structured. The sections commonly found in a report are shown below. These can, of course, be varied to suit the situation. There is no 'right' or 'wrong' format.

decimal numbering systems

Some reports which have a complex structure of headings, subheadings and sub-subheadings, use a decimal numbering system for the various sections. Although you are unlikely to get involved in such complexities in the presentation of short formal reports, you should be aware of the system used as you may encounter it when reading longer reports.

Each section is given a number (eg 1.0) and any subsection within that section is given a number after a decimal point (ie 1.1, 1.2, 1.3), and subdivisions of that are given a further decimal point and a number (eg 1.1.1, 1.1.2). As you will see in the illustration on the next page, each section is indented from the left margin.

2.0	**Procedure**
2.1	Source material
	2.1.1 Sales budget
	2.1.2 Production budget

CONTENTS OF A REPORT

When reading this section, refer to the report format shown opposite.

title and preliminaries

A report is always given a title. It is also common practice for a report, like a memorandum, to be addressed from one person to another. Job titles are normally added to these names. The report should also be dated.

introduction

This section, sometimes called 'Terms of Reference' will set out the circumstances and scope of the report:

• the person who requested it

• the ground it has to cover

• the date by which it has to be submitted

• whether it has to make any recommendations

For example: "This report, requested by the Finance Director, will analyse the revenues and costs for the three divisions of Sphere Paints for the last three financial years and will make recommendations for improving future performance. The report is due for completion by March 30."

procedure

This section will set out the methods used, eg "Data produced by the Accounts Department was used for this report. A table of financial data is included in the body of this report."

findings

This will set out the main findings and trends, highlighting figures and commenting on performance indicators; these can be set out in the form of tables, graphs and charts (see the next chapter).

This section can also be used to point out any *limitations* of the data, eg "this was an exceptional year because the accounting policies changed" or "the factory was burnt down" or "the business was taken over" . . . and so on.

report to ....(name + job title)   report date ....

report from ....(name + job title)

REPORT TITLE (in capitals)...

introduction/terms of reference
Circumstances and scope of the report – what it covers, why it is being written, for whom, and when.

procedure
Where the data comes from and how it is used.

findings
The data is set out and analysed. Any limitations of the findings will be highlighted.

conclusions
A summary of the findings – with comments.

recommendations
Recommendations made on the basis of the conclusions reached.

appendices
Extra data included here if there is not room for it in the findings.

short formal report format

conclusions

This section summarises and makes comments on the findings so that recommendations may follow if required.

recommendations

If required by the report, recommendations should be made based on the conclusions reached.

appendices

If some of the data is too bulky to go in the main 'findings' section, it can be included in an appendix – eg three years' profit and loss statements and balance sheets, stock reports or budget reports. An appendix can also be used for graphs and charts imported from a spreadsheet. If there is more than one appendix, the appendices are normally numbered.

HINTS ON REPORT WRITING

Writing a successful report is an exercise in communication. You have to get a message across clearly, accurately and on time.

Before starting the actual report, make sure that:

- you have all the facts and figures needed – you may need to construct or complete a table or speadsheet which sets out performance indicators
- you have checked all the calculations
- you have planned out the report – you may need to 'rough out' a series of points on a separate piece of paper, a process which will help you come to a reasoned conclusion
- you know what format of report is to be used

When putting pen to paper (or fingers to keyboard), bear in mind the following points:

be clear   Avoid using complex words and phrases when simple ones will do – for example:

'Sales have improved at Citro North'

is far preferable to:

'The recorded level of turnover has seen a significant uplift at the Citro North operating division.'

be brief   Remember that the person reading the report will not have hours to spare. Keep the text brief – for example:

'The stock level will need examining'

is preferable to:

'It is my view that the levels of stock maintained should become the subject of a thorough investigation.'

be objective   Avoid using 'I' and 'We' which are *subjective*, but instead be *objective* – for example:

'Citro West's low liquidity is likely to be the result of a high stock level' is far preferable to

'In my view, Citro West's poor liquidity may be a result of their having too much stock.'

Giving opinions is a form of subjectivity and should be avoided. Statements beginning 'In my view. . . ' or 'I think that . . .' should be avoided as they suggest that what follows is based on guesswork rather than on fact.

avoid slang	Using slang is lazy and should be avoided at all costs. For example:

'It is recommended that management should take measures to improve profitability'

is far better than

'I think that these results are total rubbish – they really could be improved a lot.'

Do not write 'don't' – which is the spoken version – but 'do not' and similarly 'could not' rather than 'couldn't'.

be accurate	Always *check that* figures quoted in the text tally with the data provided. If you are calculating ratios and percentages, always carry out the calculation twice and make sure you are using the right figures. If you are using a spreadsheet check that the input is correct – and get someone else to check it for you – remember that 'garbage in . . . garbage out'.

PRODUCING THE REPORT

If you refer to the Citro Plc Case Study in the Chapter 11 (see page 291) you will see that all the performance indicators have been set out in a table that is reproduced on the next page, and 'comments' have been added. These comments are a rough and ready form of report to management: they highlight the main trends and pinpoint weaknesses. They conclude with recommendations relating to the weakest performing division of the business. These comments could be rewritten in the form of a structured short report, as shown on the pages which follow the table of results.

using a word-processing program

The report will normally be word-processed, as the format 'template' will then be on file in the organisation. The following checklist sets out word-processing techniques with which you should be familiar and be prepared to use in a report where appropriate:

• setting out headings – emboldening and enlarging
• setting out data in tables and formatting tables
• indenting text and numbering paragraphs, if this is required
• importing ('pasting') graphics into the text, eg graphs and charts

CITRO PLC: PERIODIC PERFORMANCE REPORT

situation

The table below shows the performance of Citro PLC's three sales divisions for the three months ended 31 March 2004. You have been asked to prepare a performance report for the Finance Director, Brian Cousins.

	CITRO NORTH	CITRO SOUTH	CITRO WEST	TOTAL
PRODUCTIVITY				
labour productivity units/employees	2667	3077	2407	2714
sales (£)/hours	£7.30	£9.60	£7.20	£8.00
capital productivity sales (£)/ capital employed	£0.30	£0.50	£0.40	£0.40
efficiency % actual output/target output	107%	111%	87%	101%
COST PER UNIT production cost*/units sold •cost, in this case = Cost of Sales	£0.78	£0.94	£1.15	£0.96
RESOURCE UTILISATION labour utilisation% actual hours/available hours	99%	99%	93%	97%
PROFITABILITY				
Gross profit margin % gross profit/sales	37.5%	37.5%	25.0%	33.3%
Net profit margin % Net profit/sales	16.3%	12.5%	5.0%	11.0%
Return on capital employed % net profit/capital employed	5.0%	6.0%	2.0%	4.3%

solution

You word process the report set out on the next few pages. The supporting numerical data (see previous page) will have been processed on a spreadsheet, and appropriate charts extracted and imported into the appendix to the report.

The text of the report will be checked for accuracy within your Department and then sent to the Finance Director. The report may then be referred to the Board of Directors and decisions made at that level if it is thought appropriate.

from Stew Dent, Accounts Assistant

to Brian Cousins, Finance Director   **date** 10 April 2004

CITRO PLC QUARTERLY PERFORMANCE REPORT

(for the three months ended 31 March 2004)

INTRODUCTION

This report, produced by the Finance Department as part of its normal reporting procedure will set out the performance indicators for the three operating divisions of Citro PLC: Citro North, Citro South and Citro West for the three months ended 31 March 2004. It will compare the performance and make recommendations based on its findings by 15 April 2004.

PROCEDURE

The data for this report has been compiled as part of the monthly management reporting process by the Finance, Production and Sales Departments. A table of financial data and approriate charts are included in the body of this report.

FINDINGS

productivity

The *labour productivity* of the three divisions follows the same pattern over the three month period: Citro North and Citro South have higher labour productivity (2,667 and 3,077 units per employee), whereas Citro West is the least productive (2,407 units per employee).

Citro West is also the least *efficient:* 87% against 107% (Citro North) and 111% (Citro South).

The *capital productivity* of the three divisions is reasonably consistent, averaging 40p of sales per £1 of capital employed.

cost per unit

The figures for cost per unit are not strictly comparable because the three divisions manufacture a different range of products, each of which will has a different level of cost.

labour utilisation

Citro South and Citro North are performing very well with 99% of available hours worked. Again Citro West is the weakest division with labour utilisition of only 93%

profitability

Gross profit margin is consistent at 37.5% at Citro North and Citro South; Citro West is less profitable at 25%. This pattern is repeated for net profit margin and return on capital employed: the margins for Citro North and Citro South are satisfactory, whereas the results for Citro West are less so.

It should be pointed out that the table does not show figures for the other financial quarters; this additional data will enable trends to be established and analysed.

CONCLUSIONS

All divisions are profitable and achieving a reasonable level of productivity. Citro West is the weakest performer in terms of efficiency, labour utilisation and profitability. Profitability in particular is weak, pointing to a higher level of costs in this division.

RECOMMENDATIONS

Management may need to investigate areas in Citro West such as:

- working practices – to improve labour utilisation and efficiency
- containing costs – to improve profitability

The results of these investigations will enable management to take measures to improve performance in these areas.

APPENDIX

The bar charts shown below demonstrate the weakness of the Citro West division in terms of its efficiency and its return on capital employed.

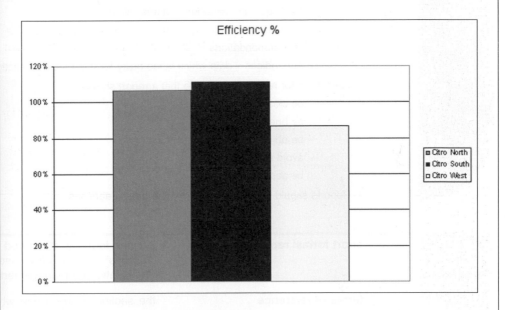

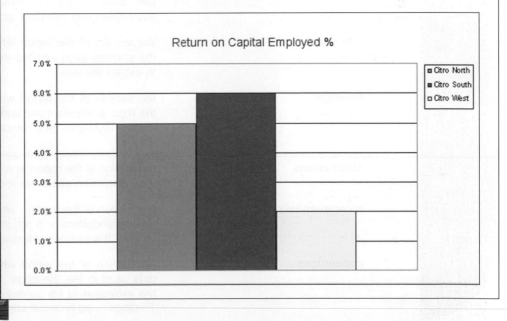

Chapter Summary

- Reports are written in a wide variety of contexts and can vary substantially in length.
- Periodic performance reports produced to present accounting data normally take the form of a short formal report.
- The sections of the report normally include:
  - report title and preliminaries (date, sender, recipient)
  - the Introduction (or 'Terms of Reference') – what it is about
  - Procedure – the sources used
  - Findings – presentation and analysis of data
  - Conclusions
  - Recommendations
  - Appendices – data which is too bulky for the 'Findings' section
- Guidelines for report writing state that a report should:
  - be clear
  - be brief
  - be objective rather than subjective
  - avoid slang
  - be accurate
- Reports should be completed within the given deadlines.

Key Terms

short formal report	a brief formally structured report (see 'sections' above), often used within an organisation for management purposes
terms of reference	the section of the report which sets out the scope and content, date of submission and intended recipient
procedure	the section of the report which sets out the sources used and the methods used to extract the data
findings	the section of the report which sets out the data, analyses it and comments on it; it also highlights any limitations of the data
conclusions	the section of the report which comes to a firm conclusion about the findings
recommendations	the section of the report which makes recommendations – if required – on the basis of the conclusions reached
appendices	the section of the report which contains data used in the 'Findings', but which is too extensive to be quoted in full in the 'Findings' – eg financial statements

Student Activities

13.1 One of the problems facing the student in writing a report is the style of language that has to be used. The common mistake is to assume that reports have to be written in some complex and 'posh sounding' language. The key points to report writing are:

- keep the language simple
- avoid slang
- avoid jargon and words which 'sound impressive' but which might obscure the meaning
- use short sentences rather than complicated long ones

To help you develop your report writing skills, turn the following two press reports into simple English. Use a word-processing package if you can, as then you can change and 'polish' your text as you go along. You will see that the style of the two reports is very different!

Confidence given a boost at Griffin Holidays

Ivor Pound Financial Correspondent

Griffin Holidays has reported some moderately encouraging financial results for the last half year, notwithstanding its disappointing performance in the corresponding period in the previous financial year, when the economic and political climates were far from encouraging for the industry.

The company has sustained its trend for profitable trading, buoyed up by a strong pound and firm demand for its products from the home market.

The reported results for the period concerned were sales of £1,345,600 (£1,289,000) and pre-tax profits of £678,000 (£550,000).

Recent commentators have made gloomy prognoses for the holiday industry as a whole and see no let-up for the present disappointing trend.

Griffin shares remain a hold in the current bear market at 165p.

Cheepflights all up in the air!

Will U Cummin Financial Correspondent

David Moorcroft, CEO of Cheepflights, the on-line cheap air ticket operation, may have caught a cold with his purchase of ten second-hand Airbus 301s from BryanAir earlier this year.

'I really am stumped by all this' said Dave, sipping champagne at a recent Savoy Hotel reception, 'these planes have been grounded for technical reasons. We stand to lose a cool £8m if we can't get them off the ground again'.

Cheepflights shares closed at 456p, down by 5%.

13.2 Refer to Student Activity 11.4 on page 298.

If you have not already done this Activity you should do it now – the text is set out below in the grey box.

When you have completed your table and drafted your comments

you are to . . .

Produce a short formal report based on your comments. Use today's date, your name (job title – Assistant, Accounts Department) and address the report to the Finance Director (invent a name). The report should be headed up with the section headings (Introduction, Procedure etc) and include a Recommendations section. The table of performance indicators should be included as an Appendix. Use a word-processing program for the report text and the table.

Trend Toys plc is a UK manufacturer planning to capture the Christmas market with its new 'RoboZapper' toy which has been heavily advertised in the pre-Christmas period.

In the month of November the marketing campaign proves very successful, demand takes off and orders flood in. In order to cope with this increased demand, extra staff are taken on and overtime is worked in the factory and in the despatch department.

The following figures are reported for the four weeks of November.

Production figures for the Trend RoboZapper:				
	Week 1	*Week 2*	*Week 3*	*Week 4*
Sales (£)	240,000	300,000	330,000	360,000
Units produced and sold	16,000	20,000	22,000	24,000
Expected output (units)	15,500	19,000	20,000	21,000
Cost of production (£)	120,000	150,000	190,000	210,000
Hours worked	4,000	4,700	4,850	5,150
Capital employed (£)	1,500,000	1,500,000	1,500,000	1,500,000

You are to calculate for each week:

(a)   labour productivity (based on output related to hours worked)

(b)   capital productivity (sales per £1 of capital employed)

(c)   efficiency percentage

(d)   cost per unit

Set out your results in the form of a table and comment on the trends shown.

13.3   Oasis Computers sells hardware and software from a chain of shops. It has representation in three towns: Kidderport, Stourminster and Persham. Each shop is self-accounting. The figures for the first six months of the year have just been brought together:

	Kidderport	Stourminster	Persham	Total
	£	£	£	£
financial information				
Sales	120,000	95,000	110,000	325,000
Cost of sales	65,000	55,000	72,000	192,000
Gross profit	55,000	40,000	38,000	133,000
Overheads	40,000	29,000	36,000	105,000
Net profit	15,000	11,000	2,000	28,000
Capital employed	150,000	120,000	135,000	405,000
non-financial information				
Employees	5	4	6	15
Hours worked	4,375	3,600	5,100	13,075
Floor space of shop	500m²	450m²	625m²	1,575m²
Units sold	2,400	1,900	2,200	6,500

You are to

Calculate appropriate ratios and percentages for all three shops and the business as a whole, covering the areas listed below; set out your results in the form of a table. Use a spreadsheet if you can to process and present the data.

(a) labour productivity – relating units to employees, and sales to hours worked

(b) capital productivity – sales per £1 of capital employed (to the nearest p)

(c) cost per unit – units sold related to cost of sales plus overheads

(d) resource utilisation – sales per square metre of floorspace

(e) gross profit percentage (to the nearest %)

(f) net profit percentage (to the nearest %)

(g) return on capital employed (to the nearest %)

Then, having discussed your findings within your student group (if this is possible), word process a short formal report to Bill Bates, General Manager of Oasis Computers. Use your own name (job title – Assistant, Accounts Department). The report should be headed up with the section headings (Introduction, Procedure etc) and include a Recommendations section. The table of performance indicators and ratios should be included as an Appendix, preferably imported from the spreadsheet.

this chapter covers . . .

In the last few chapters we have explained and illustrated:

* the ways in which performance indicators can be applied to data which has been extracted from an organisation

* the statistical techniques that can be appled to this data, producing graphs and charts to illustrate situations and trends.

* the use of spreadsheets to help in these processes

Your studies also require that you are able to consolidate this data, which may come from different operating divisions of a business. You will also need to make adjustments to the data. You may then be required to bring data together to produce a single profit and loss account, for example, and then to analyse the figures, extract performance indicators and produce graphs and charts to incorporate in a short report.

NVQ PERFORMANCE CRITERIA COVERED

unit 7: PREPARING REPORTS AND RETURNS

element 7.1

prepare and present periodic performance reports

A   consolidate information derived from different units of the organisation into the appropriate form

B   reconcile information derived from different information systems within the organisation

D   account for transactions between separate units of the organisation in accordance with the organisation's procedures

E   calculate ratios and performance indicators in accordance with the organisation's procedures

CONSOLIDATING INFORMATION

Reporting on the performance of a business which is based in one location, or which has a simple product range, is a straightforward affair. Financial and production data can be brought together to produce interim financial statements such as profit and loss accounts and balance sheets for the benefit of management. Many computer accounting programs can do this automatically and spreadsheets can be set up to process the data so that sales, profits and stock levels can be monitored, and action taken if the need arises.

the 'branch' situation

But what if the organisation consists of a number of separate 'branches' – for example travel agents, shops, hotels – all of which keep separate accounting records of sales and expenses, and in some cases stock? The accounting data will need to be consolidated to produce a single financial statement or report which will provide 'the whole picture'. This is normally a case of simple arithmetic, and can easily be set up on a spreadsheet.

Take, for example, a business which runs a chain of small shops in three separate locations – A and B and C – and has the main office at one of them. The profitability for a period such as a month can easily be calculated by consolidating the figures for all three branches:

ABC RETAIL LIMITED			
Profit and Loss Account for March 2004			
	Branch A	Branch B	Branch C	Total
	£	£	£	£
Sales	50,000	65,000	75,000	190,000
Opening Stock	20,000	22,000	25,000	67,000
Purchases	25,000	30,000	36,000	91,000
Closing stock	18,000	21,000	24,000	63,000
Cost of goods sold	27,000	31,000	37,000	95,000
Gross Profit	23,000	34,000	38,000	95,000
Wages	12,000	18,000	20,000	50,000
Other overheads	8,000	8,000	8,000	24,000
Total overheads	20,000	26,000	28,000	74,000
Net Profit	3,000	8,000	10,000	21,000

reporting the data

The data in the profit and loss account on the previous page can be analysed to provide performance indicators such as:

- gross profit percentage
- net profit percentage

A report could be set up on a spreadsheet as follows:

	A	B	C	D	E	F
1	ABC RETAIL LTD - Performance Report for March 2004					
2						
3		Branch A (£)	Branch B (£)	Branch C (£)	Total (£)	
4	Sales	50,000	65,000	75,000	190,000	
5	Cost of goods sold	27,000	31,000	37,000	95,000	
6	Gross Profit	23,000	34,000	38,000	95,000	
7	Gross Profit %	46%	52%	51%	50%	
8	Total overheads	20,000	26,000	28,000	74,000	
9	Net Profit	3,000	8,000	10,000	21,000	
10	Net Profit %	6%	12%	13%	11%	
11						
12						
13						

Charts can then be produced from this data to illustrate the comparative levels of profitability of the three branches (pie chart below) and the uses put to the sales revenue received (bar chart on the next page)

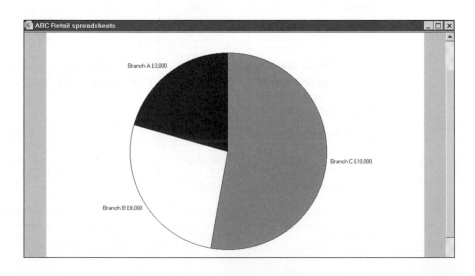

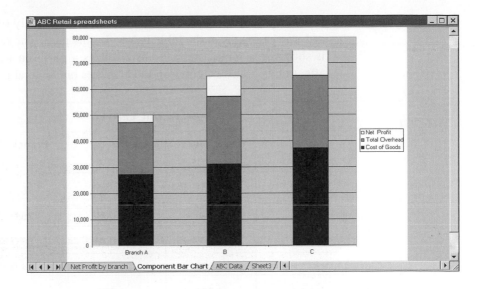

DEALING WITH STOCK TRANSFERS

transfers of stock with added margin

It is not uncommon for different divisions of a business to transfer stock between themselves as the need arises. Individual companies in large manufacturing groups may even 'sell' stock or manufactured items to each other and add on a profit margin. For example, a company manufacturing car engines may transfer them to another company in the group which produces the finished vehicles, charging the engine at cost plus an agreed margin.

transfers of stock at cost

In some businesses which involve divisions or 'branches', the transfer of the stock may be carried out *at cost*. No margin will be added on. Examples of this include transfers of stock between shops and transfers between divisions of a company, eg transfers of finished products between a manufacturing division and a sales division. Your studies of Unit 7 will always deal with such transfers *at cost*.

recording transfers of stock

These transfers need to be recorded by the individual branches or divisions, together with the sales, purchases, expenses and stock figures as appropriate. But the important point is that *transfers should not be included in the sales or purchases of the group*. If the transfers are recorded as part of sales (transfers out) or purchases (transfers in) for branches or divisions, *they should be deducted or excluded when compiling the group figures.*

It is likely that the transfers will be recorded separately (not as part of sales and purchases), as in the table below. In this particular case a 'transfer out' is shown as a minus and a 'transfer in' as a plus. You will see that the net effect of the transfers between the branches on the total group is zero.

ABC RETAIL LIMITED				
	Branch A	**Branch B**	**Branch C**	**Total**
	£	£	£	£
Sales	50,000	65,000	75,000	190,000
Opening Stock	20,000	22,000	25,000	67,000
Purchases	25,000	30,000	36,000	91,000
Closing stock	18,000	21,000	24,000	63,000
Stock transfers	– 2,000	+ 800	+ 1,200	zero

the problem of stock in transit

But what would happen, if at the end of the month, £200 of stock from Branch A had been sent off to Branch B, but had not yet arrived, or had not yet been recorded by Branch B? You would be able to detect this because the total figure for transfers out would not equal the total for transfers in. In the case of the table shown above the transfer total column would not be zero, but would shown as – £200.

dealing with stock in transit

The situation in the case mentioned in the paragraph above is:

- Branch A has recorded the stock as having been despatched and so will have reduced its closing stock figure by £200

- Branch B will not have made any adjustments to its figures at all

- There will be £200 of stock missing from the total group closing stock

The rule is therefore that the value of stock in transit should be:

- *added back to the closing stock of the branch which sent it*

- *deducted from the total of the stock transferred by that branch*

In other words, stock in transit should be treated as if it is still at the branch which sent it. In this case the closing stock of Branch A will be £18,000 + £200 = £18,200 and the transfer figures will become:

– £1,800 (Branch A)   + £600 (Branch B)   + £1,200 (Branch C) = zero

We will now look at two Case Studies. The first involves the three branches of a clothing store 'CoolTime' and shows how the **profit and loss data** is combined, adjusted and consolidated, and appropriate performance indicators extracted and illustrated. The second looks at the combining of **sales data** from two divisions of a manufacturing company, Potter PLC.

Case Study

COOLTIME: CONSOLIDATING INFORMATION

situation

CoolTime is a chain of three fashion shops, owned by Julie Mye. The main shop and the office is in Staines, and the other two shops are in Bracknell and in Slough. You work as an accounts assistant in Staines and report directly to Julie Mye.

Part of your job requires you to compile information every Monday on the financial performance of the three shops for the previous trading week. The data from Bracknell and Slough is sent to you by email.

The data for last week is as follows:

	Staines £	Bracknell £	Slough £
Sales	20,200	10,590	11,850
Purchases	9,800	3,100	4,220
Wages	3,200	2,200	2,300
Other overheads	2,750	2,800	2,600
Opening stock	18,000	10,500	14,250
Closing stock	16,900	9,800	12,900
Stock transfers to Bracknell and Slough	1,200		
Transfers from Staines		450	550

Julie Mye, trading as CoolTime
Transactions for the week ended 3 April 2004

Notes

- On 3 April £200 of stock was transferred to Bracknell from Staines. This was not recorded in the books of Bracknell until 5 April.

- No adjustments for the stock transfers that were recorded (see table above) need to be made to the sales or purchases figures of the three branches.

required

1   Check the data received from the three shops and adjust the appropriate figures for any stock in transit.

2   Using the data produced in (1), draw up a profit and loss account for the week ended 3 April 2004.

3   Draw up a performance report on a spreadsheet which calculates the following performance indicators (use percentages correct to two decimal places):
    (a)   gross profit margin
    (b)   net profit margin

4   Produce charts to illustrate the performance report:
    (a)   a pie chart showing the comparative sales of the three shops
    (b)   a component bar chart, divided into three segments, showing the use of the sales revenue by each of the three shops. The segments consist of:
        •   the cost of goods sold
        •   overheads
        •   net profit

5   Compile a short word-processed report addressed to Julie Mye, commenting on the performance of the three shops and incorporating the data and chart produced in tasks 1 to 4.

solution

1 adjusting the data for stock transfers

Before the profit and loss account can be drawn up, adjustment must be made for the £200 of stock in transit from Staines to Bracknell which is causing a discrepancy. Transfers 'out' total £1,200 and transfers 'in' total £1,000 (£550 plus £450), a difference of £200.

The solution is to treat the stock as if it has not left Staines:

•   add £200 back to the Staines closing stock figure:
    £16,900 + £200 = £17,100

•   deduct £200 from the Staines transfer figure:
    £1,200 − £200 = £1,000

The group total closing stock figure will now be correct and the net total effect of the transfers will be zero:

    − £1,000 (Staines) + £450 (Bracknell) + £550 (Slough) = zero

Tutorial note
No stock transfer adjustments need to be made to the sales and purchases figures in this Case Study, as they have already been carried out.

2 drawing up the profit and loss account

The profit and loss account can now be drawn up.

Note that the closing stock figure of the Staines branch has been adjusted upwards by £200 to £17,100 for the stock in transit, which is now treated as being back at Staines again. Otherwise all the other figures are unaltered.

Julie Mye, trading as CoolTime				
Profit and Loss Account Account for the week ended 3 April 2004				
	Staines £	*Bracknell* £	*Slough* £	*Total* £
Sales	20,200	10,590	11,850	42,640
Opening Stock	18,000	10,500	14,250	42,750
Purchases	9,800	3,100	4,220	17,120
Closing stock	17,100	9,800	12,900	39,800
Cost of goods sold	10,700	3,800	5,570	20,070
Gross Profit	9,500	6,790	6,280	22,570
Wages	3,200	2,200	2,300	7,700
Other overheads	2,750	2,800	2,600	8,150
Total overheads	5,950	5,000	4,900	15,850
Net Profit	3,550	1,790	1,380	6,720

3 drawing up the performance report

Julie will want to see the performance indicators which can be extracted from these figures. She will be particularly interested in:

• sales revenue from each of the branches

• gross profitability

• net profitability

The tables shown on the next page show:

• the spreadsheet file format with the appropriate formulas

• the completed performance report

	A	B	C	D	E	F
1						
2						
3		Staines (£)	Bracknell (£)	Slough (£)	Total (£)	
4	Sales	20200	10590	11850	=SUM(B4:D4)	
5	Cost of goods sold	10700	3800	5570	=SUM(B5:D5)	
6	Gross Profit	9500	6790	6280	=SUM(B6:D6)	
7	Gross Profit %	=B6/B4*100%	=C6/C4*100%	=D6/D4*100%	=E6/E4*100%	
8	Total overheads	5950	5000	4900	=SUM(B8:D8)	
9	Net Profit	3550	1790	1380	6720	
10	Net Profit %	= B9/B4*100%	= C9/C4*100%	= D9/D4*100%	= E9/E4*100%	
11						
12						
13						
14						

spreadsheet formulas used for the performance report

	A	B	C	D	E	F	G	H
1	Cooltime - Performance Report: week ending 3 April 2004							
2								
3		Staines (£)	Bracknell (£)	Slough (£)	Total (£)			
4	Sales	20,200	10,590	11,850	42,640			
5	Cost of goods sold	10,700	3,800	5,570	20,070			
6	Gross Profit	9,500	6,790	6,280	22,570			
7	Gross Profit %	47.03%	64.12%	53.00%	52.93%			
8	Total overheads	5,950	5,000	4,900	15,850			
9	Net Profit	3,550	1,790	1,380	6,720			
10	Net Profit %	17.57%	16.90%	11.65%	15.76%			
11								
12								
13								
14								

completed performance report

4 the charts

These charts have been produced from the spreadsheet shown on the previous page.

(a)   pie chart showing comparative sales by branch

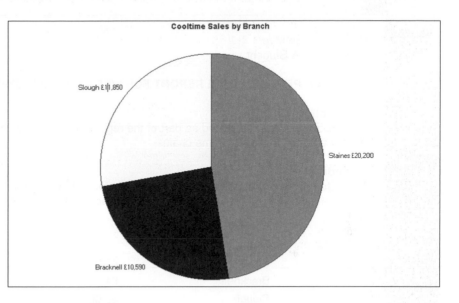

(b)   component bar chart

Note that each bar is divided into three segments representing what use has been made of the sales revenue from each of the three branches:

- the cost of goods sold
- overheads
- net profit

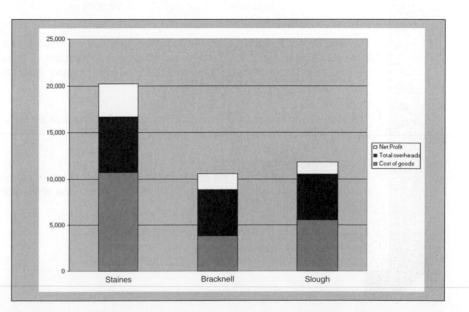

5 the short report

The short report interprets the data, performance indicators and bar chart produced in tasks 1 to 4. These will be included as appendices to the short report, the purpose of which is to highlight points that should be brought to the proprietor's attention.

Report to Julie Mye   7 April 2004
Report from A Student

COOLTIME PERFORMANCE REPORT FOR WEEK ENDED 3 APRIL 2004

Introduction
This report has been produced as part of the regular weekly performance reporting of the three shops in the CoolTime chain.

Procedure
The data for this report has been received from each of the three branches: Staines, Bracknell and Slough. The data has been processed at the Staines office.

Findings
The gross profit percentages are as follows:

Staines	47.03%
Bracknell	64.12%
Slough	53.00%

The Bracknell and Slough results are comfortably above the 50% minimum figure recommended by management. The Staines result of 47.03% may reflect a number of sales promotions (sales price reductions) offered by that store last week in order to stimulate sales, and so does not give cause for concern.

The net profit percentages are as follows:

Staines	17.57%
Bracknell	16.90%
Slough	11.65%

The only figure that gives cause for concern here is the Slough figure of 11.65% which falls well short of the 15% minimum targeted by management. The ratio of overheads to net profit for Slough shown on the enclosed bar chart clearly illustrates this problem.

Conclusions
The profitability of the CoolTime group of stores continues to be very satisfactory, with the exception of the net profitability of the Slough branch.

Recommendations
The Slough branch should be asked to provide a breakdown of its overheads for the last month so that they can be analysed and discussed with the shop manager, with a view to improving bottom line net profit.

Appendices
Data tables and charts.

POTTER PLC: CONSOLIDATING SALES FIGURES

situation

Potter PLC manufactures high quality bone china products such as dinner plates and tea sets. Most of its sales are carried out by its Sales Division, but it also sells through its popular factory shop, operated by its Manufacturing Division in Dursley.

The quarterly sales figures produced by the two divisions are as follows:

2003	Sales Division	Manufacturing Division		
	Total	Factory shop	to Sales Division	Total
	£000	£000	£000	£000
Jan - Mar	510	50	250	300
Apr - Jun	650	64	315	379
Jul - Sep	540	88	270	358
Oct - Dec	496	48	251	299

You have been asked to consolidate the sales figures to produce total sales figures for the company for each quarter, and also on a cumulative basis for the year.

solution

To produce quarterly sales figures for the whole company you will need to add together the sales figures for the Sales Division and the factory shop sales figures from the Manufacturing Division. (Note that the 'to Sales Division' figures of the Manufacturing Division are internal transfers and so will not be included).

The quarterly figures also need to be added together on a cumulative basis (for example the cumulative figure for the end of June is the total of the first two quarters' sales).

A table can then be drawn up as follows:

POTTER PLC		
Combined sales figures for Sales and Manufacturing Divisions 2003		
	Total Sales by Quarter	Cumulative Sales
	£000	£000
Jan - Mar	560	560
Apr - Jun	714	1,274
Jul - Sep	628	1,902
Oct - Dec	544	2,446

The management of Potter PLC will then be able to compare these figures with the figures for the previous year to see how the company is performing. Line graphs or bar charts can be drawn to present the figures and the trends more clearly.

Chapter Summary

- Businesses which operate separate branches or divisions will have to consolidate data from those separate divisions when compiling financial statements and performance reports.

- Businesses which operate separate branches or divisions and which deal with stock or finished products may get involved in transferring the stock or products between the branches or divisions.

- Transfers may be at cost, or they may be at cost plus a margin.

- The net total of all transfers at cost should be zero as a transfer into one branch or division (a positive figure) is numerically equal to the same transfer from another branch or division (a negative figure).

- When compiling financial data for performance reports, businesses must take care to account for stock or products 'in transit' as these can cause discrepancies.

- Any stock in transit must be accounted for by the branch or division sending it. This may involve adding it back into the closing stock of that branch or division and deducting it from the total of transfers out of the branch or division.

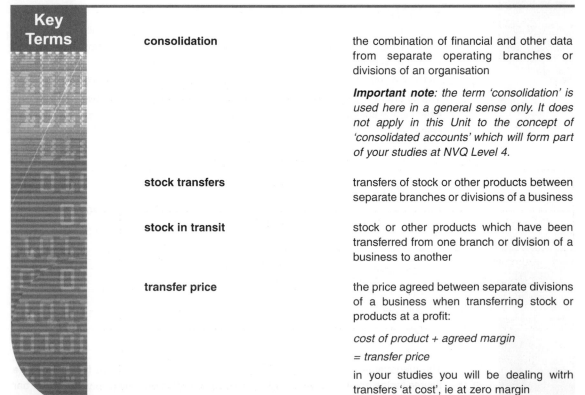

Key Terms

consolidation	the combination of financial and other data from separate operating branches or divisions of an organisation
	Important note: the term 'consolidation' is used here in a general sense only. It does not apply in this Unit to the concept of 'consolidated accounts' which will form part of your studies at NVQ Level 4.
stock transfers	transfers of stock or other products between separate branches or divisions of a business
stock in transit	stock or other products which have been transferred from one branch or division of a business to another
transfer price	the price agreed between separate divisions of a business when transferring stock or products at a profit:
	cost of product + agreed margin
	= transfer price
	in your studies you will be dealing witrh transfers 'at cost', ie at zero margin

Student Activities

14.1 FitMan Wholesale Limited is a mens clothes supplier which has two branches.

On 28 March 2004 £1,000 of stock was transferred from the Hornchurch branch to the Basildon branch at cost. This was not recorded in the books of the Basildon branch until 2 April.

Complete the gross profit calculations for FitMan Wholesale Limited, having made appropriate adjustments for stock in transit.

FITMAN WHOLESALE LIMITED			
Profit and Loss Account (extract) for week ended 28 March 2004			
	Hornchurch	**Basildon**	**Total**
	£	£	£
Sales	71,000	55,000	
Opening Stock	32,000	24,000	
Purchases	35,000	25,000	
Closing stock	31,000	23,000	
Cost of goods sold			
Gross Profit			

14.2 Complete the gross profit calculations for the retail group shown below. Make appropriate adjustments for stock in transit. No adjustments need to be made to the sales or purchases figures.

XYZ RETAIL LIMITED				
Profit and Loss Account (extract) for week ended 28 March 2004				
	Branch X	**Branch Y**	**Branch Z**	**Total**
	£	£	£	£
Sales	80,000	75,000	80,000	
Opening Stock	30,000	22,000	25,000	
Purchases	40,000	37,000	38,000	
Closing stock	28,000	21,000	24,000	
Cost of goods sold				
Gross Profit				
Transfers from X	2,000			
Transfers to Y and Z		1,000	500	

Note: On 27 March £500 of stock was transferred from Branch X to Branch Y. This was not recorded in the books of Branch Y until 1 April.

14.3   Your name is Owen Gerrard and you work as an accounts assistant for Anne Field Enterprises, a sole trader business which operates two sports shops in the North West, one in Liverpool and one in Southport. You work in the Liverpool office and are currently collecting the quarterly financial figures for the two branches so that you can consolidate them into a single profit and loss account.

The figures provided by the two branches are shown below. They include net transfers of stock at cost price between the two shops. Your line manager has told you that these transfers, which are included among the sales and purchases, should not be included in the consolidated figures.

The records from the Liverpool shop show that £200 of stock was sent to the Southport branch on 30 June. This stock in transit was not recorded in the Southport records until 2 July.

Anne Field Enterprises: Profit and Loss Account data for 3 months ended 30 June 2004

	Liverpool Branch		Southport Branch	
	£	£	£	£
Sales		120,000		100,500
Transfers to Southport at cost		5,100		-
		125,100		
Opening stock	56,000		46,000	
Purchases	61,000		53,000	
Transfers from Liverpool at cost	-		4,900	
	117,000		103,900	
Less closing stock	52,500		48,500	
Cost of goods sold		64,500		55,400
Gross Profit		60,600		45,100
Overheads		48,000		39,400
Net Profit		12,600		5,700

You note from the records that the combined profit and loss account figures for the two shops for the same period in 2003 were as follows:

	£
Sales	185,000
Cost of goods sold	112,000
Gross profit	73,000
Overheads	62,000
Net profit	11,000

You are to:

(a)   Consolidate the figures from the two shops into a profit and loss account for the business for the three months ended 30 June 2004, making the necessary adjustments to exclude transfers of stock, and stock in transit. No further adjustments need be made.

(b)   Draw up a table setting out comparative figures for the two years, including: sales, cost of goods sold, gross profit, gross profit percentage, overheads, net profit, net profit percentage (percentages should be calculated to two decimal places). Use a spreadsheet if possible.

(c)   Draw up (or extract from a spreadsheet) a compound bar chart showing for the two years

- sales revenue
- gross profit
- net profit

(d)   Write comments on the combined performance of the two shops over the two years.

14.4   Eveshore Farms Limited is a company which supplies the big supermarkets with speciality produce such as asparagus and soft fruit. Most of its sales are carried out by its Sales Division, but its also sells through its local farm shop, operated by its Production Division in Eveshore.

The quarterly sales figures produced by the two separate divisions are as shown below. In the column on the far right are set out the total quarterly sales figures for the previous year.

	Sales Division	**Production Division**			
2004	Total	Farm shop	Transfers to Sales Division	Total	Total Sales 2003
	£000	£000	£000	£000	£000
Jan-Mar	125	25	62	87	130
Apr-Jun	146	26	73	99	151
Jul-Sep	139	35	72	107	165
Oct-Dec	119	29	58	87	138

You are to

(a)   Draw up a table (or spreadsheet) which shows:

- the consolidated total sales figures for Eveshore Farms Limited for each quarter of 2004
- comparative total sales figures for 2003
- the cumulative sales figures for each quarter of 2004
- comparative cumulative sales figures for each quarter of 2003

(b)   Draw a line graph (or derive one from the spreadsheet) which shows the cumulative total sales figures for 2003 and 2004.

(c)   Write brief comments on your findings.

Reports and returns to outside agencies

In this chapter we examine a range of reports that organisations may have to complete and send to external bodies. These are required from time-to-time by a variety of external agencies:

- regulatory bodies such as HM Revenue & Customs
- organisations that award grants and provide finance, eg the Department of Trade and Industry and banks
- information-collecting organisations, eg Chambers of Commerce
- trade associations

We also stress the need to make sure that reports being sent off are:

- authorised by the appropriate person
- checked carefully for accuracy
- sent off on time and as required by the outside body

NVQ PERFORMANCE CRITERIA COVERED

unit 7: PREPARING REPORTS AND RETURNS

element 7.2

prepare reports and returns for outside agencies

A   identify, collate and present relevant information in accordance with the conventions and definitions used by outside agencies

B   ensure calculations of ratios and performance indicators are accurate

C   obtain authorisation for the despatch of completed reports and returns from the appropriate person

D   present reports and returns in accordance with outside agencies' requirements and deadlines

WHO NEEDS REPORTS?

As well as the requirement for internal reporting seen so far in this book, organisations will need from time-to-time to complete returns to external agencies. As you will see, some of these returns are covered elsewhere in your studies, eg a VAT Return. In this chapter we will present a series of Case Studies covering all the main types of return, showing how information held by the organisation is entered onto the form.

Most returns are on 'pro-forma' forms – ie the information is entered in boxes or on defined lines on pre-printed pages. This makes the information easier to identify and to collect by the organisation completing the return, and easier to process by the body asking for it. Occasionally a return may require a written report – eg part of a business plan submitted for a grant application – but the majority of returns will be straightforward forms, and these will be illustrated in detail in the Case Studies.

grant awarding bodies

If an organisation needs to raise money there are banks and other financial companies which will provide loans and public sector (government owned or controlled) bodies which will provide grants, and, in some cases, loans. Details of these sources of finance are available through Chambers of Commerce and Business Link offices. Any application for finance or a grant will invariably involve sending the organisation financial and non-financial details, as we will see in the Case Studies. Examples of finance and grant-awarding bodies include:

- banks
- local authorities
- the Department of Trade and Industry
- the European Commission

statistical information collectors

Organisations may from time-to-time be asked to complete questionnaires sent them by government agencies or Chambers of Commerce. These will cover areas such as economic trends, employment trends, skills shortages, transport, information technology, and so on. These are not like the regulatory returns which *have to be* returned, but many organisations do complete them. Although much of the required detail is not 'accounting' data as such, these returns may well involve financial aspects such as sales trends and wage rates which will involve input from the accounting function.

trade associations

A trade association is basically a membership 'club' for businesses in a particular trade, eg ABTA (Association of British Travel Agents) and the Publishers Association. As well as safeguarding and promoting the interests of businesses in those sectors, trade associations collect data from their individual members for statistical purposes and in some cases to produce directories. This data, for a retailing organisation might include details such as the level of annual sales (within certain bands), terms of trade (discounts given) and the number of employees. The accounting function of a retailer – whether it be a small shop or a major retail chain – may well have to send in these details on a regular basis.

regulatory bodies

Organisations are subject by law to a variety of external regulations and need periodically to provide returns to the bodies that administer those regulations. Examples include:

- *HM Revenue & Customs* which requires details of payroll (employer's P35 annual return), tax liabilities (self-assessment form for sole traders, accounts for larger businesses) and regular completion of a VAT 100 (VAT return) by VAT-registered businesses (see page 408)

- *Companies House* which regulates the running of limited companies and requires an annual return from companies and the filing of accounts for larger companies

authorisation of returns

All reports and returns sent to external agencies should go through a rigorous checking and authorisation procedure. There should be no short cuts in the process. Checks should ensure that all the information required is present and in the correct format. External reports and returns should also be sent off on time; most organisations will set up a diary system to ensure that this happens. Some returns will require an authorised signature; this should not be overlooked.

This aspect of reports and returns cannot be stressed too highly: there are fines for late company returns and also for errors on VAT returns, even if the error was accidental. Late submission of VAT returns can sometimes trigger off a VAT inspection. No more need be said!

CASE STUDIES

The remainder of this chapter is made up of Case Studies which explain what reports and returns are likely to be encountered and how they will be completed. They are:

- Trading figures for a bank – Design Furniture Limited
- Application for an Export Award – Helios Vision
- Chamber of Commerce Questionnaire – Villas of Italy
- Trade Association return – Microwise Publications
- VAT Return – Pomona Garden Supplies

It must be stressed that the businesses on which the Case Studies are based are entirely fictitious. The bodies to which the returns are sent are real. Osborne Books is grateful to these bodies for permission to reproduce material which they have supplied.

Case Study

TRADING FIGURES FOR THE BANK: DESIGN FURNITURE LIMITED

situation

Design Furniture Limited is a small shop selling quality design furniture to a wide range of commercial and private customers. Much of the furniture is imported; many of the customers pay on credit.

Two years ago Design Furniture Limited took out a long-term loan of £50,000 from the bank to help set up its present premises.

As part of the financing arrangements Design Furniture Limited undertook to provide trading figures for the bank on a monthly basis so that the bank could monitor the progress of the company. Clearly if the company was running into any difficulties, the bank could pick up the warning signs from the trading figures.

The trading figures show:

Current assets (money due to the company in the short term)

less **Current liabilities** (money owed by the business in the short term)

The bank would want to know that current assets were greater than current liabilities. The difference between the two (the 'working capital' of the business) enables the business to pay bills as they fall due.

source of the trading figures

The figures for the return (shown opposite) will be found in the accounting records of the company.

Trade debtors are listed in the Aged Debtor Summary, an extract from which is shown below. The summary – often produced as a monthly report on a computer accounting program – lists all customers to whom the business sells on credit. It is essentially the Sales Ledger summarised to show who owes what, and when. Its balance total will equal the total of debtors' control account. It lists in columns:

• customer names

• credit limits

• balances

• amounts not yet due – ie 'current' – assuming the company gives 30 days' credit

• amounts outstanding over 30 days

• amounts outstanding over 60 days

An extract from this schedule, with some sample entries, is shown below. It is the total line which will be used to complete the return

AGED DEBTOR SCHEDULE (extract)				date:	31 March 2003
Customer	**limit**	**balance**	**current**	**over 30 days**	**over 60 days**
	£	£	£	£	£
Adams Trading	2,000	1,457.67	1,457.67		
Braswell Ltd	2,000	1,590.50	1,000.00	590.50	
Duff Limited	1,000	1,300.00			1,300.00
TOTAL		75,060.00	35,431.00	23,906.00	15,723.00

The remaining figures are provided by the accounts office:

• the stock figure will be taken from the total of the Stores Ledger Records.

• the following figures will be taken from the monthly trial balance (list of account balances): cash account, creditors control, VAT due

• creditors figures will be taken from an aged creditor summary – constructed on the same principle as the aged debtor summary shown above

• prepayments and accruals will be noted in the records

• PAYE – income tax and National Insurance due to the Inland Revenue by the 19th of the following month – the figures will be known by the payroll office

solution

These figures are inserted on the form shown opposite and are then checked carefully. When all is in order and authorised, the form will be sent to the bank within the stipulated deadline – early in the next month. A copy will be taken for the records.

Statement of Current Trading Position
("Quick Figures")

Business Name	*DESIGN FURNITURE LTD*
As at (date)	*31 MARCH 2003*

Current Assets

a. Total Trade Debtors (ie. funds owed to you by your customers)   £   *75,060*

Please give a breakdown of your trade debtors according to how long they have been outstanding:

Up to 30 days	£	*35,431*
31 to 60 days	£	*23,906*
Over 60 days	£	*15,723*

b. Stock and Work in Progress   £   *36,107*

c. Cash Held and Total of all Bank and Building Society Credit Balances in your books   £   *5,920*

d. Other Current Assets (please specify, eg. prepayments)   *PHONE RENTAL PREPAID*

    £   *120*

Total Current Assets   (a)+(b)+(c)+(d)   £   *117,207*

Current Liabilities

e. Trade Creditors (ie. funds you owe your suppliers)   £   *59,235*

Please give a breakdown of your trade creditors according to how long they have been outstanding:

Up to 30 days	£	*45,165*
31 to 60 days	£	*12,107*
Over 60 days	£	*1,963*

f. Total of all Overdrawn Bank Balances in your books   £   *NIL*

g. Pay As You Earn (PAYE) Owed by the Business   £   *1,483*

h. Value Added Tax (VAT) Owed by the Business   £   *6,270*

i. Other Current Liabilities (please specify, eg. accruals)   *AUDIT FEE ACCRUED*

    £   *1,500*

Total Current Liabilities   (e)+(f)+(g)+(h)+(i)   £   *68,488*

Case Study

APPLICATION FOR AN EXPORT AWARD: HELIOS VISION

situation

Helios Vision Plc is a fast-growing UK manufacturer of fashion sunglasses. This company has been particularly successful in exporting to the USA and Australia. One of its success stories is the distinctive 'Cool Shade' brand which was adopted by Brad Street, star of the American TV soap 'Sunrise Park'.

The Board of Directors has decided to apply for a Government-backed Export Award for smaller businesses – over £50,000 worth of cash and professional services are available. Applications for awards are competitive. Eligible businesses must be: independent UK-based businesses, manufacturers or providers of services, employers of no more than 250 people and not a previous award winner.

On the financial side, applicants must:

• show growth in export earnings over the last 3 years

• achieve at least £100,000 in export earnings over the most recent year

The application involves:

• an entry form signed by the Managing Director (see opposite)

• a Statement of Export Achievement on one side of A4 paper

John Brandon, the MD, has asked the Sales Department to provide the written statement. It is your job to complete the figures in Part 2b of the form shown opposite.

solution

You research the accounting records and extract the following figures, which you set out in a table ready for checking and transferring to the form. You also contact the payroll supervisor for employee numbers over the last three years.

HELIOS VISION PLC			
Year to:	31.12.00	31.12.01	31.12.02
	£	£	£
UK Sales	487,612	542,373	680,063
Export Sales	105,961	189,731	249,500
Total Sales	593,573	732,104	929,563
Net profit (after tax)	71,725	93,763	121,811

When the figures have been checked and authorised, the form should be completed and passed to the MD's office for signature by John Brandon and submission by 20 May – the stipulated deadline.

ENTRY FORM
(Please type or print clearly using a ball point pen)

PART 1 Full name and address

Chairman/Managing Director	JOHN BRANDON
Company Name	HELIOS VISION
Company Address	UNIT 17 HARTBURY ESTATE
	MEREFORD
County & Postcode	MR2 5HN Tel: 01902 743193 Fax: 01902 743748
Parent Company (if any)	—
Subsidiaries (if any)	—
Total number of employees in Group (incl. Directors & employees of parent & subsidiary companies)	120

Type of Company: Manufacturing ✓   Service ◇   (Please tick)

Description of products or services exported from the UK: SUNGLASSES

PART 2 Figures *(Please tick one box to show which Award you are applying for)*

2a **Entry for Regional Award** ✓
The Best Exporting Company of the Year will be selected from the Regional Winners. Figures must be provided for the latest three complete financial years,

2b **Entry for Best Newcomer Award** ◇
Figures must be provided for the first full year of exporting

Full financial years ended MONTH	YEAR	Number of employees (Applicant firm only)	Export earnings	Whole annual turnover	Net profit after tax
DEC	2000	98	£105,961	£593,573	£71,725
DEC	2001	107	£189,731	£732,104	£93,763
DEC	2002	120	£249,500	£929,563	£121,811

PART 3 Statement of Export Achievement

A Statement of Export Achievement (not exceeding one side of A4 paper) must be submitted with this entry. Its scope is at the discretion of the entrant company but should include a short resume of the business, a description of its products/services and most importantly, details of how current export success has been achieved. Points of particular interest are sales and marketing methods, market research methods and export management.

Statement attached *(Please tick)* ✓

PART 4 Certification

◆ We submit this entry and attach a TYPED ONE-PAGE statement of export achievement. We undertake to submit immediately our latest audited Report and Accounts and an Auditor's Certificate supporting the figures in Part 2 above, in the event of our company being included on the preliminary shortlist.

◆ We hereby certify that all the particulars supplied by us in our entry are correct to the best of our knowledge and belief and comply with definitions set out and that no material information has been withheld.

◆ We accept the rules and conditions of entry A to D and agree to abide by the decisions of the Panel of Judges and the sponsors on all matters relating to these Awards.

Date 11 April 2003   Signature (of Chairman or Managing Director) J. Brandon

The Award Administrator will acknowledge receipt of your entry and will advise you whether or not you have been included on the preliminary shortlist in due course. You will be provided with a reference number which you should quote in any correspondence concerning this application.

Case Study

CHAMBER OF COMMERCE QUESTIONNAIRE: VILLAS OF ITALY

the business

You work as an accounts assistant for Villas of Italy, a Bristol-based agency which arranges Italian villa holidays for UK clients. The business is owned and managed by Luigi Ferrini. The typical holiday is two weeks spent in a luxury Tuscan hilltop villa with swimming pool and maid service. Villas of Italy hires the properties from Italian landowners and their agents, arranges charter flights to local airports and car hire and insurance as required.

Villas of Italy employs nine staff, most of them based at its Bristol headquarters. They have just been given a well-deserved pay rise. Although business performance has been steady for the last year, the fall in value of the pound against the Italian Lira has resulted in a rise in costs.

the questionnaire

Villas of Italy is a member of the local Chamber of Commerce, which Luigi finds useful, not only for its discounts on business services, but also for the opportunity he has to meet up with other business owners.

He has recently received a questionnaire from the Chamber of Commerce asking for a wide range of business information, including details of:

- market trends
- the labour market
- business investment plans
- business cash flow
- business sales and profitability
- details of influences on prices and costs

The text of the questionnaire is set out on the next three pages.

Although no financial figures are requested in the questionnaire, he asks you as accounts assistant to extract figures which provide evidence for the trends enquired about in the questionnaire. In particular you find out details of:

- sales and profit performance (Questions 2 and 7)
- cash flow (Question 5)
- investment plans (Question 6)
- sales budgets (Question 7)
- cost budgets (Question 9)

It is likely that Luigi will then complete the form with your help. The office will ensure that the form is sent off on time, to the correct person at the correct address.

BRITISH CHAMBERS OF COMMERCE

QUARTERLY ECONOMIC SURVEY

All responses are treated in the strictest confidence

1) Your Business

a) How many people do you currently employ? .....9.....

b) Please state your postcode (this is so we can break results down by area) MR1 2JF

c) What is your main activity ?   VILLA   LETTINGS

Manufacturing

Energy and Water Supply
Minerals and Chemicals
Metal Goods and Engineering
Other Manufacturing
Construction
Don't Know (please describe)

Services

Distribution, Hotels/Catering, repairs [✓]
Transport and Communication
Financial and Business Services
Other Services
Agriculture
Don't Know (please describe)

2) For Businesses involved in the UK market, excluding seasonal variations, over the past 3 months

a) Sales / Custom / Bookings have ...
increased [✓]
remained constant
decreased

b) Orders / Advance Custom / Bookings have ...
increased [✓]
remained constant
decreased

3) For Businesses involved in Overseas Markets, excluding seasonal variations, over the past 3 months N/A

a) Overseas Sales / Custom / Bookings have ...
increased
remained constant
decreased

b) Overseas Orders / Advance Custom / Bookings have..
increased
remained constant
decreased

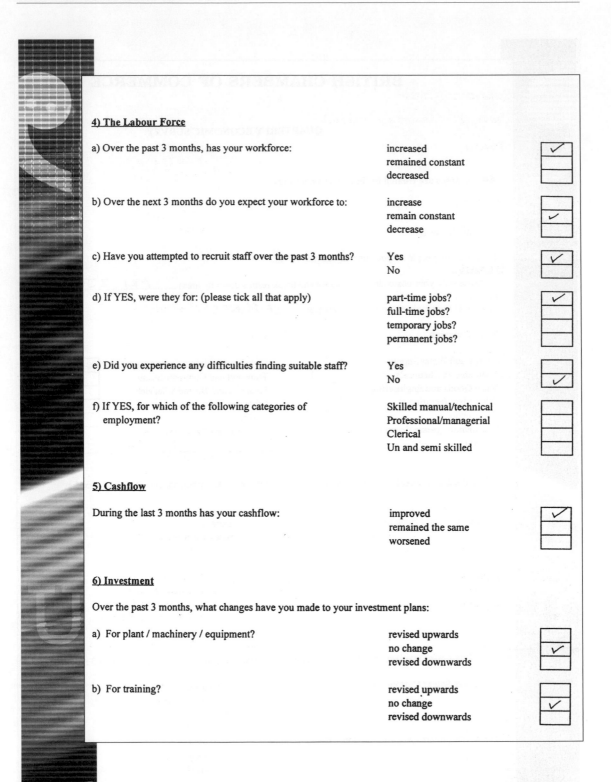

4) The Labour Force

a) Over the past 3 months, has your workforce:

increased ✓
remained constant
decreased

b) Over the next 3 months do you expect your workforce to:

increase
remain constant ✓
decrease

c) Have you attempted to recruit staff over the past 3 months?

Yes ✓
No

d) If YES, were they for: (please tick all that apply)

part-time jobs? ✓
full-time jobs?
temporary jobs?
permanent jobs?

e) Did you experience any difficulties finding suitable staff?

Yes
No ✓

f) If YES, for which of the following categories of
   employment?

Skilled manual/technical
Professional/managerial
Clerical
Un and semi skilled

5) Cashflow

During the last 3 months has your cashflow:

improved ✓
remained the same
worsened

6) Investment

Over the past 3 months, what changes have you made to your investment plans:

a) For plant / machinery / equipment?

revised upwards
no change ✓
revised downwards

b) For training?

revised upwards
no change
revised downwards ✓

7) Business Confidence

Do you believe that over the next 12 months:

Turnover	will improve	
	remain the same	✓
	worsen	.

Profitability	will improve	
	remain the same	✓
	worsen	

8) Capacity

Are you currently operating at :	full capacity ?	✓
	below full capacity ?	

9) Prices / Costs

a) Over the next 3 months, do you expect the price of your goods / services to	increase	
	remain the same	✓
	decrease	

b) Is your business currently suffering pressures to raise its prices from any of the following ?	pay settlements	✓
	raw material prices	
	finance costs	
	other overheads	

10) External Factors

Please indicate which of these following factors are more of a concern to your business than 3 months ago. (please tick all that apply)

Interest rates		Competition	
Exchange rates	✓	Corporate taxation	
Business rates		Better Industrial Relations	
Inflation		Improved cash availability	

Case Study

TRADE ASSOCIATION RETURNS: MICROWISE PUBLICATIONS

Microwise is the trade name of Microwise Publications Limited, a small company which publishes books and manuals explaining how to operate computers and use computer programs.

Microwise supplies wholesalers and bookshops and also operates a mail order department which advertises in computer magazines and sells direct to the general public.

Microwise has dealings with two Trade Associations:

- it is a member of the Independent Publishers Guild which looks after the interests of small publishers
- it provides information to the Booksellers Association, which looks after the interests of bookshops and wholesalers

The returns it has to make contain basic statistics which are important for trading. The data will be readily available in the accounts and sales departments of the company. An extract from the annual return to the Independent Publishers Guild is shown below.

INDEPENDENT PUBLISHERS GUILD ANNUAL RETURN

```
Microwise Publications Limited
Laurel House
Heathcote
Lincs
PE14 6TR
```

COMPANY DETAILS

Year Started Trading:	1987
Number Titles in Print:	153
Turnover Range*:	D

NUMBER OF STAFF

Working Owners
No. Full Time:	2
No. Part Time:	1

Other Staff
No. Full Time:	8
No. Part Time:	3
No. Freelances Used:	6

*TURNOVER RANGES
A: Under £25,000
B: £25,000 to £100,000
C: £100,000 to £500,000
D: £500,000 to £1,000,000
E: £1,000,000 to £5,000,000
F: £5,000,000 +

Case Study

VAT REGULATION: POMONA GARDEN SUPPLIES

Note: you should have encountered VAT in your studies and will study it in greater detail in the two chapters which follow. This Case Study helps to put the VAT Return into context as a return required by an external agency, HM Revenue & Customs.

Pomona Garden Supplies, based in the East Midlands, grows shrubs and trees which it sells to garden centres throughout the region. The business is VAT-registered, which means that it has to charge VAT on goods which it sells, and can reclaim VAT which it has to pay when it purchases goods and services. Every three months it has to complete a VAT Return on Form VAT 100. This provides details of sales and purchases for the period and totals of VAT charged and paid. The object of the exercise is to calculate how much VAT is due to be paid by the business to HM Revenue & Customs for the three months January to March.

The details entered on the form from the accounting records of the business are:

- Sales of £102,901 and VAT of £18,007.67 charged on these sales.

* Purchases of £63,726 and VAT of £10,748.23 charged on most of these (a few transactions are zero-rated – no VAT is payable).

- VAT due to HM Revenue & Customs of £7,259.44; a cheque for this amount will be sent with the tax return (note that the box in the bottom left-hand side is ticked).

The illustration below shows the bottom half of the VAT 100 form completed by the business. The signature is that of an authorised employee – very probably the Finance Director. The form, which covers the three months January to March, must be checked carefully and sent off by the end of April.

Before you fill in this form please read the notes on the back and the VAT leaflet *"Filling in your VAT return"*. Fill in all boxes clearl in ink, and write 'none' where necessary. Don't put a dash or leave any box blank. If there are no pence write **"00"** in the pence column. **Do not** enter more than one amount in any box.

For official use **SPECIMEN**		£	p
VAT due in this period on **sales** and other outputs	**1**	18,007	67
VAT due in this period on **acquisitions** from other **EC Member States**	**2**	–	
Total VAT due (**the sum of boxes 1 and 2**)	**3**	18,007	67
VAT reclaimed in this period on **purchases** and other inputs (including acquisitions from the EC)	**4**	10,748	23
Net VAT to be paid to Customs or reclaimed by you (**Difference between boxes 3 and 4**)	**5**	7,259	44
Total value of **sales** and all other outputs excluding any VAT. **Include your box 8 figure**	**6**	102,901	00
Total value of **purchases** and all other inputs excluding any VAT. **Include your box 9 figure**	**7**	63,726	00
Total value of all **supplies** of goods and related services, excluding any VAT, to other **EC Member States**	**8**	–	00
Total value of all **acquisitions** of goods and related services, excluding any VAT, from other **EC Member States**	**9**	–	00

Retail schemes. If you have used any of the schemes in the period covered by this return, enter the relevant letter(s) in this box.   –

If you are enclosing a payment please tick this box.   ✓

DECLARATION: You, or someone on your behalf, must sign below.

I, ... ARTHUR JAMES HENSON ....declare that the
(Full name of signatory in BLOCK LETTERS)

information given above is true and complete.

Signature ....Date .... 8 APRIL 2003

A false declaration can result in prosecution.

L

Chapter Summary

- Organisations may from time-to-time need to make returns to outside bodies.

- The returns are normally on pre-printed forms, but occasionally an additional written text may be required.

- The types of bodies requiring returns are

    - grant awarding bodies and providers of finance, eg banks

    - collectors of statistical information

    - trade associations

    - regulatory bodies such as HM Revenue & Customs

- The returns should be completed in the format and manner in which they are requested by the outside agency.

- It is essential that all completed returns are carefully checked, authorised and sent off within the stipulated deadline.

Key Terms

pro-forma	a preprinted form with a defined format
public sector bodies	organisations which are government-owned or government controlled
Department of Trade & Industry	the DTI is the UK government agency responsible for administering business incentive schemes
European Commission	the Brussels-based body which is responsible for administering the law and regulations of the European Union
trade association	a membership 'club' for a particular trade, responsible for safeguarding interests and, in some cases, regulation
Inland Revenue	the body responsible for the regulation administration and collection of tax (but not VAT)
HM Revenue & Customs	the government body responsible for the regulation and administration of import and export duties and Value Added Tax

Student Activities

15.1 Romona Smith is the owner/manager of a franchised gift shop in Stourford. The business is called 'Cute Ideas' and is supplied from the franchisor in Kettering.

The franchisor in Kettering requires a regular return of information from its franchisees (shops). Each shop is set an agreed quarterly sales target. Sales are divided into:

- Category A (books and cards)

- Category B (novelties)

Each quarter a form (see next page) is sent to shop owners requesting

- sales figures

- variances from targets (amounts)

- variances from target in the form of percentage deviation from the targets

A box is also supplied for comments by the shop owner.

The franchisor takes as commission 10% of the sales figure each quarter as part of the franchise agreement, and a box is included on the form for calculation of this payment.

When the form is completed it is returned to the franchisor together with a commission cheque within fifteen days of the end of the quarter.

It is the first week in April. Romona has just reached the end of her January - March trading quarter and has to fill in the form from the accounting information she has printed out from her computer:

	Target (£)	Actual (£)
Sales A	15,000	13,500
Sales B	21,000	18,000

Romona tells you that the last three months have not been good for a number of reasons – bad weather keeping customers away, a similar shop opening up two doors away, road works and customers being short of cash after Christmas.

You are to:

(a)   Enter the sales figures on the form

(b)   Calculate the variances (amounts and percentages – to the nearest £ and %)

(c)   Calculate the commission due

(d)   Provide comments in the space

(e)   Sign and date the form in Romona's name (assume the current year, first quarter)

CUTE IDEAS	Trading Report		Quarter ended ..../........./.......	
£		£	£ variance	% variance
Sales A (actual)	Sales Target A			
Sales B (actual)	Sales Target B			
Total Sales (actual)	Total Sales Target			
10% Commission on sales £		(cheque enclosed)		
Comments				
signature		**date**		

15.2 Heather Springer runs 'Just Desserts' a pudding and dessert manufacturing company which supplies local pubs and restuarants. She has recently borrowed £45,000 from the bank to extend her baking facilities and has just been sent a 'Statement of Current Trading Position' (shown opposite) to complete and return to the bank. The date is today's date.

You are to:

(a)   Complete the form for her. She provides you with the following information:

AGED DEBTOR SCHEDULE (extract)				
Customer	balance	current	over 30 days	over 60 days
	£	£	£	£
TOTALS	29,216.00	21,075.00	4,629.00	3,512.00

- Stock held is valued at £8,760; there is £5,631 in the bank business account.
- She is due to pay £8,920 corporation (company) tax shortly.
- She owes £1,720 to the Inland Revenue from a recent payroll run.
- No VAT is due because her goods are zero-rated. She is due a refund of £890.
- She owes £7,329 to suppliers (up to 30 days) and £8,160 (31 to 60 days).

(b)   State whether you think the bank will be happy with her return.

Statement of Current Trading Position
("Quick Figures")

Business Name _____

As at (date) _____

Current Assets

a. Total Trade Debtors (ie. funds owed to you by your customers)   £ _____

Please give a breakdown of your trade debtors according to how long they have been outstanding:

Up to 30 days   £ _____

31 to 60 days   £ _____

Over 60 days   £ _____

b. Stock and Work in Progress   £ _____

c. Cash Held and Total of all Bank and Building Society Credit Balances in your books £ _____

d. Other Current Assets (please specify, eg. prepayments) _____

_____   £ _____

Total Current Assets   **(a)+(b)+(c)+(d)**   **£** _____

Current Liabilities

e. Trade Creditors (ie. funds you owe your suppliers)   £ _____

Please give a breakdown of your trade creditors according to how long they have been outstanding:

Up to 30 days   £ _____

31 to 60 days   £ _____

Over 60 days   £ _____

f. Total of all Overdrawn Bank Balances in your books   £ _____

g. Pay As You Earn (PAYE) Owed by the Business   £ _____

h. Value Added Tax (VAT) Owed by the Business   £ _____

i. Other Current Liabilities (please specify, eg. accruals) _____

_____   £ _____

Total Current Liabilities   **(e)+(f)+(g)+(h)+(i)**   **£** _____

In this chapter we explain what Value Added Tax (VAT) is and how it works in practice. We cover the following areas:

- a definition of Value Added Tax
- the law that regulates VAT
- the various rates of VAT
- registration for VAT
- VAT on sales (ouput tax) and VAT on purchases (input VAT)
- the timing of VAT – the 'tax point'
- VAT invoices – the different types and what they involve
- VAT on imports and exports

In the next chapter we will examine the accounting records that need to be kept for VAT and how they provide the information for the VAT return.

Note: you will still often see references to 'EC' (European Community) in publications; in this chapter we will use the more recent term 'EU' (European Union).

NVQ PERFORMANCE CRITERIA COVERED

unit 7: PREPARING REPORTS AND RETURNS

element 7.3

prepare VAT returns

A   complete and submit VAT returns correctly, using data from the appropriate recording systems, within the statutory time limits

B   correctly identify and calculate relevant inputs and outputs

C   ensure submissions are made in accordance with current legislation

D   ensure guidance is sought from the VAT Office when required, in a professional manner

VAT AND REGULATION OF VAT

a definition

Value Added Tax (VAT) is a tax on the sale of goods and services

VAT is not only charged in the UK: many countries charge VAT (or a similar sales tax), and at varying rates. VAT – essentially a tax on spending – is an important source of revenue for any government. In the UK, VAT is also a tax on *imports* into the country. VAT is charged at a standard percentage rate (currently 17.5% in the UK) on *business* transactions.

VAT regulation and sources of information

The body which regulates and collects VAT in the UK is HM Revenue & Customs, which combines the operations of the Inland Revenue and what was formerly HM Customs & Excise.

VAT law in the European Union is governed by Directives which are brought into effect in the UK by statute law: the Value Added Tax Act (1994), the annual Finance Acts, and other regulations issued by the government, including sections of the 'The VAT Guide' issued by HM Revenue & Customs which explains and interprets the VAT regulations. The 'VAT Guide' is available free of charge from local VAT offices and is *essential reading*. HM Revenue & Customs also publishes a series of supplementary leaflets and booklets. These are available on the HM Revenue & Customs website – www.hmrc.gov.uk – which is an invaluable source of information for keeping up-to-date with the changes in VAT regulations.

You will not be expected in your studies to know all the 'ins and outs' of the VAT regulations, but you will be required to know *where* to find the required information, as would any practising accountant.

It should also be mentioned that the accounting treatment of VAT is set out in Statement of Standard Accounting Practice (SSAP) 5 'Accounting for Value Added Tax'. This is covered elsewhere in your Level 3 studies – see Osborne Books' *Financial Records & Accounts Tutorial*. The unit covered by this book concentrates on the administration of VAT and the VAT records needed for the VAT return.

an overview of VAT

Before explaining VAT in detail we will first take a brief look at the whole VAT process.

Most suppliers of goods and services charge VAT, unless, of course, there is no VAT payable, as in the case of the sale of food and young childrens clothes (see page 382 for zero-rated and exempt supplies). There is a registration threshold set by the government each year, normally in the Budget. From April 2008 the threshold was set at £67,000. If at the end of any month a supplier's total sales (turnover) for the past *year* exceeds this figure, or is *likely to exceed this figure during the next 30 days*, that supplier must by law register with HM Revenue & Customs to become what is known as a *taxable person.*

The effect of this registration means that the supplier (taxable person)

* *must* charge VAT on chargeable supplies (ie goods and services)
    – this is known as *output tax*

* can *reclaim* VAT paid on most supplies received
    – this is known as *input tax*

As most businesses are run to make a profit – ie more money will be received from sales than is spent on supplies – most businesses will charge more VAT (output tax) than they pay (input tax). The difference between these two must be paid to HM Revenue & Customs.

If a business trades in goods or services on which no VAT is payable (eg books or sewerage services) the business will pay more VAT than it will charge, so it can reclaim the difference from HM Revenue & Customs.

The business owner will have to complete a VAT Return (Form VAT 100) or make an Electronic VAT Return (EVR) on a regular basis – normally quarterly – to account to HM Revenue & Customs for the amount of VAT due or refundable. This is covered in the next chapter.

VAT – a tax on the final consumer

VAT is a tax which is paid by the final consumer of the goods.

If we take, for, example, a member of the public buying a computer for £705, the amount paid includes VAT of £105 (ie 17.5% of £600). The buyer stands the cost of the VAT, but the VAT is actually *paid* to HM Revenue & Customs by all those involved in the manufacturing and selling process.

This procedure is illustrated by the flow chart shown on the opposite page. You will see that the right hand column shows the amount of VAT paid to HM Revenue & Customs at each stage in the process. The supplier of raw materials, the manufacturer and the shop all pay over to HM Revenue & Customs the difference between VAT on sales (outputs) and VAT on purchases (inputs), but this amount is collected from the next person in the process. It is the *consumer* who foots the VAT bill at the end of the day. The VAT is paid to the shop, but as you can see from the diagram, the tax has already been paid (or will soon be paid) to HM Revenue & Customs.

collection of Value Added Tax

manufacture and sale of a computer

supplier of materials

sells materials for £200 plus £35 VAT = £235

manufacturer

adds on margin and sells computer for £440 plus £77 VAT = £517

shop

adds on margin and sells computer for £600 plus £105 VAT = £705

final consumer

buys computer for £600 plus £105 VAT = £705

- keeps £200
- pays £35 to HM Revenue & Customs

- keeps £440
- pays £42 to HM Revenue & Customs (difference between £77 collected and £35 paid to supplier)

- keeps £600
- pays £28 to HM Revenue & Customs (difference between £105 collected and £77 paid to supplier)

- pays nothing <u>directly</u> to HM Revenue & Customs (the £105 has all been paid to the shop)

VAT payments to HM Revenue & Customs

£35

plus

£42

plus

£28

plus

£0

equals

£105

RATES OF VAT

There are currently three rates of VAT in the UK:

- standard rate   17.5%
- reduced rate (eg on energy-saving products)   5%
- zero rate   0%

Zero-rated supplies are *not* the same as exempt supplies, although the result is the same – no VAT is charged. We will now look at these types of supply.

zero-rated supplies

Zero-rated supplies are goods and services taxed at 0%. This may sound odd, but all it means is that the supplies are taxable, but the government has decided that no tax should be charged, normally because the goods are an essential part of spending and to tax them would place a burden on the less well-off. Examples of zero-rated supplies are:

- food bought in shops, but not in restuarants
- young childrens' clothes and shoes
- transport – eg bus and train fares
- newpapers, magazines and books
- pedal cycle helmets

An important point here is that businesses that sell zero-rated goods *can reclaim the VAT charged* (the input tax) on supplies that they have bought. For example, there was no VAT charged on this book, but the publisher was able to reclaim the VAT paid on the cost of the book, eg the paper used, the marketing costs and so on. The situation with *exempt supplies* is quite different.

exempt supplies

Whereas zero-rated supplies are chargeable – at 0% – exempt supplies are not chargeable at all. Also, *a supplier who supplies only VAT-exempt goods or services cannot reclaim any input VAT*. Examples of supplies that are exempt include:

- certain types of insurance
- postal services from the Post Office
- education and healthcare
- betting and gambling, burials and cremations

You should read the 'VAT Guide' which illustrates these points further. (This is available on www.hmrc.gov.uk as Notice 700).

REGISTRATION FOR VAT

who should register?

A person in business selling goods and services on which VAT is chargeable must apply to HM Revenue & Customs on Form VAT 1 to become VAT registered:

- when the value of the taxable supplies (the *taxable turnover*) over a twelve month period *has exceeded* a registration limit set annually by the Government (£67,000 from April 2008) – the person must apply within 30 days of the end of the 12 months
- when the value of the taxable supplies (before VAT is added on) *is likely within the next thirty days* to exceed the annual registration limit

In short, a person must apply to the local VAT Office to register (within 30 days) if taxable supplies have exceeded, or are likely to exceed the annual limit. If this registration is not carried out within the 30 day time limit the person can be fined – the reason being that the supplier will be failing to collect tax due to HM Revenue & Customs.

Suppliers of zero-rated goods and services are included in these regulations, although they *may* apply for exemption from registration. It is unlikely that they will do so, however, because then they will lose the right to reclaim any VAT on goods and services they have purchased, and will be out of pocket!

It is critical that a person should register for VAT if the supplies are chargeable. There have been cases of profitable businesses which have not registered and have been 'discovered' by HM Revenue & Customs after a period of years: they have had to pay *from their own resources* all the VAT they should have charged and have been bankrupted in the process.

a business or not a business?

A business is defined by the VAT authorities as an activity which involves selling goods or a service for money over a period of time. Note that:

- it is only a *business* activity which can be VAT-registered – hobbies cannot normally be registered and business owners are *not* able to reclaim VAT on private expenses
- it is the person running the business who applies for registration – this term 'person' is fairly wide ranging and includes:
  - sole proprietors
  - partnerships
  - limited companies or groups of companies
  - clubs and associations
  - charities

non-registered businesses

Businesses that have a turnover below the annual limit do not have to register for VAT. This can be useful for a business owner, for example, because he or she can in effect become more competitive and charge less for goods and services, although there is the downside that the trader cannot reclaim VAT paid on supplies he or she has bought. This is *not* the same as the practice adopted by some 'shady' VAT-registered businesses saying to their customers "If you pay me cash in hand you won't have to pay the VAT". This is illegal and an attempt to defraud HM Revenue & Customs of VAT due.

voluntary registration

A supplier whose taxable turnover falls below the annual limit may register for VAT. This is normally because he or she will benefit from claiming back input tax on purchases, eg if the business deals in zero-rated goods.

deregistration

If a business finds that annual turnover falls – or is likely to fall – below a certain limit (normally slightly less than the registration limit) that business can apply to HM Revenue & Customs and *deregister,* if it seems advantageous to do so.

practicalities of registration

- When a person has been registered for VAT a registration certificate will be issued giving full details of registration, including the *VAT number* which must be quoted on VAT invoices.

- VAT paid by the person on expenses in setting up the business may normally be reclaimed.

- VAT must be charged on sales as soon as registration takes place.

OUTPUT TAX AND INPUT TAX - FURTHER POINTS

output tax value

The *tax value* of a supply is the value on which the VAT percentage rate is calculated. This seems a fairly obvious point, but there are situations where this value is not clear.

- *cash discounts* – as you may have seen in your previous studies, if a supplier offers a percentage discount for prompt payment (eg within 7 days), the VAT will be calculated on the *discounted* amount, even if the purchaser does not take up the offer and takes 30 days or more to pay

- *foreign currency values* – importers of goods and services into the UK invoiced in a foreign currency must always work out the VAT on the *sterling equivalent* of the foreign currency converted using a consistent method (the rates used can be the newspaper rates or the rates published by HM Revenue & Customs)

input tax exceptions

A VAT-registered business will obviously try to claim back input tax on as many expenses as it legitimately can. There are however a number of items on which VAT *cannot* be reclaimed. These include:

- purchase of a car for a business (unless the business sells cars or the car is to be used as a taxi and exclusively by the business)
- business entertainment expenses
- goods and services purchased, but *not* used in the business

It is quite common for a business owner to have the benefit of goods and services which are used *partly* for the business and *partly* for personal domestic use, eg home telephone, heating and lighting in a home office. In these instances, the business owner can *apportion* the tax, ie split the input VAT between business and private use and claim back only the input tax relating to business use.

TAX POINTS

The *tax point* of a taxable supply is the date on which it is recorded as taking place for the purposes of the tax return.

For *goods* the *basic tax point* is normally when the goods are sent to the customer or taken away by the customer. For *services* the basic tax point is normally when the service is performed.

It is usual practice for the tax point to be *fixed:*

- if a VAT invoice (see page 387) is issued or payment is received *before* the basic tax point (the supply of the goods or service) then the date of the invoice or payment – whichever happens first – becomes the *actual tax point*
- if a VAT invoice is issued *up to 14 days* after the basic tax point (date of supply) the date of issue of the invoice becomes the tax point

The 14 day rule may be varied – with the written approval of the local VAT Office. For example, a supplier may issue monthly invoices on a regular basis for goods or services supplied during the whole of the month. The date of the invoice or the last day of the month – consistently applied – can then become the *actual tax point.*

The principle of the tax point is important to the VAT-registered business:

- it results in a consistent and accurate method of recording VAT transactions

- it can help cash flow in a business – an early tax point helps a business purchasing goods because the input tax can be reclaimed earlier, eg for a purchase in the last week of a VAT quarter, rather than in the next week – this will make a three month (VAT quarter) difference in cash flow

VAT INVOICES

When a VAT-registered supplier sells standard-rated goods or services to another VAT-registered person, the supplier must give or send to the purchaser within 30 days of the supply a VAT invoice (see opposite page) which contains information about the goods or services supplied. A copy of the invoice should be kept on file (paper or electronic) by the supplier.

The requirements for the contents of a VAT invoice are laid down by HM Revenue & Customs and were amended in January 2004, following the issue of EC Invoicing Directive 2001/115/EC. The information on the invoice should include:

- an invoice number

- the name and address of the supplier

- the VAT number of the supplier

- the date of the invoice

- the purchaser's name and address

- a description (the 'details') of the goods or services supplied, eg shirts or hours of an accountant's time

- the quantity of goods (eg 4 shirts) or the extent of the service (eg 4 hours of accountant's time)

- the unit price, eg the cost of each shirt or hour (or consultation) – this is a new requirement from 2004

- the total charge made, excluding VAT

- the total amount of VAT charged – this must be in sterling (but note that the VAT rate and VAT amounts for individual items do not now have to be shown)

- the total charge made, including VAT – this also has to be in sterling

Study the invoices shown on the next two pages and see how they differ.

SALES INVOICE

Trend Designs

Unit 40 Elgar Estate, Broadfield, BR7 4ER
Tel 01908 765365 Fax 01908 7659507 Email lisa@trend.u-net.com
VAT Reg GB 0745 4172 20

invoice to

Crispins Fashion Store
34 The Arcade
Broadfield
BR1 4GH

invoice no	**787906**
account	**3993**
your reference	**1956**
date/tax point	**21 04 05**

deliver to

as above

details	quantity	unit price	amount (excl VAT)	VAT rate %	VAT amount £
Schwarz 'T' shirts (black)	20	5.50	110.00	17.5	19.25
Snugtight leggings (black)	15	12.50	187.50	17.5	32.81

terms
Net monthly
Carriage paid
E & OE

Total (excl VAT)	**297.50**
VAT	**52.06**
TOTAL	**349.56**

This invoice has been issued by a supplier of fashion clothes, Trend Designs, to Crispins Fashion Store on 21 April (the tax point). Note that all the requirements of a VAT invoice are met: both items sold are charged at the standard rate of tax and the unit price is shown (but showing the VAT rate for each item is optional). The VAT total of £52.06 will recorded as output tax for Trend Designs and as input tax for Crispins Fashion Store. There is no cash discount offered and the buyer has to settle the full £349.56 a month after the invoice date, at the end of May.

━ SALES INVOICE ━

Paragon Printers

Partners: Edwin Parry, George Dragon
Unit 43 Elgar Estate, Broadfield, BR7 4ER
Tel 01908 765312 Fax 01908 7659551 Email Ed@paragon.u-net.com VAT Reg GB 0745 4672 71

invoice to

Prime Publicity Ltd	
4 Friar Street	
Broadfield	
BR1 3RG	

invoice no	**787923**
account	**3993**
your reference	**47609**
date/tax point	**07 05 05**

deliver to

as above

details	unit price	amount (excl VAT)	VAT rate %	VAT amount £
Printing 2,000 A4 leaflets	189.00	189.00	zero	00.00
Supplying 2,000 C4 envelopes	75.00	75.00	17.5	13.12

terms
Net monthly
Carriage paid
E & OE

Total (excl VAT)	264.00
VAT	13.12
TOTAL	277.12

This invoice has been issued by a commercial printer, Paragon Printers, to Prime Publicity Limited on 7 May (the tax point) for goods delivered. Note that in this case there are two rates of VAT involved: printing is zero-rated and stationery is standard rated. Where there are mixed VAT rates, as here, the two rates and VAT amounts must be quoted. The VAT total of £13.12 will be recorded as output tax for Paragon Printers and as input tax for Prime Publicity Ltd. There is no cash discount offered and the buyer has to settle the full £277.12 a month after the invoice date, at the beginning of June.

calculations on VAT invoices

VAT is calculated as a percentage of the cost of the goods. If invoiced goods cost £100, the VAT (at the standard rate of 17.5%) is calculated as:

$$\frac{£100 \times 17.5}{100} = £17.50$$

If the amount of VAT calculated comes out at more than 2 decimal places, you should round *down* to the nearest penny. On the invoice opposite:

$$\frac{£75 \times 17.5}{100} = £13.125 \text{ (rounded down to £13.12)}$$

Guidance relating to rounding may be found in the 'VAT Invoices' section of the 'VAT Guide'. For example, there are rules relating to complex rounding methods when calculating VAT on individual items or 'lines' on a VAT invoice.

The important factor is that any rounding is *consistently applied*. The method of rounding down shown here is simple, and tried and tested.

zero-rated and exempt supplies

If you supply goods which are zero-rated or exempt, invoices issued must show this fact and also that no VAT amount is payable. Note that an invoice for zero-rated or exempt supplies is only compulsory if there is a mixture of rates (as on the opposite page) or if the customer is in another EU state.

situations where VAT invoices are not needed

There are a number of situations where VAT invoices are not needed:

- where the purchaser is not registered for VAT
- if the purchaser is on a *self-billing* system (ie the *purchaser* issues the invoice and sends it with the payment)

The first point mentioned above is sometimes ignored: businesses cannot realistically be expected to enquire if every buyer is VAT-registered, so they will issue a VAT invoice for all routine sales.

There are also situations where invoices may just show the VAT-inclusive amount. These are

- where the transaction total is less than £250
- where the buyer agrees to a modified format – any amount

less detailed invoices – amounts under £250

If the amount charged for the supply is £250 or less (including VAT) a less detailed invoice may be issued. This type of invoice must show:

- the name and address of the supplier
- the date of supply
- a description of the goods or services
- the total charge payable for each item, *including* VAT

To work out the VAT element in a VAT inclusive price the buyer should use the *VAT fraction*.

If you are given a figure which includes VAT and you need to work out the VAT amount you multiply the amount by the VAT fraction – which for 17.5% is $7/47$.

For a total of £117.50 the calculation is:

$$\frac{£117.50 \times 7}{47} \quad = \quad £17.50 \text{ VAT included in the } £117.50$$

This is particularly useful if you receive a less detailed invoice or a receipt, eg for petrol, which includes VAT but does not state the amount.

modified invoices – any amount

If a buyer agrees to the arrangement, a business supplying standard-rated goods or services may issue a modified invoice showing only the VAT-inclusive amount (the charge for the supply plus the VAT amount) *for each item sold*. This type of invoice must, however, show separately – at the bottom of the document:

- the VAT-inclusive total of the supplies – ie the overall total
- the total amount of VAT charged (included in the overall total)
- the total value of the supplies before VAT is added on
- the total value of any zero-rated and exempt supplies on the invoice

This type of invoice will be useful for a supplier that includes a large number of items on each invoice, eg a wholesaler supplying a shop.

other types of invoice – pro-forma invoice

The 'VAT Guide' explains a number of different type of invoice which you would only find in specialised business situations, eg large purchases of petrol or diesel, and cash-and-carry wholesalers. If you encounter these you should refer to the 'VAT Guide'.

A further type of invoice, which is more common, is the *pro-forma invoice*. This is a document issued by a seller offering goods at a certain price and inviting the buyer to send a payment in return for which the goods will then be supplied. This is a common arrangement when a seller receives an order from a new customer, but does not want to sell on credit – because there may well be a credit risk – and so needs payment up front.

A proforma invoice (see illustration below) may well look exactly like an invoice, but because it does not relate to a firm sale, *cannot be used as evidence to reclaim input tax.* Pro-forma invoices should be clearly marked 'THIS IS NOT A VAT INVOICE'. Should a sale result from a pro-forma invoice a separate invoice (the VAT invoice) should then be issued.

PRO-FORMA INVOICE

SPICER STATIONERY
45 High Street
Mereford MR1 3TR
Tel 010903 443851
VAT Reg 422 8371 78

R U Dodgy Limited
56 Larches Walk
Mereford MR5 8UH

13 May 2003

Your ref Purchase Order 2934234

45 x A4 Box files (burgundy) @ £4.99 each	£224.55
VAT @ 17.5%	£39.29
TOTAL PAYABLE	£263.84

This is not a VAT invoice.
A VAT invoice will be issued on receipt of the amount in full.

VAT ERRORS ON INVOICES

With the increasing use of computer accounting systems (which automatically calculate the VAT) errors on invoices should become less common. If a VAT invoice is issued by hand, mistakes can occur:

- the wrong rate of VAT could be used
- the calculation of the VAT amount could be wrong

Whatever happens, the invoice should never be altered and sent out to the customer in its amended state. Instead a debit note or credit note should be issued, showing full details of the error and a numerical reference to the faulty invoice.

If the amount of VAT calculated is too high . . .

Issue an adjusting credit note to the customer, or accept an adjusting debit note from the customer. If this is not done, the higher amount must go through the VAT records of the business and be accounted for accordingly.

If the amount of VAT calculated is too low . . .

Issue an adjusting invoice to the customer, billing him/her for the underpaid VAT. If this is not done the supplier must still account for the higher and correct amount to HM Revenue & Customs, ie stand the loss. This could be the case if the supplier is too embarrassed to admit the mistake!

IMPORTS AND EXPORTS

So far we have dealt with VAT as it affects business dealings within the UK. VAT must also be accounted for in dealings with overseas states, both within the EU (European Union, formerly European Community) and also outside the EU (formerly EC).

The basic principle, which applies to exports and imports, is that VAT is a tax on imported goods and some services – it is paid where appropriate by the importer and is treated as an input tax.

VAT and countries outside the EU

- when goods are *imported* into the UK from countries outside the EU, VAT is normally due at the same rate that would apply to a supply of those goods within the UK – it is treated in the same way as input tax

- when goods are *exported* from the UK to countries outside the EU, the goods are normally zero-rated, as long as documentary evidence of export is obtained and retained by the supplier within 3 months of the date of supply

VAT and the Single Market (the EU)

The Single Market is the phrase used to describe trading within the states that make up the European Union (EU). Since the beginning of 1993 the EU has become an area in which movements of goods are no longer called 'imports' and 'exports' but 'acquisitions'. VAT is no longer collected at the frontiers but from the *buyer:*

- *if the buyer is VAT registered* – the goods are zero-rated on despatch and VAT is collected from the buyer at the rate which applies in the buyer's country and accounted for on the buyer's VAT Return as input tax
- *if the buyer is not VAT registered* – the goods will normally be charged by the supplier at the VAT rate which applies in the country of the supplier

the conditions for zero-rating of EU supplies

In the first case above – the supply of goods from one EU state to another between two VAT registered businesses or individuals – the goods can only be zero-rated by a UK supplier if certain conditions are met:

- the buyer's valid VAT registration number must be obtained by the supplier and quoted on the VAT invoice – the number must include the two letter country prefix (eg DE for Germany, GB for Great Britain)
- the goods are sent to a destination in another EU state
- the supplier holds documentary evidence that the goods have been sent (the evidence must be obtained within 3 months of despatch)

tax points for goods supplied to the EU

The tax point for goods despatched by a UK supplier to another EU state is the earlier of:

- the date on the invoice covering the goods
- the 15th of the month following the month of supply

tax treatment for goods sent to UK buyers

When a UK buyer receives goods from another EU state:

- the tax point follows the same rules as above (ie the date of the invoice received or the 15th of the month following supply)
- VAT is payable at the rate applicable to those goods within the UK (eg books will be zero-rated, adult clothes will be standard rated) – the amount will be entered on the VAT Return (see next chapter)

free zones and warehousing

Mention must be made of warehousing and free zones. These are storage facilities for goods, normally at or near ports and airports; they can be used for storage of goods received from overseas.

No VAT is due on these goods until the goods are released from storage to the UK buyer. Goods received from EU states, as mentioned above, are not *imports* but *acquisitions* and are not subject to the import requirements imposed on non-EU goods.

Single Market documentation – sales lists

UK VAT-registered traders who supply other EU states with goods are required to send lists of their EU supplies to HM Revenue & Customs, normally on a quarterly basis. The standard form VAT 101 is shown below. Traders with low volumes of EU sales may be exempted from completing these forms.

	Value Added Tax **EC Sales list** For the period To		SPECIMEN	
H M Customs and Excise		VAT Registration Number		Branch/subsidiary Identifier
		GB	You could be liable to a financial penalty If your completed listing is not received by the due date. Due date:	Calendar Quarter
	Your Vat Office telephone number is .... Before you fill in this form please read the notes overleaf.		For official use D O R only	

	Country Code	Customer's VAT Registration Number	Total value of supplies £	p	Indi-cator
1				0 0	
2				0 0	
3				0 0	
4				0 0	
5				0 0	
6				0 0	
7				0 0	
8				0 0	
9				0 0	
10				0 0	
11				0 0	
12				0 0	
13				0 0	
14				0 0	
15				0 0	

Number of pages completed

Lines completed (this page only)

Declaration: You, or someone on your behalf, must sign below.

I, ... declare that the
(Full name of signatory in BLOCK LETTERS)

information given above and on any continuation sheets is true and complete.

Signature .... Date .... 19 ....
A false declaration can result in prosecution

Could you please supply a

Contact Name: .... Telephone number: ....
VAT 101 CD 3382/N3(06/93)   F8613   PDD3A HQ Manchester

Form VAT 101 – Sales List

Single Market statistics – Intrastat

Intrastat has replaced customs declarations as a means of supplying statistics on EU trade. It applies only to goods and not to services. The figures are gathered from suppliers' figures entered in boxes on VAT Returns (see the next chapter). Suppliers whose EU trade in goods exceeds a certain threshold (£260,000) have to provide further information in returns known as *Supplementary Declarations* (see below).

Instratat – Supplementary Declaration Form

- Value Added Tax (VAT) is a sales tax on most goods and services imposed by governments in a number of different countries to raise revenue.

- VAT is regulated in the UK by the Value Added Tax Act (1994) and other regulations, in the EU generally it is governed by Directives.

- VAT is administered and collected in the UK by HM Revenue & Customs.

- VAT is paid by the final consumer but is collected and paid to HM Revenue & Customs by the businesses involved in the selling and manufacturing processes.

- VAT is charged at different rates: standard, reduced (domestic fuel) and zero. These (except for zero rate) may be changed from time-to-time.

- A person must register for VAT if annual sales liable to VAT exceed (or are likely to exceed within 30 days) an annual threshold.

- A VAT-registered person must pay to HM Revenue & Customs the VAT charged on sales (output tax) less tax on purchases (input tax). If input tax exceeds output tax a refund is due. The payment or refund is calculated on the regular VAT return (VAT 100).

- The recording of the date of the sales and purchases is important in this calculation – the date of payment is the tax point.

- A VAT-registered supplier must in most circumstances issue a VAT invoice to the buyer. The VAT invoice must contain defined items of information relating to the transaction.

- VAT is also a tax on the import or acquisition of goods and services from overseas states.

- Exports to EU and non-EU countries are normally zero-rated.

- Acquisitions and imports are normally subject to VAT at the rate applicable in the country to which the goods are sent.

- VAT registered businesses sending significant quantities of goods within the EU record the sales statistics on sales lists and Intrastat returns.

Value Added Tax	a tax on the sale of goods and services
VAT Guide	the book published by HM Revenue & Customs which explains the workings of VAT
supplier	a person who sells goods and services
taxable person	a supplier who has been registered for VAT; a person can be a sole trader, a partnership, a limited company, a group of companies, a club or association, a charity

output tax	VAT on sales of goods and services
input tax	VAT on purchases of goods and services
VAT 100	the HM Revenue & Customs VAT Return, which calculates VAT to be paid or refunded by off setting input tax and output tax
standard rate	the basic percentage rate at which VAT is calculated – currently 17.5% in the UK
reduced rate	a reduced rate allowed for domestic fuel – currently 5% in the UK
zero-rated goods	supplies which are liable to VAT, but at zero %
exempt goods	supplies which are not liable to VAT
basic tax point	the date on which the supply is made
actual tax point	the date on which the supply is recorded for the purposes of the VAT Return – normally the date of the invoice
VAT invoice	an invoice recording the taxable supply (the sale) containing specific required details; for lower value transactions (under £250) the invoice may be less detailed
pro-forma invoice	a document issued by a supplier, inviting a buyer to pay for goods before they are supplied – this document is not a VAT invoice
VAT fraction	the fraction used to work out the VAT content of an amount which contains VAT: the procedure is to multiply the amount by the fraction. For the 17.5% rate the fraction is $7/47$.
Single Market	trading within the states of the European Union (EU)
acquisitions	imports within the Single Market
free zone	a defined area within a country into which goods can be imported and stored, VAT only being due when the goods are taken out of that area
sales lists	lists of sales made by UK VAT-registered suppliers of goods to other EU states, sent on a regular basis to HM Revenue & Customs
Intrastat	periodic figures relating to supplies to other EU states supplied by completing boxes on the VAT Return, or in the case of larger traders on Supplementary Declaration forms

Student Activities

16.1 What does VAT tax?

16.2 State three sources of VAT regulation in the UK.

16.3 Define a 'taxable person'.

16.4 What is the difference between input tax and output tax?

16.5 In what circumstances may a supplier reclaim VAT from HM Revenue & Customs?

16.6 Why does the final consumer pay all the VAT on chargeable goods and services, but pay nothing personally to HM Revenue & Customs?

16.7 What are the three rates of VAT currently charged in the UK?

16.8 Explain the difference between the terms 'zero-rated' and 'VAT-exempt'. Give three examples of each.

16.9 State two circumstances in which a person must register for VAT.

16.10 Which of the following are likely to be registered for VAT?

    (a)   a sole proprietor with an annual sales turnover of £35,000

    (b)   a partnership with an annual turnover of £150,000

    (c)   a public limited company with a sales turnover of £1.5 million

    (d)   a local sports club with an annual bar turnover of £95,000

    (e)   a national charity which raises money for cancer research and has an annual income from commercial fundraising activities of £1.2 million

16.11 A VAT invoice offers 2.5% cash discount for early settlement. If the total invoice amount before VAT is £100, the VAT charged (at 17.5%) should be:

    (a)   £17.06

    (b)   £17.07

    (c)   £17.50

    (d)   £17.05

16.12 On which of the following purchases (all paid through the business bank account of a VAT-registered company) can VAT be reclaimed?

(a)   a new computer for use in the business

(b)   a new company car for the managing director

(c)   business entertainment expenses

(d)   the managing director's home telephone bill – the home telephone is often used for business calls in the evenings and at weekends

16.13 The invoice below has been issued as a VAT invoice. What is wrong with it?

SALES INVOICE

Trend Designs

Unit 40 Elgar Estate, Broadfield, BR7 4ER
Tel 01908 765365 Fax 01908 7659507 Email lisa@trend.u-net.com

invoice to

Persephone Fashion
45 The Broads
Broadfield
BR1 8UH

details	quantity	amount (excl VAT)	VAT rate %	VAT amount £
Bianca 'T' shirts	42	209.58	17.5	36.68

terms

Net monthly

Carriage paid

E & OE

Total (excl VAT)	209.58
VAT	36.68
TOTAL	273.26

16.14 When is the tax point in the following circumstances?

    (a)   a tax invoice is issued before the delivery of the goods sold; payment is made 30 days later

    (b)   a pro-forma invoice is issued and payment is made before the delivery of the goods and issue of the VAT invoice

    (c)   a VAT invoice is issued and dated 7 days after the date of the supply of goods

    (d)   a supplier issues regular monthly invoices to cover supplies made during the month; the invoices are dated the last day of the month

16.15 Your business receives five invoices from a VAT registered trader. The amounts are:

£87.50, £41.12, £47.00, £55.75, £99.05

Your colleague notes that

- none of the invoices has the VAT amount listed separately – there is just a total on each which includes the amount for the goods and VAT combined (ie the figures quoted above)

- the invoices have all the other details you would expect to see on a VAT invoice

You are to:

    (a)   state whether the invoices are valid VAT invoices

    (b)   calculate the VAT on each invoice so that you can enter up the purchases day book

16.16 A trader running a plant nursery business has just registered for VAT. He supplies garden centres with bedding plants, shrubs and small trees. Often his invoices to the garden centre purchasing departments are long – often having over thirty items, and totalling thousands of pounds. He asks if he has to show the VAT on every single invoice line, as his computer stationery is set up for showing just the overall VAT total for each rate of VAT charged at the bottom of the invoice. What would be your advice?

16.17 You work as Accounts Supervisor at ABC Wholesalers, Unit 3 Severn Estate, Mereford MR4 7AS. Your invoicing clerk had rather a bad day recently and exactly seven days ago two invoices went out to customers showing incorrect VAT amounts – the wrong rates had been used in the calculations. The rate that should have been used was 17.5% standard rate. The details are:

    (1)   Invoice 4562 issued to Bradley Supplies, 41 Stroud Road, Bagley MR3 6YH, for £250 net shows VAT of £46.25. The contact there is Miss Sharon Pitts, Purchasing Manager.

    (2)   Invoice 4566 issued to J Simpson, 56 Cathedral View, Mereford MR1 2JF, for £400 net shows VAT of £60. The contact there is Ms Janice Simpson.

You are to:

    (a)   work out the correct amounts (VAT and invoice totals) and the differences for each invoice

    (b)   state what ABC Wholesalers should do with the errors to comply with VAT regulations

    (c)   draft appropriate letters to the customers, using your own name and the current date; if you decide not to send a letter to a customer you should write a memo to the Accounts Manager (John Penny) explaining your reasons

16.18 Fabricius Furniture of Farnham, UK, plans to sell its range of luxury hand-made furniture to a VAT-registered dealer in Leipzig, Germany. The UK Sales Manager has a number of questions:

(a)   What happens to the payment of VAT on the goods? Furniture is standard-rated in the UK.

(b)   What conditions (relating to VAT) have to be complied with by the supplier on the supply of the goods?

(c)   When is the tax point for the supply of the goods?

(d)   Would it make any difference if the dealer in Leipzig was not VAT registered?

16.19 Biblios Books is a VAT-registered specialist bookshop which imports books from Spanish-speaking Ruritania. Books in the UK are zero-rated, but in Ruritania they attract a VAT rate of 10%.

(a)   Will VAT be payable on the books imported into the UK from Ruritania?

(b)   Will VAT be payable on the books sold in the UK?

16.20 (a)   What form has to be completed by a business that supplies goods within the EU and needs to provide Sales Lists?

(b)   What figures and returns have to be made by a VAT-registered business in respect of Instrastat?

17 VAT records and the VAT Return

this chapter covers . . .

In this chapter we explain:

- the records a VAT-registered business needs to keep to satisfy the requirements of HM Revenue & Customs

- the treatment of VAT in manual accounts and computer accounts

- the way the figures are collected from the accounting records to supply information for the VAT Return

- the need for a VAT control account

- the completion of the VAT Return Form VAT 100

- how to deal with errors in the VAT records and how to avoid default situations

- the implications of special schemes – annual accounting, flat rate, cash accounting, bad debt relief, retail schemes

- dealings with the local VAT office

Note: you will still often see references to 'EC' (European Community) in publications; in this chapter we will use the more recent term 'EU' (European Union).

NVQ PERFORMANCE CRITERIA COVERED

unit 7: PREPARING REPORTS AND RETURNS

element 7.3

prepare VAT returns

A   complete and submit VAT returns correctly, using data from the appropriate recording systems, within the statutory time limits

B   correctly identify and calculate relevant inputs and outputs

C   ensure submissions are made in accordance with current legislation

D   ensure guidance is sought from the VAT Office when required, in a professional manner

KEEPING VAT RECORDS

VAT and VAT records

The accounting system of a VAT-registered business should record:

- input tax on purchases and expenses
- output tax on sales

It must be appreciated that accounting systems vary substantially from business to business, but the basic *principles* will remain the same: data has to be collected periodically (normally quarterly) so that input tax can be set off against output tax for the completion of the VAT Return.

It is important to have a working knowledge of the records that have to be maintained by a VAT-registered business. They are set out in the 'Records and accounts' section of the 'VAT Guide' and also in the shorter 'VAT: Keeping records and accounts' published by HM Revenue & Customs. The basic records that relate specifically to VAT include:

- *copies of sales invoices* (ideally in numerical/date order) – these are the tax invoices which set out the output tax charged (if it is charged)
- *originals of purchase invoices* (ideally given a consecutive reference number) – these are the tax invoices which set out the input tax which the business can reclaim
- *credit notes* and *debit notes* relating to adjustments made to tax invoices
- documentation relating to *imports and exports* – eg proof of despatch
- a *VAT control account* – which records or summarises all items of input and output tax and acts as the source of data for the VAT Return

'flat rate' scheme – less documentation required

In April 2002 a new 'flat rate' scheme was introduced. This currently allows businesses with an annual turnover of up to £150,000 to base their VAT liability on a flat percentage of the total of their receipts rather than on individual transactions. The percentage depends on the trade sector in which the business operates. This scheme is described on detail on pages 416-417.

other business records

VAT-registered businesses may be visited by VAT officers from time-to-time for *VAT inspections* to ensure that the records are being correctly maintained and administered. Businesses may also be investigated by the Inland Revenue, by the Department of Social Security, and, depending on the level of sales turnover, they may require an audit of their accounts. Accurate business record keeping is therefore critically important if the owner wants to avoid accountants' fees for the reconstruction of incomplete records. The business records that should be kept – in addition to those listed above – include:

- bank statements, paying-in slips and cheque book stubs
- purchase orders and delivery notes
- cash books and petty cash books
- purchases and sales day books
- ledger accounts
- payroll records
- computer printouts and reports
- annual accounts

We will now look in more detail at the records needed for sales (output tax) and purchases and expenses (input tax). For the purposes of your studies we will initially look at a business that buys and sells on credit and maintains a manual accounting system. You should always bear in mind that there are other businesses that trade on cash terms (immediate payment) and which have computer accounting programs which automate many of the processes that we will be describing. We will cover these later in the chapter.

records for output tax (sales)

Records for output tax include:

sales day book

This lists all sales made on credit and has an analysis column for VAT which is totalled periodically.

credit notes issued and debit notes received

Any credit given (eg for returned goods, adjustments for overcharges) may involve VAT and deduction should be made from output tax. Sometimes a separate sales returns day book, with a VAT analysis column, will be kept by the business.

cash book

This includes a VAT analysis column and records details of other receipts *not on credit* which involve output tax, eg cash sales. Receipts for credit sales should be ignored.

records for input tax (purchases and expenses)

Records for input tax include:

purchases day book

This lists all purchases made on credit and has an analysis column for VAT which is totalled periodically.

credit notes received and debit notes issued

Any credit received (eg for returned goods, adjustments for overcharges) may involve VAT and deduction should be made from input tax. Sometimes a separate purchases returns day book, with a VAT analysis column, will be kept by the business.

cash book

This lists all the expenses paid by the business; VAT *for non-credit items* should be taken from the cash book analysis column. VAT on payments for credit purchases should be ignored. A petty cash book with a VAT column may also be used to list small expenses and will need to be accounted for.

VAT control account

The central record for any VAT-registered business book-keeping system is the VAT control account into which all input and output tax is entered. The balance of VAT control account represents the amount owing to (or due from) HM Revenue & Customs. The diagram below is based on the layout recommended by HM Revenue & Customs in the 'VAT Guide'. It shows entries for a supplier who normally has a surplus of output tax over input tax, ie the supplier pays VAT every quarter to HM Revenue & Customs.

VAT control account – summary of entries

VAT deductible (input tax)	VAT payable (output tax)
Purchases Day Book VAT monthly totals, *less* any credit notes received/debit notes issued	Sales Day Book VAT monthly totals, *less* any credit notes issued/debit notes received
Cash Book – items not in Purchases Day Book	Cash Book – items not in Sales Day Book
Petty Cash Book – VAT on small expenses	
Acquisitions from EU states	Acquisitions from EU states
Corrections of errors from previous periods (not exceeding £2,000 net)	Corrections of errors from previous periods (not exceeding £2,000 net)
Adjustments from special schemes*	Adjustments from special schemes*
= TOTAL TAX DEDUCTIBLE	= TOTAL TAX PAYABLE
	less TOTAL TAX DEDUCTIBLE
	equals TAX PAYABLE ON VAT RETURN

* special schemes are discussed on pages 415 to 419.

You should note that the control account shown is not a double-entry account in the strict sense, for example, items such as credit notes are deducted on each side rather than being entered on the opposite side. In practice the VAT control account will be maintained in whatever way the accounting system – manual or computerised – requires. The important point is that the entries used for the VAT Return are *all accounted for in a consistent way*.

treatment of VAT paid and reclaimed

One omission from the diagram on the previous page is the VAT actually paid or reclaimed *for the previous VAT period*. Most businesses which sell standard-rated supplies will pay the VAT surplus to HM Revenue & Customs; other businesses – eg bookshops – which sell zero-rated supplies, will end up paying more VAT on inputs than they charge on outputs, and so will *reclaim* VAT from HM Revenue & Customs each VAT period.

The reason the entries are not shown in the control account is that they cancel each other out and so have *no effect on the VAT due or owing* at the end of the period.

At the beginning of each VAT period the VAT Control account will have an opening balance, *either*

- VAT due to be paid to HM Revenue & Customs – shown on the right-hand side of the account as a credit balance brought forward (this is the figure at the bottom of the diagram on the previous page), *or*

- VAT reclaimable from HM Revenue & Customs – shown on the left-hand side as a debit balance brought forward

When the VAT payment is made by the supplier (or received, if VAT is reclaimable) during the VAT period, the opening balance will be cancelled out. The net effect of the two entries on the account balance will be nil. The examples below show how VAT paid and reclaimed is treated:

VAT CONTROL ACCOUNT (extract) – VAT payable by supplier

VAT deductible (input tax)	£	VAT payable (output tax)	£
Bank (VAT paid by supplier)	12,400	Balance brought forward (previous period's VAT due to be paid by supplier)	12,400

VAT CONTROL ACCOUNT (extract) – VAT reclaimable by supplier

VAT deductible (input tax)	£	VAT payable (output tax)	£
Balance brought forward (previous period's VAT reclaimable by supplier)	10,000	Bank (VAT received by supplier from HM Revenue & Customs)	10,000

computer accounts – VAT Control Account

The VAT control account shown on page 405 assumes that all the VAT data is transferred manually from the accounting records. If a business operates a computer accounting program, normally *every transaction* that involves VAT will automatically post the VAT element to VAT control account, eg sales, purchases, journal entries, payment or repayment of VAT.

The reports available will vary according to the sophistication of the program. Up-to-date programs will do all the work for the supplier, including the production of a screen and a printout at the end of the VAT period with figures needed for the VAT Return. The business which relies on this system must make sure that the VAT data is correct before VAT Return is processed. A computer VAT Return screen is shown below.

Value Added Tax Return		
J SMITH LIMITED 54 HIGH STREET STOURFORD ST1 4TY	For the period	01 01 08
	to	31 03 08
VAT due in this period on sales	1	18,007.67
VAT due in this period on EC acquisitions	2	00.00
Total VAT due (sum of boxes 1 and 2)	3	18,007.67
VAT reclaimed in this period on purchases	4	10,748.23
Net VAT to be paid to Customs or reclaimed by you	5	7,259.44
Total value of sales, excluding VAT	6	102,901.00
Total value of purchases, excluding VAT	7	63,726.00
Total value of EC sales, excluding VAT	8	00.00
Total value of EC purchases, excluding VAT	9	00.00

Calculate   Reconcile   Print   ☐ Include Reconciled   ⓘ   Close

Less sophisticated programs may merely produce summaries of sales and purchases day books and cash books, and a transaction history of VAT Account over the VAT period. If this account history of VAT Account is used for extracting the data for the VAT Return, care must be taken to adjust for payment or repayment of VAT relating to the previous period during the VAT quarter (see the previous page) as this will automatically post to VAT account, but is clearly is not classed as a taxable output or input (you cannot tax tax!). If this is the case:

- payment of VAT to HM Revenue & Customs must be deducted from the input tax total
- repayment of VAT received from HM Revenue & Customs must be deducted from the output tax total

THE VAT RETURN – FORM VAT 100

When the VAT figures have been transferred to the VAT control account and the amount of VAT due or reclaimable has been calculated, the VAT Return can then be completed. The form is illustrated on the next page, and a Case Study follows. The boxes are completed as follows:

1   The total VAT due on sales and other outputs. This total should be adjusted for any credit notes issued and any underdeclarations (£2,000 net or less) on previous returns.

2   VAT due on acquisitions from other EU states.

3   The total of boxes 1 and 2.

4   The total VAT reclaimed on purchases and other inputs (less any credit notes). This total includes tax on acquisition of goods from other EU states and overdeclarations (£10,000 net or less) on previous returns.

5   Take the figures in boxes 3 and 4, deduct the smaller from the larger and enter the difference in box 5. If the figure in box 3 is more than the figure in box 4, this is the amount payable to HM Revenue & Customs. If the figure in box 3 is smaller than the figure in box 4, the amount in box 5 will be repaid to the supplier completing the form.

6   The total of sales and outputs *excluding* any VAT. This will include exempt, standard and zero-rated supplies and supplies to EU member states. Remember to adjust the total for any credit notes/debit notes.

7   The total of purchases (inputs) excluding any VAT. This includes standard, zero and exempt supplies, imports and acquisitions from EU states. Remember to adjust the total for any credit notes/debit notes.

8   The total of supplies of goods and related services, excluding VAT, to EU states (note that 'related services' refers to items such as freight and insurance charges for the goods).

9   The total of acquisition of goods and related services, excluding VAT, from EU states (as above, 'related services' refers to items such as freight and insurance charges for the goods).

notes on completion of VAT 100

- if a VAT payment is being enclosed, the relevant box should be ticked
- the form should be signed by an authorised person
- the form should be returned by the due date shown on the form in the envelope provided (normally one month after the end of the VAT period)
- do not leave any boxes blank – enter 'none' if there is no figure to insert

- always have the arithmetic and figures checked
- mistakes should be crossed through and correct figures inserted; the amendments should be initialled
- for retail schemes, please see page 419

Note that VAT registered organisations now have the option of sending the VAT Return electronically by Electronic VAT Return (EVR).

		£	p
VAT due in this period on **sales** and other outputs	**1**	31,353	61
VAT due in this period on **acquisitions** from other **EC Member States**	**2**	183	05
Total VAT due **(the sum of boxes 1 and 2)**	**3**	31,536	66
VAT reclaimed in this period on **purchases** and other inputs (including acquisitions from the EC)	**4**	14,826	92
Net VAT to be paid to Customs or reclaimed by you **(Difference between boxes 3 and 4)**	**5**	16,709	74
Total value of **sales** and all other outputs excluding any VAT. **Include your box 8 figure**	**6**	179,163	00
Total value of **purchases** and all other inputs excluding any VAT. **Include your box 9 figure**	**7**	84,725	00
Total value of all **supplies** of goods and related services, excluding any VAT, to other **EC Member States**	**8**	none	00
Total value of all **acquisitions** of goods and related services, excluding any VAT, from other **EC Member States**	**9**	1,046	00

a completed VAT Return Form VAT 100

FANCY THAT LTD – COMPLETING THE VAT RETURN

situation

Fancy That Limited is a wholesaler of fancy goods – gifts and cards – which are supplied on credit terms to shops in the UK, although a small proportion is sold for cash. Most of the goods are sourced in the UK, but some are imported from Italy and Spain. Fancy That Limited is VAT-registered and its VAT quarters run from January to March, April to June, July to September and October to December. Most of the goods sold are standard-rated, but a few stock lines – mainly books – are zero-rated.

It is now the first week in April. The data for the January-March VAT Return have been compiled. You have been asked to complete the VAT Control Account and prepare the VAT 100 ready for checking and signature by Dan Brookshaw, Finance Director.

The VAT 100 is due back to HM Revenue & Customs by 30 April, but the company's practice is to submit it by the middle of the month.

The data is taken from the manual accounting system and summarised as follows:

SALES DAY BOOK SUMMARY				
	Zero-rated sales £	Standard-rated sales £	VAT £	Total sales (standard-rated) £
January	2,930.50	15,170.15	2,654.77	17,824.92
February	1,923.81	21,689.03	3,795.58	25,484.61
March	2,706.61	22,729.50	3,977.66	26,707.16
TOTAL	7,560.92	59,588.68	10,428.01	70,016.69

PURCHASES DAY BOOK SUMMARY				
	Zero-rated purchases £	Standard-rated purchases £	VAT £	Total purchases (standard-rated) £
January	00.00	8,791.60	1,538.53	10,330.13
February	00.00	12,326.50	2,157.13	14,483.63
March	00.00	9,731.95	1,703.09	11,435.04
TOTAL	00.00	30,850.05	5,398.75	36,248.80

CASH BOOKS – NON CREDIT ITEMS

	NET £	VAT £	GROSS £
from main cash book			
Cash sales (Jan-Mar)	4,926.80	862.19	5,788.99
Cash purchases (Jan-Mar)	3,500.00	612.50	4,112.50
from petty cash book			
Expenses (Jan-Mar)	456.90	79.95	536.85

ADDITIONAL INFORMATION

- Fancy That's purchases and expenses in the period in question are all standard-rated.

- EU acquisitions for the period totalled £17,794.03, VAT due £3,113.95.

- The business has issued the following sales credit notes to its customers:
  £491.50 + £86.01 VAT = £577.51

- The business has received the following credit notes from its suppliers:
  £579.21 + £101.36 VAT = £680.57

- In January Fancy That paid VAT of £4,106.52 for the last quarter to HM Revenue & Customs; as the amount cancelled out the balance brought down in VAT Control Account, it is ignored for the purposes of the current period VAT calculations.

- The accounts office made an error on a VAT calculation on an invoice during the last VAT quarter: a customer has been undercharged £75.29 output tax. Fortunately he has agreed to accept an invoice for this amount (he can reclaim it as input tax anyway). The problem for you is that the last quarter's VAT Return was £75.29 short on output tax. This error needs correcting on the current VAT Return.

solution

The data will be entered in VAT Control Account in order to calculate the amount of VAT due to HM Revenue & Customs. The summary shown at the top of the next page is not the way the ledger account will *actually* appear in the double-entry system of the business, but it is displayed here in summary form to make the entries clearer.

The VAT Control Account Summary shows:

- totals for input tax and output tax – and the source of the figures

- the calculation for the VAT due to HM Revenue & Customs for the period

When the VAT Control Account has been checked, the figures can then be used to work out the totals for the VAT 100 form – see the calculations that follow the account summary. The data that will be entered on the VAT 100 are shown here with a grey background. The first five boxes use *VAT amounts* and work out the total amount due to HM Revenue & Customs. Note that pence are omitted in boxes 6, 7 and 9.

VAT control account – summary of entries

VAT deductible: input tax		VAT payable: output tax	
	£		£
Purchases Day Book £5,398.75 *less* credit notes £101.36	5,297.39	Sales Day Book £10,428.01 *less* credit notes £86.01	10,342.00
Cash Book	612.50	Cash Book	862.19
Petty Cash Book	79.95		
EU Acquisitions	3,113.95	EU Acquisitions	3,113.95
		Correction of error	75.29
TOTAL INPUT TAX	9,103.79	TOTAL OUTPUT TAX	14,393.43
		less TOTAL INPUT TAX	9,103.79
		equals VAT DUE	5,289.64

data entered in the VAT Return

			£	£
Box 1	Sales Day Book (adjusted for credit notes)		10,342.00	
	Correction of error		75.29	
	Cash sales		862.19	
				11,279.48
Box 2	EU Acquisitions			3,113.95
Box 3	Box 1 plus Box 2			14,393.43
Box 4	Purchases Day Book (less credit notes)		5,297.39	
	Cash book		612.50	
	Petty cash book		79.95	
	EU Acquisitions		3,113.95	
				9,103.79
Box 5	Net VAT due (box 3 less box 4)			5,289.64

Boxes 6 to 9 deal with sales/purchases *before VAT*. Note that pence are omitted.

			£	£
Box 6	Zero-rated credit sales		7,560.92	
	Standard-rated credit sales		59,588.68	
	less credit notes		(491.50)	
	Cash sales		4,926.80	
				71,584.90
Box 7	Purchases on credit		30,850.05	
	less credit notes		(579.21)	
	Cash book		3,500.00	
	Petty cash		456.90	
	EU Acquisitions		17,794.03	
				52,021.77

Box 8   'none'

Box 9   EU Acquisitions: £17,794.03

	For the period
HM Customs and Excise	01 01 03 to 31 03 03

SPECIMEN

625 454 7108 51 100 03 99 Q25147

FANCY THAT LIMITED
UNIT 4 BAYTREE ESTATE
BROADFIELD
BR3 7GH

Registration Number	Period
454 7108 51	03 03

You could be liable to a financial penalty if your completed return and all the VAT payable are not received by the due date.

Due date: 30 04 03

For Official Use

Before you fill in this form please read the notes on the back and the VAT leaflet *"Filling in your VAT return"*. Fill in all boxes in ink, and write 'none' where necessary. Don't put a dash or leave any box blank. If there are no pence write "00" in the pence column. **Do not** enter more than one amount in any box.

			£	p
VAT due in this period on **sales** and other outputs	1		11,279	48
VAT due in this period on **acquisitions** from other **EC Member States**	2		3,113	95
Total VAT due (**the sum of boxes 1 and 2**)	3		14,393	43
VAT reclaimed in this period on **purchases** and other inputs (including acquisitions from the EC)	4		9,103	79
Net VAT to be paid to Customs or reclaimed by you **(Difference between boxes 3 and 4)**	5		5,289	64
Total value of **sales** and all other outputs excluding any VAT. **Include your box 8 figure**	6		71,584	00
Total value of **purchases** and all other inputs excluding any VAT. **Include your box 9 figure**	7		52,021	00
Total value of all **supplies** of goods and related services, excluding any VAT, to other **EC Member States**	8		none	00
Total value of all **acquisitions** of goods and related services, excluding any VAT, from other **EC Member States**	9		17,794	00

Retail schemes. If you have used any of the schemes in the period covered by this return, enter the relevant letter(s) in this box.

If you are enclosing a payment please tick this box. ✓

DECLARATION: You, or someone on your behalf, must sign below.
I, ...DANIEL BROOKSHAW... declare that the
(Full name of signatory in BLOCK LETTERS)
information given above is true and complete.
Signature .... Date 15 April 2003
A false declaration can result in prosecution.

L

0038584

VAT 100 (Half)   PCU (June 1996)

VAT ERRORS AND DEFAULTS

net errors of £10,000 to £50,000 or less

Net errors made in previous VAT periods of £10,000 or less (or 1% of quarterly turnover, subject to a maximum of £50,000) can be adjusted in later VAT returns through the VAT Control Account (as we have just seen in the Case Study).

'Net error' is the difference between the total of errors in output tax and the total of the errors in input tax. In the majority of cases, hopefully, there will only be one error, and this will be the 'net error'. Typical errors are failure to charge output tax on chargeable supplies, charging at the wrong rate, or arithmetical errors in the accounts.

net errors over the limit – voluntary disclosure

If there should be a net error of more than £10,000 (or 1% of quarterly turnover, subject to a maximum of £50,000), this should be advised to the local VAT Office on Form VAT 652 or in a letter as a *voluntary disclosure*. The details that will need to be disclosed are:

- the amount(s)
- the VAT period in which the error occurred
- whether the errors involved input or output tax (or both)
- whether the error was in favour of the business or HMRC

Failure to disclose errors, however innocent they may be, can have serious consequences. A HM Revenue & Customs investigation could result in a misdeclaration penalty, which could mean a 15% charge on unpaid VAT. No misdeclaration penalty can be charged if a voluntary disclosure is made.

defaults

If a trader fails to return the VAT 100 and any due payment within the set time limit (normally a month after the end of the VAT period), the trader is *in default* and a *surcharge liability notice* will be issued fixing a 12 month surcharge period. If there is a *further* default during this period, a *default surcharge* will be levied.

This surcharge, subject to certain minimum limits, is calculated as a percentage of the VAT amount owing and can increase from 2% to 15% during the surcharge period.

SPECIAL SCHEMES

The illustration of the VAT Control Account on page 405 included entries for *special schemes*. These vary the way in which VAT is collected. They are designed to help businesses which may be put at a disadvantage if VAT is collected in the normal way.

annual accounting scheme

This scheme enables businesses to make VAT Returns *annually* rather than quarterly. This is a great advantage to the small trader for whom time is valuable; the only downside being that the accounts must be kept very accurately over the year – errors tend to compound themselves over time!

The main features of the scheme are:

- it is available to traders with an annual taxable turnover of £1.35 million or less at the time the scheme starts

- the scheme can be operated in conjunction with the flat rate scheme (see next page)

- if annual taxable turnover is up to £150,000, the scheme can start any time after VAT registration

- if annual taxable turnover is between £150,000 and £1.35million, the trader can only come onto the scheme 12 months after VAT registration

- the trader must pay 90% of an estimate made of the likely annual VAT payment, normally by nine equal monthly instalments (by standing order or direct debit) starting in the fourth month of the VAT year

- alternatively the trader can pay using 3 interim payments, each of 25% of the likely annual VAT liability, in months 4, 7 and 10 of the annual accounting period

- the trader must pay the balance due with the annual VAT Return, due *two* months after the end of the VAT year

The timing of the payments made is summarised in the table below.

Months	1	2	3	4	5	6	7	8	9	10	11	12	13	14
Payments (9 interim)				1	2	3	4	5	6	7	8	9		10
Payments (3 interim)				1			2			3				4

Full details of this scheme are contained in the 'Annual Accounting' pamphlet published by HM Revenue & Customs. This is also available on www.hmrc.gov.uk as Notice 732.

flat rate scheme (FRS)

The flat rate scheme is designed for small businesses whose annual taxable turnover does not exceed £150,000, and whose total turnover (including income on which no VAT is paid) does not exceed £187,500 a year.

It is radically different from normal VAT schemes in which input VAT and output VAT are identified and recorded, resulting either in net VAT being paid over to HM Revenue & Customs, or reclaimed (if tax on expenses [inputs] is greater than that on sales [outputs]).

With the **flat rate scheme** the business does not have to identify and record every single VAT transaction in order to calculate the net amount of VAT due. Instead a **flat percentage rate** is charged on the total supplies (sales) – including VAT-exempt supplies – for each VAT period. This calculation produces the amount of VAT due.

The flat rate varies with the trade sectors. Some common examples are shown in the table below.

type of business	flat rate
retailers of food and newspapers	2%
pubs	5.5%
sports facilities	7%
private detectives	10%
entertainment	11%
beauty treatment	12%
book-keeping services	13%

The calculation of the flat rate VAT is simple. Suppose you are a book-keeper and your quarterly supplies (ie income from customers) is £12,000, including VAT. Your flat rate is 13% and so your quarterly VAT liability is:

£12,000 x 13% = £1,560

If you ran a pub and your quarterly turnover was the same amount (obviously a quiet pub), your VAT liability (see table above) would be:

£12,000 x 5.5% = £660

Note also that there is a 1% reduction in the flat rate during the first year of VAT registration.

Remember that the flat rate is used only to calculate the amount of VAT you owe, because an allowance is made for input tax in the percentage. **You will not charge VAT at the flat rate**, but instead at the normal rate for the supplies. You will issue VAT invoices showing the normal VAT rate charged.

Also, if your supplies are **zero rated** (for example if you sell books) and you normally reclaim VAT because your inputs are higher than your outputs, you would not use the flat rate scheme (unless you want to give money away!)

Another point to note is that if you purchase a **capital asset**, eg a computer, with an invoice value (including VAT) of £2,000 or more, you can claim the input VAT paid on this asset. If you sell it again, you will have to pay back to HM Revenue & Customs the VAT you receive. This extra VAT on purchases (inputs) and sales (outputs) will be recorded on the VAT Return.

The records that you will need to keep for the flat rate scheme are:

- the flat rate turnover for the VAT accounting period
- the flat rate percentage used
- the VAT calculated as due
- a VAT account – recording VAT paid under the scheme and any VAT involved in the purchase or sale of a capital asset

Note that the flat rate scheme may be operated with the annual accounting scheme. This makes dealing with VAT far simpler for the small business. Not only is VAT calculated as a basic percentage, it is only calculated once a year. Details of the scheme are available on www.hmrc.gov.uk as Notice 733.

cash accounting scheme

This scheme allows businesses to account for VAT on the basis of the date of *payments* received and made rather than on the tax point on *invoices* received and issued. In other words a business under this scheme does not have to account for output tax on the date of the supply, but only when (and if!) payment is received, which could be many months later. This is an enormous help to traders who have to pay their suppliers promptly but may have to wait a long time before receiving payment. It also provides automatic relief for VAT on bad debts: if the buyer does not pay up, no output VAT is declarable (as it would be if VAT was assessable on invoices rather than payments). To qualify for this scheme a business must:

- anticipate annual taxable turnover of £660,000 or less
- have a 'clean' VAT record – ie all VAT Returns made on time, no assessments for VAT evasion or convictions for VAT fraud

When registered under this scheme a supplier will continue to issue VAT invoices but will need to keep accounting records in a specific way:

- the tax point for payments in cash, by cheque, credit card, bank transfer is always the transaction date (eg the date on the credit card voucher)

- a cash book (or similar record) must be maintained summarising all payments made and received, with *a separate column for VAT*, suitable for providing the data for the VAT Return

- invoices issued or received for any payments made *in cash* must be receipted and dated

Details of this scheme are in the 'Cash Accounting' pamphlet published by HM Revenue & Customs or on www.hmrc.gov.uk (Notice 731).

bad debt relief

A *bad debt* is an amount owing which a supplier writes off in the books because he/she is unlikely ever to be paid – the buyer may have 'gone bust' for example. The cash accounting scheme explained above automatically protects the small trader against *bad debts*: if an invoice is not paid, no output VAT will have to be declared because no payment will be received.

This clearly does not apply to businesses not on the cash accounting scheme; what happens if output VAT paid over to HM Revenue & Customs on the VAT Return is not received six or more months later by the supplier because the debt goes bad? HM Revenue & Customs allows a refund to all suppliers through the VAT Return – this is known as *bad debt relief*.

Bad debt relief is available:

- for debts which are more than six months overdue (six months from the due date of the payment, or six months after the date of supply if it was later than the due payment date)

- when the output VAT has already been paid to HM Revenue & Customs

- when the debt has been written off in the supplier's accounts and transferred to a separate bad debt account

The supplier must retain a copy of the unpaid VAT invoice, but does not have to advise the buyer of the bad debt relief claim. The buyer must in any event repay to HM Revenue & Customs any input tax claimed on unpaid invoices which have been outstanding more than six months.

Bad debt relief is accounted for on the VAT Return by adding it to the Box 4 total (VAT reclaimed on purchases). As noted above, this figure must have been processed through a separate bad debt account. It will appear in the VAT control account on the left-hand side, as an addition to input tax.

Full details of this scheme are contained in the 'Relief from VAT on bad debts' pamphlet published by HM Revenue & Customs or can be downloaded from www.hmrc.gov.uk (Notice 700/18).

retail schemes

VAT accounting for shops who may make a mixture of standard-rated, zero-rated and exempt supplies is potentially very complex. HM Revenue & Customs has introduced a series of *retail schemes* to help retail suppliers. You will have seen the box on the VAT 100 form for completion by suppliers operating these schemes. There are five schemes for businesses with taxable turnover up to £10m. Larger businesses will have 'tailor-made' *bespoke* retail schemes arranged by HM Revenue & Customs.

You do not at this stage in your studies need to know all the 'ins and outs' of retail schemes but you should note that the five standard schemes fall into three categories:

- *point of sale scheme*

  This is used when the VAT rate can be identified when the goods are sold at the till – the till will record the rate for each transaction.

- *apportionment schemes*

  These schemes apply when a retailer cannot realistically separate zero-rated and standard-rated goods at the till (eg buying food [zero-rated] and video tapes [standard-rated] at the corner shop). These schemes relate:

  - the proportion of VAT rates on outputs (sales at the tills) to the proportion of rates on inputs (what the retailer pays the wholesaler) *or*
  - an estimate is made of the expected selling price of goods at different rates and an appropriate percentage applied to the total takings

- *direct calculation schemes*

  The takings for the goods at the VAT rate which provides the smallest proportion of overall takings is calculated and deducted from the total takings on a daily basis.

DEALING WITH THE VAT OFFICE

The normal point of contact with HM Revenue & Customs is the local VAT office. The staff are willing to help suppliers with advice and as regulatory bodies they are also likely to want to make sure that a supplier keeps accurate VAT records.

From time-to-time a supplier may receive an inspection visit from VAT officers who will go through the records with the proverbial 'toothcomb' to ensure that all the necessary documentation and accounting records are in order, VAT Returns are being submitted on time and VAT is not being underpaid or overpaid. If the officer(s) consider that VAT has been underpaid, HM Revenue & Customs can raise an *assessment* demanding the VAT that they consider to be due. There are channels for formal appeals and tribunals to deal with disputes, should they occur.

In your studies it is stressed that guidance should be sought from the VAT office 'in a professional manner'. This means that any queries or problems should be referred to the local office through the appropriate channels. If your firm's accounts office is involved, this means an authorised official (supervisor or section head) should telephone or write to the VAT office. If the business is run by a sole trader, the enquiry will come from the owner.

Typical queries might include:

"Are these goods standard-rated or zero-rated"

"The business is being wound down and will close next year. Do we have to de-register for VAT?"

"We have discovered that we have underpaid output VAT by £3,000 on the last VAT Return. What should we do?"

"My acquisitions from USA are invoiced in US$. What sterling figures should I use in the VAT records?"

The rule is: if in doubt, ask; but in a professional manner

Chapter Summary

- It is important that an organisation maintains accurate and comprehensive accounting records, keeping the records for at least six years. They may be needed for inspection by the Inland Revenue, by the Department of Social Security, by auditors and (for VAT registered businesses) by HM Revenue & Customs.

- VAT records that must be kept include

  - copies of sales invoices

  - originals of purchase invoices

  - credit notes and debit notes issued and received

  - VAT control account

  - other associated records

- VAT-registered businesses may use manual or computerised accounting systems. The normal sources of accounting data for the completion of the VAT Return are:

- sales and purchases day books (for credit items)

- cash book and petty cash book (for non-credit items)

- This data is compiled in a VAT control account which is structured as follows:

VAT control account – summary of entries

VAT deductible (input tax)	VAT payable (output tax)

Purchases Day Book VAT total, *less*
    any credit notes received/ debit notes issued
	Sales Day Book VAT total, *less*
	    any credit notes issued/debit notes received

Cash Book – items not in Purchases Day Book	Cash Book – items not in Sales Day Book
Petty Cash Book – VAT on small expenses	
Acquisitions from EU states	Acquisitions from EU states

Corrections of errors from previous periods
    (not exceeding £2,000 net)
	Corrections of errors from previous periods
	    (not exceeding £2,000 net)

Bad debt relief	
= TOTAL TAX DEDUCTIBLE	= TOTAL TAX PAYABLE *less* TOTAL TAX DEDUCTIBLE *equals* TAX PAYABLE ON VAT RETURN

- In addition the VAT control account will record VAT owing and paid to HM Revenue & Customs (or VAT owed and paid by HM Revenue & Customs) – but payments are not entered on the VAT Return.

- Computer accounting systems will normally keep a running VAT account to which all transactions involving VAT are posted. Some programs will additionally produce a VAT return printout.

- The VAT Return and payment (if required) should be completed and despatched within the timescale allowed (normally a month from the end of the VAT period); the VAT 100 should be signed by an authorised person.

- Net VAT errors of £10,000 or less (or 1% of quarterly turnover, subject to a £50,000 maximum limit) can be corrected on a subsequent VAT Return. Errors over these limits should be advised as a 'voluntary disclosure' to HM Revenue & Customs in a letter or Form VAT 652.

- If a VAT Return is not returned within the stipulated timescale, HM Revenue & Customs will issue a twelve month surcharge liability notice; a further default within the twelve months may result in a default surcharge.

- To help businesses which may be put at a disadvantage by the standard VAT Return system, HM Revenue & Customs has introduced a number of special schemes to help businesses: annual accounting, flat rate scheme, cash accounting, bad debt relief and retail schemes.

- Suppliers dealing with HM Revenue & Customs should do so professionally; to give HM Revenue & Customs confidence in them.

Key Terms		
VAT inspection	a visit by VAT officers to ensure that adequate VAT records are being maintained and that the correct amount of VAT is being collected and reclaimed
VAT Control Account	an essential account which collects all the accounting data needed for the VAT Return; it may be maintained manually or by a computer accounting system
VAT Return	Form VAT 100 is completed by VAT-registered suppliers at the end of each VAT period in order to calculate the amount of VAT due to HM Revenue & Customs or reclaimable from them; it also records statistical data about EU acquisitions
voluntary disclosure	disclosure of a net error (over set limits) in VAT calculations to HM Revenue & Customs by a registered supplier
misdeclaration penalty	a penalty imposed on a VAT-registered supplier who is found by HM Revenue & Customs to have errors and irregularities in the VAT records
surcharge liability notice	a notice issued by HM Revenue & Customs to a VAT-registered supplier who has failed to make a VAT Return within the stipulated period (12 months)
default surcharge	a percentage charge on an amount of unpaid VAT
annual accounting scheme	a scheme which enables businesses (with annual taxable turnover of £1.35million or less) to make VAT returns annually rather than quarterly – VAT owing is paid in regular instalments and the VAT 100 is due two months after the end of the VAT period
flat rate scheme	a scheme which enables businesses with an annual taxable turnover of up to £150,000 to pay VAT at a flat percentage rate based on tax inclusive turnover

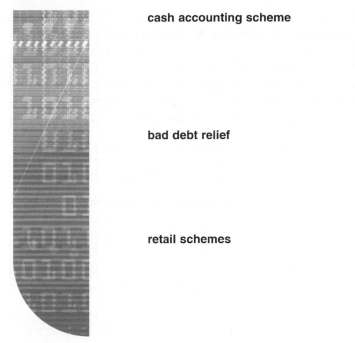

cash accounting scheme	a scheme which allows businesses (with annual taxable turnover of £660,000 or less) to account for VAT on the basis of payments received and made rather than the tax point on invoices received and issued; it provides automatic relief for VAT on bad debts
bad debt relief	a scheme available for any registered supplier whereby output VAT paid over to HM Revenue & Customs on a debt which has subsequently (over 6 months after the due date) gone bad is reclaimable through the VAT 100
retail schemes	a variety of schemes for businesses in the retail trade where it is difficult to account to different rates of VAT at the point of sale; there are three main types of scheme: point of sale, apportionment and direct calculation

Student Activities

17.1 Make a checklist of

(a) the basic records that must be maintained by a business in order to account for VAT

(b) additional accounting records which should be maintained to support the records mentioned in (a) above

17.2 What would be the problem as far as VAT is concerned if a VAT-registered business had not kept

(a) copies of sales invoices issued

(b) originals of purchase invoices received

17.3 In a manual accounting system what is the danger, as far as VAT calculation is concerned, in extracting VAT entries from the Sales Day Book and also from the Cash Book?

17.4 Construct VAT control accounts from the VAT figures shown on the next page. The figures have been extracted from the accounting records of four different businesses; in each case ensure that you calculate the VAT due or reclaimable for the VAT period. Note: any VAT payable or reclaimable for the previous period is to be ignored.

VAT FIGURES	Business A £	Business B £	Business C £	Business D £
Purchases Day Book	2,720.00	3,239.50	5,726.05	3,923.50
Sales Day Book	5,961.70	5,906.33	9,176.23	521.30
Credit notes received	326.50	107.60	195.50	170.90
Credit notes issued	501.29	321.90	391.80	81.25
Cash book purchases (non-credit)	275.60	179.29	173.76	1,256.81
Cash book sales (non-credit)	329.73	260.75	356.25	723.80
Petty cash book purchases	13.85	nil	18.92	41.20
EU Acquisitions	796.30	78.00	1,523.90	nil
VAT overpaid previous period	nil	nil	271.20	17.50
VAT underpaid previous period	nil	32.65	86.30	nil
Bad debt relief	nil	85.50	89.23	29.50

The format shown below can be used to set up the VAT Control Account. You will need to calculate the final amount of VAT due or reclaimable. If the final total is reclaimable it should be shown in brackets.

VAT deductible (input tax)	**VAT payable (output tax)**
Purchases Day Book VAT total, *less* any credit notes received/ debit notes issued	Sales Day Book VAT total, *less* any credit notes issued/debit notes received
Cash Book – items not in Purchases Day Book	Cash Book – items not in Sales Day Book
Petty Cash Book – VAT on small expenses	
Acquisitions from EU states	Acquisitions from EU states
Corrections of errors from previous periods (not exceeding £2,000 net)	Corrections of errors from previous periods (not exceeding £2,000 net)
Bad debt relief	
= TOTAL TAX DEDUCTIBLE	= TOTAL TAX PAYABLE
	less TOTAL TAX DEDUCTIBLE
	equals TAX PAYABLE/(RECLAIMABLE)

17.5 You work as an assistant in a firm of accountants and have been asked to draw up VAT Returns for four clients. You have extracted the relevant data from their accounting records and have set it out on a spreadsheet shown below.

You are to calculate the totals for all nine boxes of the four VAT Returns ready for checking. If you wish, you can use the table set out on the next page for entering the figures.

	Business 1 £	Business 2 £	Business 3 £	Business 4 £
VAT FIGURES EXTRACTED				
Sales day book	11,099.17	17,180.86	3,196.37	3,436.25
Credit notes issued	213.12	693.89	54.63	98.34
Cash sales	1,388.10	304.29	686.93	302.15
Purchases day book	6,297.83	10,806.39	1,104.75	10,166.32
Credit notes received	152.37	368.87	28.50	188.44
Cash purchases	321.81	1,014.70	52.50	nil
Petty cash expenses	nil	91.17	33.41	48.26
Bad debt relief	639.80	850.00	nil	250.00
Overpayment (previous period)	nil	258.92	nil	365.12
Underpayment (previous period)	nil	nil	95.20	109.90
EU acquisitions	nil	3,281.28	216.31	8,791.96
NET SALES AND RECEIPTS				
Zero-rated sales	126.75	8,326.18	1,507.29	75,800.00
Standard-rated sales	63,423.86	98,176.35	18,265.00	19,635.75
Credit notes issued	1,217.85	3,965.10	312.18	561.95
Cash sales (standard-rated)	7,932.01	1,738.81	3,925.37	1,726.58
Zero-rated purchases	1,290.00	3,706.70	295.80	2,560.22
Standard-rated credit purchases	35,987.60	61,750.80	6,312.87	58,093.30
Credit notes received	870.72	2,107.83	162.91	1,076.84
Cash payments (standard-rated)	1,838.96	5,798.32	300.00	nil
Petty cash expenses	nil	521.00	190.95	275.81
EU acquisitions	nil	18,750.21	1,236.09	50,239.80

Suggested answer layout for 17.5:

VAT 100 Box No.	Business 1	Business 2	Business 3	Business 4
1				
2				
3				
4				
5				
6				
7				
8				
9				

17.6   You are working in an accountant's office and receive a number of VAT enquiries from clients. What would your advice be in each case?

(a)   Oriental Supplies Limited overcharged VAT on an invoice during the previous VAT quarter and the VAT 100 has already been sent off. The amount involved is £350.00.

(b)   Olly Moore is a VAT-registered freelance computer consultant. Six months ago he started selling space on his Web site to advertisers. This has been very successful and sales during the first VAT quarter were higher than expected. Unfortunately in the rush to get this side of his business going, he omitted to charge VAT on the first batch of sales invoices. He reckons that during the first quarter he has failed to charge £4,200 of VAT. The relevant VAT 100 was sent off over two months ago.

(c)   Helen Underhill telephones to say that she has just realised that the book-keeper she hired last VAT quarter has failed to send off the VAT 100 in time. It has been incorrectly filed in the pending tray and is now over a month overdue. She has fired her book-keeper but is concerned about the late submission of the form which she hopes to get into the post this week.

17.7   What special VAT schemes would you recommend to VAT-registered businesses in the following circumstances? State in each case:

•   how the scheme differs from the normal arrangements

•   the advantages of the scheme to the business

•   the practical accounting requirements of the scheme

(a)   Gilbert Gumbert is a busy sole trader, who has been registered for VAT for two years. He has an annual taxable turnover of £250,000. He also has a 'clean' VAT record with no records of default. He has problems however:

•   the time it takes him to fill in his VAT returns

•   the strain on cash flow of having to make quarterly VAT payments with his VAT 100

(b)   Samuel Mugosa has just started in business as a sole trader. He repairs household electrical goods. He estimates that his annual turnover for his first year will be £125,000. What VAT scheme in addition to the annual accounting scheme would you recommend him to use?

Would your advice to him be the same if he sold books (which are zero-rated)?

(c)   Fiona Strong is a successful 'trouble-shooting' management consultant with an annual taxable turnover of £150,000. She also has a 'clean' VAT record with no records of default. She has a wide range of clients but is constantly running into cash flow problems, largely because some of her clients are financially insecure:

- her clients often demand long credit terms

- her clients do not pay up on time

- some of her clients do not pay up at all

- she has to pay most of her expenses and overheads straightaway or within 30 days

17.8   Seamus O'Deah, a VAT-registered trader, has just been informed that a customer with six overdue invoices outstanding has been made bankrupt. Seamus wants to know:

(a)   which of the invoices listed below is eligible for bad debt relief (and why)

(b)   how any claim will be adjusted in his accounts and on the VAT 100 (state any VAT amount involved in the process)

The VAT invoices in question date over two years: 2003 and 2004. It is currently 30 June in the year 2004. Seamus' financial year-end of 30 June is also the end of his VAT quarter.

Invoice 7773, due for payment 30 March 2004, goods supplied 14 February 2004, VAT £45.00

Invoice 7645, due for payment 20 February 2004, goods supplied 21 January 2004, VAT £21.00

Invoice 7578, due for payment 28 December 2003, goods supplied 4 January 2004, VAT £34.40

Invoice 7510, due for payment 20 December 2003, goods supplied 20 November 2003, VAT £35.00

Invoice 7415, due for payment 30 November 2003, goods supplied 30 October 2003, VAT £45.20

Invoice 7200, due for payment 20 August 2003, goods supplied 22 July 2003, VAT £56.40

Answers to student activities

CHAPTER 1: AN INTRODUCTION TO COST ACCOUNTING

1.1　(a)　•　The principle behind this Student Activity is the identification of relevant costs
　　　　•　Whilst the type of organisation selected may well not fit with the exact layout for a manufacturing business, as shown on page 17, the Activity should generate thought and discussion of costs involved
　　　　•　As an example, an outline of the costs incurred by a school or college is as follows:

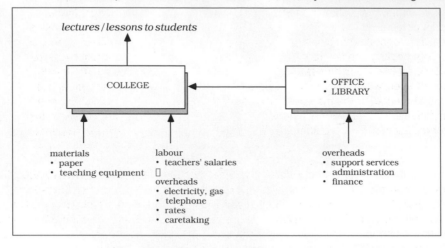

lectures / lessons to students

COLLEGE

• OFFICE
• LIBRARY

materials
• paper
• teaching equipment

labour
• teachers' salaries

overheads
• electricity, gas
• telephone
• rates
• caretaking

overheads
• support services
• administration
• finance

　　(b)　•　What are the units of output of the organisation to which costs can be charged?
　　　　•　The main sections of the organisation should be identified. Does the costing system in use charge costs to these sections, whether or not they are formally called cost centres?
　　　　•　In the school/college described above, the example cost unit is student hours, and cost centres examples are teaching departments, learning resources, administration.

1.2　Suggestions to include:

	COST UNIT	COST CENTRE
college of further education	student hour	teaching department learning resources administration
mixed farm	kilo of wheat head of cattle	field cattle shed

1.3　(a)　See text, pages 21 and 22
　　(b)　•　raw materials: variable
　　　　•　factory rent: fixed
　　　　•　telephone: semi-variable
　　　　•　direct labour: variable
　　　　•　indirect labour: fixed
　　　　•　commission to sales staff: variable

Classifying costs by nature identifies them as being fixed, or semi-variable, or variable. This helps with decision making – the business might be able to alter the balance between fixed and variable costs in order to increase profits.For example, a furniture manufacturing business will have to make decisions on whether to use direct labour (variable cost) or machinery (fixed cost) for many of the production processes. The decision will be based very much on the expected level of sales, ie for lower sales it is likely to make greater use of direct labour, while for higher sales a more machine-intensive method of production might be used.

1.4

tubular steel	direct materials
factory supervisor's salary	indirect labour
wages of employee operating moulding machine	direct labour
works canteen assistant's wages	indirect labour
rates of factory	indirect expenses
power to operate machines	indirect expenses*
factory heating and lighting	indirect expenses
plastic for making chair seats	direct materials
hire of special machinery for one particular order	direct expenses
cost of grease for the moulding machine	indirect materials
depreciation of factory machinery	indirect expenses
depreciation of office equipment	indirect expenses

* Note: the cost of power to operate machines has been classified above as an indirect expense. This is often the case because it is not worthwhile analysing the cost of power for each unit of production. An industry that uses a lot of power will often have meters fitted to each machine so that costs may be identified and allocated to production as a direct expense. Other, lesser users of power, are unlikely to calculate the separate cost and will consider power to be an indirect expense. Whichever treatment is used, it is important that it is applied consistently.

1.5

COST ITEM	CLASSIFICATION (write your answer)
Dressings	direct materials
Disposable scalpels	direct materials
Surgeon's salary	direct labour
Floor cleaning materials	indirect materials
Laundry	indirect expenses*
Depreciation of staff drinks machine	indirect expenses*
Theatre heat and light	indirect expenses*
Porter's wages	indirect labour
Anaesthetic gas	direct materials
Depreciation of theatre equipment	indirect expenses
Maintenance of theatre equipment	indirect expenses
Cost of CDs for music in theatre	indirect expenses
Anaesthetist's salary	direct labour

* These items have been classified as indirect expenses – this is the most likely classification. If the money amount of any item was large, it would be worthwhile looking at the costing system to see if the item could be identified as a direct expense.

1.6

Cost item	Total cost	Prime cost	Production overheads	Admin costs	Selling and distribution costs
	£	£	£	£	£
Wages of employees working on the bottling line	6,025	6,025			
Wages of employees in the stores department	2,750		2,750		
Cost of bottles	4,050	4,050			
Safety goggles for bottling line employees	240		240		
Advertisement for new employees	125			125	
Depreciation of bottling machinery	500		500		
Depreciation of sales staff's cars	1,000				1,000
Royalty paid to local farmer	750	750			
Cost of trade exhibition	1,500				1,500
Computer stationery	210			210	
Sales staff salaries	4,095				4,095
TOTALS	21,245	10,825	3,490	335	6,595

1.7 (a)

Hughes Limited
Total cost statement for the year ended 31 December 2004

	£	£
Direct materials		118,830
Direct labour		117,315
PRIME COST		236,145
Production overheads		
rent and rates	16,460	
factory power	3,825	
factory heat and light	1,185	
factory expenses and maintenance	4,095	
depreciation of factory plant and machinery	3,725	
		29,290
PRODUCTION COST		265,435

Non-production overheads

Selling and distribution costs:

advertising		11,085
Administration costs:		
office salaries and wages	69,350	
office expenses	3,930	
		73,280
TOTAL COST		349,800

Note: It has been assumed in the cost statement that:

• all of the raw materials used in the factory are direct materials

• all of the factory wages are direct labour – with additional information, it would be possible to split the cost between direct and indirect labour

(b)

Hughes Limited
Profit statement for the year ended 31 December 2004

		£
Sales		426,350
less Total cost		349,800
PROFIT		76,550

CHAPTER 2: MATERIALS COSTS

2.1   *Stock item D*

• maximum space = 350 units; maximum usage = 95 days x 3 units per day = 285 units; therefore maximum stock is 285 units

• minimum stock = 10 days x 3 units per day = 30 units

• re-order level = 30 units + (7 days x 3 units per day) = 51 units

• re-order quantity = 285 units – 30 units = 255 units

Stock item E

• maximum space = 350 units; maximum usage = 95 days x 4 units per day = 380; therefore maximum stock is 350 units

• minimum stock = 10 days x 4 units per day = 40 units

• re-order level = 40 units + (7 days x 4 units per day) = 68 units

• re-order quantity = 350 units – 40 units = 310 units

2.2

STOCK RECORD						
Stock Description	*A4 yellow card*					
Stock units	*reams*		Minimum	*36 reams*		
Stock Ref. No.	*A4/Y3*		Maximum	*105 reams*		
Location	*row7, bin5*		Re-order level	*66 reams*		
			Re-order quantity	*69 reams*		

DATE	GOODS RECEIVED		GOODS ISSUED		BALANCE
	Reference	Quantity	Reference	Quantity	
2004					
1 May					*84*
4 May			*MR184*	*18*	*66*
6 May			*MR187*	*20*	*46*
10 May			*MR188*	*10*	*36*
14 May	*GRN4507*	*69*			*105*
17 May			*MR394*	*20*	*85*
20 May			*MR401*	*11*	*74*
26 May			*MR422*	*6*	*68*

2.3   (a)   stock record

(b)   stock list

(c)   stock reconciliation

(d)   cost and net realisable value

2.4

FIFO

STORES LEDGER RECORD

Date	Receipts			Issues			Balance		
2004	Quantity	Cost	Total Cost	Quantity	Cost	Total Cost	Quantity	Cost	Total Cost
		£	£		£	£		£	£
January	20	3.00	60.00				20	3.00	60.00
February	10	3.50	35.00				20	3.00	60.00
							10	3.50	35.00
							30		95.00
March				8	3.00	24.00	12	3.00	36.00
							10	3.50	35.00
							22		71.00
April	10	4.00	40.00				12	3.00	36.00
							10	3.50	35.00
							10	4.00	40.00
							32		111.00
May				12	3.00	36.00			
				4	3.50	14.00	6	3.50	21.00
							10	4.00	40.00
							16		61.00

LIFO

STORES LEDGER RECORD

Date	Receipts			Issues			Balance		
2004	Quantity	Cost	Total Cost	Quantity	Cost	Total Cost	Quantity	Cost	Total Cost
		£	£		£	£		£	£
January	20	3.00	60.00				20	3.00	60.00
February	10	3.50	35.00				20	3.00	60.00
							10	3.50	35.00
							30		95.00
March				8	3.50	28.00	20	3.00	60.00
							2	3.50	7.00
							22		67.00
April	10	4.00	40.00				20	3.00	60.00
							2	3.50	7.00
							10	4.00	40.00
							32		107.00
May				10	4.00	40.00			
				2	3.50	7.00			
				4	3.00	12.00	16	3.00	48.00

AVCO

STORES LEDGER RECORD

Date	Receipts			Issues			Balance		
2004	Quantity	Cost	Total Cost	Quantity	Cost	Total Cost	Quantity	Cost	Total Cost
		£	£		£	£		£	£
January	20	3.00	60.00				20	3.00	60.00
February	10	3.50	35.00				20	3.00	60.00
							10	3.50	35.00
							30	3.17	95.00
March				8	3.17	25.33	22	3.17	69.67
April	10	4.00	40.00				22	3.17	69.67
							10	4.00	40.00
							32	3.43	109.67
May				16	3.43	54.84	16	3.43	54.83

Note: some figures have been rounded to the nearest penny

2.5

FIFO

STORES LEDGER RECORD: TYPE X

Date	Receipts			Issues			Balance		
2004	Quantity	Cost	Total Cost	Quantity	Cost	Total Cost	Quantity	Cost	Total Cost
		£	£		£	£		£	£
January	100	4.00	400.00				100	4.00	400.00
February				80	4.00	320.00	20	4.00	80.00
March	140	4.20	588.00				20	4.00	80.00
							140	4.20	588.00
							160		668.00
April	100	3.80	380.00				20	4.00	80.00
							140	4.20	588.00
							100	3.80	380.00
							260		1,048.00
May				20	4.00	80.00			
				120	4.20	504.00	20	4.20	84.00
							100	3.80	380.00
							120		464.00
June	80	4.50	360.00				20	4.20	84.00
							100	3.80	380.00
							80	4.50	360.00
							200		824.00

LIFO

STORES LEDGER RECORD: TYPE X

Date	Receipts			Issues			Balance		
2004	Quantity	Cost	Total Cost	Quantity	Cost	Total Cost	Quantity	Cost	Total Cost
		£	£		£	£		£	£
January	100	4.00	400.00				100	4.00	400.00
February				80	4.00	320.00	20	4.00	80.00
March	140	4.20	588.00				20	4.00	80.00
							140	4.20	588.00
							160		668.00
April	100	3.80	380.00				20	4.00	80.00
							140	4.20	588.00
							100	3.80	380.00
							260		1,048.00
May				100	3.80	380.00	20	4.00	80.00
				40	4.20	168.00	100	4.20	420.00
							120		500.00
June	80	4.50	360.00				20	4.00	80.00
							100	4.20	420.00
							80	4.50	360.00
							200		860.00

AVCO

STORES LEDGER RECORD: TYPE X

Date	Receipts			Issues			Balance		
2004	Quantity	Cost	Total Cost	Quantity	Cost	Total Cost	Quantity	Cost	Total Cost
		£	£		£	£		£	£
January	100	4.00	400.00				100	4.00	400.00
February				80	4.00	320.00	20	4.00	80.00
March	140	4.20	588.00				20	4.00	80.00
							140	4.20	588.00
							160	4.17	668.00
April	100	3.80	380.00				160	4.17	668.00
							100	3.80	380.00
							260	4.03	1,048.00
May				140	4.03	564.20	120	4.03	483.80
June	80	4.50	360.00				120	4.03	483.80
							80	4.50	360.00
							200	4.22	843.80

Note: some figures have been rounded to the nearest penny

FIFO STORES LEDGER RECORD: TYPE Y

Date	Receipts			Issues			Balance		
2004	Quantity	Cost	Total Cost	Quantity	Cost	Total Cost	Quantity	Cost	Total Cost
		£	£		£	£		£	£
January	200	10.00	2,000.00				200	10.00	2,000.00
February	100	9.50	950.00				200	10.00	2,000.00
							100	9.50	950.00
							300		2,950.00
March				200	10.00	2,000.00			
				40	9.50	380.00	60	9.50	570.00
April	100	10.50	1,050.00				60	9.50	570.00
							100	10.50	1,050.00
							160		1,620.00
May	140	10.00	1,400.00				60	9.50	570.00
							100	10.50	1,050.00
							140	10.00	1,400.00
							300		3,020.00
June				60	9.50	570.00			
				40	10.50	420.00	60	10.50	630.00
							140	10.00	1,400.00
							200		2,030.00

LIFO STORES LEDGER RECORD: TYPE Y

Date	Receipts			Issues			Balance		
2004	Quantity	Cost	Total Cost	Quantity	Cost	Total Cost	Quantity	Cost	Total Cost
		£	£		£	£		£	£
January	200	10.00	2,000.00				200	10.00	2,000.00
February	100	9.50	950.00				200	10.00	2,000.00
							100	9.50	950.00
							300		2,950.00
March				100	9.50	950.00			
				140	10.00	1,400.00	60	10.00	600.00
April	100	10.50	1,050.00				60	10.00	600.00
							100	10.50	1,050.00
							160		1,650.00
May	140	10.00	1,400.00				60	10.00	600.00
							100	10.50	1,050.00
							140	10.00	1,400.00
							300		3,050.00
June				100	10.00	1,000.00	60	10.00	600.00
							100	10.50	1,050.00
							40	10.00	400.00
							200		2,050.00

AVCO

STORES LEDGER RECORD: TYPE Y

Date 2004	Receipts			Issues			Balance		
	Quantity	Cost	Total Cost	Quantity	Cost	Total Cost	Quantity	Cost	Total Cost
		£	£		£	£		£	£
January	200	10.00	2,000.00				200	10.00	2,000.00
February	100	9.50	950.00				200	10.00	2,000.00
							100	9.50	950.00
							300	9.83	2,950.00
March				240	9.83	2,360.00	60	9.83	590.00
April	100	10.50	1,050.00				60	9.83	590.00
							100	10.50	1,050.00
							160	10.25	1,640.00
May	140	10.00	1,400.00				160	10.25	1,640.00
							140	10.00	1,400.00
							300	10.13	3,040.00
June				100	10.13	1,013.00	200	10.13	2,027.00

Note: some figures have been rounded to the nearest penny

Balance sheet valuation at 30 June 2004:

	£	
Type X	824.00	(cost price, using FIFO)
Type Y	1,950.00	(net realisable value)
	2,774.00	

2.6   **Task 1**

STORES LEDGER RECORD

Product: **Wholewheat flour**

Date 2004	Receipts			Issues			Balance	
	Quantity kgs	Cost per kg £	Total Cost £	Quantity kgs	Cost per kg £	Total Cost £	Quantity kgs	Total Cost £
Balance at 1 May							10,000	2,500
6 May	20,000	0.30	6,000				30,000	8,500
10 May				20,000	10,000 x 0.25 10,000 x 0.30	2,500 3,000 5,500	10,000	3,000
17 May	10,000	0.35	3,500				10,000 10,000	3,000 3,500
20 May				15,000	10,000 x 0.30 5,000 x 0.35	3,000 1,750 4,750	5,000	1,750

Task 2

2004	Code	Debit	Credit
6 May	3000	£6,000	
6 May	5000		£6,000
10 May	3000		£5,500*
10 May	3300	£5,500	
17 May	3000	£3,500	
17 May	5000		£3,500
20 May	3000		£4,750**
20 May	3300	£4,750	

* £2,500 + £3,000   ** £3,000 + £1,750

CHAPTER 3: LABOUR COSTS

3.1

N Ball:	35 hours x £8.00 per hour = £280.00 (no bonus)
T Smith:	37 hours x £9.00 per hour = £333.00 + bonus £9.00 = £342.00
L Lewis:	40 hours x £10.00 per hour = £400.00 + bonus £13.75 = £413.75
M Wilson:	38 hours x £7.00 per hour = £266.00 + bonus £4.08 = £270.08

3.2

MEMORANDUM	
To:	Office Manager
From:	Accounts Assistant
Date:	Today

Remuneration of production-line workers

I have been asked to produce a report on remuneration methods for production-line workers.

At present the company pays these workers on a time-rate basis. The main advantages of such a system from the viewpoint of both employer and employees are as follows:

• it is easy to calculate and understand

• there is no requirement to establish time allowances and piecework rates

• employees receive a regular wage, which is unaffected by fluctuations in output

• the system can be applied to all direct labour employees

• the quality of finished output does not suffer as a result of hurried work

The disadvantages of time rate are that:

• all production-line employees are paid the same, whether they work efficiently or inefficiently

• no incentive is given to employees to work harder

• the company needs to employ supervisors to ensure that output is maintained

• slow working by employees does not affect the basic wage, but could lead to the company having to pay overtime rates to ensure that output is completed.

Employee representatives have approached the company management with a request that other remuneration methods be considered. In particular piecework systems, or a time rate with a production bonus system have been suggested.

A *piecework system* is where payment is based on the quantity of output.

The main advantages of this are that:

• payment of wages is linked directly to output

• more efficient workers earn more than those who are less efficient

• work is done quicker and less time is wasted

The main disadvantages are that:

• the system is not suitable for all direct labour employees

• there may be difficulty in agreeing piecework rates between employer and employees

- the quality of the finished product may be low and more inspectors may be needed
- control system will be needed to check the amount produced by each worker
- from the employer's point of view, the quality of the finished product may be low
- pay calculations will be more complex

Employees need to be aware that pay is reduced if there are production problems, eg machine breakdown, or shortage of materials. A way around this is to use a piecework system with a guaranteed time rate. A further disadvantage is that there may be difficulties in agreeing piecework rates.

A time rate with a production bonus is a system used to encourage employees to be more efficient where work is not so repetitive. There are a number of variations of bonus including increased bonuses for higher levels of output, and group bonuses paid to groups of employees.

The main advantages of bonus systems are that:

- wages are linked to output, but a minimum wage – the time rate – is guaranteed each week
- work is done quicker and less time is wasted
- the more efficient workers earn more
- a bonus system can often be applied to the entire workforce

The disadvantages are that:

- from the employee's point of view, the bonus is not paid if circumstances such as machine breakdown, or shortage of materials occur
- from the employer's point of view, the quality of the finished product may be low and more inspectors will be needed
- there may be difficulty in agreeing bonus rates with employees
- control procedures are needed, and pay calculations will be more complex

Conclusion

Each of the three main methods of remuneration has advantages and disadvantages. In selecting a suitable system both employer and employee must consider that:

- reward should be related to effort and fair to all staff
- the system should be easy to manage and administer, and be cheap and efficient to run
- it should be easy for employees to understand how pay is calculated
- payment should be made at regular intervals and soon after the event
- the principles of the scheme should remain constant, but there should be flexibility to deal with changes in production techniques

---

3.3   (a) • L Fry: £400.00 (time rate)
- R Williams: £315.00 (piecework rate)
- P Grant: £362.50 (piecework rate)

(b) • not suitable for all direct labour employees
- employees' pay is reduced if there are production problems
- quality of the finished product may be low
- more inspectors may be needed

- control systems needed to check the amount produced by each worker
- more complex pay calculations
- may be difficulty in agreeing piecework rates with employees

3.4 Gross wages

			£
•	Steve Kurtin:	35 hours at £5.50 per hour =	192.50
		4 hours overtime at £7.333 per hour =	29.33
		production bonus 45 x 25p =	11.25
			233.08
•	Pete Singh:	35 hours at £6.50 per hour =	227.50
		3 hours overtime at £8.667 per hour =	26.00
		4 hours overtime at £9.75 per hour =	39.00
		production bonus 57 x 25p =	14.25
			306.75

Piecework rate for Steve Kurtin
£233.08 ÷ 45 = £5.18 per 1,000 copies printed

3.5

	MOULDING	FINISHING
• Standard hours saved	–	500
• Bonus (£)	–	2,025*
• Total labour cost (£)	31,160	38,475

* £36,450 ÷ 4,500 hours = £8.10 x 500 hours = £4,050 ÷ 2 = £2,025

3.6 (a) Week 1: 400 hours at £6.20 per hour = £2,480

50 hours at 1.5 x £6.20 = 50 x £9.30 = £465

Total gross earnings for Week1 = £2,480 + £465 = £2,945

Week 2: 400 hours at £6.20 per hour = £2,480 = Total gross earnings

(b) Week 1: Normally treated as indirect labour cost would be overtime premium on 50 hours, ie 50 x 0.5 x £6.20 = £155

Week 2: Normally treated as indirect labour cost would be 20 hours of non-production work at basic pay, ie 20 x £6.20 = £124

3.7
- *work-in-progress £2,100:* the cost of direct labour incurred by the company for the work on manufacturing the product
- *production overheads £900:* the cost of indirect labour incurred by the company for the week
- *non-production overheads £700:* the administration labour costs for the week
- *total payroll for the week £3,700:* the total of net wages paid to employees, income tax and National Insurance Contributions, and pension contributions

3.8 **Task 1**

Dr		Wages Control Account		Cr
	£			£
Cash/bank (net wages)	7,500	Work-in-progress (direct labour)		6,500
Inland Revenue (income tax and NIC)	1,450	Production overheads		
Pension contributions	750	(indirect labour)		2,700
		Non-production overheads		
		(administration)		500
	9,700			9,700

Task 2

2004	Code	Debit	Credit
26 March	3300	£6,500	
26 March	5200		£6,500
26 March	3500	£2,700	
26 March	5200		£2,700
26 March	3700	£500	
26 March	5200		£500

3.9 Total cost of direct labour for October:

			£
14,400 hours	x £8 per hour	=	115,200
1,600 hours	x £12 (£8 + £4) per hour	=	19,200
16,000 hours			134,400

Cost book-keeping entries:

	Debit	Credit
	£	£
• work-in-progress – 'Mulligan' clubs (1500)	134,400	
• wages control (5000)		134,400

CHAPTER 4: EXPENSES

4.1 (a) *Capital expenditure:* expenditure incurred on the purchase, alteration or improvement of fixed assets. Examples: purchase of premises, vehicles, machinery; legal costs of buying property; installation and setting up of a machine.

(b) *Revenue expenditure:* expenditure incurred on running costs. Examples: fuel for vehicles; repairs to premises; labour costs of running the business.

4.2   (a)   *Direct expenses:* those expenses that are attributable to particular units of output. Examples: royalties payable to the designer of a product; special items bought in for a particular product or job; power costs metered to output; depreciation methods linked directly to output (such as units of output or service method).

(b)   *Indirect expenses:* those expenses that are not attributable directly to particular units of output. Examples: rent and rates, heating and lighting, depreciation methods not linked directly to output (such as straight-line and reducing balance methods).

4.3   Fred Jarvis' wages will be shown in wages control account as:

–   *debit* cash/bank, income tax and NIC, and pension contributions

–   *credit* property account

Thus the cost of his labour is debited to the fixed asset account of property (rather than work-in-progress, as would be the usual case for production-line employees). As he is building an extension to the warehouse, his wages (and also the cost of the materials he uses) are treated as capital expenditure because he is adding to the value of a fixed asset.

4.4   **Graph A**
- shows a *fixed cost,* which remains constant over a range of output levels
- as output increases, the *cost per unit* falls
- at an output beyond the limit of the graph, the fixed cost will increase as another factory needs to be rented; the nature of such a cost is known as a *stepped fixed cost.*

Graph B
- shows a *variable cost,* which alters directly with changes in output levels
- as output increases then the cost increases, ie the cost per unit remains the same

4.5

		capital expenditure	revenue expenditure
(a)	purchase of motor vehicles	✓	
(b)	depreciation of motor vehicles		✓
(c)	payment of office rent		✓
(d)	salaries of office staff		✓
(e)	legal fees relating to the purchase of property	✓	
(f)	re-decoration of office		✓
(g)	installation of air-conditioning in office	✓	
(h)	wages of own employees used to build extension to the stockroom	✓	
(i)	installation and setting up of a new machine	✓	

4.6

	direct expenses	indirect expenses	either*
(a) hire of machinery for a particular job	✓		
(b) office rent		✓	
(c) cleaning materials		✓	
(d) power costs			✓
(e) royalty paid to designer for each unit of output	✓		
(f) sales staff car expenses		✓	
(g) depreciation of production machinery			✓
(h) consultant's fees relating to a particular job	✓		
(i) heating and lighting		✓	

(d) Power costs are direct expenses where machinery is separately metered and used for a particular product or job; otherwise, they are indirect expenses.

(g) Depreciation of production machinery is a direct expense when the depreciation method is linked directly to output (such as units of output or service method; it is an indirect expense when the depreciation method is not linked directly to output (such as straight-line and reducing balance methods).

4.7

	fixed	semi-fixed	variable
(a) rates of business premises	✓		
(b) royalty paid to designer for each unit of output			✓
(c) car hire with fixed rental and charge per mile		✓	
(d) employees paid on piecework basis			✓
(e) straight-line depreciation	✓		
(f) units of output depreciation			✓
(g) direct materials			✓
(h) telephone bill with fixed rental and charge per unit		✓	
(i) office salaries	✓		

4.8 (a) cleaning materials for the machines: indirect materials
(b) wages of factory supervisor: indirect labour
(c) clay from which pots are made: direct materials
(d) royalty paid to designer: direct expenses
(e) salary of office assistant: indirect expenses*
(f) electricity used to heat the kilns: indirect expense (or possibly a direct expense – see note to question 4.6(d) above)
(g) rates of factory: indirect expense
(h) depreciation of office equipment: indirect expense
(i) wages of production line workers: direct labour
(j) salesperson's salary: indirect expenses*
(k) interest charged on bank overdraft: indirect expenses

* Note: Both the salary of the office assistant and the salesperson's salary have been classified as indirect expenses, rather than indirect labour. This is because neither of them work in the factory and so the cost cannot be attributed directly to production. By contrast, the wages of the factory supervisor are classified as indirect labour – here the employee does work in the factory, and the cost is more closely linked to production.

- *production overheads:* (a), (b), (f), (g)
- *selling and distribution overheads:* (j)
- *administration overheads:* (e), (h)
- *finance overheads:* (k)

4.9 Task 1

Dr **General Expenses Account** Cr

2004		£	2004		£
30 June	Balance b/d	28,250	30 June	Work-in-progress: treadmill	5,450
			30 June	Work-in-progress: exercise cycles	3,170
			30 June	Production overheads	12,950
			30 June	Non-production overheads: selling and distribution	3,860
			30 June	Non-production overheads: administration	2,820
		28,250			28,250

Task 2

2004	Code	Debit	Credit
30 June	2100	£5,450	
30 June	5150		£5,450
30 June	2200	£3,170	
30 June	5150		£3,170
30 June	3500	£12,950	
30 June	5150		£12,950
30 June	4200	£3,860	
30 June	5150		£3,860
30 June	4400	£2,820	
30 June	5150		£2,820

4.10 •

	high output	15,000 units	£65,000
less	low output	10,000 units	£50,000
equals	difference	5,000 units	£15,000

• amount of variable cost per unit:

$$\frac{£15,000}{5,000} = £3 \text{ variable cost per unit}$$

• at 10,000 units of output the cost structure is:

	total cost	£50,000
less	variable costs (10,000 units x £3 per unit)	£30,000
equals	fixed costs	£20,000

• check at 15,000 units of output when the cost structure is:

	variable costs (15,000 units x £3 per unit)	£45,000
add	fixed costs (as above)	£20,000
equals	total costs	£65,000

• therefore fixed costs, at these levels of output, are £20,000

4.11

2005	**BUDGETED PRODUCTION COSTS**		
Units	250,000	300,000	350,000
Costs	£	£	£
Variable costs:			
Materials	400,000	480,000	560,000
Labour	325,000	390,000	455,000
Expenses	100,000	120,000	140,000
	825,000	990,000	1,155,000
Fixed costs:			
Labour	96,500	96,500	96,500
Overheads	107,500	107,500	107,500
	204,000	204,000	204,000
TOTAL PRODUCTION COST	1,029,000	1,194,000	1,359,000
COST PER UNIT	£4.12	£3.98	£3.88

- Variable costs per unit are:
  - materials, £1.60 (ie £400,000 ÷ 250,000 units)
  - labour, £1.30
  - expenses, £0.40
- Fixed costs remain fixed at the higher levels of output
- The costs at higher levels of output are on the basis that
  - there is a linear relationship for variable costs
  - there are no stepped fixed costs
- The fall in cost per unit as output increases occurs because the fixed costs are being spread over a greater number of units, ie the fixed cost per unit falls

CHAPTER 5: OVERHEADS

5.1
- allocation of overheads – the charging to a cost centre of those overheads that have been directly incurred by that cost centre
- apportionment of overheads – the charging to a cost centre of a proportion of overheads

5.2 (a)

OVERHEAD ANALYSIS SHEET		
	MOULDING	FINISHING
Budgeted total overheads (£)	9,338	3,298
Budgeted machine hours	1,450	680
Budgeted overhead absorption rate (£)	6.44*	4.85**

*   £9,338 ÷ 1,450 hours

**   £3,298 ÷ 680 hours

(b)

JOB OVERHEAD ANALYSIS SHEET		
	MOULDING	FINISHING
Job machine hours	412	154
Budgeted overhead absorption rate (£)	6.44	4.85
Overhead absorbed by job (£)	2,653.28*	746.90**

*   412 hours x £6.44 per hour

**   154 hours x £4.85 per hour

(c) **Units of output**
- Using this method, production overhead is absorbed on the basis of each unit of output.
- This would be appropriate where units of output are identical and where each spend the

same amount of time in the departments.
• It does not seem appropriate for use by Wyvern Fabrication as the company appears to have different types and sizes of jobs passing through its two departments – to use units of output, each job would be charged the same rate.

Direct labour hour
• With this method, production overhead is absorbed on the basis of the number of direct labour hours worked.
• While this is a commonly-used method, it is inappropriate where some output is worked on by hand while other output passes quickly through a machinery process and requires little direct labour time.
• This method may be appropriate for Wyvern Fabrication; however, much depends on the balance between direct labour hours and machine hours in the two production departments.

5.3 (a)

cost	basis of apportionment	total	dept A	dept B	dept C
		£	£	£	£
Rent and rates	Floor area	7,210	3,090	1,545	2,575
Depn. of machinery	Value of machinery	10,800	5,400	3,240	2,160
Supervisor's salary	Production-line employees	12,750	6,800	3,400	2,550
Machinery insurance	Value of machinery	750	375	225	150
		31,510	15,665	8,410	7,435

(b) 37 hours x 48 weeks = 1,776 direct labour hours per employee
Dept A: 8 employees = 14,208 hours = £1.10 per direct labour hour
Dept B: 4 employees = 7,104 hours = £1.18 per direct labour hour
Dept C: 3 employees = 5,328 hours = £1.40 per direct labour hour

5.4 (a) and (b)

cost	basis of apportionment	total	machining	finishing	maintenance
		£	£	£	£
Rent and rates	Floor area	5,520	2,760	1,840	920
Buildings insurance	Floor area	1,320	660	440	220
Machinery insurance	Value of machinery	1,650	1,200	450	–
Lighting and heating	Floor area	3,720	1,860	1,240	620
Depn of machinery	Value of machinery	11,000	8,000	3,000	–
Supervisory salaries	No. of employees	30,000	18,000	9,000	3,000
Maintenance dept salary	Allocation	16,000	–	–	16,000
Factory cleaning	Floor area	4,800	2,400	1,600	800
		74,010	34,880	17,570	21,560
Re-apportionment of maintenance dept	Value of machinery	–	15,680	5,880	(21,560)
		74,010	50,560	23,450	–

(c)   35 hours x 47 weeks = 1,645 direct labour hours per employee
Machining Dept: 6 employees = 9,870 hours = £5.12 per direct labour hour
Finishing Dept: 3 employees = 4,935 hours = £4.75 per direct labour hour

(d)   Depending on the method and type of production, the company is most likely to use overhead absorption rates based on:
- direct labour hour, or
- machine hour

These are discussed in the text (pages 129 to 130). Alternative methods could be based on a percentage of certain costs, eg direct materials, direct labour, prime cost.

5.5

	total	business studies	general studies	administration	technical support
		£	£	£	£
Overheads	81,600	40,000	20,000	9,600	12,000
Technical support	–	6,000	3,000	3,000	(12,000)
				12,600	–
Administration	–	8,400	4,200	(12,600)	–
	81,600	54,400	27,200	–	–

5.6   (a) $\dfrac{\text{total overheads}}{\text{total hours}}$ $= \dfrac{£59,900}{3,290}$ =   £18.21 per partner hour

(b) $\dfrac{£59,900 + £60,000}{3,290}$ =   £36.44 per partner hour

(c)   2 hours x 47 weeks x £18.21   =   £1,711.74 per partner
(ie £3,423.48 in total)

5.7   (a)   Direct labour hour: (3 hours x 80 seats) + (3.5 hours x 40 seats)
= 380 direct labour hours per month = £2.63 per hour.

Machine hour: (1 hour x 80 seats) + (2.5 hours x 40 seats)
= 180 machine hours per month = £5.56 per hour.

Alternative methods could be based on a percentage of certain costs, eg direct labour.

(b)   *Direct labour hour*

'Standard'   £36.50 + £7.89   =   £44.39

'De Luxe'   £55.00 + £9.21   =   £64.21

Machine hour

'Standard'   £36.50 + £5.56   =   £42.06

'De Luxe'   £55.00 + £13.89   =   £68.89

Note: some figures have been rounded to the nearest penny

(c)   See text. The machine hour rate charges most to 'de luxe' model. On balance, direct labour hours may be the best method to use because the products are more labour-intensive than machine-intensive.

5.8 Task 1

Fixed overheads for November 2004	Basis	Total £	Warehouse £	Manufacturing £	Sales £	Administration £
Depreciation	Net book value	9,150	1,830	6,100	305	915
Rent	Floor space	11,000	1,650	6,600	1,100	1,650
Other property overheads	Floor space	6,200	930	3,720	620	930
Administration overheads	Allocated	13,450				13,450
Staff costs	Allocated	27,370	3,600	9,180	8,650	5,940
		67,170	8,010	25,600	10,675	22,885

Task 2

Budgeted fixed overhead absorption rate for the manufacturing department:

£25,600 ÷ 10,000 hours = £2.56 per machine hour

5.9   Task 1

Fixed overheads for August 2004	Basis	Total £	Accommodation £	Restaurant £	Bar £	Kitchen £	Administration £
Bedroom repairs	Allocated	3,200	3,200				
Electricity	Metered	1,700	550	250	150	700	50
Rent	Floor space	9,000	5,850	1,350	900	450	450
Kitchen repairs	Allocated	1,025				1,025	
Staff costs	Allocated	23,595	4,550	6,740	3,045	2,310	6,950
Other property overheads	Floor space	4,000	2,600	600	400	200	200
		42,520	16,750	8,940	4,495	4,685	7,650
Administration			4,590	1,530	765	765	(7,650)
		42,520	21,340	10,470	5,260	5,450	—

Task 2

Budgeted fixed overhead absorption rate for the kitchen:

£5,450 ÷ 1,000 hours = £5.45 per labour hour

5.10

| Dr | Production Overheads Account: Moulding Department | | Cr |

Dr			Cr
	£		£
Bank (overheads incurred)	5,000	Work-in-progress	4,800
		Profit and loss (under-absorption)	200
	5,000		5,000

Dr	Production Overheads Account: Finishing Department		Cr
	£		£
Bank (overheads incurred)	7,000	Work-in-progress	7,500
Profit and loss (over-absorption)	500		
	7,500		7,500

2004	Code	Debit	Credit
26 May	3000	£4,800	
26 May	3400		£4,800
26 May	3000	£7,500	
26 May	3500		£7,500
26 May	6000	£200	
26 May	3400		£200
26 May	3500	£500	
26 May	6000		£500

CHAPTER 6: METHODS OF COSTING

6.1 The method of costing for each business should be justified; however, the following are the most likely methods:

- *accountant* – job costing, because each job will take a different length of time and is likely to involve a number of staff, each with different skill levels
- *bus company* – service costing, where the object is to find the cost per unit of service, eg passenger mile; job costing used for 'one-offs', eg quoting for the transport for a trip to the seaside for an old people's home
- *baker* – batch costing, where identical units are produced in batches, eg loaves; job costing could be used for 'one-off' items, eg a wedding cake
- *sports centre* – service costing, or job costing for 'one-off', eg hire of the main sports hall for an exhibition
- *hotel* – different methods of costing are likely to be used, eg service costing for the rooms, batch costing in the restaurant, and job costing for special events
- *construction company* – contract costing for large, complex projects which last for a long period of time; job costing for smaller, more routine work

6.2

		£	£
Direct materials:	100m x £7.50	750.00	
	75m x £4.00	300.00	
			1,050.00
Direct labour:	35 hours x £6.00		210.00
Overheads:	35 hours x £8.50		297.50
(a) TOTAL COST			1,557.50
Profit (20% of total cost)			311.50
(b) SELLING PRICE			1,869.00

6.3

JOB COST SHEET
Replacement Cylinder Head

		£
Direct Materials		
100 kg of high-strength steel at £10 per kg		1,000.00
Direct Labour		
Foundry:	10 hours at £10.00 per hour	100.00
Finishing:	15 hours at £12.00 per hour	180.00
Overheads		
Foundry:	80% of direct labour cost	80.00
Finishing:	12 machine hours x £20 per hour	240.00
TOTAL COST		1,600.00
Profit (25% of total cost)		400.00
SELLING PRICE		2,000.00

6.4 *Total costs:*

	£
Depreciation of diesel trains £30,000* x 6 trains	180,000
Leasing charges for track	500,000
Maintenance charges for trains	455,000
Fuel for trains	105,000
Wages of drivers and conductors	240,000
Administration	260,000
	1,740,000

* (£650,000 – £50,000) ÷ 20 years = £30,000 per train per year

Cost per passenger mile:

$$\frac{£1,740,000}{2.5m\ journeys \times 5\ miles} = £0.1392 \text{ per passenger mile}$$

6.5

Cost element	Costs	Completed Units	Work-in-progress			Total Equivalent Units	Cost per Unit	WIP valuation
			Units	% complete	Equivalent Units			
	A	B	C	D	E	F	G	H
					C x D	B + E	A ÷ F	E x G
	£						£	£
Direct materials	11,500	20,000	5,000	100	5,000	25,000	0.46	2,300
Direct labour	9,000	20,000	5,000	50	2,500	22,500	0.40	1,000
Production overheads	18,000	20,000	5,000	50	2,500	22,500	0.80	2,000
Total	38,500						1.66	5,300

(a)   Cost per toy is £1.66 each

(b)   Work-in-progress valuation is £5,300:   £

20,000 completed units at £1.66 each   33,200

work-in-progress valuation   5,300

total costs for month   38,500

6.6

Dr   **Process Account**   Cr

	Quantity (litres)	Unit cost £	Total £		Quantity (litres)	Unit cost £	Total £
Materials	22,000	0.25	5,500	Normal loss			
Labour		0.15	3,300	(scrap sales)	2,000	–	400
Overheads		0.10	2,200	Finished goods	20,000	0.53	10,600
	22,000		11,000		22,000		11,000

Dr   **Normal Loss Account**   Cr

	£		£
Process account	400	Bank/debtors	400

Tutorial note:

The cost per unit of the expected output is:

$$\frac{£11,000 - £400}{20,000 \text{ litres}} = £0.53 \text{ per litre}$$

6.7

Dr				Process Account				Cr
	Quantity	Unit cost	Total		Quantity	Unit cost	Total	
	(kilos)	£	£		(kilos)	£	£	
Materials	42,000	0.25	10,500	Normal loss	2,000	–	400	
Labour		0.10	4,200	Finished goods	39,500	0.41	16,195	
Overheads		0.05	2,100	Abnormal loss	500	0.41	205	
	42,000		16,800		42,000		16,800	

Dr		Normal Loss Account		Cr
	£			£
Process account	400	Bank/debtors		400

Dr		Abnormal Loss Account		Cr
	£			£
Process account	205	Bank/debtors (500 kilos x 20p)		100

Tutorial note:

The cost per unit of the expected output is:

$$\frac{£16,800 - £400}{40,000 \text{ kilos}} = £0.41 \text{ per kilo}$$

6.8

Dr				Process 1 Account				Cr
	Quantity	Unit cost	Total		Quantity	Unit cost	Total	
	(litres)	£	£		(litres)	£	£	
Materials	10,000	0.50	5,000	Normal loss (10%)	1,000	–	400	
Labour		0.40	4,000	Transfer to				
Overheads		0.20	2,000	process 2	9,000	1.18	10,600	
	10,000		11,000		10,000		11,000	

Dr   **Process 2 Account**   Cr

	Quantity (litres)	Unit cost £	Total £		Quantity (litres)	Unit cost £	Total £
Transfer from				Normal loss (5%)	450	–	225
process 1	9,000	1.18	10,600	Finished goods	8,300	1.58	13,130
Labour		0.20	1,800	Abnormal loss	250	1.58	395
Overheads		0.15	1,350				
	9,000		13,750		9,000		13,750

Dr   **Normal Loss Account**   Cr

	£		£
Process 1 account	400	Bank/debtors	400
Process 2 account	225	Bank/debtors	225
	625		625

Dr   **Abnormal Loss Account**   Cr

	£		£
Process 2 account	395	Bank/debtors (250 litres x 50p)	125

Tutorial notes:

- In process 1, the cost per unit of the expected output is:

$$\frac{£11,000 - £400}{9,000 \text{ litres}} = £1.18 \text{ per litre}$$

- In process 2, the cost per unit of the expected output is:

$$\frac{£13,750 - £225}{8,550 \text{ litres}} = £1.58 \text{ per litre}$$

Dr   **Process Account**   Cr

	Quantity (litres)	Unit cost £	Total £		Quantity (litres)	Unit cost £	Total £
Materials	11,000	0.50	5,500	Normal loss	1,000	–	300
Labour		0.35	3,850	Finished goods	10,200	1.18	12,036
Overheads		0.25	2,750				
			12,100				
Abnormal gain	200	1.18	236				
	11,200		12,336		11,200		12,336

6.9

Dr	Abnormal Gain Account		Cr
	£		£
Normal loss account	*60	Process account	236

Dr	Normal Loss Account		Cr
	£		£
Process account	300	Bank/debtors	240
		Abnormal gain account	*60
	300		300

* 200 litres at 30p per litre

Tutorial note:

The cost per unit of the expected output is:

$$\frac{£12,100 - £300}{10,000 \text{ litres}} = £1.18 \text{ per litre}$$

CHAPTER 7: BOOK-KEEPING FOR COSTING

7.1   (c)

7.2   (d)

7.3   (a)   factory rent – manufacturing account

(b)   production supervisors' wages – manufacturing account

(c)   insurance of factory buildings – manufacturing account

(d)   depreciation of office equipment – profit and loss account

(e)   sales commission – profit and loss account

(f)   raw materials purchased – manufacturing account

(g)   advertising – profit and loss account

7.4

CROWN HEATH MANUFACTURING COMPANY
MANUFACTURING AND PROFIT AND LOSS ACCOUNT
for the year ended 31 December 2004

	£	£
Opening stock of raw materials		10,500
Add Purchases of raw materials		27,200
		37,700
Less Closing stock of raw materials		10,200
COST OF RAW MATERIALS USED		27,500
Direct labour		12,600
PRIME COST		40,100
Add Production overheads:		
Indirect labour	3,900	
Rent and rates	1,200	
Power	2,000	
Depreciation of factory machinery	900	
Repairs to factory buildings	300	
Sundry factory expenses	900	
		9,200
PRODUCTION COST OF GOODS COMPLETED		49,300
Sales		60,400
Opening stock of finished goods	4,300	
Production cost of goods completed	49,300	
	53,600	
Less Closing stock of finished goods	3,200	
COST OF SALES		50,400
Gross profit		10,000
Less Non-production overheads		6,500
Net profit		3,500

7.5

BARBARA FRANCIS

MANUFACTURING AND PROFIT AND LOSS ACCOUNT

for the year ended 31 December 2004

	£	£
Opening stock of raw materials		31,860
Add Purchases of raw materials		237,660
		269,520
Less Closing stock of raw materials		44,790
COST OF RAW MATERIALS USED		224,730
Direct labour		234,630
PRIME COST		459,360
Add Production overheads:		
Rent and rates	24,690	
Power	7,650	
Heat and light	2,370	
Sundry expenses and maintenance	8,190	
Depreciation of plant and machinery	7,450	
		50,350
PRODUCTION COST OF GOODS COMPLETED		509,710
Sales		796,950
Opening stock of finished goods	42,640	
Production cost of goods completed	509,710	
	552,350	
Less Closing stock of finished goods	96,510	
COST OF SALES		455,840
Gross profit		341,110
Less Non-production overheads:		
Rent and rates	8,230	
Salaries	138,700	
Advertising	22,170	
Office expenses	7,860	
		176,960
Net profit		164,150

7.6 Note that transactions are recorded in the integrated book-keeping system in the order in which they took place.

Dr		Capital Account		Cr
	£			£
Balance c/d	67,000	Bank		50,000
		Profit and loss		17,000
	67,000			67,000
		Balance b/d		67,000

Dr		Bank Account		Cr
	£			£
Capital	50,000	Machinery		20,000
Debtors	25,000	Labour		10,000
		Production overheads		5,000
		Non-production overheads		4,000
		Creditors		7,000
		Balance c/d		29,000
	75,000			75,000
Balance b/d	29,000			

Dr		Machinery Account		Cr
	£			£
Bank	20,000			

Dr		Materials Account		Cr
	£			£
Creditors	7,500	Work-in-progress		6,000
		Balance c/d		1,500
	7,500			7,500
Balance b/d	1,500			

Dr		Creditors' Account		Cr
	£			£
Bank	7,000	Materials		7,500
Balance c/d	500			
	7,500			7,500
		Balance b/d		500

Dr	**Labour Costs Account**		Cr
	£		£
Bank	10,000	Work-in-progress	10,000

Dr	**Production Overheads Account**		Cr
	£		£
Bank	5,000	Work-in-progress	5,000

Dr	**Non-Production Overheads Account**		Cr
	£		£
Bank	4,000	Profit and loss	4,000

Dr	**Sales Account**		Cr
	£		£
Profit and loss	37,000	Debtors	37,000

Dr	**Debtors' Account**		Cr
	£		£
Sales	37,000	Bank	25,000
		Balance c/d	12,000
	37,000		37,000
Balance b/d	12,000		

Dr	**Work-in-Progress Account**		Cr
	£		£
Direct materials	6,000	Finished goods	19,000
Direct labour	10,000	Balance c/d	2,000
Production overheads	5,000		
	21,000		21,000
Balance b/d	2,000		

Dr	**Finished Goods Account**		Cr
	£		£
Work-in-progress	19,000	Cost of sales	16,000
		Balance c/d	3,000
	19,000		19,000
Balance b/d	3,000		

Dr		**Cost of Sales Account**		Cr
	£			£
Finished goods	16,000	Profit and loss		16,000

Dr		**Profit and Loss Account**		Cr
	£			£
Non-production overheads	4,000	Sales		37,000
Cost of sales	16,000			
Net profit (to Capital account)	17,000			
	37,000			37,000

Trial balance at 31 July 2004

	Dr	Cr
	£	£
Capital		67,000
Bank	29,000	
Machinery	20,000	
Materials	1,500	
Creditors		500
Debtors	12,000	
Work-in-progress	2,000	
Finished goods	3,000	
	67,500	67,500

7.7 • work-in-progress account £16,500: the cost of direct labour incurred by the company for the week on manufacturing the product

• production overheads accounts £5,900: the cost of indirect labour incurred by the company for the week

7.8 • Debit: profit and loss account £125

• Credit: production overheads account £125

The amount of under-absorbed overhead is debited to profit and loss account where it adds to the total costs of the business, and so reduces profit.

7.9 • Debit: production overheads account (finishing department)

• Credit: profit and loss account

The amount of over-absorbed overhead is credited to profit and loss account where it increases profit.

7.10   **Department A**

- overhead absorbed by cost units £3.00 x 1,240 hours = £3,720
- actual cost of production overhead = £3,800
- under-absorption of overhead = £   80

Department B

- overhead absorbed by cost units £6.00 x 1,660 hours = £9,960
- actual cost of production overhead = £9,040
- over-absorption of overhead = £ 920

Dr	**Production Overheads Account: Department A**		Cr
	£		£
Bank (overheads incurred)	3,800	Work-in-progress	3,720
		Profit and loss (under-absorption)	80
	3,800		3,800

Dr	**Production Overheads Account: Department B**		Cr
	£		£
Bank (overheads incurred)	9,040	Work-in-progress	9,960
Profit and loss (over-absorption)	920		
	9,960		9,960

7.11

Dr			**Process Account**				Cr
	Quantity	Unit cost	Total		Quantity	Unit cost	Total
	(litres)	£	£		(litres)	£	£
Materials	22,000	0.70	15,400	Normal loss	1,800	–	900
Labour			6,600	Finished goods	20,300	1.25	25,375
Overheads			4,150				
			26,150				
Abnormal gain	100	1.25	125				
	22,100		26,275		22,100		26,275

Dr	Abnormal Gain Account		Cr
	£		£
Normal loss account	*50	Process account	125

Dr	Normal Loss Account		Cr
	£		£
Process account	900	Bank/debtors	850
		Abnormal gain account	*50
	900		900

* 100 litres at 50p per litre

Tutorial note:

The cost per unit of the expected output is:

$$\frac{£26,150 - £900}{20,200 \text{ litres}} = £1.25 \text{ per litre}$$

7.12

Dr			Process 1 Account				Cr
	Quantity	Unit cost	Total		Quantity	Unit cost	Total
	(kilos)	£	£		(kilos)	£	£
Materials	4,000	3.00	12,000	Normal loss (10%)	400	–	200
Labour			1,840	Transfer to			
Overheads			2,150	process 2	3,700	4.39	16,229
			15,990				
Abnormal gain	100	4.39	439				
	4,100		16,429		4,100		16,429

Dr			Process 2 Account				Cr
	Quantity	Unit cost	Total		Quantity	Unit cost	Total
	(kilos)	£	£		(kilos)	£	£
Transfer from				Normal loss (20%)	1,180	–	590
process 1	3,700	4.39	16,229	Finished goods	4,600	5.70	26,225
Materials	2,200	4.00	8,800	Abnormal loss	120	5.70	684
Labour			1,420				
Overheads			1,050				
	5,900		27,499		5,900		27,499

Dr		Normal Loss Account		Cr
	£			£
Process 1 account	200	Bank/debtors		150
Process 2 account	590	Abnormal gain account		*50
		Bank/debtors		590
	790			790

Dr		Abnormal Gain Account		Cr
	£			£
Normal loss account	*50	Process 1 account		439

* 100 kilos at £0.50 per kilo

Dr		Abnormal Loss Account		Cr
	£			£
Process 2 account	684	Bank/debtors (120 kilos x £0.50)		60

Tutorial notes:

- In process 1, the cost per unit of the expected output is:

$$\frac{£15,990 - £200}{3,600 \text{ kilos}} = £4.39 \text{ per kilo}$$

- In process 2, the cost per unit of the expected output is:

$$\frac{£27,499 - £590}{4,720 \text{ kilos}} = £5.70 \text{ per kilo}$$

- At the end of the financial year:
  - the balance of abnormal loss account is debited to profit and loss account
  - the balance of abnormal gain account is credited to profit and loss account

CHAPTER 8: SHORT-TERM DECISIONS

8.1

units of output	fixed costs	variable costs	total cost	sales revenue	profit/(loss)*
	£	£	£	£	£
0	7,500	0	7,500	0	(7,500)
500	7,500	2,500	10,000	5,000	(5,000)
1,000	7,500	5,000	12,500	10,000	(2,500)
1,500	7,500	7,500	15,000	15,000	nil
2,000	7,500	10,000	17,500	20,000	2,500
2,500	7,500	12,500	20,000	25,000	5,000
3,000	7,500	15,000	22,500	30,000	7,500

* brackets indicate a loss

8.2 **Graphical method**

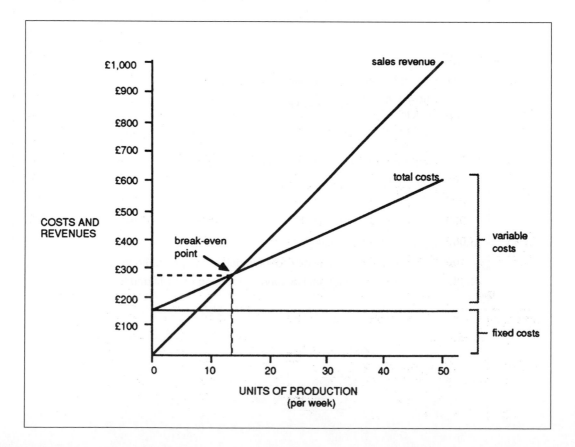

Calculation method

The contribution per unit is:

		£
	selling price per unit	20
less	variable costs* per unit	9
equals	contribution per unit	11

* materials £4 + direct labour £5

The break-even calculation is:

$$\frac{\text{fixed costs (£)}}{\text{contribution per unit (£)}} = \frac{£154^{**}}{£11} = 14 \text{ units (teddy bears) per week}$$

** factory rent and rates £100 + fuel and power £20 + other costs £20

8.3 (a) table method

units of output	fixed costs	variable costs	total cost	sales revenue	profit/(loss)*
	£	£	£	£	£
100	12,000	2,000	14,000	3,500	(10,500)
200	12,000	4,000	16,000	7,000	(9,000)
300	12,000	6,000	18,000	10,500	(7,500)
400	12,000	8,000	20,000	14,000	(6,000)
500	12,000	10,000	22,000	17,500	(4,500)
600	12,000	12,000	24,000	21,000	(3,000)
700	12,000	14,000	26,000	24,500	(1,500)
800	12,000	16,000	28,000	28,000	nil
900	12,000	18,000	30,000	31,500	1,500
1,000	12,000	20,000	32,000	35,000	3,000
1,100	12,000	22,000	34,000	38,500	4,500
1,200	12,000	24,000	36,000	42,000	6,000

* brackets indicate a loss

(b)   graph method

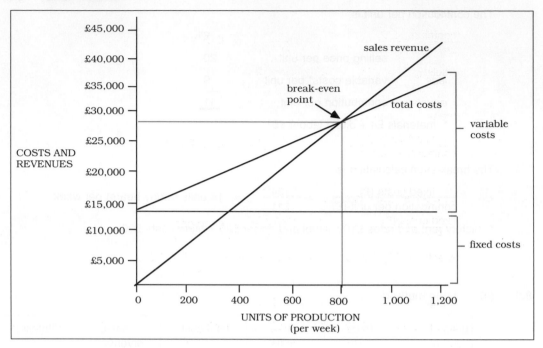

(c)   calculation method

Fixed costs of £12,000 ÷ contribution of £15 per bat = 800 bats to break-even.

(d)   profit/(loss)

*   200 bats

	£
Sales (£35 per bat)	7,000
Less variable costs (£20 per bat)	4,000
Contribution	3,000
Less fixed costs	12,000
Loss for month	(9,000)

*   1,200 bats

	£
Sales (£35 per bat)	42,000
Less variable costs (£20 per bat)	24,000
Contribution	18,000
Less fixed costs	12,000
Profit for month	6,000

(e)   margin of safety

$$\frac{\text{current output} - \text{break-even output}}{\text{current output}} \times \frac{100}{1} = \frac{1,000 - 800}{1,000}$$

= 20 per cent, or 200 units

8.4   Task 1

- profit volume ratio

$$\frac{\text{contribution (£)}}{\text{selling price (£)}} = \frac{£15^*}{£25} = 0.6 \text{ or } 60\%$$

* selling price £25 – variable cost £10

- break-even point in units

$$\frac{\text{fixed costs (£)}}{\text{contribution per unit (£)}} = \frac{£300,000}{£15} = 20,000 \text{ units}$$

- break-even point in sales revenue

$$\frac{\text{fixed costs (£)}}{\text{PV ratio}} = \frac{£300,000}{0.6} = £500,000$$

check: 20,000 units x selling price £25 per unit = £500,000

- margin of safety at output of 30,000 units

$$\frac{\text{current output – break-even output}}{\text{current output}} = \frac{30,000 - 20,000}{30,000} \times \frac{100}{1}$$

= 33.3%, or 10,000 units, or £250,000 of sales revenue

- number of units to generate a target profit of £100,000

$$\frac{\text{fixed costs (£) + target profit (£)}}{\text{contribution per unit (£)}} = \frac{£300,000 + £100,000}{£15} = 26,667 \text{ units}$$

Task 2

		forecast output (30,000 units)	maximum output (40,000 units)
		£	£
	sales revenue (at £25 each)	750,000	1,000,000
less	variable costs (at £10 each)	300,000	400,000
equals	contribution (to fixed costs and profit)	450,000	600,000
less	monthly fixed costs	300,000	300,000
equals	forecast profit for month	150,000	300,000

Task 3

- profit volume ratio

$$\frac{£10^*}{£20} \quad = \quad 0.5 \text{ or } 50\%$$

* selling price £20 – variable cost £10

- break-even point in units

$$\frac{£300,000}{£10} \quad = \quad 30,000 \text{ units}$$

- break-even point in sales revenue

$$\frac{£300,000}{0.5} \quad = \quad £600,000$$

check: 30,000 units x selling price £20 per unit = £600,000

- margin of safety at maximum output of 40,000 units

$$\frac{40,000 - 30,000}{40,000} \times \frac{100}{1} \quad = 25\%, \text{ or } 10,000 \text{ units, or } £200,000 \text{ of sales revenue}$$

- forecast profit at sales of 40,000 units

		£
	sales revenue (at £20 each)	800,000
less	variable costs (at £10 each)	400,000
equals	contribution (to fixed costs and profit)	400,000
less	monthly fixed costs	300,000
equals	forecast profit for month	100,000

REPORT

To: General Manager

From: Accounts Assistant

Date: Today

Proposal to reduce selling price

Introduction

- You asked me to report on the suggestion from one of the managers that the selling price for our product should be reduced from £25 per unit to £20.

- The manager has suggested that the effect of this reduction would be to increase output from the forecast of 30,000 units per month to our maximum output of 40,000 units per month.

Report

- As can be seen from the workings at current levels of output of 30,000 units per month:
  - profit volume ratio is 60%
  - break-even point is 20,000 units
  - margin of safety is 33.3%
  - forecast profit is £150,000 per month
- If the manager's suggestion is adopted sales will increase to our maximum output of 40,000 units per month; this will give us:
  - profit volume ratio of 50%
  - break-even point of 30,000 units
  - margin of safety of 25%
  - forecast profit of £100,000 per month

Conclusion

- From the data summarised above it can be seen that the manager's suggestion would reduce our profit volume ratio, increase the break-even point, and reduce the margin of safety. All of these are all movements in the wrong direction.
- The main point to note is that forecast profit will fall by £50,000 per month to £100,000 per month, and the volume of output will need to be higher.
- Although we would be working at maximum output if the suggestion is adopted, this does mean that there is no scope to increase output and sales in the future without major changes to our cost structure. We would not be able to meet requests for additional sales from our existing customers, and this could cause them to seek all of their supplies from our competitors.
- For these reasons, I would recommend that the manager's suggestion is not undertaken.

8.5   **Task 1**

Product	'Madrid' £	'Paris' £	'Rome' £
Selling price per unit	30	40	60
Less: Unit variable costs			
Direct materials	10	15	20
Direct labour	5	8	12
Variable overheads	2	3	2.50
Contribution per unit	13	14	25.50

Task 2

Break-even point for the 'Madrid' range is:

$$\frac{\text{fixed costs (£)}}{\text{contribution per unit (£)}} = \frac{£72,800}{£13} = \underline{5,600 \text{ units}}$$

Task 3

Product	'Madrid'	'Paris'	'Rome'
Contribution per unit	£13	£14	£25.50
Machine hours per unit	0.5	0.4	0.75
Contribution per machine hour	£26	£35	£34

Task 4

- Machine hours are the limiting factor here, with only 3,000 hours available.

- To maximise profits, the company should maximise the contribution from each machine hour.

- The preferred order is 'Paris' (at £35 contribution per machine hour), 'Rome' (at £34), and 'Madrid' (at £26).

- The company's production plan will be:

'Paris', 3,000 units x 0.4 hours per unit	=	1,200	hours
'Rome', 500 units x 0.75 hours per unit	=	375	hours
'Madrid', 2,850 units x 0.5 hours per unit	=	1,425	balance of hours available
		3,000	hours

Note that this production plan does not allow for full production of the 'Madrid' range.

8.6

REPORT

To: Production Manager

From: Accounts Assistant

Date: Today

Production of products A and B

Introduction

- You asked for my recommendations for next week's production.

- Materials used in the production of both products are in short supply and we are currently only able to obtain 500 kgs each week. We therefore need to use these materials to the best advantage of the company.

Report

- With insufficient direct materials we have a limiting factor (or a scarce resource). To make best use of this limiting factor to produce profits for the company, we must maximise the contribution (selling price – variable costs) from each kg of direct material.

- The contribution from producing each unit of A is £30. As this product requires two kgs of material, the contribution per kg is £30 ÷ 2 kgs = £15.

- The contribution from producing each unit of B is £50. As this product requires four kgs of material, the contribution per kg is £50 ÷ 4 kgs = £12.50.

- To make best use of the limiting factor of direct material, the company should produce all of product A that can be sold, ie 200 per week. This will take 400 kgs of materials (200 units x 2 kgs each) and will leave 100 kgs available to produce 25 of product B (25 units x 4 kgs each).

- Please note that, if this production plan is followed, insufficient of product B will be produced to meet demand. This may make it difficult to re-establish it in the market when full production of this product can be resumed once the shortage of direct materials has been resolved.

Conclusion

• Based on the concept of maximising the contribution from each kg of material (the limiting factor), I recommend that the production for next week should be:

      200 units of product A

      25 units of product B

• This will give a forecast profit statement for next week as follows:

		product A £	product B £	total £
	Sales revenue:			
	200 product A at £150 per unit	30,000		30,000
	25 product B at £200 per unit		5,000	5,000
		30,000	5,000	35,000
less	Variable costs:			
	200 product A at £120 per unit	24,000		24,000
	25 product B at £150 per unit		3,750	3,750
equals	Contribution	6,000	1,250	7,250
less	Fixed overheads			4,000
equals	Profit			3,250

8.7   Task 1

DURNING FOODS LIMITED: Production line for Indian meals

Planned results for November 2004

Number of meals to be sold	36,000
	£
Direct materials at 75p per meal	27,000
Direct labour at 45p per meal	16,200
Direct expenses at 20p per meal	7,200
Overheads for Indian meals production line	
at £7,500 + 15p per meal	12,900
Other production overheads	4,000
Total cost	67,300
Sales revenue at £2.00 per meal	72,000
Profit	4,700

Workings (using figures for July):

- direct materials per meal   = £25,125 ÷ 33,500 meals = £0.75
- direct labour per meal   = £15,075 ÷ 33,500 meals = £0.45
- direct expenses per meal   = £6,700 ÷ 33,500 meals   = £0.20
- overheads for Indian meals production line

	meals	£
high	34,700	12,705
low	31,000	12,150
difference	3,700	555

variable cost per meal   = £555 ÷ 3,700 meals   = £0.15

fixed cost   = £12,525 – (£0.15 x 33,500 meals) = £7,500

- other production overheads: fixed cost = £4,000 per month
- sales revenue per meal = £67,000 ÷ 33,500 meals = £2.00

Task 2

DURNING FOODS LIMITED: Production line for Indian meals

Planned results for November 2004: increased activity

Number of meals to be sold	40,000
	£
Direct materials at 75p – 20% = 60p per meal	24,000
Direct labour at 45p per meal	18,000
Direct expenses at 20p per meal	8,000
Overheads for Indian meals production line at £7,500 + 15p per meal	13,500
Other production overheads	4,000
Total cost	67,500
Sales revenue at £2.00 per meal	80,000
Profit	12,500

Break-even point

		£	£
Contribution per meal:			
	selling price		2.00
less	variable costs:		
	direct materials	0.60	
	direct labour	0.45	
	direct expenses	0.20	
	production line overheads	0.15	
			1.40
equals	contribution per meal		0.60
Fixed costs:			
	production line overheads		7,500
	other production overheads		4,000
			11,500

Break-even point:

$$\frac{£11,500}{£0.60} = 19,167 \text{ meals}$$

Margin of safety

$$\frac{40,000 - 19,167}{40,000} \times \frac{100}{1} = 52\%$$

8.8 The marginal cost per unit of Exe is £5 (direct materials £3 + direct labour £2), and so any contribution, ie selling price less marginal cost, will be profit:

• *200 units at £6 each*

The offer price of £6 is above the marginal cost of £5 and increases profit by the amount of the £1 extra contribution, ie (£6 – £5) x 200 units = £200 extra profit.

• *500 units at £4 each*

This offer price is below the marginal cost of £5; therefore there will be a fall in profit if this order is undertaken of (£4 – £5) x 500 units = £500 reduced profit.

WESTFIELD LIMITED
monthly profit statements

	Existing production of 2,000 units	Existing production + 200 units @ £6 each	Existing production + 500 units @ £4 each
	£	£	£
Sales revenue (per month):			
2,000 units at £12 each	24,000	24,000	24,000
200 units at £6 each	–	1,200	–
500 units at £4 each	–	–	2,000
	24,000	25,200	26,000
Less production costs:			
Direct materials (£3 per unit)	6,000	6,600	7,500
Direct labour (£2 per unit)	4,000	4,400	5,000
Production overheads (fixed)	8,000	8,000	8,000
PROFIT	6,000	6,200	5,500

The conclusion is that the first special order should be accepted, and the second declined.

8.9

POPCAN LIMITED
monthly profit statements

	Existing production of 150,000 cans	Existing production + 50,000 cans at 18p each
	£	£
Sales revenue (per month):		
150,000 cans at 25p each	37,500	37,500
50,000 cans at 18p each	–	9,000
	37,500	46,500
Less production costs:		
Direct materials (5p per can)	7,500	10,000
Direct labour (5p per can)	7,500	10,000
Production overheads – variable (4p per can)	6,000	8,000
– fixed*	9,000	9,000
PROFIT	7,500	9,500

* 6p x 150,000 cans = £9,000

The offer from the supermarket chain should be accepted because:

•   the marginal cost of producing each can is 14p (direct materials 5p, direct labour 5p, variable production overheads 4p)

•   the offer price is 18p per can, which is above marginal cost, and gives a contribution of 4p

•   profits increase by the amount of the extra contribution, ie (18p − 14p) x 50,000 cans = £2,000 extra profit

8.10

MAXXA LIMITED

Profit statement for the month ended 31 January 2004

	MARGINAL COSTING		ABSORPTION COSTING	
	£	£	£	£
Sales 3,000 units at £8 each		24,000		24,000
Variable costs				
Direct materials at £1.25 each	5,000		5,000	
Direct labour at £2.25 each	9,000		9,000	
	14,000			
Less Closing stock (marginal cost)				
1,000 units at £3.50 each	3,500			
	10,500			
Fixed production overheads	6,000		6,000	
			20,000	
Less Closing stock (absorption cost)				
1,000 units at £5 each			5,000	
Less Cost of goods sold		16,500		15,000
PROFIT		7,500		9,000

Working notes:

Closing stock is calculated on the basis of this year's costs:

marginal costing, variable costs only, ie £1.25 + £2.25 = £3.50 per unit

absorption costing, variable and fixed costs, ie £20,000 ÷ 4,000 units = £5 per unit

The difference in the profit is caused only by the closing stock figures: £3,500 under marginal costing, and £5,000 under absorption costing. With marginal costing, the full amount of the fixed production overheads has been charged in this year's profit statement; by contrast, with absorption costing, part of the fixed production overheads (here £6,000 x 25%* = £1,500) has been carried forward in the stock valuation.

*   1,000 units in stock out of 4,000 units manufactured

CHAPTER 9: LONG-TERM DECISIONS

9.1 (a) payback period

Year	PROJECT EXE Cash Flow £000	PROJECT EXE Cumulative Cash Flow £000	PROJECT WYE Cash Flow £000	PROJECT WYE Cumulative Cash Flow £000
0	(80)	(80)	(100)	(100)
1	40	(40)	20	(80)
2	40	–	30	(50)
3	20	20	50	–
4	10	30	50	50
5	10	40	40	90

As can be seen from the above table:
- Project Exe pays back after two years
- Project Wye pays back after three years

(b) net present value

Year	Discount Factor	PROJECT EXE Cash Flow £000	PROJECT EXE Discounted Cash Flow £000	PROJECT WYE Cash Flow £000	PROJECT WYE Discounted Cash Flow £000
0	1.000	(80)	(80)	(100)	(100)
1	0.893	40	35.72	20	17.86
2	0.797	40	31.88	30	23.91
3	0.712	20	14.24	50	35.60
4	0.636	10	6.36	50	31.80
5	0.567	10	5.67	40	22.68
Net Present Value (NPV)			13.87		31.85

REPORT

To:	Robert Smith
From:	Accounts Assistant
Date:	Today

Capital investment projects: Exe and Wye

I have carried out an appraisal of these two projects, based on the information provided. I have used two techniques:

• payback

• net present value

The first of these, payback, sees how long it takes for the initial outlay of the project to be repaid by the net cash flow coming in. For Project Exe, the payback period is two years; for Project Wye, it is three years. Using this technique, Project Exe is more favourable.

Payback is an easy technique both to calculate and understand. However, it does have the disadvantage of ignoring all cash flows after the payback period. With these two projects, Wye has strong cash inflows in years 4 and 5, after the payback period (however, these could be a disadvantage if the project is likely to go out-of-date soon).

The net present value (NPV) technique relies on discounting relevant cash flows at an appropriate rate of return, which is 12 per cent for these projects. Net present value is a more sophisticated technique than payback in that it uses all cash flows and takes the timing of cash flows into account. However, the meaning of NPV is not always clear, and the rate of return required on the projects may vary over their life.

Project Wye has a higher NPV (but also a higher initial cost) at £31,850, when compared with Exe at £13,870. The fact that both figures are positive means that either project will be worthwhile. However, in view of the differing initial costs, it would be appropriate to calculate the internal rate of return, so that a comparison can be made directly between the two projects.

9.2 Task 1

The net cash flows are:

	£000
year 1	(95)
year 2	30
year 3	40
year 4	50
year 5	25

(a)   payback period

Year	Cash Flow	Cumulative Cash Flow	
	£000	£000	
1	(95)	(95)	
2	30	(65)	
3	40	(25)	
4	50	25	∴ £25,000 required
5	25	50	

The design costs are recovered half-way through year 4: £30,000 + £40,000 + (£25,000/£50,000 x 12 months). Thus the payback period is 3 years and 6 months from the start of the project; in terms of revenue, the payback period is 2 years and 6 months. Note that these assume even cash flows during the year.

(b)   net present value

Year	Cash Flow		Discount Factor	Discounted Cash Flow
	£000			£000
1	(95)	x	0.909	(86.35)
2	30	x	0.826	24.78
3	40	x	0.751	30.04
4	50	x	0.683	34.15
5	25	x	0.621	15.52
		Net Present Value (NPV)		18.14

Task 2

- For this new project IRR, at almost 20 per cent, is much higher than the 10% return required on new projects.

- This means that, in financial terms, the new project is acceptable – the wider the margin of IRR above the return required, the better.

9.3 Task 1

DURNING FOODS LIMITED

Working paper for the financial appraisal of purchase of delivery vehicles

DISCOUNTED CASH FLOW

Year	Cash Flow	Discount Factor at 12%	Discounted Cash Flow
	£		£
2004	(80,000)	1.000	(80,000)
2005	28,300	0.893	25,272
2006	28,300	0.797	22,555
2007	28,300	0.712	20,150
2008	*38,300	0.636	24,359
Net Present Value (NPV)			12,336

* £28,300 + £10,000 resale value

PAYBACK PERIOD

Year	Cash Flow	Cumulative Cash Flow	
	£	£	
2004	(80,000)	(80,000)	
2005	28,300	(51,700)	
2006	28,300	(23,400)	
2007	28,300	4,900	£23,400* required
2008	38,300	43,200	

* £28,300 − £4,900

Payback period = 2 years + (£23,400/£28,300) = 2.8 years, ie 2 years and 10 months

Task 2

REPORT
To: General Manager   **From:**   Accounts Assistant   **Date:**   12 November 2004
<u>Purchase of delivery vehicles</u>   The proposal to purchase delivery vehicles is acceptable from a financial viewpoint because it returns a positive net present value of £12,336 at a discount rate of 12 per cent. This calculation assumes that all cash flows occur at the end of each year.   The payback period is during 2007. If we assume even cash flows during the year, the payback period can be calculated as 2.8 years (or 2 years and 10 months) from the start. This is acceptable since it is shorter than the company requirement of three years, although there is not a great deal of room for error in the cash flow calculations.

9.4   Task 1

The net cash flows are:

	£000
year 0	(40)
year 1	(60)
year 2	45
year 3	54
year 4	90
year 5	60

(a)   payback period

Year	Cash Flow	Cumulative Cash Flow	
	£000	*£000*	
0	(40)	(40)	
1	(60)	(100)	
2	45	(55)	
3	54	(1)	
4	90	89	∴ £1,000 required
5	60	149	

The development costs are recovered in the very early part of year 4: £45,000 + £54,000 + (£1,000/£90,000 x 12 months). Thus the payback period is 3 years and 0.13 months (ie less than one week into the next year) from the start of the project; in terms of revenue, the payback period is 2 years and 0.13 months. Note that these assume even cash flows during the year.

(b)   net present value

Year	Cash Flow		Discount Factor	Discounted Cash Flow
	£000			£000
0	(40)	x	1.000	(40)
1	(60)	x	0.893	(53.58)
2	45	x	0.797	35.86
3	54	x	0.712	38.45
4	90	x	0.636	57.24
5	60	x	0.567	34.02
			Net Present Value (NPV)	71.99

Task 2

REPORT

To: Managing Director

From: Accounts Assistant

Date: Today

Introduction of a new range of bikes

I have carried out an appraisal on the project, based on the information provided.

The net present value technique relies on discounting relevant cash flows at an appropriate rate of return. It would be helpful to know:

1.   whether there are any additional cash flows beyond year 5

2.   whether the introduction of a new range of bikes will affect sales of our existing bikes

On the basis of the information provided, the project has a positive net present value of £71,990 and should be carried out.

9.5   numerical assessments using net present value methods

Year	Cash Flow		Discount Factor		Discounted Cash Flow
	£				£
Outright purchase					
0	(10,000)	x	1.000	=	(10,000)
5	1,000	x	0.621	=	621
			Net Present Value (NPV)	=	(9,379)
Hire purchase					
0	(4,000)	x	1.000	=	(4,000)
1	(4,000)	x	0.909	=	(3,636)
2	(4,000)	x	0.826	=	(3,304)
5	1,000	x	0.621	=	621
			Net Present Value (NPV)	=	(10,319)
Leasing					
1	(2,500)	x	0.909	=	(2,272.50)
2	(2,500)	x	0.826	=	(2,065.00)
3	(2,500)	x	0.751	=	(1,877.50)
4	(2,500)	x	0.683	=	(1,707.50)
5	(2,500)	x	0.621	=	(1,552.50)
			Net Present Value (NPV)	=	(9,475.00)

Tutorial note: We are using NPV here with <u>costs</u>: therefore the best project (in financial terms) has the <u>lowest</u> NPV, which is the least cost to the business.

advice to Ken Jones

- Outright purchase is marginally more attrractive than leasing the equipment.
- Hire purchase ranks third.
- Much depends on the financial position of your business – although outright purchase comes out the best, you will have to have the cash to pay for the equipment at the beginning.
- On balance, leasing may be the most suitable option for you, with regular annual payments being made over the period you plan to use the equipment.

CHAPTER 10: REPORTING INFORMATION

10.1 See pages 269 and 270.

10.2 Costs and revenue.

10.3 False. See page 271.

10.4 See pages 272 and 273.

10.5 (a) revenue, running costs, number of beds, number of employees, number of out-patients, number of in-patients

(b) revenue, running costs, number of employees, number of clients, number of hours worked, types of jobs carried out

(c) revenue, cost of production, overheads, units produced (by product), employees, hours worked

(d) figures for *each site*: revenue, costs, number of employees, opening hours, floor area, number of clients signed up, number of clients using facilities

10.6 The first paragraph should state that business investment has declined over the last 12 months, quoting some figures. Some indication of the trend in different industrial sectors should be made.

The second paragraph should reiterate the fact that the general trend is downwards. Examples should be given, comparing the sectors from best to worst and giving an appropriate recommendation.

The style throughout should be simple and to the point. Students should not copy out text from the original.

10.7 This is a communications skills developing exercise. The main object here is for the student to be able to identify the main points and to be able to write them down in plain English and to discuss them. The original article may be from a national daily paper, or it may be a local report (which may be more interesting for overseas centres).

CHAPTER 11: MEASURING PERFORMANCE

11.1 (a) 61%   ([716 ÷ 1182] x 100)

(b) 39%   ([76 ÷ 196] x 100)

(c) 17%   ([120 ÷ 716] x 100)

(d) £341,000   (£310,000 x [100 + 10] ÷ 100)   or   £310,000 x 1.1

(e) £102,000   (£120,000 x [100 - 15] ÷ 100) or £120,000 x 0.85

(f) GB£0.72   ([10 ÷ 9] x GB£0.65)
Profits are likely to be reduced, as income for the business is likely to be in GB£.

11.2

	(a) units	(b) %
January	120	96
February	109	87
March	131	105
April	136	109
May	110	88
June	123	98
July	178	142
August	135	108
September	93	74
October	150	120
November	134	107
December	112	90
Total	1,531	1,224

(c)   128 and 102% respectively.

Comments:

- There are seasonal fluctuations, eg more policies than average in July, ready for the summer registrations.
- Average productivity is 128 units (target 125), reflected in efficiency of 102%.

11.3   (a)

	cost (£)
January	200
February	192
March	200
April	183
May	175
June	186
July	200
August	200
September	188
October	179
November	187
December	192

(b)   Average annual cost per unit = £58,200/308 units = £189

Comments:

- Seasonal fluctuations (more installed just before holiday period and just before Christmas).
- Costs are lower when larger numbers of units are sold – economies of scale.

11.4 (a)

		daily utilisation %
Monday	56/56	100
Tuesday	50/56	89
Wednesday	28/56	50
Thursday	56/56	100
Friday	48/56	86

(b) Weekly hours available = 8 x 7 x 5 = 280
Hours worked during the week = 238
Labour utilisation for week 238/280 x 100 = 85%

Because the business is highly dependent on computers, idle time is likely to be the result of computer breakdown, or power cut, or even poor time recording (less likely). Idle time is high on Wednesday, which suggests that the management has not utilised the staff time efficiently – the staff could have used the time for administrative tasks, or contacting existing or prospective customers. Friday, is of course, Friday – there may have been an extended lunchtime for some form of celebration.

11.5

		Week 1	Week 2	Week 3	Week 4
(a)	labour productivity	£60	£64	£68	£70
(b)	capital productivity	16p	20p	22p	24p
(c)	efficiency %	103%	105%	110%	114%
(d)	cost per unit	£7.50	£7.50	£8.64	£8.75

Comments:
*   the level of production is rising over the period to meet demand
*   productivity is rising over the period
*   capital productivity and efficiency are also increasing, reflecting the same trend
*   cost per unit is rising sharply – reflecting the overtime worked and rising material costs
*   this rise in costs is not a cause for immediate concern as the extra sales more than compensate; in the long term the company will need to look at its working practices and supplier situation

11.6

	Jan-March	April-June	July-Sept	Oct-Dec	Total
Sales (£)	280,000	350,000	375,000	210,000	1,215,000
Cost of sales (£)	168,000	217,000	221,250	128,100	734,350
Gross profit (£)	112,000	133,000	153,750	81,900	480,650
Gross profit %	40%	38%	41%	39%	40%
Overheads (£)	70,000	77,000	80,000	65,000	292,000
Net profit (£)	42,000	56,000	73,750	16,900	188,650
Net profit %	15%	16%	20%	8%	16%
ROCE %	-	-	-	-	15%

Comments:

- sales are very seasonal – as one would expect in the agricultural industry
- gross profit remains steady, reflecting a stable gross profit margin – a healthy sign
- net profit varies with the seasonal fluctuation in sales – the main reason being overheads staying at more or less the same level, but sales being variable

CHAPTER 12: CHARTS, AVERAGES AND INDICES

12.1 Errors:

- no heading to table
- there are two years 3 – year 4 in extreme right-hand column
- £ labels missing
- gross profit Year 3 should be £650
- Year 1 total £150, year 2 £250, Year 3 £270

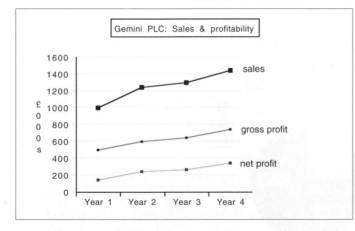

12.2 (a)

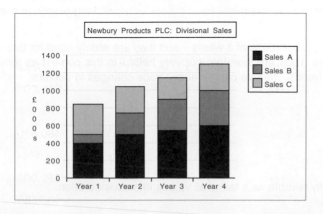

This chart shows clearly the upward trend in sales, but is less helpful in showing the *comparative* sales trends. A compound bar chart or line graph will do this more clearly (see [b]).

(b)

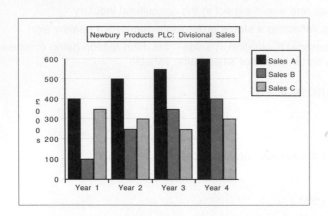

This chart makes it easy to see the divisional sales trends, but less easy to see any group sales trend (for which the component bar chart is more suitable)

(c)

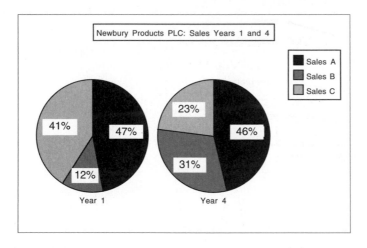

Pie charts are excellent for showing proportions of a whole – and they are widely used for this – but they do not show relative quantities. They are therefore not very helpful in this context as they are clumsy in illustrating year-to-year trends: the eye cannot easily trace changes in sectors.

12.3
- mean   £10.20
- median   £5.90
- mode   £10.00

The mean is the most arithmetically reliable as it takes all values into consideration.

12.4   (a)   Moving average calculation:

Week	unit sales units (M)	moving average units (M)
1	3	-
2	5	6
3	10	6.7
4	5	7.3
5	7	8
6	12	8.7
7	7	9.3
8	9	11
9	17	11.3
10	8	11.7
11	10	12
12	18	

(b)   Average weekly increment 0.7M, ie (12-6) ÷ (10-1)

(c)   Forecast trend line: from week 12: 12.7, 13.4, 14.1, 14.8

Graph:

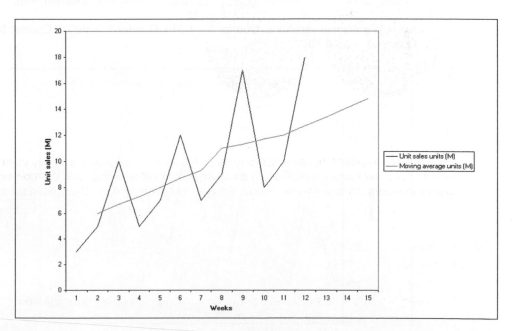

12.5 (a) & (b) Calculation of moving averages and seasonal variations.

Year	Quarter	Historical Sales Data	4-point Moving Average	Averaged Pairs (Trend)	Seasonal Variation
2001	1	2,000			
	2	4,500			
			3,625		
	3	6,000		3,750	+ 2,250
			3,875		
	4	2,000		3,937.5	– 1,937.5
			4,000		
2002	1	3,000		4,187.5	– 1,187.5
			4,375		
	2	5,000		4,500	+ 500
			4,625		
	3	7,500		4,750	+ 2,750
			4,875		
	4	3,000		5,062.5	– 2,062.5
			5,250		
2003	1	4,000		5,375	– 1,375
			5,500		
	2	6,500		5,625	+ 875
			5,750		
	3	8,500		5,875	+ 2,625
			6,000		
	4	4,000		6,187.5	– 2,187.5
			6,375		
2004	1	5,000		6,562.5	– 1,562.5
			6,750		
	2	8,000		6,875	+ 1,125
			7,000		
	3	10,000			
	4	5,000			

(c) Average quarterly increment $\frac{(6,875 - 3,750)}{(12 - 1)}$ = 284 units (nearest unit).

(e) Average seasonal variations: Quarter 1 – 1,375, Quarter 2 + 833.3, Quarter 3 + 2,541.7 Quarter 4 – 2,062.5.

(d)

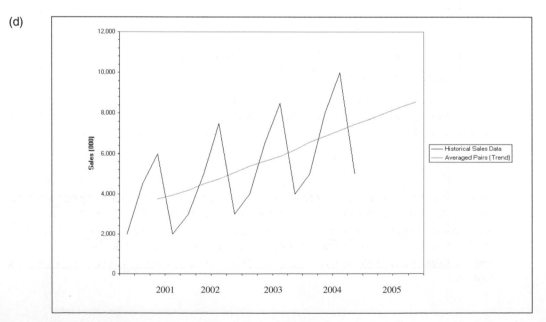

12.6 (a)   Cumulative frequency: 4, 16, 37, 49, 52

(b)   Graph drawn from this data (see page 319 for the format).

(c)   The graph is steepest between cumulative frequencies of 110 and 120. This indicates that the most common frequencies are in the range 110 to 120.

12.7 (a) - (d)

month	sales (£M) year 1	sales (£M) year 2	cumulative sales (£M) year 2	moving half-year total (£M)
January	6	8	8	55
February	7	9	17	57
March	9	10	27	58
April	10	12	39	60
May	11	12	51	61
June	10	11	62	62
TOTAL	53	62		

(e)

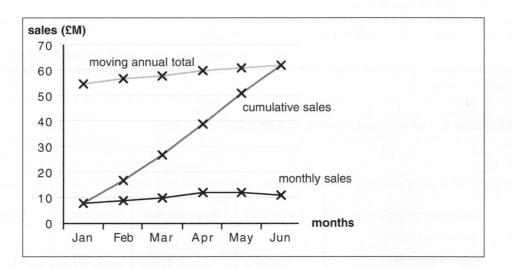

The chart shows that sales (Year 2) level off in May and fall in June (lower trend line). This appears to be a seasonal trend because the same happened in Year 1 (see table).

The moving half-year total line (top line) shows a consistently healthy upwards slope, indicating an increase on the previous year for each of the first six months of Year 2.

The cumulative total (middle line) shows a steady rise, which is consistent with a steady sales pattern.

12.8 (a)

	Year 1	Year 2	Year 3	Year 4	Year 5
Sales	100	101	104	109	111
Net profit	100	102	107	108	109

Both sales and profits are increasing each year in line with each other, steadily rather than rapidly.

(b)

	Year 1	Year 2	Year 3	Year 4	Year 5
Sales (£)	350,000	337,577	334,763	334,659	319,841
Net profit (£)	45,000	43,742	44,024	42,713	40,185

When adjusted for the RPI, both sales and profits are declining significantly in real terms.

CHAPTER 13: REPORT WRITING

Tutors may wish to adopt the short formal report with headings, or the more simple report without headings. We would recommend the former, as it brings the concept of structure more forcibly to mind.

13.1 The two reports should be redrafted in simple English.

The first report is written in overblown and pompous language and could be condensed to a few sentences. The results figures and the share price should be quoted.

The second report is written in casual language which uses slang and unimportant detail. This report could also be condensed to a few sentences. The £8m cost of grounding figure and the share price should be quoted.

13.2 See chapter for headings and answer to 11.5 for points to be raised.

13.3

	performance indicator	Kidderport	Stourminster	Persham	Total
(a)	labour productivity:				
	units/employees	480	475	367	433
	sales/hours	£27	£26	£22	£25
(b)	sales/£1 capital employed	80p	79p	81p	80p
(c)	cost per unit	43.75	44.21	49.09	45.69
(d)	sales per m^2	£240.00	£211.11	£176.00	£206.35
(e)	gross profit %	46%	42%	35%	41%
(f)	net profit %	13%	12%	2%	9%
(g)	return on capital employed	10%	9%	1%	7%

The report should *assess* the performance indicators (not just say figure A is bigger than figure B etc). In particular the poor performance of Persham and its effect on the group performance should be highlighted. Students should note:

productivity

Labour productivity is about 20% - 25% lower at Persham than at the other shops; this is not too serious; in fact capital productivity is highest at Persham at 82p. These indicators result from the fact that sales are buoyant at Persham – 2,200 units sold (more than Stourminster). The problems seem to lie elsewhere.

cost per unit

Persham has the highest cost per unit (£49.09). This again points to the root problem.

resource utilisation

Persham has the lowest sales per square metre of floorspace. Better use could perhaps be made of merchandising.

profitability

Gross profit percentage is lowest at Persham. One possible reason is that they are not getting the best terms from suppliers; alternatively they could be giving greater discounts to stimulate sales.

Net profit percentage and ROCE are poor at Persham (only 1%). Overhead costs are clearly too high here and should be investigated.

CHAPTER 14: CONSOLIDATING AND REPORTING INFORMATION

14.1 Figures that have been calculated and adjusted are shown in bold type.

FITMAN WHOLESALE LIMITED			
Profit and Loss Account (extract) for week ended 28 March 2004			
	Hornchurch	Basildon	Total
	£	£	£
Sales	71,000	55,000	**126,000**
Opening Stock	32,000	24,000	**56,000**
Purchases	35,000	25,000	**60,000**
Closing stock	**32,000**	23,000	**55,000**
Cost of goods sold	**35,000**	**26,000**	**61,000**
Gross Profit	**36,000**	**29,000**	**65,000**

14.2 Figures that have been calculated and adjusted are shown in bold type.

	Branch X £	Branch Y £	Branch Z £	Total £
Sales	80,000	75,000	80,000	**235,000**
Opening Stock	30,000	22,000	25,000	**77,000**
Purchases	40,000	37,000	38,000	115,000
Closing stock	**28,500**	21,000	24,000	73,500
Cost of goods sold	**41,500**	**38,000**	**39,000**	118,500
Gross Profit	**38,500**	**37,000**	**41,000**	116,500
Transfers from X	**1,500**			
Transfers to Y and Z		1,000	500	**nil**

Table title:
XYZ Retail Limited
Profit and Loss Account (extract) for week ended 28 March 2004

14.3

(a) **Anne Field Enterprises: Profit and Loss Account data for 3 months ended 30 June 2004**

	£	£
Sales		220,500
Opening stock	102,000	
Purchases	114,000	
	216,000	
Less closing stock	101,200*	
Cost of goods sold		114,800
Gross Profit		105,700
Overheads		87,400
Net Profit		18,300

*Includes £200 added back to the Liverpool closing stock in respect of stock in transit.

(b)   **Anne Field Enterprises: Comparison of data for 3 months ended 30 June**

	2003	2004
Sales	185,000	220,500
Cost of goods sold	112,000	114,800
Gross Profit	73,000	105,700
Gross Profit percentage	39.46%	47.94%
Overheads	62,000	87,400
Net Profit	11,000	18,300
Net Profit percentage	5.95%	8.30%

(c)   **compound bar chart**

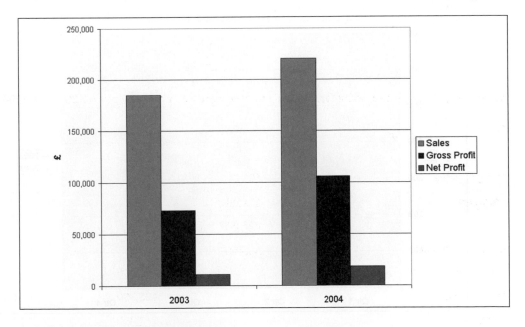

(c)   **Comments** are generally very positive:

- Sales have increased by 19%
- Gross profit percentage has increased by 8.48%
- Net profit percentage has increased by 2.35%

The management has clearly improved the overall sales and profitability of the business. The substantial increase in gross profit would suggest that merchandise is being successfully marked up, and this with the increase in sales has helped to improve net profitability by 39%. The only penalty has been a sharp rise in overheads by 41%. This may need investigating and the goal for 2005 should be to trim this increase.

14.4

(a)

EVESHORE FARMS LIMITED				
Combined sales figures for Sales and Production Divisions 2003 and 2004				
	Total Sales 2003 £000	Total Sales 2004 £000	Cumulative Sales 2003 £000	Cumulative Sales 2004 £000
Jan - Mar	130	150	130	150
Apr - Jun	151	172	281	322
Jul - Sep	165	174	446	496
Oct - Dec	138	148	584	644

(b) **line graph**

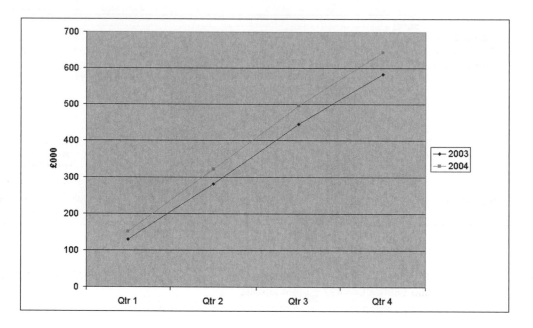

(c) **comments**

Annual sales have increased by 10.3%, which is encouraging, given the low underlying rate of inflation.

Analysis of the quarterly sales shows that the increase in the first two quarters (15.4% and 13.9%) is higher than in the last two quarters (5.5% and 7.3%). This is not a problem in itself, but management would be advised to investigate the reason for the slowdown in sales growth.

CHAPTER 15: REPORTS AND RETURNS TO OUTSIDE AGENCIES

15.1

CUTE IDEAS	Trading Report			Quarter ended ....31./.03..../.year	
£			£	£ variance	% variance
Sales A (actual)	13,500	Sales Target A	15,000	1,500	10
Sales B (actual)	18,000	Sales Target B	21,000	3,000	14
Total Sales (actual)	31,500	Total Sales Target	36,000	4,500	13

10% Commission on sales £3,150   (cheque enclosed)

Comments
Points to include: acknowledgment of fall in sales (mentioning variance) and attributing the factors mentioned in the question; future performance could be estimated in general terms.

signature   *R Smith*   **date** (in first week of April + year)

15.2 (a) Total trade debtors £29,216 (split into 3 time periods) + stock £8,760 + bank £5,631 + VAT due £890 = £44,497 current assets.

Trade creditors £15,489 (split into 2 time periods) + PAYE due £1,720 + corporation tax due £8,920 = £26,129 current liabilities.

(b) The bank should be happy with her figures: current assets comfortably exceed current liabilities (by £18,368, ie the working capital of the company).

CHAPTER 16: THE PRINCIPLES OF VAT

16.1 Sales of chargeable supplies and imports – sales of business goods and services by VAT registered persons.

16.2 Three from EC Directives, VAT Act, Finance Acts, VAT Guide, HM Revenue & Customs, SSAP 5.

16.3 A person registered for VAT, eg sole trader, partnership, limited company, club, charity.

16.4 Input tax is a tax on purchases and expenses and may normally be reclaimed by the supplier; output tax is tax charged on chargeable supplies and is due to HM Revenue & Customs. The arithmetic difference between the two is payable to HM Revenue & Customs on the VAT Return.

16.5 A supplier may reclaim VAT if the amount of input tax in any VAT period exceeds the amount of output VAT. VAT is also reclaimable in the case of bad debt relief (covered in Chapter 15).

16.6 The VAT is paid to the supplier, who is accountable, together with other businesses involved in the production process, to HM Revenue & Customs for the VAT (see diagram on page 287).

16.7 In July 1998: standard 17.5%, reduced 5%, zero 0%.

16.8 Zero-rated VAT is VAT at 0% charged on taxable supplies. Exempt supplies are supplies which are not taxable. See page 288 or the 'VAT Guide' for examples.

16.9 When the annual VAT threshold has been reached. When the annual VAT threshold is likely to be reached within the next 30 days.

16.10 (b) (c) (d) (e).

16.11 (a) £17.06

16.12 (a), (d) in respect of the proportion of the bill which relates to business expense

16.13 Unit price missing, invoice number missing, VAT number missing, issue date missing, VAT amount has been rounded up (should be £36.67). Wrong cast in total: £36.68 taken as £63.68.

16.14 (a) the date of issue of the tax invoice

    (b) the payment for the goods (the pro-forma invoice is not a tax invoice)

    (c) the date of issue of the tax invoice (the 14 day rule)

    (d) the date of the invoice (as this is a regular practice); strictly speaking this should be approved by the local VAT office

16.15 (a)   the invoices are valid VAT invoices as they are all under £250 and fall into the 'less detailed' category which can quote VAT-inclusive totals

(b)   using the VAT fraction of $^7/_{47}$, the net and VAT amounts are:

£74.47 + £13.03 VAT = £87.50

£35.00 + £6.12 VAT = £41.12

£40.00 + £7.00 VAT = £47.00

£47.45 + £8.30 VAT = £55.75

£84.30 + £14.75 VAT = £99.05

16.16 There is no problem with this request. He can use a 'modified invoice' which totals rather than itemises VAT

16.17 (a)   VAT @ 17.5% on £250 should be £43.75 (invoice total £293.75),ie £2.50 overcharge

VAT @ 17.5% on £400 should be £70 (invoice total £470.00), ie £10 undercharge.

(b)   *Overcharge:* either issue a credit note or accept a debit note from the customer for £2.50, or if this is not done, account to HM Revenue & Customs as excess output tax. The former is preferable.

Undercharge: either ABC Wholesalers should issue an adjusting invoice or pay the £10 due to HM Revenue & Customs themselves.

(c)   The letter in the first case should contain an apology and possibly enclose a credit note.

In the second case either a letter of apology should be sent to the customer (together with an adjusting invoice), or if the supplier is going to stand the loss, an appropriate memo should be sent to the Accounts Manager, explaining the circumstances and stating the importance of maintaining good customer relations.

16.18 (a)   The goods are zero-rated on despatch and VAT is collected from the German buyer by the German tax authorities at the prevailing German rate.

(b)   The buyer's valid VAT registration number must be quoted on the VAT invoice (this number will be prefixed GE). The goods are sent to Germany and documentary evidence of despatch must be obtained by the supplier within 3 months of despatch.

(c)   The earlier of the date on the VAT invoice, or the 15th of the month following the month of supply. The first is the most likely of these.

(d)   VAT will have to be charged on the goods by the supplier at the appropriate UK rate.

16.19 (a)   No   (b) No

16.20 (a)   Form VAT 101.

(b)   Appropriate boxes on the VAT 100 (all suppliers), and Supplementary Declaration forms if the annual Instrastat threshold is reached.

CHAPTER 17: VAT RECORDS AND THE VAT RETURN

17.1   See text; (a) page 403 (b) page 404

17.2   (a)   there is no evidence (as required by HM Revenue & Customs) for collection of output VAT

(b)   there is no evidence (as required by HM Revenue & Customs) for claiming back of input VAT

17.3   Danger of double counting of output VAT – both in the Sales Day Book and also in the Cash Book when the money is received from the customer. VAT collected from the Cash Book VAT column should be for supplies *not* sold on credit.

17.4

VAT control account – Business A			
VAT deductible: input tax		**VAT payable: output tax**	
	£		£
Purchases Day Book £2,720.00 *less* credit notes £326.50	2,393.50	Sales Day Book £5,961.70 *less* credit notes £501.29	5,460.41
Cash Book	275.60	Cash Book	329.73
Petty Cash Book	13.85		
EU Acquisitions	796.30	EU Acquisitions	796.30
TOTAL INPUT TAX	3,479.25	TOTAL OUTPUT TAX	6,586.44
		less TOTAL INPUT TAX	3,479.25
		equals VAT DUE	3,107.19

VAT control account – Business B			
VAT deductible: input tax		**VAT payable: output tax**	
	£		£
Purchases Day Book £3,239.50 *less* credit notes £107.60	3,131.90	Sales Day Book £5,906.33 *less* credit notes £321.90	5,584.43
Cash Book	179.29	Cash Book	260.75
EU Acquisitions	78.00	EU Acquisitions	78.00
Bad debt relief	85.50	Undercharge (previous period)	32.65
TOTAL INPUT TAX	3,474.69	TOTAL OUTPUT TAX	5,955.83
		less TOTAL INPUT TAX	3,474.69
		equals VAT DUE	2,481.14

VAT control account – Business C

VAT deductible: input tax	£	VAT payable: output tax	£
Purchases Day Book £5,726.05 *less* credit notes £195.50	5,530.55	Sales Day Book £9,176.23 *less* credit notes £391.80	8,784.43
Cash Book	173.76	Cash Book	356.25
Petty cash book purchases	18.92		
EU Acquisitions	1,523.90	EU Acquisitions	1,523.90
Bad debt relief	89.23		
Net overpayment (previous period)	184.90		
TOTAL INPUT TAX	7,521.26	TOTAL OUTPUT TAX	10,664.58
		less TOTAL INPUT TAX	7,521.26
		equals VAT DUE	3,143.32

VAT control account – Business D

VAT deductible: input tax	£	VAT payable: output tax	£
Purchases Day Book £3,923.50 *less* credit notes £170.90	3,752.60	Sales Day Book £521.30 *less* credit notes £81.25	440.05
Cash Book	1,256.81	Cash Book	723.80
Petty cash book purchases	41.20		
Bad debt relief	29.50		
Overpayment (previous period)	17.50		
TOTAL INPUT TAX	5,097.61	TOTAL OUTPUT TAX	1,163.85
		less TOTAL INPUT TAX	5,097.61
		equals VAT RECLAIMABLE	(3,933.76)

17.5

VAT 100 Box No.	Business 1	Business 2	Business 3	Business 4
1	12,274.15	16,791.26	3,923.87	3,640.06
2	none	3,281.28	216.31	8,791.96
3	12,274.15	20,072.54	4,140.18	12,432.02
4	7,107.07	15,933.59	1,378.47	19,323.32
5	5,167.08	4,138.95	2,761.71	(6,891.30)
6	70,264	104,276	23,385	96,600
7	38,245	88,419	8,172	110,092
8	none	none	none	none
9	none	18,750	1,236	50,239

17.6 (a) The overcharge being under £2,000, and there being no other similar errors, can be adjusted in the next VAT Return by adding the £350 to the input side of the VAT Control Account. The £350 will have to be credited to the customer on a credit note (unless the customer has already issued a debit note).

(b) This undercharge is over the £2,000 limit and so Olly will have to make a voluntary disclosure by letter or on Form VAT 652 to the local VAT office. This will avoid the possibility of a later misdeclaration penalty.

(c) Any VAT 100 which is submitted late will be subject to a 12 month surcharge liability notice for the fiirst default and to a default surcharge if there is a further default during that period. Further details can be found in the Revenue & Customs booklet 'Default Surcharge'.

17.7 (a) The annual accounting scheme (see page 415)

(b) The flat rate scheme for the household repair business, but not for a business selling zero-rated goods, because the input VAT could not then be reclaimed. (See pages 416-417)

(c) The cash accounting scheme (see pages 417-418)

17.8 (a) Invoices 7773, 7645 outside time period. Invoice 7578 not eligible (date of supply within 6 months).

Invoices 7510, 7415 and 7200 eligible (due date and date of supply over 6 months)

Total bad debt relief reclaimable £136.60

(b) The total bad debt (net sales figure) must be entered in a bad debts account and written out of the sales ledger.

The VAT element must be entered in the VAT Control Account (inputs side) and then, when the VAT Return is processed, be added to the VAT 100 Box 4 total (VAT reclaimed on purchases). The VAT due or reclaimable will thus be adjusted for the VAT which was not paid to the supplier by the bankrupt customer.

Appendix
Photocopiable documents

STOCK RECORD

Stock description ....

Stock units ....

Stock ref. No. ....

Location ....

Minimum ....

Maximum ....

Re-order level ....

Re-order quantity ....

DATE	GOODS RECEIVED		GOODS ISSUED		BALANCE
	Reference	Quantity	Reference	Quantity	

STOCK RECORD

Stock description ....

Stock units ....

Stock ref. No. ....

Location ....

Minimum ....

Maximum ....

Re-order level ....

Re-order quantity ....

DATE	GOODS RECEIVED		GOODS ISSUED		BALANCE
	Reference	Quantity	Reference	Quantity	

STORES LEDGER RECORD

Date	Receipts			Issues			Balance		
	Quantity	Cost	Total Cost	Quantity	Cost	Total Cost	Quantity	Cost	Total Cost
		£	£		£	£		£	£

REPORT/MEMORANDUM
To:
From:
Date:

Index